Recordable
CD Bible

Recordable CD Bible

Mark L. Chambers

IDG Books Worldwide, Inc.
An International Data Group Company
Foster City, CA ✦ Chicago, IL ✦ Indianapolis, IN ✦ Southlake, TX

Recordable CD Bible

Published by
IDG Books Worldwide, Inc.
An International Data Group Company
919 E. Hillsdale Blvd.
Suite 400
Foster City, CA 94404
http://www.idgbooks.com (IDG Books Worldwide Web site)

Library of Congress Catalog Card No.: 97-073219

ISBN: 1-7645-3078-X

Printed in the United States of America

10 9 8 7 6 5 4 3 2 1

DD/QX/QZ/ZX/FC

Distributed in the United States by IDG Books Worldwide, Inc.

Distributed by Macmillan Canada for Canada; by Transworld Publishers Limited in the United Kingdom; by IDG Norge Books for Norway; by IDG Sweden Books for Sweden; by Woodslane Pty. Ltd. for Australia; by Woodslane Enterprises Ltd. for New Zealand; by Longman Singapore Publishers Ltd. for Singapore, Malaysia, Thailand, and Indonesia; by Simron Pty. Ltd. for South Africa; by Toppan Company Ltd. for Japan; by Distribuidora Cuspide for Argentina; by Livraria Cultura for Brazil; by Ediciencia S.A. for Ecuador; by Addison-Wesley Publishing Company for Korea; by Ediciones ZETA S.C.R. Ltda. for Peru; by WS Computer Publishing Corporation, Inc., for the Philippines; by Unalis Corporation for Taiwan; by Contemporanea de Ediciones for Venezuela; by Computer Book & Magazine Store for Puerto Rico; by Express Computer Distributors for the Caribbean and West Indies. Authorized Sales Agent: Anthony Rudkin Associates for the Middle East and North Africa.

For general information on IDG Books Worldwide's books in the U.S., please call our Consumer Customer Service department at 800-762-2974. For reseller information, including discounts and premium sales, please call our Reseller Customer Service department at 800-434-3422.

For information on where to purchase IDG Books Worldwide's books outside the U.S., please contact our International Sales department at 415-655-3200 or fax 415-655-3295.

For information on foreign language translations, please contact our Foreign & Subsidiary Rights department at 415-655-3021 or fax 415-655-3281.

For sales inquiries and special prices for bulk quantities, please contact our Sales department at 415-655-3200 or write to the address above.

For information on using IDG Books Worldwide's books in the classroom or for ordering examination copies, please contact our Educational Sales department at 800-434-2086 or fax 817-251-8174.

For press review copies, author interviews, or other publicity information, please contact our Public Relations department at 415-655-3000 or fax 415-655-3299.

For authorization to photocopy items for corporate, personal, or educational use, please contact Copyright Clearance Center, 222 Rosewood Drive, Danvers, MA 01923, or fax 508-750-4470.

ABOUT IDG BOOKS WORLDWIDE

Welcome to the world of IDG Books Worldwide.

IDG Books Worldwide, Inc., is a subsidiary of International Data Group, the world's largest publisher of computer-related information and the leading global provider of information services on information technology. IDG was founded more than 25 years ago and now employs more than 8,500 people worldwide. IDG publishes more than 275 computer publications in over 75 countries (see listing below). More than 60 million people read one or more IDG publications each month.

Launched in 1990, IDG Books Worldwide is today the #1 publisher of best-selling computer books in the United States. We are proud to have received eight awards from the Computer Press Association in recognition of editorial excellence and three from *Computer Currents'* First Annual Readers' Choice Awards. Our best-selling *...For Dummies*® series has more than 30 million copies in print with translations in 30 languages. IDG Books Worldwide, through a joint venture with IDG's Hi-Tech Beijing, became the first U.S. publisher to publish a computer book in the People's Republic of China. In record time, IDG Books Worldwide has become the first choice for millions of readers around the world who want to learn how to better manage their businesses.

Our mission is simple: Every one of our books is designed to bring extra value and skill-building instructions to the reader. Our books are written by experts who understand and care about our readers. The knowledge base of our editorial staff comes from years of experience in publishing, education, and journalism — experience we use to produce books for the '90s. In short, we care about books, so we attract the best people. We devote special attention to details such as audience, interior design, use of icons, and illustrations. And because we use an efficient process of authoring, editing, and desktop publishing our books electronically, we can spend more time ensuring superior content and spend less time on the technicalities of making books.

You can count on our commitment to deliver high-quality books at competitive prices on topics you want to read about. At IDG Books Worldwide, we continue in the IDG tradition of delivering quality for more than 25 years. You'll find no better book on a subject than one from IDG Books Worldwide.

John Kilcullen
CEO
IDG Books Worldwide, Inc.

Steven Berkowitz
President and Publisher
IDG Books Worldwide, Inc.

*Eighth Annual
Computer Press
Awards ≥1992*

*Ninth Annual
Computer Press
Awards ≥1993*

*Tenth Annual
Computer Press
Awards ≥1994*

*Eleventh Annual
Computer Press
Awards ≥1995*

IDG Books Worldwide, Inc., is a subsidiary of International Data Group, the world's largest publisher of computer-related information and the leading global provider of information services on information technology. International Data Group publishes over 275 computer publications in over 75 countries. Sixty million people read one or more International Data Group publications each month. International Data Group's publications include: **ARGENTINA:** Buyer's Guide, Computerworld Argentina, PC World Argentina; **AUSTRALIA:** Australian Macworld, Australian PC World, Australian Reseller News, Computerworld, IT Casebook, Network World, Publish, Webmaster; **AUSTRIA:** Computerwelt Osterreich, Networks Austria, PC Tip Austria; **BANGLADESH:** PC World Bangladesh; **BELARUS:** PC World Belarus; **BELGIUM:** Data News; **BRAZIL:** Annuario de Informática, Computerworld, Connections, Macworld, PC Player, PC World, Publish, Reseller News, Supergamepower; **BULGARIA:** Computerworld Bulgaria, Network World Bulgaria, PC & MacWorld Bulgaria; **CANADA:** CIO Canada, Client/Server World, ComputerWorld Canada, InfoWorld Canada, NetworkWorld Canada, WebWorld; **CHILE:** Computerworld Chile, PC World Chile; **COLOMBIA:** Computerworld Colombia, PC World Colombia; **COSTA RICA:** PC World Centro America; **THE CZECH AND SLOVAK REPUBLICS:** Computerworld Czechoslovakia, Macworld Czech Republic, PC World Czechoslovakia; **DENMARK:** Communications World Danmark, Computerworld Danmark, Macworld Danmark, PC World Danmark, Techworld Denmark; **DOMINICAN REPUBLIC:** PC World Republica Dominicana; **ECUADOR:** PC World Ecuador; **EGYPT:** Computerworld Middle East, PC World Middle East; **EL SALVADOR:** PC World Centro America; **FINLAND:** MikroPC, Tietoverkko, Tietoviikko; **FRANCE:** Distributique, Hebdo, Info PC, Le Monde Informatique, Macworld, Reseaux & Telecoms, WebMaster France; **GERMANY:** Computer Partner, Computerwoche, Computerwoche Extra, Computerwoche FOCUS, Global Online, Macwelt, PC Welt; **GREECE:** Amiga Computing, GamePro Greece, Multimedia World; **GUATEMALA:** PC World Centro America; **HONDURAS:** PC World Centro America; **HONG KONG:** Computerworld Hong Kong, PC World Hong Kong, Publish in Asia; **HUNGARY:** ABCD CD-ROM, Computerworld Szamitastechnika, Interneto online Magazine, PC World Hungary, PC-X Magazin Hungary; **ICELAND:** Tolvuheimur PC World Island; **INDIA:** Information Communications World, Information Systems Computerworld, PC World India, Publish in Asia; **INDONESIA:** InfoKomputer PC World, Komputek Computerworld, Publish in Asia; **IRELAND:** ComputerScope, PC Live!; **ISRAEL:** Macworld Israel, People & Computers/Computerworld; **ITALY:** Computerworld Italia, Macworld Italia, Networking Italia, PC World Italia; **JAPAN:** DTP World, Macworld Japan, Nikkei Personal Computing, OS/2 World Japan, SunWorld Japan, Windows NT World, Windows World Japan; **KENYA:** PC World East African; **KOREA:** Hi-Tech Information, Macworld Korea, PC World Korea; **MACEDONIA:** PC World Macedonia; **MALAYSIA:** Computerworld Malaysia, PC World Malaysia, Publish in Asia; **MALTA:** PC World Malta; **MEXICO:** Computerworld Mexico, PC World Mexico; **MYANMAR:** PC World Myanmar; **NETHERLANDS:** Computer! Totaal, LAN Internetworking Magazine, LAN World Buyers Guide, Macworld Netherlands, Net, WebWereld; **NEW ZEALAND:** Absolute Beginners Guide and Plain & Simple Series, Computer Buyer, Computer Industry Directory, Computerworld New Zealand, MTB, Network World, PC World New Zealand; **NICARAGUA:** PC World Centro America; **NORWAY:** Computerworld Norge, CW Rapport, Datamagasinet, Financial Rapport, Kursguide Norge, Macworld Norge, Multimediaworld Norge, PC World Ekspress Norge, PC World Nettverk, PC World Norge, PC World ProduktGuide Norge; **PAKISTAN:** Computerworld Pakistan; **PANAMA:** PC World Panama; **PEOPLE'S REPUBLIC OF CHINA:** China Computer Users, China Computerworld, China InfoWorld, China Telecom World Weekly, Computer & Communication, Electronic Design China, Electronics Today, Electronics Weekly, Game Software, PC World China, Popular Computer Week, Software Weekly, Software World, Telecom World; **PERU:** Computerworld Peru, PC World Profesional Peru, PC World SoHo Peru; **PHILIPPINES:** Click!, Computerworld Philippines, PC World Philippines, Publish in Asia; **POLAND:** Computerworld Poland, Computerworld Special Report Poland, Cyber, Macworld Poland, Networld Poland, PC World Komputer; **PORTUGAL:** Cerebro/PC World, Computerworld/Correio Informático, Dealer World Portugal, Mac*In/PC*In Portugal, Multimedia World; **PUERTO RICO:** PC World Puerto Rico; **ROMANIA:** Computerworld Romania, PC World Romania, Telecom Romania; **RUSSIA:** Computerworld Russia, Mir PK, Publish, Seti; **SINGAPORE:** Computerworld Singapore, PC World Singapore, Publish in Asia; **SLOVENIA:** Monitor; **SOUTH AFRICA:** Computing SA, Network World SA, Software World SA; **SPAIN:** Communicaciones World España, Computerworld España, Dealer World España, PC World España, PC World, Macworld, DOS World, Federal Computer Week, GamePro Magazine, InfoWorld, I-Way, Macworld, Network World, PC Games, PC World, Publish, Video Event, THE WEB Magazine, and WebMaster; online webzines: JavaWorld, NetscapeWorld, and SunWorld Online; **URUGUAY:** InfoWorld Uruguay; **VENEZUELA:** Computerworld Venezuela, PC World Venezuela; and **VIETNAM:** PC World Vietnam.

Credits

Acquisitions Editor
John Read

Development Editor
Matthew Lusher

Copy Editors
Richard H. Adin
Anne Friedman

Technical Editors
Mike Aquilina
Deirdré Straughan

Production Coordinator
Katy German

Book Design
Drew R. Moore

Graphics and Production Specialists
Ritchie Durdin
Stephanie Hollier
Dina F Quan
Andreas F. Schueller

Quality Control Specialist
Mick Arellano

Proofreader
David Wise

Indexer
James Minkin

About the Author

Mark L. Chambers has been a freelance author, computer consultant, technical writer, BBS sysop, and game programmer for over a decade. He spends entirely too much time on the Internet. His favorite pastimes include LSU football, collecting gargoyles, playing his pinball machines, and listening to just about every type of music imaginable. You can reach him on the Internet at:

markc@computerland.net

This book is gratefully dedicated to my wife, Anne, and my two daughters, Erin and Chelsea — thanks for giving me both the freedom to reach for my dream and the strength I needed to hang on to it!

Foreword

In the Beginning

The advent of the audio CD in the mid-1980s heralded the beginning of the digital revolution in the home, providing music lovers with a new standard of music quality. And while there is still some debate among audiophiles about whether vinyl LPs or CDs more truly represent the utmost in sonic realism, the fact is the crystal clear sound and durable compact format of the audio CD have made it arguably *the* most popular consumer electronics product in history.

Soon after the introduction of the audio CD, the same low cost and reliable CD technology first used in the audio world began to show up in computer systems as a method of storing computer data (the so-called CD-ROM, or *compact disc-read only memory*). With a seemingly limitless capacity for rich graphics, audio, and data, the CD-ROM soon supplanted the venerable floppy disk as the preferred method of software distribution, helping bring the multimedia revolution to the desktop personal computer.

For all of its advantages, CD technology has historically had one major disadvantage — it has been a read-only format. While CD-recordable (CD-R) devices actually did exist, their exorbitant cost (upwards of $30,000) and bulky size (often as large as a washing machine) meant they remained the exclusive domain of high-end professionals. In addition, the technology was somewhat unreliable and prone to the dreaded "buffer underrun" (a discontinuity in the data flow to the recorder, rendering the CD worthless) if a user so much as looked the wrong way.

CD Recorders Show Up on the Desktop

But, seemingly overnight, CD-recordable technology underwent a metamorphosis. CD recorders are now compact, affordable, and reliable. Leading CD recording software packages such as Adaptec's Easy-CD Pro and CD Creator are much more intuitive, enabling users to quickly and easily create and publish data (spreadsheets, presentations, and so on), record music, and back up important files. And unlike proprietary storage devices (such as ZIP drives, magneto-optical devices, and various tape peripherals), data written with a CD recorder in ISO 9660 mode is standardized and compatible across computer platforms (including DOS, Windows, Macintosh, and UNIX). So the CDs you create can be distributed to the estimated 100 million personal computers with a CD-ROM or CD-R drive. In addition, all you wannabe rock and roll stars can now can record your hottest original hits to CD and distribute them to the hundreds of millions of people worldwide with audio CD players!

An Exciting Future

The future of CD-R looks bright. In fact, the installed base of CD recorders has zoomed from a few thousand units in 1994 to nearly one and a half million units in 1996, with an anticipated three million more CD recorders expected to ship in 1997. With large multinational firms such as Hewlett-Packard, Sony, Philips, and Yamaha leading the way, the next few years may see the inclusion of a low-cost CD recorder as standard equipment on desktop PCs. More affordable CD recorders and the advent of packet writing technology such as Adaptec's DirectCD promise to make the storing of information to CD-R as easy as storing to a floppy drive by providing drive letter access and making buffer underruns a thing of the past. Got a 10MB file loaded with graphics, animation, and audio? Just drag and drop the file to your CD-R drive, and then distribute!

The Shape of Things to Come

CD-recordable technology is the precursor to other exciting technologies such as DVD (digital versatile disc). Sporting the same size and format as today's CD-ROM, DVD will initially provide 4.7GB (about seven CDs worth) of information, enabling consumers to watch full-length movies incorporating spectacular video, awesome five-channel surround sound, and even different versions of a movie (for example, PG and R) on the same DVD disc. With its enormous storage capacity, DVD will also become the choice for software distribution (enabling more dynamic audio and more lifelike video capabilities). Subsequently, the initial 4.7GB DVD format (which is single-layered and single-sided) will give way to dual-layer and dual-sided versions of DVD, which will provide a breathtaking 18GB worth of data. Like CD-recordable today, there will also be recordable versions of DVD that enable users to store and distribute tremendous volumes of information.

It is clear that with DVD offering 18GB of storage space, this technology promises to be the end all for data, audio, and video storage. And as the oft-repeated saying in the computer industry goes, "Who would ever need *that* much storage space!?"

About the Book

In this book, Mark Chambers continues in the excellent tradition of other IDG Books Worldwide Bibles by taking the mystery out of CD recording. Mark does an excellent job explaining the somewhat complex underpinnings of CD-recordable technology in a concise, easy-to-understand way. Whether you are a seasoned CD-R veteran or contemplating buying your first CD recorder, Mark helps walk you through the buying decision and process of creating your own CDs, providing thorough insight and helpful advice to get the most out of CD recording.

Mike Aquilina
Product Manager,
CD-Recording Software
Software Products Group, Adaptec, Inc.

Preface

If you enjoy the bare necessities of writing, here's the no-frills description of this book: It has been designed to cover every angle of the art of CD recording.

To be more precise, this book explains how to purchase a recorder, how to install it, and what software to select. This book teaches you how to organize your material, what recording format to use, and how to create various types of discs. It explains all of the technical aspects of CD recording in simple English, and it discusses tips and tricks that I've learned over the last three years of recording.

However, that isn't the *real* reason why I wrote this book. The real reason was to save you time, money, and trouble — to make sure that you, the reader, will never experience the trials and tribulations that typically await most owners of a CD recorder. CD recording is a truly amazing technology — but only after your hardware and software is installed and running correctly, your system has been optimized for recording, and you're aware of the potential problems! Consider this book to be your bridge over those pitfalls, and as you advance it will provide you with more information on improving your finished CDs.

It is my sincere hope that in the months and years ahead, someone will bring up the topic of CD recording to you, and because of this book you'll be able to smile and say, "What's the big deal? There's nothing to it!"

Who Should Read This Book?

You're an ideal candidate if you're:

+ Considering purchasing a CD recorder

+ Ready to install a recorder and its accompanying software

+ Trying to determine which recording software to buy

+ Currently recording data, audio, and multimedia CDs (or trying to, anyway)

+ Simply interested in the technology of CD recording

+ Experiencing problems with recording

Because this book was developed as a comprehensive "Bible" series book, your CD recording experience level doesn't matter. Of course, a novice will naturally appreciate the introductory chapters, especially those covering the purchase and installation of a SCSI CD recorder. But even if you've been recording for years, you're likely to find something new, including information on upcoming improvements in recording technology and CDs themselves.

What hardware and software do you need? This book centers on CD recording under Windows 95, but I do address Macintosh owners whenever the two platforms differ substantially. We'll cover the Windows 95 versions of three recording programs in-depth: Easy CD Creator, Easy CD Pro 95, and CD Creator.

If you're not an expert with Windows 95, don't worry — no previous knowledge of Windows 95 is required. We will perform a number of different steps to optimize your Windows 3.1 or Windows 95 system for recording, but each of these steps is fully explained and illustrated to make the process as easy as possible. "Does it matter which recorder I have?" I've avoided hardware-specific material wherever possible. As an avid reader of other computer books, nothing irritates me quite so much as buying a book and suddenly discovering that the author has different equipment and no coverage for my hardware! The methods I outline and the information I supply throughout the book should work well no matter what brand or model of recorder you own.

Organization

This book is organized into the following four parts:

+ **CD Recording 101 (Chapters 1–6).** These chapters introduce you to compact disc technology — how everything works, why you would want to record a disc, buying and installing your hardware, and installing Easy CD Creator under Windows 95.

+ **Recording a CD (Chapters 7–14).** This section is the heart of the book, and it contains most of the information that pertains directly to CD recording. In this section, you'll learn how to select and organize your data for recording, how to prepare your computer, and how to record different types of discs with Easy CD Creator, Easy CD Pro 95, and CD Creator. In particular, two chapters are dedicated to Easy CD Creator; the first, Chapter 9, takes you through the basics and shows you how to create data, audio, and multimedia discs, while Chapter 10 explains advanced recording, including Photo CDs and Video CDs.

+ **Advanced Topics (Chapters 15–17).** This final section explores some of the avenues you may wish to pursue once you've mastered the art of CD recording. Chapter 15 describes some of the professional touches you can add to your finished projects with HTML. You'll also be introduced to a typical multimedia authoring program, Corel's Click & Create, and I'll outline the improvements in disc technology that you can look forward to in the future.

+ **The Appendixes.** The appendixes include a hardware and software vendor list, descriptions of popular recorders and recording programs, a glossary, technical information, and a description of the contents of the accompanying CD-ROM.

Although I designed the book to be read from cover to cover, this arrangement should help you select those portions of the book that interest you the most. For example, if you've already installed your recorder and software, you may want to review the first section to see exactly what's happening behind the scenes as you record.

Navigating Through This Book

Because of the size and scope of this book and the number of processes I describe, it's important that you're aware of the various signposts we've placed throughout to help guide you. Each chapter begins with an overview of the information it contains, and each ends with a quick summary of what you learned.

Icons have also been placed in the margins to indicate something special or highlight specific text. Here's a list of these icons and what they represent:

 Tips provide you with the extra knowledge that separates the novice from the veteran; make use of the tips spread throughout this book to get the most out of your hardware and software.

 Notes along the way provide additional information or technical data on the subject at hand.

 The Warning icon is your sign of a potential problem, usually encountered during a process.

 The Cross Reference icon points the way to additional information you'll find in other locations throughout the book.

Finally, you'll also encounter sidebars throughout the book that give you more extensive background knowledge on particular topics.

Acknowledgments

No one could possibly write a book of this size and scope without help from an entire group behind the scenes, and I had the best help an author could possibly want!

First, I'd like to thank those who allowed me to include their software in the text and on the companion CD-ROM: John Battista, John Hornick, Bob Ellison, Chris Anderson, Jan Brondum, and Dimitri Bragin.

I would have never been able to provide the latest information on Easy CD Creator and DirectCD without the timely assistance I received from the good folks at Adaptec.

Thanks are due to Tim Kilgore and Bryan Chilcutt for their technical help and recording tips, as well as my good friend Phil James for his moral support.

I am very grateful to Mike Aquilina, Product Manager at Adaptec, and Deirdré Straughan. Their enthusiasm, comprehensive knowledge of CD recording, and genuine interest in my work was invaluable, and I'm happy to say that this book is much better because of their help and their fine technical editing.

Finally, I owe an unending debt of gratitude to three very special people at IDG Books Worldwide: John Read, who supported my idea for this book; Rebecca Morgan, who delivered the goods; and, last but not least, Matt Lusher, the best Development Editor I've ever had, and without whom this book would have faltered a hundred times over.

My sincere thanks to all of you!

Contents at a Glance

Table of Contents

● ●

CD-ROM Recording 101

Part I introduces compact disc technology. You learn how your CD-ROM drive reads data and how a CD recorder stores data. We also discuss the process of buying a CD recorder and the process of installing your new hardware and software.

How Does a CD-ROM Work?

For most computer owners today, a CD-ROM drive is a familiar sight, and loading and running a program from a CD-ROM disc is second nature. Like the telephone, the television, and your computer, it's simply an electronic device that works — or if you're unlucky, it doesn't work and you're on the way to the shop to have it checked. There's really no need to understand how it does what it does, unless you delight in that sort of arcane knowledge.

Everything changes, however, when you begin recording your own CDs. If you're not intimately familiar with the inner workings of a typical CD-ROM drive and the construction of the CD-ROM disc itself, you're going to waste a lot of time (and potentially quite a bit of money as well). There are just too many variables involved, too many steps required, and too many opportunities for mistakes for CD recording to be an easy "plug-and-play" process. In other words, to record your own compact discs successfully, you must become a CD-ROM guru (although that word may make you shudder). Don't worry, I'll try to make the transition as easy as possible for you!

There's no better place to begin than with the basics, so in this chapter, you learn about the physical construction of CD-ROM discs and CD-ROM read-only drives — you learn about CD recorders in Chapter 3. We discuss how CD-ROMs store information and how the drive reads that data. Finally, we discuss how to handle and care for CD-ROMs, both those you have bought and those that you've recorded yourself.

By the time you finish this chapter, you'll have a good working knowledge of exactly what goes on when you run a program or listen to music recorded on a CD. Here we go . . . if you have any questions, just raise your hand!

The CD-ROM Itself

First, for the explanation that everyone knows: a compact disc is a thin, round plastic platter 12 centimeters in diameter and approximately a millimeter thick, usually with the program name or some sort of logo printed on the top, and a shiny underside that reflects light in a prism effect. Like traditional vinyl record albums, it also has a hole in the center for a spindle. Figure 1-1 shows the "business side" of a typical disc.

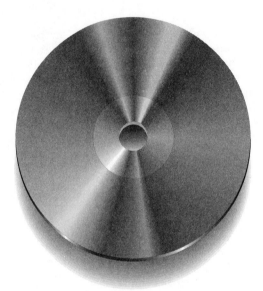

Figure 1-1: A typical compact disc.

Sony and Philips introduced compact discs to the public in 1980 as a replacement for vinyl record albums. Once CDs took off in the music industry and production costs dropped sufficiently, computer manufacturers began selling CD-ROM drives in earnest, and the first CD-ROM titles began to appear.

You may be asking, "Why are audio compact discs called CDs and computer compact discs called CD-ROMs?" Because experts like to point out that a compact disc used in a computer is actually a form of memory storage, just like the memory in your PC. Therefore, they call a computer compact disc a CD-ROM, which is short for Compact Disc - Read-Only Memory. This indicates that you can only read data from a CD-ROM, and you can't write new data to it like you can a hard drive or your computer's memory. The difference is really one in name only, as compact disc music and computer data are stored and retrieved exactly the same way.

You've probably also noticed by now that I've been referring to CD-ROM and audio discs, instead of "disks." That's another standard practice; it helps keep it clear whether we're talking about magnetic disk technology or digital compact discs.

Now let's get technical: a CD-ROM disc stores data on the surface of a polycarbonate disc, which is in turn covered by a thin layer of reflective aluminum film and a layer of lacquer for protection. Later in this chapter, you learn how that data is encoded and decoded, but for now, just remember that this is digital data, which is essentially a very long series of ones and zeros (rather like the settings for a light switch, which can be either ON or OFF). Both computers and your stereo's audio CD player understand this digital "language."

Here's an important point: the aluminum film layer is present only on mass-produced CD-ROMs, like the audio CDs and prerecorded computer CD-ROMs you buy at the store. The CDs that you record yourself store the same digital data, but they do it in a different manner. Confused yet? Don't panic; we cover the differences between the two types of discs in the next chapter.

The plastic coating that covers the entire underside of the disc serves an important purpose as well — it protects the data stored on the disc from damage from scratches and normal wear and tear, making CD-ROMs quite durable. As an example, I remember a typical gimmick that audio salesmen used to demonstrate how rugged compact discs were during the introduction of compact discs to the public in the early '80s: they would drop the disc on the carpeted floor and stand on it, while telling the skeptical customer just how good digital audio really was, especially if they had small children. After the pitch, the salesman would pick up the disc, wipe it off and play it, just to prove that it was undamaged!

There are different sizes of CD-ROMs, each of which can hold a different amount of data. The most common recordable CD-ROM can hold approximately 74 minutes of audio, or about 650 megabytes. Although they're much rarer and harder to find, there are also 63-minute discs that can hold 553 megabytes, and a disc 8 centimeters in diameter that can hold 184 megabytes.

How Is CD-ROM Data Stored?

As we've said, CD-ROMs store digital data on a thin metallic film embedded within the plastic; but how is the data stored on this film? Does the film hold an electric charge or is it magnetic like a floppy disk?

Actually, the answer has nothing to do with electricity or magnetism; compact disc technology uses the reflective quality of light to interpret a series of microscopic pits and smooth surfaces, called *lands*, in the film, rather like a computer version of Braille that your CD-ROM drive "reads" with a laser beam. Figure 1-2 illustrates a cross-section of a factory-made compact disc.

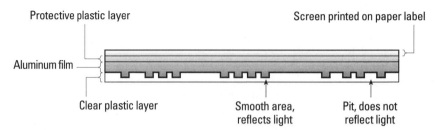

Figure 1-2: A cross-section of a mass-produced CD-ROM.

How is digital data stored on this thin metallic film? Those two possible values of 0 and 1 are represented by a pattern of microscopic cavities, or pits, that appear in the otherwise smooth surface of the metal. These pits can be read by your CD-ROM drive's laser beam. A sophisticated computer program converts the computer data or digital sound into this series of pits. These pits are then transferred to the compact disc at the factory.

The data appears on the disc in a single long track, much like a vinyl record album, but this digital "groove" moves in the opposite direction: it starts at the center, around the spindle, and as data is recorded it moves out towards the edge of the disc. To give you an idea of the size of this groove, if it was "unraveled" into a straight line, it would be approximately three miles long! As shown in Figure 1-3, the smooth surface returns one kind of signal to your drive, while the pits return another. We describe the process of reading and decoding performed by your CD-ROM drive in more detail later in this chapter.

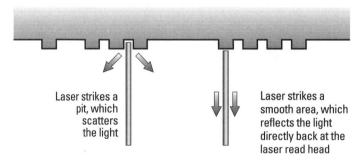

Figure 1-3: Reflected laser light is converted to digital data.

Mass-Producing Compact Discs

Now that compact discs are such a popular medium, there are dozens of factories throughout North America that specialize in replicating (or mass-producing) compact discs. Let's run through the process of mass-producing compact discs at one of these factories:

1. Using a laser or a photoetching process, a glass master disc is created that acts as the prototype for the entire production run.

2. Reverse metal molds called *stampers* are created from that master disc.

3. Presses use the stampers to mold the identical positive pattern of microscopic pits into the surface of a polycarbonate disc. The polycarbonate is injected directly into the mold and allowed to cool.

4. The disc is covered with a thin layer of aluminum.

5. The reflective film is covered by a layer of lacquer to protect it. At this point, the CD-ROM is essentially finished; you could put it into your CD-ROM drive and use it.

6. Each disc is screen-printed with a label and packaged in a jewel box or a protective sleeve.

Once again, remember that this process is radically different than the one you'll use to record your own CD-ROMs! Generally, only software developers and record companies need mass-produced compact discs, and the large majority of those are music discs.

CD Standards

You may be wondering how a manufacturer can be certain that any drive can read any disc produced at the factory; after all, audio compact disc players have no need for computer data! Luckily, computer manufacturers around the world follow a series of standards that ensure that every disc of a certain type "speaks the same language," and the manufacturers of different types of disc players can be certain of what will be on the discs we buy in the store.

These standards — commonly referred to as "books" — dictate how the data is physically arranged on different types of discs:

✦ Yellow Book — the standard for computer CD-ROMs.

✦ Red Book — the standard for digital audio CDs.

✦ Blue Book — the standard for CD Extra, also called CD Enhanced.

✦ Green Book — the standard for CD-I (short for *compact disc interactive*) discs.

✦ White Book — the standard for video CDs that carry MPEG-1 format digital video.

✦ Orange Book — the standard for recordable CDs. Naturally, this is the standard we'll mention the most!

Components of a CD-ROM Drive

OK, now that we know what CD-ROMs are and how they are made, let's get down to the business of reading them. In this section, the main components of the typical CD-ROM drive used by both Intel-based PCs and Macintosh computers are introduced; and, as mentioned earlier, audio CD players also use the same technology.

Every compact disc player has these major parts:

✦ **The laser read head.** This low-power laser is focused upward at the underside of the CD-ROM and is mounted on a moving arm that enables it to cover the entire disc surface.

✦ **The motor.** A CD-ROM disc is held firmly by a spindle system that is connected to a drive motor, very similar to a vinyl record album on a record player. Unlike a record player, however, the motor in a CD-ROM drive must have very precise control over the discs' speed, as it will vary while the CD-ROM is read.

✦ **The prism and light sensor.** This prism arrangement channels the laser light returned from the smooth areas of the disc surface back to the light sensor. It moves in tandem with the laser read head. The light sensor is the component that actually determines whether the laser light was reflected by the disc.

✦ **The disc caddy or tray.** Older CD-ROM drives required a disc caddy, which is a thin plastic box with a door that opens to hold the disc. It has a sliding bottom panel that moves to one side after you've inserted the caddy into the drive, much like the metal cover on a floppy disk moves to expose the disk. CD-ROM changers, which can hold and switch between 4 and 10 discs, typically use cartridges, which are caddies that can hold multiple discs in separate slots. CD-ROM "jukeboxes" can hold 100 discs or more, individually mounted in multiple cartridges. Figure 1-4 illustrates a CD-ROM caddy, while Figure 1-5 shows a changer cartridge. Although caddies do protect the disc somewhat from scratches and dust (and some manufacturers believe that caddy mechanisms are more durable), they're considered unnecessary for single-disc drives; almost all CD-ROM drives provide a tray that holds the disc when you load or unload it.

✦ **Front panel controls.** Every CD-ROM drive has an eject button, but many new drives also feature audio CD-style controls for play, pause, and jump to the next or previous track. Most players also have an earphone/external speaker plug for computer owners who prefer headphones.

We shouldn't forget software. Depending on which operating system your PC uses, you may have to load a software driver that enables your computer to recognize and use a CD-ROM drive. For MS-DOS and Windows 3.x users, it is the MSCDEX driver that enables the operating system to read the CD's ISO 9660 format, and it's usually loaded as part of your AUTOEXEC.BAT file. Your CD-ROM drive also has a device driver that's installed within your CONFIG.SYS file. If you're using Windows 95 or Windows NT, your CD-ROM drive is probably supported directly within the operating system, so you shouldn't have to load any external software drivers.

Figure 1-4: A caddy for a single-disc CD-ROM drive.

Figure 1-5: A cartridge for a multi-CD changer.

Retrieving Data From a CD-ROM

Let's delve into the details of how your CD-ROM drive actually reads the data encoded on a compact disc. Here is the process step-by-step:

1. You place a CD-ROM into the tray (or caddy) and it slides into the drive. The spindle locks the disc into place and it starts spinning.

   Unlike a hard drive that always spins at the same speed, a CD-ROM drive varies the speed at which the disc spins. Why? Since data is written to a compact disc in a single continuous track, the portion of the disc directly above the laser read head must always be moving at the same speed. If you recall your science, you'll remember that the outside edge of a spinning disc is actually moving faster relative to the inside edge — so, as the laser read head moves closer to the center of the disc to read the data there, the motor spins faster to maintain the same speed (as shown in Figure 1-6).

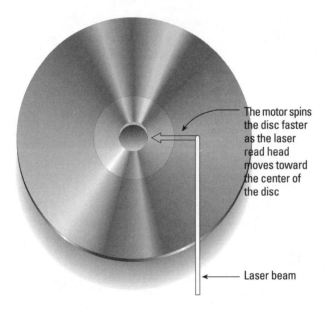

The motor spins
the disc faster
as the laser
read head
moves toward
the center of
the disc

Laser beam

Figure 1-6: The motor in a CD-ROM drive varies speed as the read head moves, spinning faster as the read head moves towards the center.

2. The drive activates the laser read head, which focuses the laser light on the underside of the compact disc.

3. The laser beam passes through the polycarbonate plastic covering the underside of the disc and reaches the metallic layer in the center of the disc.

4. If the laser beam strikes a depression in the metal surface, the light is dispersed in all directions, effectively returning no signal as shown in Figure 1-7. However, if the beam strikes a smooth portion of the metal surface, it's reflected directly back towards the laser read head, as shown in Figure 1-8. The transition between a land and a pit indicates a one in the digital data stream.

5. The reflected light passes through the prism system within the laser read head, which sends it at a 90-degree angle to a light sensor. The sensor reacts to the light by generating a current that is relayed to the computer as part of the data stream.

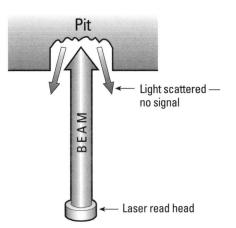

Figure 1-7: Light does not reflect from a pit.

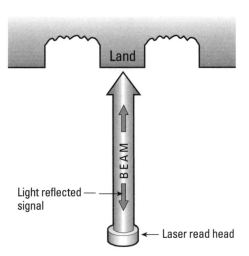

Figure 1-8: Light reflects directly from a smooth surface.

This process repeats until all of the file has been read by the CD-ROM drive. As you might imagine, the faster the CD-ROM drive spins the disc and reads these signals, the faster it can send the stream of electrical signals and pauses to your computer; this is why a drive that's advertised as a "10 speed" drive costs significantly more than a "4 speed" drive.

By the way, your CD-ROM drive will always read a particular area of the disc first. Once it reaches the proper speed, the drive automatically searches for a section of the disc called the *table of contents*. The table of contents lists all the files and directories on the disc and where they are located. When the drive locates and reads the disc table of contents, it appears as a drive on your system and you can display the directory, just as if it was a hard drive.

The ISO 9660 Standard

All right, now you know how data is retrieved from a CD; but how is that data arranged? As you might have expected, the logical format of each file on a CD-ROM is described by yet another international standard, the ISO 9660 standard. Because of ISO 9660, a disc can be read by most computers around the world, regardless of the country of its manufacture.

Before ISO 9660 was accepted, many CD-ROM manufacturers used their own proprietary file formats, which usually meant that the discs they made were incompatible with many computers and operating systems. To combat this "Tower of Babel" effect, a number of the most prominent companies banded together to form the High Sierra Group, and they created a standard format that they all used called the *High Sierra Format*.

Because of the obvious need for a standard CD-ROM file format, the international community soon accepted the High Sierra Format as a standard, and it eventually developed into the ISO 9660 standard in use today. You'll find additional information on the ISO 9660 standard in the technical appendix at the back of this book.

Proper Handling and Care of CD-ROMs

Now that you know how data is retrieved from a CD-ROM, you can see just how important it is to handle your blank and recorded compact discs as carefully as possible. Laser light must be able to pass directly through the polycarbonate surface, and it must be reflected correctly.

When picking up a compact disc, try not to touch the surface, because oil and fingerprints build up over time and can become problems. It's best to hold the disc by the outside edge. Some people even use their finger for a spindle by sticking it through the hole in the disc.

To avoid picking up dust, dirt, or liquid contaminants, never place a CD-ROM on a table or on the ground. If you smoke, try to reduce the amount of smoke and ash around your drive. Never bend a disc, and I wouldn't recommend using them as pet toys either!

Now, let's review the six deadly dangers facing any compact disc:

✦ **Scratches.** The CD-ROM itself is designed to minimize the damage caused by rough handling — for example, that protective layer of plastic that covers the metal surface of the disc is scratch-resistant — but a very deep scratch is likely to interfere with the reflection of laser light, or it could damage the metallic layer. In either case, you may end up with a disc that is readable only with a large number of errors, or not readable at all. Keep all sharp objects away from your compact discs; this includes any cloth with a heavy weave that you may use for wiping and any ballpoint pens or pencils you may use for marking the contents of the disc! That ballpoint pen may very well scratch right through the lacquer surface.

✦ **Stains.** It makes sense that stains like paint and ink would interfere with the laser beam, but actually just any liquid stain — clear or otherwise — can ruin a compact disc. Even the oil from your hands can interfere with recording and playing a CD-ROM. If you do have to remove a sticky stain, make sure you use a soft, lint-free cloth, because scratches from a paper towel or a dustrag will only do more damage!

✦ **Dust and dirt.** Dust and dirt cause the most common problems with recording and playing CD-ROMs. A single speck of dust or grain of sand can wreak havoc with the laser beam; if you've ever had a problem with "skipping" when you listen to an audio CD, it's likely due to dust on the underside of the disc.

✦ **Vibration.** Another cause of skipping — especially while traveling in a car — is undue vibration. Most audio compact disc players have a built-in "read-ahead/read-again" feature that minimizes the effects of vibration by either storing a few seconds of music or automatically rereading data; either method enables your music to continue uninterrupted. In most cases, your computer's CD-ROM drive will never experience vibration like this, but it's still not a good idea to shake or vibrate your PC while it's recording a disc!

✦ **Heat.** Here's a problem that CD-ROMs do share with traditional magnetic media. Exposure to heat can warp the disc or, in the worst case, melt it. Make sure you keep your CD-ROMs away from direct sunlight, and if you're transporting them in a hot car in summer, take them with you as you leave — don't leave them locked in that greenhouse! Exposure to any temperature above 100 degrees Fahrenheit for any length of time is sure to damage a CD-ROM.

✦ **Chemicals.** We're talking about more than solvents and glues that decompose plastic; you should never wipe a CD-ROM with glass cleaning fluid or any type of abrasive cleanser. Avoid alcohol like the plague when it comes to CD-ROMs.

If you'd like to spend the extra money, there are commercial "CD cleaning systems" available at most electronics and department stores. These usually are some sort of velvet pad that moves across the surface of the disk in a circular motion. They typically require a small amount of cleaning liquid that is a mixture of alcohol and water.

In my opinion, these gadgets are overkill; compact discs are designed to be easy-to-clean, and unless you use CD-ROMs in a particularly dusty environment they shouldn't often require cleaning. In addition, buying refills of that cleaning liquid is expensive. You really only need the cleaning liquid if your toddler has gotten into your CD collection and smeared peanut butter all over the CDs!

To clean a CD-ROM safely, I recommend a lint-free photographer's lens cloth. You can buy one in any photography shop; the cloth is made from a very fine and soft weave that won't leave a scratch. The cloth is specially made to clean expensive photographic lenses, and doesn't require any chemicals.

Got your lens cloth? Good! Holding the disc by the edges, wipe it as shown in Figure 1-9, with a straight motion that moves from the center of the disc to the edge. Never wipe a CD-ROM in a circular motion; this can cause scratches aligned with the track that obscure long stretches of data.

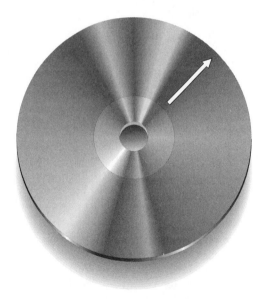

Wipe a CD from the center to the edge in a straight motion

Figure 1-9: The proper method of cleaning a compact disc.

I also recommend you buy a CD-ROM lens cleaning disc as well. This nifty invention looks just like a CD-ROM from the top, but the underside has a tiny lint-free brush embedded in the middle of the disc. To clean your laser read head, you listen to the audio track on the disc, which will prompt you to change tracks at the proper time. As the laser head moves, the brush moves across the laser lens and wipes it clean of any dust or dirt. Check first to see whether your CD-ROM drive has a self-cleaning lens, and you should **never** use this cleaning disc on your CD-recorder.

Summary

In this chapter, we discussed:

✦ the components of both compact discs and CD-ROM read-only drives;

✦ how digital information is stored on CD-ROMs;

✦ how your drive reads digital data recorded on mass-produced CD-ROMs;

✦ how you can safely handle your CD-ROMs;

✦ what products are available to help keep your discs and CD-ROM drive clean and trouble-free.

In the next chapter, you learn why CD-ROM technology has become so popular with computer manufacturers, software developers, and computer owners around the world, as well as a number of possible applications for recorded CD-ROMs.

✦   ✦   ✦

Why Record a CD-ROM?

As mentioned earlier, CD-ROMs have increased dramatically in popularity within the last two to three years, and now they rank as the primary distribution media for most commercial computer programs of any size; in fact, even some of the more popular shareware game and utility programs are now being distributed on CD-ROM. Step up to a newsstand that carries computer magazines, and you'll be swamped with CD-ROMs that include game demos, online service programs, and Internet material. Computer books are almost universally equipped with CD-ROMs full of shareware and commercial applications. It's getting to the point where you feel cheated if you get a program on one of those old-fashioned floppy disks!

Sales statistics for CD-ROM recording hardware reflect that same growth and popularity. In 1995, approximately 20 million recordable discs and 200,000 CD recorders were sold. A year later, those numbers had jumped to nearly 50 million recordable discs and over 2 million CD recorders. In 1997, projected sales are for 80 million blank discs and a whopping 5 million CD recorders!

Why do CD-ROMs suddenly enjoy this enormous popularity among software developers and the general public? What's wrong with the traditional magnetic storage that PC users have been using comfortably for the last decade?

In this chapter, we discuss the important factors that have contributed to the rise of the CD-ROM, and why even novice PC owners are now recording their own discs. We also discuss a number of possible applications for recorded CD-ROMs of interest to everyone, from casual users to corporate employees and professional multimedia developers.

The Byte Explosion

A major factor in the popularity of CD-ROMs among software developers is the rapid growth of today's applications and games. In years past, programs and all their accompanying data files could easily fit on one or two 3-inch floppy disks, usually with room to spare. Only a few years ago, the IBM PC architecture supported CGA and EGA low-resolution graphics, an internal speaker, and a 2400-baud modem connection. A mere four megabytes of RAM provided all the elbow room you were likely to need, and your dot matrix line printer did just that — it printed lines of text in black and white.

Today's PCs are a whole different ball game! To be competitive in today's market, even utility programs need fancy, disk-gobbling graphics and a 16-bit stereo sound file to accompany each click of the mouse, all of which require ever more hard disk space to store. The continued growth of Windows illustrates this dramatic increase in space requirements. MS-DOS 6.22 requires all of three floppies to install, while Windows 3.1 requires seven, and Windows 95 more than doubles the number of floppies yet again! Even a partial hard drive installation of a popular multimedia game like MECHWARRIOR 2 or WING COMMANDER 4 is likely to take 30 megabytes of space.

In fact, a growing number of applications and games today are no longer distributed on 3-inch disks; you either have a CD-ROM drive, or you simply don't run the program. Some individual file sizes have grown so immense — especially digital video in .AVI or .MOV format — that it's no longer practical to consider shipping them on floppy disks.

Due to the rapid rise of the multimedia PC, the switch to 32-bit operating systems, and the appearance of higher-capacity storage media like the Iomega ZIP disk, the 3-inch floppy disk certainly seems doomed to the hardware graveyard — and it's been replaced by, for the most part, the CD-ROM, which offers the spacious surroundings needed by those same applications. It's still unusual to see an application that requires more storage space than a single CD-ROM, and often a developer will fill up the 200 or 300 megabytes left to spare with demo programs, images, clip art, or sound files.

Permanent Storage

Another common problem with magnetic storage like floppy disks and tapes is the eventual loss of data due to mechanical wear, a dirty drive, exposure to magnetic fields, or damage to the media itself. Whether the data is a spreadsheet file or a ZIP archive saved to disk, the loss of just a few bytes usually results in the loss of the entire file.

Although most PC owners don't know it, magnetic media usually has a shelf life of less than a decade. That may sound like plenty of time, but it's certainly a best case where the disk simply sits on a shelf. In real life, no one should depend on magnetic media for permanent storage; for example, if you retrieve the same data from a floppy disk several times a day, there's a good chance it will fail within a few months. Many computer owners have learned the hard way that you should never leave your priceless collection of floppy disks on top of your stereo speakers for a week or so!

Most of us tend to consider hard drives as "permanent" storage, too. It's true that today's hard drives are much more reliable and sturdy than those made a few years ago, but it's no accident that smart PC owners with important files back up often, and that corporations invest in multiple-disk systems that can preserve file integrity even after a drive fails completely.

On the other hand, the CD-ROM represents storage that's about as foolproof and permanent as possible. There are no moving parts to wear out, and a CD-ROM cannot be erased by a strong magnetic source. Practically the only way to damage a CD-ROM is to deliberately break it or melt it; however, if you're not familiar with handling CD-ROMs, you should review the section "Proper Handling and Care of CD-ROMs" in Chapter 1. By the way, if you need to permanently destroy the data on a disc, you can actually microwave it; however, doing so might damage the microwave oven, so I usually cut discs into small pieces with a pair of heavy bolt cutters from my toolbox.

The durability of CD-ROMs makes them an ideal storage media for recording archival information you're likely to need several years from now. I've often used CD-ROMs while traveling; if you're carrying a laptop with you and it has a CD-ROM drive, why fill up its hard drive with 300 megabytes of data that could be lost if it's damaged or stolen? That same data would fit on a single CD-ROM with room to spare, and you can carry it in your briefcase!

Random Access

If you've ever used a standard QIC tape drive for storing your files, you've likely fallen asleep at least once or twice waiting for it to store, restore, or compare files. Most tape drives are sequential storage devices, meaning that they must wind and rewind the tape, moving through other files to find a specific file. For example, if the file you're trying to restore from tape was one of the last written, the tape drive has to perform these steps:

1. Rewind the tape completely to reach the catalog file.

2. Read the catalog file to determine where on the tape your file was stored.

3. Fast-forward to that point on the tape, skipping all the other files.

4. Read the file.

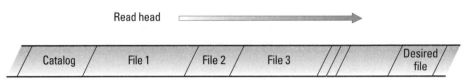

Figure 2-1: An illustration of sequential file access.

Figure 2-1 shows this process. Even though you're not reading those files, your tape drive still has to cover that area, usually resulting in a long wait.

Floppy disk drives, hard drives, and CD-ROM drives are different; they are random access devices, meaning that they can jump directly to a specific file and read it immediately. Oh, by the way, you might have also guessed that your computer's memory is actually a form of random access storage as well — hence the acronym RAM, for Random Access Memory — but it really doesn't fit in with the rest, since you lose the data stored in your PC's RAM each time you turn it off.

To illustrate, your drive performs these steps when retrieving that same file from a backup on a CD-ROM:

1. Read the directory (or, more properly, the table of contents) to determine where your file is stored on the disc.

2. Jump directly to that point on the disc.

3. Read the file.

Figure 2-2 shows this process. As you can see, random access is much more efficient than sequential access, especially since there's no fast-forward step!

This doesn't make the CD-ROM the perfect random access storage solution, though. As mentioned in Chapter 1, relatively slow access time and raw kilobyte/second throughput still hampers current CD-ROM technology. The hard drive is still king of the random access storage crowd, with the CD-ROM drive second, and the lowly floppy drive taking last place. A typical hard drive reads over 10 times more data in a single second than today's fastest CD-ROM drive, and the hard drive's read head is much faster as it moves across the magnetic surface of the drive. We discuss the speed factor, access time, and throughput of CD-ROMs in Chapter 4.

However, today's 12x and 16x speed CD-ROM drives can easily sustain the data throughput needed for demanding digital video, with the fastest drives surpassing 1500KB/second throughput — making the CD-ROM the ideal media for commercial multimedia software. Let's be honest; it's hard to imagine software developers shipping multimedia titles on individual hard drives!

WHEN TAPE WAS KING

You may be asking, "Why would anyone use a tape drive to actually load and run programs?" In the ancient days of 8-bit hardware like the Atari 800, the Radio Shack Model III, and the Commodore 64, cassette tape drives were much less expensive than floppy drives, which were even sold separately from the computer! For this reason, many older computer owners will remember that wonderful moment when they could invest in their first floppy drive (or, if you were really a trendsetter, an honest-to-goodness **hard drive!**) and banish their cassette drive to the closet.

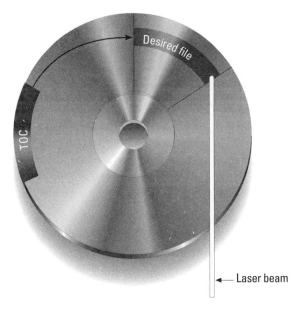

Figure 2-2: An illustration of random file access.

Widespread Acceptance

If you've priced a new computer these days, you already know another reason CD-ROM recording is growing so fast in popularity. Today, no one would think of buying a desktop PC — or even one of the more expensive portables or laptops — without a CD-ROM drive. CD-ROM drives are a required part of the MPC (short for *Multimedia Personal Computer*) level 2 standard, which also defines the minimum sound card, processor, and video requirements needed to run multimedia software. More and more applications are assuming that you're running a computer that meets this standard.

Therefore, the CD-ROM has reached the status of "household word," especially among game players and those that enjoy educational titles. Most of the children in school today can tell you where a CD-ROM goes in a computer and which side goes up, and Windows 95 can automatically launch applications from a CD-ROM without requiring you to press a key or touch the mouse. Not much else is really needed! If you record a CD-ROM on your computer, you can bet that most of the computers built within the last several years are able to read it.

This acceptance is all-important to software developers, who must ship software on media that the customer is likely to request (and the fewer types of media, the better). As little as three years ago, you were safe shipping software on 5-inch floppy disks; however, most PCs no longer ship with a 5-inch drive, so today there would be a good chance the program would be returned.

Low Cost

In the early days of audio CDs, audiophiles commonly paid $25 or more for a single disc. There were very few CD manufacturing plants in operation, compact discs were not well-known, and the perceived value of high-quality digital sound all contributed to such high prices. In fact, some wondered whether audio compact discs would ever be widely accepted because of their expense compared to vinyl albums.

The same was true during the introduction of the computer CD-ROM. Only a handful of programs were available, CD-ROM drives were priced far too high for the average consumer, and the cost of manufacturing and mastering the discs themselves added to the cost of the program.

Those days are gone forever. The overwhelming popularity of the CD-ROM has lowered prices dramatically across the board, from the cost of manufacturing and mastering the media to the CD-ROM drives themselves (including, of course, CD recorders). The same CD recorder that once sold for $2,000 today sells for $500 to $800, and prices continue to drop.

Calculating Cost per Megabyte

The most important cost savings with a recorded CD-ROM, however, is its tremendously low cost per megabyte of storage. If you read computer magazines, you're probably familiar with this well-known yardstick, which usually appears in advertisements for hard drives. As an example, an inexpensive two-gigabyte hard drive might run $200, which works out to ten cents per megabyte. Let's apply this same calculation to a CD recordable blank, which can store 650 megabytes for about $6.50 at bulk prices: that works out to an impressive one cent per megabyte!

Of course, our example two-gigabyte drive can be erased and used again, but if you're looking to save information permanently and as inexpensively as possible, the CD-ROM is definitely the best solution available to computer owners today!

Other Low-Cost Storage

There are competitors looming on the horizon that attempt to combine the interchangeable quality of a CD-ROM with the speed and read/write capability of a hard drive. Within the last year or two, Iomega introduced two low-cost removable magnetic media drives, the ZIP and JAZ drives, that range in price from $150 to $450, respectively. The JAZ drive, in fact, is actually a removable hard drive cartridge which operates just like a standard hard drive. These drives are the second generation of removable magnetic media, able to hold much more than the original Bernoulli drives made by the same company. They can hold anywhere from 100 megabytes to an entire gigabyte of data on a single cartridge, and the JAZ drive shown in Figure 2-3 is as fast as a standard fixed hard drive.

Figure 2-3: A JAZ removable cartridge drive, which can hold up to one gigabyte of data.

However, those cartridges are very expensive compared to a recordable CD. Plus, the ZIP and JAZ removable drives are nowhere near as popular and commonplace as the CD-ROM drive, making them impractical for mass distribution. It's not likely that they will ever reach the same "critical mass" of popularity that the CD-ROM reached a couple of years ago.

Flexibility

Another advantage of the recorded CD-ROM is its versatility at storing vastly different types of media. As you have already learned, CD-ROMs can easily hold computer data, digital audio, or a mixture of both; but, to be fair, so can hard drives, and even magnetic tape has been used to store both programs and audio. Of course, no one expects distribution of a multimedia encyclopedia on a magnetic tape cartridge!

Part of the attraction in recording CD-ROMs, though, is the ability to create inexpensive audio CDs that are as good as those you can buy in your local record store. Only the recordable CD-ROM will work in a standard CD audio drive. In fact, some musicians buy CD recorders simply for their audio capabilities, and never save a byte of computer data.

Cross Reference Plus, the CD recorder offers another format that no other media can offer — Video CDs. Discs written by a program like VCD Creator contain digital video and stills playable by any video CD player. Chapter 10 discusses creating your own Video CDs with VCD Creator.

Possible Applications

Let's examine some of the applications, both common and uncommon, for recorded CD-ROMs.

✦ **Archival backup.** As discussed earlier, the CD-ROM is far superior to standard tape backups in every area but one — tapes can be re-used. However, if you want to remove seldom-used programs and data from your hard drive, or if you'd like to create a permanent backup as a "snapshot" of your hard drive, a CD-ROM is practically perfect. You can even access your data directly from the CD-ROM, while a tape backup needs to be restored first. For example, I often run programs directly from archival CD-ROMs that I've recorded; as long as the program doesn't attempt to write data to the CD-ROM (and you save your files to your hard drive), it will probably work! However, system files currently in use by your computer can't be backed up to disc; this is a common problem with most tape backup programs as well.

✦ **Audio CDs.** If you're a music lover, you can create your own audio CDs for every occasion, taking songs directly from other audio CDs (and, with a sound card, you can record from your stereo). If you have hard-to-find albums on vinyl, keep them in mint condition; connect your stereo to your sound card to record them in digital format and then create CDs.

Warning As you might imagine, copyright law protects records, tapes, and prerecorded audio CDs. Before you unwittingly commit a crime, check to make sure you're allowed to copy the music; for example, most audio CDs carry a restriction against unauthorized duplication. If you're at all uncertain of the legality of copying any material, contact your lawyer!

✦ **Transporting data.** The low cost, durability, storage space, and physical size of recorded CD-ROMs make them ideal for transporting large amounts of data from one place to another. For example, a network administrator for a company's branch office might need to send hundreds of megabytes of files to the home office on a regular basis. Those files could be sent over a modem, but it would take several hours (even with the fastest modems available today), and a broken telephone connection will interrupt the transfer. Instead, why not take half an hour to record the files on a single CD-ROM and send it to the home office in a disk mailer?

✦ **Unattended "session" discs for radio stations.** The majority of radio stations has switched from vinyl albums and tapes to CD-ROMs, and many have also invested in CD recorders to create "session" discs for unattended play. Commercials recorded in digital format on a PC's hard drive through a sound card are able to be included on "session" discs.

✦ **Distribution.** Of course, when we think of data distributed on CD-ROM, we think of commercial software; however, those CD-ROMs are mass-produced instead of recorded individually. Software developers often use recorded CD-ROMs to distribute beta copies of a new product. Internal distribution is another possibility; for example, some companies record a copy of a CD-ROM containing common network files, software patches, word processing templates, company clip art, and so forth for each department that uses a standard set of applications. Using this CD-ROM, new employees can install everything they need from a single source instead of searching the company network for each file. If you belong to a computer club or user group, there's probably a member who maintains a club library of shareware and public domain software who would like to dump that collection of floppy disks!

✦ **Electronic photo albums.** If you have a bookshelf dedicated to photo albums, consider creating an electronic copy of those pictures that you can give to another family member! All you need is a scanner to capture the photos in digital format and one of many shareware or public domain "slide show" programs, which you can include in a separate directory on the disc. Again, don't forget the multimedia advantages of recorded CD-ROMs; why not record your children and add the sound files to your permanent album as well? In Chapter 10, you learn all the details on how you can use PCD Creator to build your own library of images from Kodak PhotoCDs.

✦ **Offline Web sites.** Do you run a World Wide Web site (a "webmaster" in cyberspace jargon)? If so, have you ever tried to demonstrate all the multimedia bells and whistles on your site on another computer, only to find out that the network is down or the connection is moving at a snail's pace? Perhaps it's time to create a snapshot of your entire web site on CD-ROM, directories and all, and load your HTML pages from it instead! Your browser will load your site much faster, no matter whether the PC has an Internet connection!

◆ **Network archive libraries.** If you'd like to offer a permanent archive of files that will benefit everyone on your office network, record those files on a CD-ROM and connect a read-only drive to your network as a shared system device. Your system administrator will thank you, since those files won't need to be backed up, yet everyone at your company can access the files whenever they're needed. Along the same lines, if you run an online bulletin board system (or *BBS*) as I do, move that huge file library you've built up over the years to a CD-ROM archive and save yourself 650 megabytes of hard drive space! Your callers will never know they're retrieving files from a CD-ROM.

Summary

In this chapter, you learned:

◆ why CD-ROM recording has become so popular and universally accepted in recent years as a means of saving time and hard drive space;

◆ the reasons CD-ROMs are superior to magnetic media like tapes, floppy disks, and hard drives;

◆ a number of applications that can take advantage of the recorded CD-ROM.

The next chapter introduces the basics of CD recording.

◆   ◆   ◆

The Basics of CD Recording

Congratulations! At this point you probably know more about the fundamentals of compact disc technology than anyone on your block. We covered the construction of the compact disc itself, as well as how data is stored on the disc at the factory and retrieved from the disc by your CD-ROM drive. You learned the properties of both audio and CD-ROM discs and why they are so popular today. You also know how to handle and store your compact discs to keep them in good shape.

We're not finished with the basics yet, because the CD-ROMs you record yourself are constructed differently, and your recorder stores data on them differently. The good news is that your CD-ROM drive will read the discs you record yourself using the same process described in Chapter 1, and you'll handle your recorded discs in the same fashion — at least you won't have to cover that ground again!

In this chapter, we describe how your CD recorder actually records a CD. This gives you an overall picture of CD recording before we get knee-deep in details and exceptions to the rules. This chapter explains the differences between the CDs you record yourself and those mass-produced in a factory. You also learn which recordable discs to buy and where you can get them. We discuss the steps involved in recording a single CD and a disc image. Finally, you learn several different methods of labeling your recorded discs, from simple and inexpensive to professional screen printing.

Recordable CD-ROMs vs. Standard CD-ROMs

As you learned earlier, the compact discs you buy in a store carry their digital information on a plastic disc covered with a thin metallic layer of aluminum. In the factory, the stamper recreates from the original master disc the pits your CD-ROM player's laser beam reads.

Of course, your PC isn't equipped with a CD-ROM press, but, because a standard CD-ROM drive can read both a factory-made compact disc and one that you've recorded yourself, something must create the equivalent of pits and smooth surfaces that will be translated into digital data. So, how are recordable discs made?

The Construction of Recordable Discs

Unlike factory-made compact discs, recordable discs do not have an aluminum layer. Instead, the cross-section of a recordable disc includes a layer of gold and a layer of light-sensitive dye, as shown in Figure 3-1. This dye is not sensitive to ordinary light, unlike the film in a camera; instead, it reacts specifically to the laser light emitted by your CD recorder, so there's no need to worry about "exposing" a blank recordable CD-ROM to the light. Also, there is no layer of aluminum to provide a reflective surface, as in a mass-produced CD-ROM. On the recordable disc, the layer of gold reflects light.

Additionally, recordable CDs have a thin groove cut into the protective plastic on the underside of the disc. This groove is so small it's invisible to the naked eye, but it performs two very important functions: the laser write head follows it as data is recorded, and your recorder uses it to determine where the laser write head is positioned on the surface of the disc, and, therefore, at what speed the disc should spin.

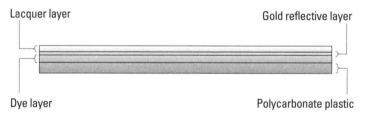

Lacquer layer   Gold reflective layer

Dye layer   Polycarbonate plastic

Figure 3-1: The cross-section of a recordable CD.

In fact, the easiest way to tell a recordable CD from a commercially made disc is by the color of the disc. A mass-produced disc has a clear protective coating and a silver or silver-gold color, depending on what metal was used, and it looks the same on both the top and bottom. A recorded CD, on the other hand, has a gold top, and the underside is usually green or yellowish green (the color of the dye), with a hint of the gold behind it. Some recordable discs use a blue-colored dye.

Buying Blank Discs

"Where can I buy recordable CDs?" As late as a year or so ago, that was a difficult question to answer, because CD recorders were considered high-end, expensive devices and no store wished to carry them or the blank discs. The only source generally available was mail order, and blanks ranged from $15 to $20 each in bulk.

Luckily, the same factors that lowered the price of CD recorders also dropped the price of blank compact discs, and you can find prices as low as $6 each in bulk through a good mail order company. It's also easier to find discs in local stores. Any large electronics store, office supply store, or computer retail store should offer blank CDs, with prices from $8 to $12 each. Prices for recordable CDs tend to reflect brand name recognition, but I recommend TDK — its quality is always high, but its prices tend to be lower in bulk than other brand names. Other excellent brands to look for are Kodak, 3M, Maxell, Verbatim, and Sony.

The standard recordable CD blank holds approximately 74 minutes of digital audio or about 650 megabytes of computer data. When buying your CD blanks, make certain that they conform to the Orange Book standard; that way, you can be certain they'll work in your recorder. The Orange Book standard specifies the format accepted worldwide for recordable CDs. Also, if you have a recorder that writes at 4x speed, the blanks you buy should be certified for 4x recording.

How Is a CD Recorded?

Now let's concentrate on the process of recording a CD on your PC. First, what happens inside the drive and how is it different from the mastering process used at the factory to mass-produce discs?

Earlier you learned that a recordable CD doesn't use thin layers of polycarbonate and aluminum to hold digital data. Instead, the recorder makes changes in the dye layer underneath a layer of gold, and the laser beam doesn't reflect light when it hits these altered areas (see Figure 3-2). For most disc blanks, the laser beam in the recorder's write head discolors the dye layer; other discs use a dye layer which melts or bubbles. These alterations in the dye layer have the same effect as the pits in the aluminum layer of a mass-produced disc.

THE PROBLEM OF MEDIA COMPATIBILITY

If you record a disc without errors but you can't, for example, read it on your CD-ROM drive at work, you're experiencing the common symptom of media incompatibility. If the manufacturer of your recorder recommends a specific brand of blank disc as tested and certified compatible, you may avoid problems reading your discs on other CD-ROM drives by using that brand.

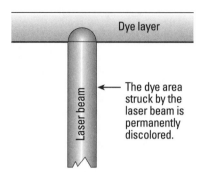

Dye layer

Laser beam

← The dye area struck by the laser beam is permanently discolored.

Figure 3-2: Changes made in the dye surface of a blank disc by the recorder.

Whatever the change, the same steps occur.

1. You place a blank CD into the tray (or caddy) and it slides into the drive. The spindle locks the disc into place and it starts spinning. Just like the motor in a standard read-only CD-ROM drive, your recorder has to vary the speed at which the disc rotates to record data properly.

2. The drive activates the write head, which focuses the laser light on the underside of the compact disc. The write head automatically aligns the laser beam with the groove I mentioned earlier.

3. The laser beam passes through the plastic covering the underside of the disc and reaches the dye layer in the center of the disc.

4. The CD recording software reads the data you want recorded in digital format, usually from your computer's hard drive, into a special section of your computer's memory called a *buffer*. Because RAM reads data much faster than a hard drive, the data in this buffer helps ensure that your recorder won't run out of signals to record, which would ruin the recording. We talk about data buffers and other software factors later in the book, as well as how you can copy data directly from a compact disc in a second CD-ROM drive to your CD recorder.

5. Your recording software works along with the electronics within your recorder to toggle the power and frequency of the laser read head to match the digital signals. When the recorder switches the laser beam to high power, it records a pit (Figure 3-3). When the recorder switches the beam to lower power, it leaves the dye intact, creating a land (Figure 3-4).

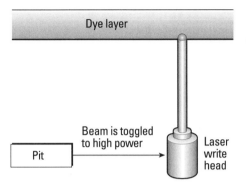

Figure 3-3: The laser is set to high power for a pit, causing a reaction on the dye layer.

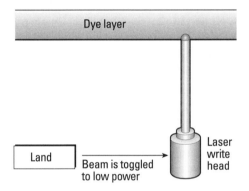

Figure 3-4: The laser is set to low power for a land, so the dye layer remains clear.

6. This process repeats until all the data is recorded. At this point, your recording software writes the disc table of contents, which allows any standard CD-ROM drive to read the data. Your disc is finished!

Most recorders today write data at either 2x speed or 4x speed, so the recording process might be completed faster than an older single-speed CD-ROM could read the same data from the disc! If your PC is equipped with a slower hard drive, however, you can still write data at single speed, but it will take longer. It doesn't matter to the drive that will read your disc at what speed the disc was recorded.

You may be asking, "Why doesn't the laser beam in a read-only CD-ROM drive affect the dye layer after the CD has been recorded?" The answer is that when your CD recorder toggles its laser write head on, it's using a laser beam of a different frequency that's 10 times more powerful than the laser read head of a standard CD-ROM drive; therefore, a standard CD-ROM read-only drive does not erase or alter the information on a recorded disc.

Recording a Single CD-ROM

It's time to discuss where the data mentioned in step 4 above comes from. There are two methods of storing information you wish to record on a CD:

✦ **On your hard drive.** This is how most of us accumulate data to be transferred to a CD. Files either already exist on your hard drive or are copied from other sources, like floppies, backup tapes, and other CDs. I reserve time to arrange these files into some sort of logical order, grouping them into directories that will make it easy for me to find them later. These files are then marked for copying when you create your disc layout, and your recording software reads them directly off the hard drive, copying them to the blank CD.

Note   For storage purposes, individual songs from an audio CD are just another type of file; however, you don't need to arrange them manually to make them easier to find, like I suggest you do with computer data files. Your CD-ROM recording software should allow you to place them in any order you like when you build your audio CD layout.

✦ **On another CD.** If you happen to have a SCSI read-only CD-ROM drive on the same SCSI connection as your CD recorder, you can copy select files or the contents of an entire disc directly from the read-only drive to the recorder. Of course, this is much quicker than copying those same files or an entire disc image to your hard drive and then copying them back as you record the CD, but this trick usually works only with a SCSI read-only CD-ROM. The typical enhanced IDE CD-ROM drive used in most computers today cannot be used as a direct source drive with most recording programs.

Recording Multiple Copies

Several applications mentioned in Chapter 2 require the recording of more than one copy of a CD-ROM; for example, a software developer might distribute several copies of a program under development to customers as part of a beta testing program. Along the same lines, you might need to make copies of the same disc within several days or weeks of each other; for instance, a shareware developer might create a copy of the same CD-ROM each time a customer orders that program over the Internet. What's the easiest way of recording more than one copy of the same disc?

Rather than laboriously copy each individual file to your hard drive each time you want to make a CD-ROM, most CD recording software allows you to create a disc image file (sometimes called a project file or a master file) on your hard drive. In essence, a disc image file contains every byte of data contained on the recorded CD, but it also contains other information specific to the creation of compact discs, such as the volume name, directory structure, extended descriptions of files, and recording format. For audio discs, a disc image will also contain the name of each song and its length in minutes and seconds. Depending on the features of the recording software you use, an image file might even contain graphics and text for the jewel box inserts.

Of course, if a disc image file contains all the data that will appear on the recorded CD, it's going to be up to 650 megabytes (depending on how full the completed disc will be)! If you create many copies of the same disc over a long period of time, I'd certainly suggest a dedicated hard drive or partition be set aside for recording — we cover hardware and software requirements later in the book.

Although reserving such a huge amount of valuable hard drive territory can involve some creative file juggling, it's convenient and fast to use a disc image file for multiple copies of a disc; you simply load the image file from your hard drive with a menu command, pop in a blank CD, start the process, and walk away.

Labeling Your Recorded CD-ROMs

Labeling a recorded CD is another of those topics that depends on personal preference and the specific application. I've known music lovers since junior high school who have never labeled a single 8-track or cassette tape; then there are those who don't consider a recording done until it's been properly labeled. There are several DOS and Windows programs available that create fancy labels for cassettes, floppy disks, and even QIC backup tapes.

How you label your recorded discs is up to you — unless you're producing them for distribution to others. If you're simply creating an archival backup of your complete hard drive, a few words will suffice to identify the contents and date you recorded them. If, however, you are distributing recorded discs, consider how important the appearance of your work is for the person who receives it. I strongly recommend that you invest in a disc labeling system, or that you order custom screen printing for your blank discs; that first impression the customer receives when seeing your CD-ROM is important, especially when your company's image is involved!

With that in mind, let's consider your three labeling options for the compact discs you record.

Hand Labeling

Whether you order blank CDs from a mail order company or buy them at a local store, check to make sure you can write on the top surface; this is usually indicated on the disc box or in the description. These discs usually cost a few cents extra, since the top of each blank is coated with an extra opaque layer of plastic or paint that insures your writing will not interfere with the reflective gold layer.

Do not use a pencil, ballpoint pen, or any pen with a hard tip to write on your discs — you risk damaging the gold reflective layer and the dye layer under that thin lacquer! The writing tool of choice for marking CDs is a felt-tip permanent marker with a sharp point.

If your discs have an obvious white space area for writing, make sure you stay within the borders of that area, as some blanks have the extra opaque layer only in that area to reduce costs. If you're unsure whether you can write on a particular blank, write a short one or two word description on the clear plastic border directly surrounding the spindle hole; your CD-ROM drive does not use this area, so it's safe to write on.

Custom Screen Printing

Most store-bought CD-ROMs have screen printed labels. Screen printing involves applying one or more layers of paint to the top of the disc, usually in at least two colors. Typically, a company will submit artwork when ordering a batch of mass-produced discs, and the design is converted into a number of stencils that allow each color of paint to reach certain parts of the disc. Figure 3-5 illustrates the application of three different colors to a disc to create a finished label.

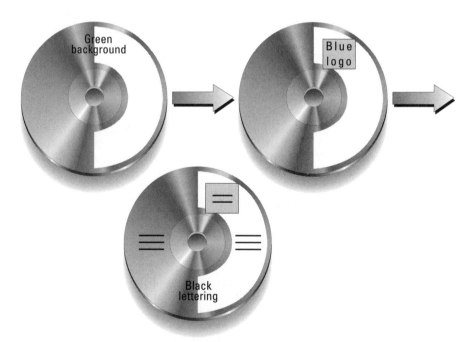

Figure 3-5: Successive applications of different colors create a screen-printed label on a compact disc.

Like CD recording software and hardware, prices on bulk screen printing have dropped considerably in the last few years. However, the process is more expensive with each color you add, and sometimes the relative size and complexity of the label design also affects the price per disc. If you're going to distribute several dozen discs, a good middle-of-the-road approach is to select a simple design containing your logo, a title, and a line or two of text, and have that printed in a single color; your discs are professionally labeled, but the cost per disc is kept as low as possible.

Printed Labels

The third possibility for identifying your discs is the printed label, which falls in between labeling your discs by hand and having them professionally screen printed; it's less expensive than two-color screen printing, but more attractive than labeling a disc by hand.

The process of printing labels usually involves designing your label with special software and printing the design on peel-off labels with a laser or inkjet printer. Although you can align labels manually, if your hand-eye coordination isn't the best you can spoil a perfectly good CD-ROM — if your label isn't applied correctly, you end up with a CD-ROM that's not balanced correctly, causing read errors in some drives. For this reason, CD-ROM labeling systems include simple machines that help you to apply those sticky labels.

The best CD-ROM labeling system for paper labels is the NEATO CD Labeling Kit, which comes with PC and Macintosh label templates and Windows 3.1/Windows 95 software for designing and printing the labels. The standard kit comes with 100 blank labels in gold, silver, and white, which should last for some time (unless you're a shareware developer or you create several copies at once). You can usually buy additional labels from the store where you bought the kit.

The Windows DesignExpress software included with the NEATO kit is excellent and allows you to design labels in color, complete with geometric designs that add accent to the disc title or your company name. You create your labels in a true WYSIWYG (short for "What You See Is What You Get") environment. Tools include text frames and effects, borders, and shading. You can also include images in bitmap, metafile, and Encapsulated PostScript (EPS) format. An assortment of clipart images and predesigned label backgrounds make it easy to add a professional touch. Figure 3-6 illustrates the DesignExpress screen and a representative label design.

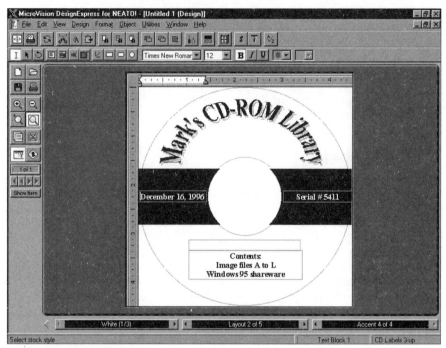

Figure 3-6: The DesignExpress screen and a NEATO label design.

If you'd rather use your favorite word processor or drawing package to create labels, the NEATO kit includes label templates for popular programs like Word, CorelDraw, and PageMaker, as well as clipart images in bitmap and CompuServe GIF formats. Future updates will include jewel box templates.

The label applicator is an simple two-piece device; one piece resembles a tube and acts as the spindle, holding the CD-ROM steady, while the other piece is a base that holds the label. The application couldn't be easier — you push the pieces together and the label is aligned and affixed in one step.

Two warnings: First, if you're going to use paper labels, use only labels that are specifically designed for use on CD-ROMs. For example, don't use a mailing label on a CD-ROM, since you could cause a balance problem and ruin the disc. Second, don't ever try to remove a label after you've put it on; tearing off the label might unbalance the disc or cause damage to the disc's top layer.

Summary

This chapter discussed:

+ how recorded CD-ROMs are different from mass-produced discs;
+ where to buy CD-ROM blanks;
+ how your recorder actually saves the digital information understood by your computer on compact disc;
+ the steps involved in recording a single disc;
+ how to create a disc image so you can conveniently record multiple copies of a disc;
+ how to label discs by hand and with paper labels;
+ the advantages of professional screen printing.

In the next chapter, it's time to purchase your CD-ROM recorder (if you haven't already)! Chapter 4 includes all you need to know about how to determine what features you need, what to buy, and where to buy it.

✦   ✦   ✦

Buying a CD Recorder

CHAPTER 4

◆ ◆ ◆ ◆

In This Chapter

The first step

Internal vs. external recorders

Selecting read/ write speeds

The data buffer

Audio support

Alternate recording formats

Recording software

Adapter cards

Cables and blank discs

Researching and buying a drive

◆ ◆ ◆ ◆

There's never been a better time to purchase a CD recorder. Prices have dropped across the entire industry, from blank CD-ROMs, to recording software, to the recorders themselves, while read-only drives are getting faster and faster. Today's programs and data files can take up hundreds of megabytes on a hard drive, but they're easily transported and permanently archived on a CD-ROM. Multimedia CD-ROMs that feature digital video are consistent top sellers in entertainment and educational software, while entire encyclopedias are being distributed on a single disc. The CD-ROM recorder is, as they say in Silicon Valley and Hollywood, "hot stuff"!

However, the task of selecting and buying a CD recorder is still as arduous as ever, even with knowledge of how a CD-ROM is made and how drives and recorders work. In the first three chapters, you learned the fundamentals, but they won't help you much in determining which features are important, what drive to buy, and how much to pay. Most mail order companies sell everything from the drive by itself to a complete package with an adapter card, cables, software, and discs. If you're unfamiliar with computer hardware, the specifications for recorders read like a foreign language, and you may not need everything offered by the top-of-the-line model. If you're a Macintosh owner, you're likely to have most of what you need already on your computer, but most PC owners can't even run a CD recorder without a hardware upgrade.

Don't panic! In this chapter, I arm you with all the knowledge you need to make an informed choice between different drives and the features they offer. I also cover the extras that a complete recording package should include — SCSI (short for *Small Computer Systems Interface*) adapter cards, cables, software, and blank discs.

The First Step

The first step in purchasing a CD recorder is the definition of exactly what you need for your specific computer. This avoids the purchase of extra hardware, software, and supplies you don't need, and ordering a CD recorder is easier when you know the details about your computer. Besides, we can do a quick check on whether your computer can handle recording as-is, or whether you need to upgrade hardware or software before you buy your recorder. We cover the specific hardware and software requirements for Easy CD Creator in more detail in Chapter 5.

Grab a sheet of paper (or, if you're really in a symbiotic relationship with your computer, open up a text editor) and jot this information:

✦ **Operating system.** Is your machine running Windows 3.x, Windows 95, Windows NT, or MacOS? If you're currently using only DOS, then be prepared for bad news — almost all of today's CD mastering software relies on Windows, so it's time to consider adding at least Windows 3.11 to your PC. Besides, you can always drop back to DOS when you're finished recording!

✦ **Processor speed.** CD recording is a power-hungry application. If you're thinking of recording CD-ROMs using a 386-based PC or a Macintosh SE, stop right where you are and consider a faster computer. At minimum, you need a PC with an 80486 processor, and the faster the better. For recording on the Macintosh, the minimum horsepower you need is a 68040-based computer or a PowerMac.

✦ **Existing I/O.** Does your PC currently have a SCSI interface for a hard drive or CD-ROM drive? If so, you've probably just saved yourself the cost of an interface card.

✦ **Existing hard drive.** Do you currently have at least 650 megabytes of hard drive space? No? Then you won't be able to create disc image files that fill an entire CD-ROM. If you're only interested in recording material that already exists on your drive — for example, creating archival backups of your hard drive — this isn't a problem. However, to get the full use out of your recorder, consider buying a larger hard drive or cleaning off 650 megabytes of data.

✦ **Existing software.** Have you already purchased a specific CD recording program? If you've already bought Easy CD Creator or another CD recording application, you're not going to require a bundled copy.

STAY AWAY FROM COMPRESSION!

So, you've bought a recorder but you find yourself low on hard drive space, and you can't afford a new hard drive; how can you record a full disc image? If you use Windows, your first idea might be to use Stacker, DoubleSpace, or DriveSpace to compress your drive — **do not do this!** Although the overhead involved in decompressing your data is slight, recording data that's buffered to a compressed drive is not recommended; it's likely to cause recording errors. Instead, consider repartitioning your current hard drive into two logical drives, and compress only your main drive (leaving the other logical drive of 650 megabytes or more uncompressed). Later, we discuss how to configure Easy CD Creator so that it will use the uncompressed drive. Even better, I recommend saving what existing archivable data you have on your hard drive onto your first recorded disc, then you can simply delete those files and run or access them from the CD-ROM!

OK, now that you've got these details in front of you, these are the questions to ask:

1. *Do I need a SCSI interface card?* If your system does not currently have a SCSI card, you're going to need one, and it should be included in a complete package. If you already have SCSI, you'll be better off buying a "bare" CD recorder (a term usually used to indicate that you're buying just a CD-ROM drive without a controller). Most mail order stores that specialize in storage devices can sell you a bare drive, and you'll always save money over a bundled kit if you already have your recording software. But remember, you won't get full documentation on how to connect the drive to your existing SCSI adapter, so you should be knowledgeable about the process.

2. *Do I need software?* Once again, if the answer is "yes," then check out a complete recording package. Recording software usually starts at around $100, so if you already have your software, it's better to buy the bare drive and a separate SCSI adapter (if you need one), and save the cost.

3. *Do I need to copy disc-to-disc directly?* If you're going to be copying data from other CD-ROMs often, buying a SCSI read-only CD-ROM drive at the same time you buy a recorder is something to consider. Remember, you don't have to have a SCSI CD-ROM source drive to transfer data from existing audio discs and CD-ROMs, but it certainly makes the task easier — you eliminate the intervening step of first copying all that data to your hard drive. Of course, if you already have a SCSI CD-ROM on your system, the problem is solved (and you have my permission to pat yourself on the back for being such a computer genius).

Answering these questions determines whether you need a bare CD recorder, a recorder, and a SCSI card, or an entire recorder package.

Internal vs. External Recorders

The next step in narrowing your choices for a CD recorder is determining whether you need an external recorder or an internal recorder; both are shown in Figure 4-1.

Figure 4-1: Internal and external CD recorders.

Note Almost all Macintosh CD recorders are external, so if you're using a Mac you can skip this section.

The Advantages of an External Recorder

First, let's discuss the advantages of owning an external recorder.

✦ **Portability.** If you're buying a recorder for an entire office that might be used with other computers, the external drive is the natural choice. Of course, each computer that uses the recorder must have an external SCSI port (which is standard issue on SCSI adapter cards), a copy of the recording software (which will probably require a site license for use on more than one PC), and all the hardware necessities mentioned earlier, like a fast processor and a sizable chunk of free hard drive space. Moving the recorder from PC to PC is quite easy, though, with only one cable connection to the PC and a power supply to the wall AC jack.

✦ **Temperature.** Although I haven't mentioned it yet, you may already know that CD recorders generate more heat than the average hard drive, or even the average CD-ROM read-only drive. This extra heat is generated by the higher-powered laser used to write data, as well as all the extra electronics built into a recorder. Usually this isn't a problem, but if your PC is already running a 486 or Pentium in a case with one fan and you've stuffed it full of adapters and devices, that extra heat could prove damaging to your PC's components. Suffice it to say that an external recorder doesn't contribute to (or suffer from) the radiated heat inside your computer.

✦ **No installation.** If your PC already has a SCSI adapter and you'd rather not attempt to install an internal drive, or your computer's case no longer has a free half-height device bay, then an external recorder is certainly more convenient. The same is true for portable computer owners who might have a SCSI PCMCIA card in their machine, but can't handle an internal recorder!

The Advantages of an Internal Recorder

On the other hand, internal hard drives and CD-ROM drives have historically been more popular with most computer owners. An internal CD recorder has these advantages.

✦ **Cost**. As you might expect, the separate case, power supply, and SCSI interface used by an external recorder make it more expensive than its internal cousin. Typically, you pay around $100 more for an external drive.

✦ **Convenience**. If you won't be recording on more than one PC, if you have a cluttered desk, or if you have a habit of spilling your morning coffee, then an internal drive is probably more attractive. I'll never forget the moment a few years ago when a good friend of mine accidentally pushed off his desk an expensive hard drive he was about to install; one sickening crunch, and it never worked again. A CD recorder is a precision instrument, and you can avoid accidents like that with an internal drive.

✦ **Security**. If you're working in an office environment and you'd rather not come to work one morning to discover that your expensive recorder has "wandered off," consider an internal drive.

Now that you know the advantages of both internal and external drives, you can make a decision based on what you need. In our experience, most people end up weighing the importance of price versus portability — and, unless you really need a drive you can easily move from one machine to another, we'd suggest an internal CD recorder.

Selecting Read/Write Speeds

As you're shopping for your recorder, you're going to encounter a strange phenomenon native to every discussion of CD-ROM drives: "the X factor." Advertisements for CD-ROM recorders almost always list either a combination of two numbers followed by Xs (for example, 4X read/2X write), or they state the drive is "quad-speed read and double-speed write." If you're not familiar with what's going on, this is likely to leave you scratching your head in confusion.

The explanation of the X factor turns out to be simple, as long as you remember our discussion of the internal workings of a CD recorder: a CD recorder can also do double-duty as a read-only drive. Those numbers represent the data transfer rates your drive can reach while reading a disc and recording (or writing) a disc, respectively. The computer industry describes the speed of today's CD-ROM drives as a multiple factor of the original transfer rate for a single-speed audio compact disc player, which is 150 kilobytes per second. Therefore, a 4x (or "quad-speed") drive can transfer data four times as fast as an original single-speed drive, or approximately 600 kilobytes a second.

How do read and write speeds influence your buying decision? Today's CD recorders are much slower than true, dedicated read-only drives when reading a prerecorded disc; for example, today's faster read-only drives are generally 10x or 12x, and at the time of this writing even 16x CD-ROM drives are appearing and 24x drives are expected soon. On the other hand, today's fastest CD recorders can only write data at 4x, and most recorders are still limited to 2x when writing data. The most common combination is currently 4x read and 2x write.

So what's to decide — just pick the fastest recorder possible, right? That makes perfect sense when applied to the write speed, since a recorder that writes information faster to the disc means time saved during the recording process. When choosing between two recorders, pick the fastest write speed you can afford.

However, paying extra for a faster read speed may not always be the best choice, because cost makes the difference once again. You pay a premium price for a drive that reads (at the most) 6x, and if you already have a 6x IDE drive on your system, the read speed doesn't really matter much. For example, I use my recorder only for creating new CDs, while I run programs and install applications from a separate 8x IDE drive.

Also, a 4x drive is currently the minimum requirement for most multimedia CD-ROMs, especially games that run directly from the disc, and future CD-ROMs will likely require a faster drive. Therefore, you should consider whether to avoid paying extra money for a recorder that will soon be slower than the multimedia standard!

More than any other factor, CD recorder cost depends on its read and write speeds, so carefully consider the tradeoff between the time you save and the money you spend; if you're a patient person, you can save a considerable amount of money by selecting a recorder that writes at 2x speed!

The Importance of the Data Buffer

The data buffer is truly the unknown component of your CD recorder. Asking a salesperson how big the buffer is on a drive is likely to get you nothing but a questioning look, and even some PC owners who already have a recorder have no idea what a buffer does or how important it is to the recording process.

As you recall from the last chapter, recording software uses a portion of your hard drive as a temporary buffer to hold data until it can be written to disc by your recorder. Because the recording process is so timing-dependent, your recorder cannot pause while writing data; in fact, the success of the recording process depends upon the CD recorder receiving a steady flow of data. Any interruption or lag in the flow of signals to your drive will result in an aborted recording (and usually a ruined disc ready for the wastebasket).

For this reason, most recorders have their own hardware buffer designed to hold data until it's ready to be written. This buffer is actually a small bank of random access memory like the RAM in your PC — but, because the access time for RAM is many times faster than the access time for a hard drive, your recorder's hardware buffer is much more efficient at retrieving data and transferring it to the laser write head. Figure 4-2 illustrates how the buffer stores data until it's recorded.

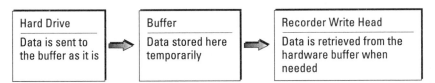

Figure 4-2: The data buffer lessens the load on your PC's hard drive.

Recorders with a larger hardware buffer are less prone to data transfer errors. The larger the buffer, the lower the demands on your PC's hard drive, so systems with slower hard drives may not be quite as likely to abort a recording because of overruns.

Most recorders on the market have at least one megabyte of hardware buffer, so I recommend you accept that as the minimum when selecting a drive. Older, less expensive drives might have 512K or 256K of buffer memory; if your PC is a Pentium and its hard drive has an access time of less than 10 milliseconds, you might be comfortable buying one of these older recorders, but I'd certainly spend the extra money for a newer recorder!

Audio Support

Another distinction between different recorders is their support for audio. Like read-only CD-ROMs, recorders can play audio CDs, and most have the same audio out cable that read-only drives have for connecting to your sound card. Many student computer owner's have decided against a portable stereo in favor of a pair of powered speakers hooked up to a PC's CD-ROM.

However, many recorders provide better support for playing audio discs, including front-mounted headphone jacks, front volume controls, and buttons to skip to the previous or next track. You usually pay extra for audiophile features, so consider whether you'll be using your recorder as an audio player; if you're planning on adding a recorder to a system with an existing CD-ROM, your read-only drive may already have everything you need and there's no reason to select a higher-priced recorder for its audio features.

You should also make sure that your recorder supports digital audio extraction, which enables you to copy audio tracks from existing audio compact discs to your hard drive or another disc.

Alternate Recording Formats

A lesser-known side of CD recording is the availability of alternate recording formats on most drives. Discs produced in these secondary formats are not usually found in stores, and you may never need to actually record one, but support for these formats does help to differentiate recorders as you shop. It's important to note that even though your drive may support an alternate format, you won't be able to create the disc unless your recording software supports it as well.

We discuss each of these formats in detail later in the book, so for now let's simply give a short list:

✦ **CD Extra.** This alternative format records audio and data on the same disc in two sessions, with the first session containing the audio and the second session containing data. These discs are designed for use both on audio CD players and computer CD-ROM drives. The audio session contains additional data for each track.

✦ **Photo CD Image Pac.** A format designed to display high-resolution images, usually used with digital camera pictures. Note that most CD recorders cannot use discs especially made for Kodak PhotoCD processing.

✦ **Video CD.** Discs created in this format can display digital video with freeze-frame on any standard video CD player.

✦ **CD-ROM XA.** Discs recorded in multisession format using Mode 1 or Mode 2 (many older CD-ROM drives can only recognize discs recorded in Mode 2). A multisession disc can contain more than one recording session, up to the total space on the disc.

WHAT ARE MODES 1 AND 2?

Although you don't really need to know all about Modes 1 and 2 to successfully record a disc, they are often mentioned and most recording programs usually allow selection of one or the other. Mode 1 CD-ROM data is recorded with error correction; it takes more space on the disc to record in Mode 1, but the error correction helps to insure that the data will be read correctly. Mode 1 is always used for text, computer programs, and data, where a single incorrectly read byte can render an entire file worthless. Mode 2 has no error correction, and is used for recording video, audio, and images — these kind of files can survive the loss of a few bytes without losing quality.

✦ **Packet writing.** Although this isn't actually an alternate recording format, you often see it listed in advertisements alongside them. Packet writing is a recording method that allows your computer to save files individually to your CD recorder as if it was a hard drive. Of course, you still can't erase recorded CD-ROMs, but this method of recording makes it much easier to save a few files at a time rather than writing the entire contents of a CD-ROM at once. We discuss packet writing later in the book; for now, just remember that it's a good feature to have.

Older recorders may not be able to write some of these formats. If the advertising for a particular recorder doesn't list the supported formats, it's certainly worth a call to the company or the drive's manufacturer, or a quick trip through cyberspace to their Web site.

Recording Software

Most of the applications available today for PCs and Macs are available in both commercial and shareware/freeware forms; you can usually find an inexpensive alternative on a bulletin board system or the Internet for most programs you buy in a store. This includes office software like word processors, databases and spreadsheets, drawing and raytracing programs, communications software, games, and even high-end software, such as CAD programs, and operating systems, such as Linux and FreeBSD.

Unfortunately, the exact opposite is true of CD recording software. Due to the complex nature of the program and the relatively small demand in the past, there are very few inexpensive shareware alternatives to full-featured, commercial CD recording software like Easy CD Creator. There are freeware utilities — for example, programs that will copy an audio track to a disc — but they are nowhere near as comprehensive as the commercial offerings. With the rapid growth in popularity of CD recording, I'm certain that we will see more recording software released as shareware.

This leaves you with a limited number of choices for recording software. In this book, we cover every detail of Easy CD Creator — which I consider to be the best by far — and introduce you to CD Creator and Easy-CD Pro. These are probably the three most popular recording software packages available today, and they are extensively bundled as part of recorder kits; manufacturers favor them because each can create discs in all of the recording formats mentioned, and they all support a wide range of existing recorders. These programs are also easy to use; each takes full advantage of the Windows 95 drag and drop functionality.

Don't forget to make sure that you receive software for your SCSI card if you're buying a kit; this can range from a single install disk with a number of drivers to several disks that also contain utilities and a device manager. If your kit happens to include EZSCSI 4.x, you may already have CD recording software (Easy-CD 95 and CD Copier).

Adapter Cards

As mentioned earlier, CD recorders require a SCSI connection to your computer. Macintosh owners are in luck, since SCSI is the device interface of choice for Macs. Most PC computers built today, however, use the IDE interface for storage devices, so it's likely that your PC requires a SCSI adapter card.

For this reason, most recorder kits come with the adapter as standard equipment. Be careful, though — not all adapter cards are created equal! Before you purchase a kit, make sure that the adapter is the proper type to fit in your PC, and that your PC has an open slot of the correct size.

The standard card offered in recorder kits is a 16-bit ISA adapter, which should fit in just about any PC, but if your machine is already using all of its ISA slots you may have to remove a card or buy a PCI SCSI adapter. Do not install an 8-bit SCSI adapter, since an 8-bit adapter will not have the throughput speed necessary for recording.

If you're unsure how many open card slots you have and what type they are, it's time to unplug your PC and unscrew the cover! You should see a row of long expansion slots (usually seven or eight) at the back of your computer. Two or three of these slots probably already contain adapter cards; just check to make sure you have at least one expansion slot empty.

Also, verify that the slot can accept a 16-bit card. If the slot is longer than one or two other slots on your motherboard, then it's likely to be 16-bit (the shorter slots accept only 8-bit cards). Also, because a 16-bit card has two sets of connectors, the slot itself should be separated into two sections by a thin divider. Figure 4-3 shows a typical 16-bit card and slot.

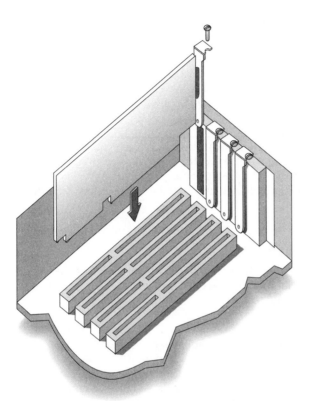

Figure 4-3: A 16-bit adapter card and matching
expansion slot.

Tip

If the idea of opening your PC makes you nervous — or if an adapter card bit you
during your childhood — don't panic! Merely enlist the aid of a family member or
friend who's digitally aware and familiar with the inside of a computer. If no one is
available to help, unplug your computer from the monitor and keyboard and bring
it to your local computer store or repair shop to determine whether you have an
open 16-bit slot.

If you already have a SCSI card in your PC, make sure you still have an open device
ID — a SCSI card can support up to eight devices at one time, but one device ID is
usually reserved for the adapter card itself.

In Chapter 5, we discuss installing your SCSI adapter and configuring it for use
with your CD recorder.

Cables and Blank Discs

If you're buying a complete recorder kit, make sure that it includes all the cables, screws, SCSI terminators, and various odds and ends needed to complete the installation. There's nothing more aggravating than finding you need to buy a six-inch cable when you're knee-deep in the bowels of your PC and components are covering your kitchen table!

Blank recordable discs are another nice feature of a kit, since you'll need at least one to perform a burn test and verify that CD Creator is working properly. If you don't buy a kit, make sure you buy at least one blank disc. Since the CD Creator burn test doesn't actually write to the disc, you can use that disc for your first recording.

Researching a Drive

Now that we've discussed what to look for when purchasing a recorder or kit, you may be asking, "Where do I look?" There are a number of resources available when researching a purchase for your computer.

✦ *Computer Shopper*. Even in this Internet age, I still prefer this magazine for quickly checking prices. If you're not familiar with *Computer Shopper*, it's the bible of mail order — a massive monthly magazine that usually weighs about three pounds, and contains advertisements from every known corner of North America. *Shopper* has a very convenient product index in the back that allows you to search by component and manufacturer, so you can jump between advertisements for the same component and compare price. Also, *Shopper* often features reviews of different components, as well as articles on new technology. You can usually find *Shopper* at newsstands and magazine counters.

✦ **Computer magazines.** Besides *Computer Shopper*, I especially recommend *PC Magazine* and *PC World* for their hardware reviews. Computer magazines often feature product comparisons between CD-ROM drives and recorders from different manufacturers, and a *PC Magazine* Editor's Choice award carries quite a bit of weight in the computer world.

✦ **The Web.** If you've got an Internet connection, you can use one of the major search engines, such as Yahoo or Webcrawler, to find web sites for different recorder manufacturers. There are three sites that I use while computer shopping on the Web: the CD Recordable section of the Adaptec site at `www.adaptec.com`, `www.netbuyer.com` (*Computer Shopper*'s NetBuyer), and `www.necx.com` (NECX Direct). The Adaptec site includes links to all CD recorder manufacturers with Web sites. The last two are great free sites that allow you to search through products from hundreds of manufacturers. Both also provide a specification search system that makes it easy to display products that match just the features you want. Figure 4-4 shows the NECX Direct specification search screen for CD recorders. If you find exactly what you're looking for at the right price, you can even order online through a secure connection!

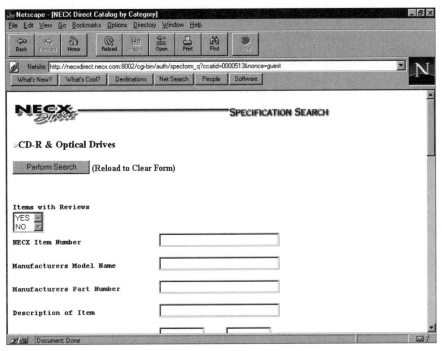

Figure 4-4: The NECX Direct search screen for CD recorders.

✦ **Local stores.** Depending on where you live, there's a good chance you can drop by a large retail computer store and find at least one or two recorders to consider.

✦ **Newsgroups and user groups.** Ask the opinions of those who are already recording CD-ROMs! If you have a local computer user group, check and see if one or two members have a recorder and find out what they think. If you have access to Internet newsgroups, you can subscribe to three popular areas for discussing CD recording: comp.publish.cdrom.hardware, comp.publish.cdrom.software, and comp.publish.cdrom.multimedia. A question on any of these groups is likely to result in an avalanche of opinions.

✦ **The Easy-CD mailing list.** This moderated forum is a service of the Adaptec Software Products Group, where those interested in CD-recordable technology can help each other with technical and general CD-R questions. I have found this list to be an invaluable source of information and solid advice! You may join the list at any time by sending a message to Listserv@listserv.adaptec.com with the following text in the body of the message:

```
sub adaptec_CDR
```

If you prefer, you can receive these in a single large message, daily, by sending a message to Listserv@listserv.adaptec.com with the following text in the body of the message:

```
sub adaptec_CDR digest
```

The digest version delivers messages in batches of 80K at a time rather than receiving them one by one — up to 50 per day — as they arrive.

Where to Buy?

At last! You've reached the end of your journey. You've assessed what features you need in a recorder and selected the brand and model that's perfect for you. Now you must make the choice that computer owners have faced since the days of the first IBM PC: mail order or a local store?

Which you choose depends, of course, on whether you can find the specific recorder you're looking for locally. If you live in a larger city, finding the right recorder in town might be possible, but CD recorders are still not standard equipment in all computer stores. However, you can probably still order the recorder you want from a computer store in town.

The Advantages of Buying Locally

These are the advantages of buying your recorder from a local store:

✦ **Personal help**. If you're a relative newcomer to the world of computers, it never hurts to enlist the aid of those more experienced. Your local computer store can help you through the entire process of installing and configuring your recorder; in fact, they will often do so for a flat hourly rate. Receiving personal, ongoing help from most catalog outlets and mail order companies is generally akin to pulling teeth.

✦ **Warranty work and returns**. There's no need to pack everything back up and ship it cross-country if you happen to purchase a defective recorder. Your local computer store will either fix it on-site or ship it for you for warranty service. To be honest, I've encountered very few problems with hardware that I've purchased through the mail, but I've heard many stories of damage that occurred in shipping and parts that weren't included.

✦ **Hands-on shopping**. Naturally, you're especially lucky if you can find the recorder you're ready to buy in a local store, since you can examine it in person — perhaps even convince the salesperson to open it up so you can see the contents firsthand and read the documentation before you buy.

The Advantages of Buying Through Mail Order

There are a few key advantages to purchasing your recorder electronically via the Web or through a mail order catalog, instead of locally.

✦ **Selection**. Today's computer catalog stores have a vast selection of hardware at prices that no local store could possibly provide. Even if the recorder you want is a lesser-known brand, chances are that you'll still be able to compare price and warranty from at least one or two companies advertising in *Computer Shopper* or on the Web.

✦ **Tax**. Depending on your state laws, a purchase made in another state through a mail order company may save you state sales tax.

✦ **Price**. Without the need for a storefront or salespeople, mail order stores have less overhead than your local computer store, and you'll almost always save a significant amount of money by ordering through the mail. You can also take advantage of mail order catalog closeouts, where older hardware is sold for much less than the original price.

As you can see, if you're experienced at buying and installing computer hardware, you're more likely to purchase your recorder through the mail. You may already have some "favorite" catalog stores that you've had good luck with in the past — buying from a known vendor is always a plus.

If you're a novice at buying and installing computer hardware, your best bet is to order the drive you want through a local computer store and pay them to install it. The extra money is worth the peace of mind.

If you do buy through a catalog, and this is your first mail order purchase, make sure you avoid the "dirty tricks" played by some companies; for example, automatically charging you extra for faster shipment without telling you of cheaper rates, selling out-of-stock merchandise, or telephone salespeople who try to sell you additional items that you don't need. As long as you're careful, you can save hundreds of dollars on a recorder through the mail!

Summary

This chapter led you through:

✦ the process of defining your recording needs;

✦ selecting the right features;

✦ determining whether you need a bare drive or a full recording package;

✦ purchasing your recorder from a local store or through the mail.

If you haven't purchased a recorder yet, you now know the basics of what to look for, where to go, and what to do!

In the next chapter, we concentrate on installing and configuring your recorder and the hardware and software it requires.

✦   ✦   ✦

Installing Your CD Recorder

◆　◆　◆　◆

Hardware and
software
requirements

Optional software
and hardware

Adding SCSI support

Installing an internal
drive

Installation problems

◆　◆　◆　◆

At this point, I'm assuming that you've selected your
CD recorder and that you're ready to install it. Once
we complete this chapter, your drive will be installed and we
can begin concentrating on the software and the recording
process.

As I mentioned in the last chapter, many PC owners are
unfamiliar with some of the tasks we perform in this chapter:
opening your PC's case, adding adapter cards, installing the
drive itself, and connecting cables. If you are nervous about
any of these steps, consider bringing your recorder and your
PC to a local computer store that performs installations; a
professional computer technician can install your drive in a
few hours. Installing a CD recorder is not a process that lends
itself to training, so I wouldn't recommend that you attempt
to "earn while you learn"!

However, if you already have experience in adding adapter
cards and installing hard drives, you probably will not find
this process difficult. One suggestion: If you haven't worked
with a SCSI device, make sure you pay close attention to the
sections covering the SCSI adapter.

A final note before we get started: the instructions I give in
this chapter are general steps to follow that are common to
most recorders, and should not be considered specific to
any one recorder! You **must** read the documentation that
accompanies your recorder and your SCSI adapter card
before we begin, and I mean read them cover-to-cover —
there may be steps specific to your drive that I don't include
here. When in doubt, or when the documentation supplied
with your hardware deviates from my instructions, follow the
documentation.

With that said, let's get to work!

Hardware and Software Requirements

In this section, I outline the specific hardware and software requirements that apply to most recorders on the market, as well as the requirements for Easy CD Creator. I mentioned requirements in general in the last chapter to help you in selecting a recorder, but if your system doesn't have these prerequisites, you won't be able to record at all. Also, the documentation that accompanied your recorder may add requirements to this basic list.

Hardware

For a standard 4x read/2x write recorder, you need this hardware:

✦ **80486 Processor.** The faster the processor the better, of course. If you're using Windows 95, I recommend nothing slower than a Pentium, but a 486DX-33 with plenty of RAM and a very fast hard drive should be able to handle double-speed recording with Windows 3.1. Macintosh owners, you'll need at least a 68040-25, but a PowerMac is preferred.

✦ **Eight megabytes of RAM.** Again, this is a definite minimum amount under Windows 3.1; if you're using Windows 95 or Windows NT, this minimum figure rises to 16 megabytes. Windows creates a "virtual" memory area, commonly called the *swapfile,* on your hard drive; in layman's terms, program data that won't fit in memory is stored in the swapfile. Since the swapfile has to be transferred to and from your hard drive — which takes much longer than it would if the data was actually read from your PC's RAM — it makes sense that the more RAM your machine has, the better! Additionally, Windows 95 and Windows NT demand extra RAM for the operating system.

THERMAL CALIBRATION EXPLAINED

Most CD-ROM manufacturers recommend a hard drive that uses intelligent thermal calibration. What the heck do those buzzwords mean? Here's the answer: All hard drives automatically adjust themselves to current temperature conditions on a regular basis. To do this, your hard drive must temporarily interrupt the flow of data for a second or so, even if you're reading or writing a file at the time. Normally, of course, you don't notice this, and your hard drive controller insures you don't lose any data during calibration; however, if this process occurs while a large file is being read from your hard drive during a recording, that interruption could return an error and abort the entire recording! Therefore, if you're buying a hard drive for recording use, see if it will delay thermal calibration until it's idle, which will prevent any interruption in the flow of data to your recorder. These drives are often described as "AV" drives. If you're in doubt about whether a particular drive uses intelligent thermal calibration, check the manufacturer's web site for specifications or call its sales department.

✦ **Hard drive.** As mentioned in Chapter 4, a one-gigabyte hard drive dedicated solely as recording space is the optimum configuration, but if you can't afford a separate drive, try to clear as much space on your drive as possible. CD recording demands a hard drive with an average seek time of 11 milliseconds or less. Do not use a compression scheme like Stacker or DriveSpace to create more room on your hard drive, because the compression process and software require too much overhead and may cause recording errors.

Software

Next, here are the software requirements for that same standard 4x read/2x write recorder.

✦ **Windows 3.1 or higher.** As you probably noticed, the question of which operating system to use for recording really depends on your hardware. If your machine fits the minimum requirements for using Windows 3.1, there's really no reason to upgrade to a PC that can record under Windows 95; discs recorded on your 16-bit system will be just as good! If your system fits the minimum requirements for Windows 95, you're probably already using it; Windows 95 does have the advantage of 32-bit speed and file access. However, in my experience the operating system of choice for CD recording is definitely Windows NT, and I have had the most success with it. NT is a rock-solid environment that really takes advantage of today's Pentium and Pentium Pro hardware, and it features the fastest disk operation and program speed of any Windows platform to date.

✦ **DOS 6.22.** Of course, DOS is only required for PCs running Windows 3.1. If you haven't upgraded to the latest DOS, this is the time to do it, since older versions have inferior support for CD-ROM players and SCSI devices. Also, the version of SMARTDRV that comes with DOS 6.22 supports caching for CD-ROM devices, making it much faster when reading files or running programs from a CD-ROM.

✦ **MSCDEX 2.2.3.** This is the latest version of the DOS extension that allows your PC to recognize and use a CD-ROM drive. MSCDEX runs from your AUTOEXEC.BAT. Typically, the installation software accompanying CD-ROM drives automatically adds it (this is because MSCDEX must specify the CD-ROM device driver shipped with your drive). Windows 95 and Windows NT owners will not need MSCDEX, as the same functionality is built into these operating systems. Some SCSI hardware and software manufacturers have a special proprietary version of MSCDEX that they install; for example, Corel Corporation's CorelCDX program provides the functionality of MSCDEX and also provides additional caching features. Check your recorder and SCSI adapter manuals for specific information on the drivers and extensions installed by their software.

✦ **SCSI ASPI Manager.** Yet another program needed only if you're using Windows 3.1, this program allows your PC to recognize and use SCSI devices. The ASPI Manager runs from your CONFIG.SYS file. The installation software accompanying SCSI adapters and SCSI devices usually adds it automatically.

Those are the hardware and software requirements for Easy CD Creator and most CD recorders. Since most of the software I mention is installed automatically, you shouldn't need to worry about manually placing drivers and extensions in your configuration files.

Tip   As soon as you receive your recorder and SCSI card, take a minute to connect to the Web page or bulletin board system maintained by each manufacturer and check for the latest revision of the drivers and extensions used by your new hardware. Typically, you'll first install the older version of the software that was packaged with your hardware, but then you can also apply a patch, or upgrade the software to the latest revision. Most manufacturers of CD recorders maintain their own Web sites, so it's also a good idea to check for updates for your recorder's drivers or firmware.

Optional Hardware and Software

Once you've gained experience with recording CDs, you'll probably find yourself wishing for one or two "luxuries" that will make the process easier. In this section, I discuss the hardware and programs that — although not required to record — can save time and effort.

Hardware

First, you may wish to consider this additional hardware:

✦ **Multimedia sound card.** If you're going to record audio from an outside source and transfer it to CD, you'll need a sound card for your PC. Even the least expensive sound cards available today can do 16-bit 44.1KHz stereo recording, and most come with software for Windows and DOS. Music and sounds are stored in WAV file format on your hard drive. With the right cables, your card should be able to record audio from your stereo or VCR. Remember, you do **not** need a sound card to create audio compact discs with tracks from existing audio CDs or WAV files that are already on your hard drive. Figure 5-1 illustrates a typical multimedia sound card.

Figure 5-1: A stereo sound card can record digital audio to your hard drive, ready for transfer to CD.

✦ **SCSI CD-ROM drive.** As mentioned earlier, adding a SCSI read-only CD-ROM drive to your computer makes it much easier to copy files from existing CD-ROMs. Because your recorder either came with a SCSI adapter or you already have one in your PC, adding a SCSI CD-ROM is as simple as installing the drive in your PC and connecting it to the cable leading to the SCSI adapter. This is certainly an addition you can make at any time; after you've used your recorder for a few months, it will be easy to tell whether you would benefit from direct CD-to-CD recording. I explain more about CD-to-CD recording later. If you'll be copying tracks from audio compact discs, check to make sure that the drive you're considering supports digital audio extraction; again, connect to the manufacturer's web site for specifications or call its sales department.

✦ **Uninterruptible power supply.** Under most circumstances, any loss of power during a recording ruins the disc. If your neighborhood has a history of power outages or "brownouts," you should consider buying an uninterruptible power supply (or UPS for short) to safeguard your computer. On average, a UPS will give you an additional 10 to 15 minutes of power, which should be enough to finish a recording. Most UPS units also protect against electrical surges which can seriously damage your PC, and some of the more expensive units even filter the power supply to your PC to prevent interference from the electronic "noise" typical of AC power. A 400-watt UPS unit should be enough to maintain power for a multimedia PC for up to 10 minutes. Figure 5-2 shows an uninterruptible power supply.

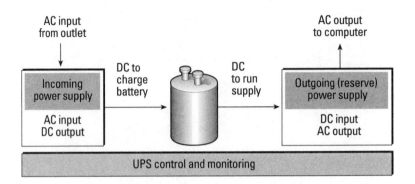

Figure 5-2: A UPS can protect your computer from brownouts and blackouts.

✦ **Inkjet or laser printer.** Adding a printer to your system allows you to create labels for your discs, print records of a disc layout for future reference, and print jewel box covers. These days, the most popular printers (and the best-supported) are either inkjet printers (like the Hewlett-Packard DeskJet series) or a personal laser printer (like the HP LaserJet series). If you'd like to print your compact disc artwork in color, color inkjet printers now sell for $200 to $300.

Software

Now let's look at software. These optional programs may prove helpful to you:

✦ **Hard drive defragmenter.** As you learn later, a badly fragmented hard drive can seriously slow down your PC as it reads files for recording, and that slowdown could cause problems. If you're running Windows 3.1 under DOS 6.22, use Microsoft's DEFRAG program from the DOS prompt. If you're running Windows 95, use the Disk Defragmenter program (found in the Accessories folder under System Tools). However, if you don't have a defragmenter on your PC, I recommend the Norton Utilities package from Symantec.

✦ **WAV file editor.** With a good WAV editor, you can add special effects like reverb and echo to your sound files, mix two files together or trim unwanted silence or static from a file. There are a number of popular shareware WAV editors available today through the Internet. Figure 5-3 illustrates the editing window from my favorite, the shareware editor Cool Edit 96 by Syntrillium Software (**www.syntrillium.com**). There's also a Windows 3.1 version. You'll find both on the CD-ROM accompanying this book. I discuss Cool Edit 96 in more detail when I cover recording audio.

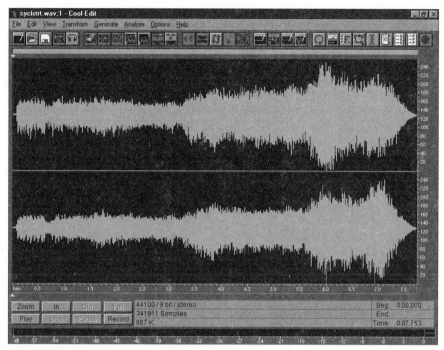

Figure 5-3: Displaying a recorded WAV file in COOL EDIT.

✦ **Image editor.** If you record GIF, JPEG, or bitmap files, you'll find an image editor absolutely essential! My editor of choice is Paint Shop Pro from JASC — actually, it's one of my top 10 favorite programs! PSP is a real shareware success story. I use PSP several times a day to convert images from one format to another, crop and resize them, add or decrease the number of colors in an image, and modify characteristics like brightness and contrast. Figure 5-4 shows a good example of PSP's brightness/contrast adjustment control. Version 4 of Paint Shop Pro is also a full-fledged painting package, so you can create your own graphics from scratch. If you create custom disc labels or jewel box covers for your projects, run — don't walk — to the CD-ROM and check it out!

Figure 5-4: The king of shareware image editing software, Paint Shop Pro.

✦ **Multimedia catalog.** Because many recorders are used to archive multimedia files, it pays to invest in a good catalog system to keep track of all those video clips, images, and sounds. In my experience, you'll quickly forget exactly what those cryptic DOS filenames mean! On the companion disc, you'll find the catalog program Media Center, another great shareware title from JASC, the makers of Paint Shop Pro. Media Center displays files in *thumbnail* format, as shown in Figure 5-5. For example, each image is reduced to a smaller version about the size of your thumb, and therefore the program can show you 20 or more images in several rows on a single screen. To view an image full size, you simply double-click on it. Organizing an entire collection of files is easy with Media Center — you can rename individual files, delete files from a catalog, or move them between catalogs. This program will save you many hours of hunting for that one file throughout an entire CD-ROM!

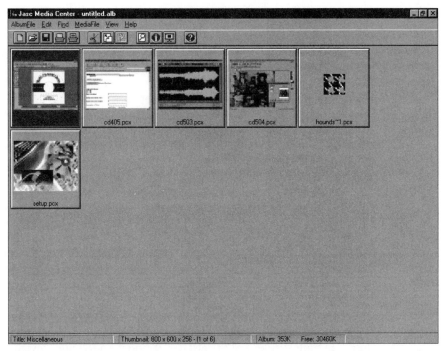

Figure 5-5: It's easy to select a single image from this thumbnail display in Media Center.

It's a good idea to check often the Internet CD-ROM newsgroups I mentioned for news of new software releases, and keep your ear to the ground on your favorite software websites for inexpensive shareware that may help you while recording. As CD recording becomes more and more popular, you'll likely find a growing shareware industry to support it. In my experience, you don't "need" these extra programs, but they sure make producing CDs easier — and if you do use them, you'll wonder how you ever got along without them!

Adding SCSI Support

Of all the different bus and interface acronyms tossed around the computer industry — the "popular" IDE, the "traditional" ISA, the "ancient" EISA — none is probably more respected and reviled at the same time than the SCSI (*Small Computer System Interface*) standard drive interface.

Why? It actually boils down to two important points.

> ✦ **The Good News**. Although it's been around for some time, SCSI is still the undisputed king of drive interfaces in terms of raw throughput speed (up to 40 megabytes/second in its newest form) and versatility. Devices of all kinds

can be hooked up to a SCSI interface; not just hard drives, CD-ROM read-only drives, and CD recorders, but scanners and tape drives as well. SCSI hard drives are traditionally more expensive, but they're much faster, and the most expensive SCSI drives can store an incredible 9 gigabytes of data! Although Intel-based PCs have never fully embraced the SCSI bus, Macintosh users have enjoyed its benefits for years as standard equipment. Today, you'll likely find SCSI adapter cards on network server PCs (which benefit from the speed of a SCSI hard drive), PC workstations, the fastest home and office desktops, and those computers that need the special device support (like CD recorders). I'm happy to say that SCSI drives are finally catching on in the mainstream PC community.

✦ **The Bad News**. Without a doubt, the SCSI interface system has the reputation of being one of the most difficult computer concepts for the novice to understand and install. If you've ever installed an IDE drive, there really wasn't that much to it; you might have to change one jumper, but the entire process probably took an hour. One of the reasons why SCSI has never been popular with PC owners in the past is because it's much more complex. Personally, I consider older SCSI adapter cards to be spoiled children who refuse to cooperate until everything is done their way. The only piece of computer hardware I have ever seen ceremoniously burned with a blowtorch was a friend's recalcitrant SCSI card, and he refuses to talk about it to this day because "the whole experience was much too painful to remember."

On the technical side, a SCSI card can support up to eight devices, assigning each device an ID number from 0 to 7 to identify it. Since most SCSI adapter cards reserve ID number 7 for themselves, that leaves seven available device IDs on most cards. Typical PC installations might include:

✦ the adapter and the CD recorder (shown in Figure 5-6). This is the most common configuration for PC owners;

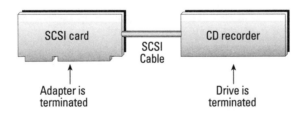

Figure 5-6: A typical CD recorder configuration for a PC with an IDE hard drive and no other SCSI devices.

✦ the adapter, a SCSI hard drive, and the CD recorder;

✦ the adapter, a SCSI CD-ROM read-only drive, and the CD recorder.

Each end of the SCSI chain on your computer must have a terminator, which in essence marks the end of the device chain to the adapter card. Figure 5-7 illustrates correct termination, while Figure 5-8 shows the effect of improper termination. The terminator can be a separate resistor pack, a series of DIP switches, or a series of jumpers on the device.

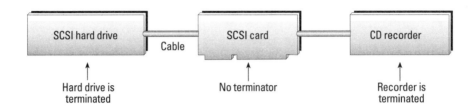

Figure 5-7: A properly terminated SCSI device chain.

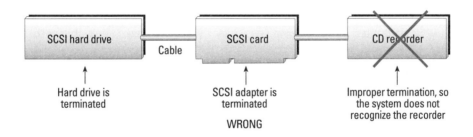

Figure 5-8: Improper termination causes devices at the end of the chain to be ignored.

Now that I've thoroughly scared you, let me reassure you that today's SCSI cards and installation software are much easier to configure and use than when my friend applied the blowtorch five years ago; in fact, my Adaptec SCSI adapter installed easily and configured itself automatically! This is especially true if you're running Windows 95 or Windows NT, which include built-in support for SCSI cards. SCSI manufacturers recognized long ago that they had to make their products easier to use, and the growing popularity of SCSI in the PC community is proof that they've been successful.

In this section, we install your SCSI card and configure it. To avoid problems along the way, make sure you pay close attention to both this book and the documentation that came with your card, especially when we configure device IDs and terminators.

I Already Have SCSI!

First, let's cover what changes you need to make if you're installing a CD recorder on a system that already has a SCSI adapter. I repeat some of these steps in the discussion on adding SCSI to an IDE system, so if your PC does not have SCSI, please skip to the next section!

1. If you have SCSI device software, run it and write down the SCSI IDs for each device on your system. If you have no way of determining IDs through software, you'll have to check each device manually once the cover is off.

2. Turn off your computer, but leave it plugged in.

 Tip   Before you unwrap any of your new toys or touch any internal components of your PC, I urge you to remove your PC's cover and touch the top of the metal case that surrounds your power supply! Why? You'll discharge any static electricity that might be lurking on your person. Any computer technician will tell you that static electricity is a leading cause of failure in electronic components, so you should always eliminate any static buildup on your body before handling computer hardware.

3. Remove your computer's cover and move it safely out of your way. In most cases, it means removing three or four screws from the rear of your computer, although some new cases feature covers removable with a single thumbscrew.

4. Determine which devices on the SCSI cable are terminated. If you only have one device, then both it and the adapter card are terminated.

5. Choose an unused SCSI ID for your CD recorder and select that number on your recorder. Typically, this is done with a series of DIP switches or a thumbwheel on the back of the drive — check your recorder's documentation for selecting an ID. If your computer is a Macintosh, remember that ID 7 is reserved for the SCSI system itself, so avoid that ID like the plague!

6. Terminate a recorder installed at the end of the SCSI chain. Do **not** terminate a recorder placed anywhere in the middle of the chain. Once again, check your recorder's documentation to determine how to set termination. **Remember to change the existing termination on your old devices if necessary!**

7. If you're installing an internal drive, see the section "Installing Your Drive" later in this chapter. If you're installing an external drive, go to the next step.

8. Close up your computer and plug it in. If you're using an external drive, connect the recorder's cable to your external SCSI port and plug your recorder in.

9. If you're running an external CD recorder, turn it on now. As a rule, always turn on external SCSI devices first before you turn on your computer.

10. Finally, run your SCSI device management software! Some "plug and play" SCSI adapters automatically recognize a new device, while others require you to configure a new device manually through software.

That completes the process for an existing SCSI system. As I said before, it's considerably easier than adding a card and a device from scratch, so relax and drink a soda while everyone else takes the long route!

Adding SCSI to an IDE System

If you're like most PC owners, your machine has one or two IDE hard drives, and perhaps even an IDE secondary port for a CD-ROM read-only drive or tape backup. Adding a new SCSI adapter to your system might involve a false start or two, but if you pay attention to details and tackle things in order, you should come out on the other side — about 60 minutes later — safe and sound, and in one piece! Follow these general steps:

1. If your SCSI adapter comes with a software diagnostic tool for determining the settings before installation, run it now. The documentation for your card will specify whether you need to run any software prior to installation.

2. Turn off your computer and unplug it.

3. Remove your computer's cover and move it safely out of your way. In most cases, it means removing three or four screws from the rear of your computer, although some new cases feature covers removable with a single thumbscrew.

4. Select an empty 16-bit ISA expansion slot (or an empty PCI card slot if you're installing a PCI SCSI card). Position doesn't matter, but I generally try to locate new cards as far away from existing cards as possible to provide better cooling.

5. Remove the screw holding the slot cover directly opposite the expansion slot your SCSI card will use. This opens the slot at the back of your PC and allows access to the external SCSI connector.

6. At this point, check your documentation and determine whether your card has any hardware jumpers or switches to set; if so, make sure you set them now, instead of trying to change them after the card has been installed! Many SCSI cards today are *jumperless*, meaning that configuration is performed entirely through software; if you're lucky enough to have one of these, you can skip this step.

7. If you have an internal drive, connect the SCSI ribbon cable to the adapter card. Pin 1 on the cable must match pin 1 on the card's cable connector. To determine which pin on the cable is pin 1, look for a wire with a stripe or colored dots along one side of the cable; pin 1 of the cable's connector is the first pin on that side. Typically, cards have pin 1 marked on their connectors with a tiny number 1 next to the right pin. As long as the colored side of the

cable is on the same side as pin 1 on the card, your cable is correctly connected.

8. Line up the bus connector on the bottom of the adapter card with the matching pattern of pins inside the expansion slot. Note the location of the plastic divider that separates the expansion slot; this divider should match the notch cut into the connector. The bottom of the bracket on the end of the adapter card should fit next to the back of your computer's case.

9. Keeping the card perpendicular to the computer's motherboard, press down across the full length of the card to insert it into the connector. Sometimes this takes a little muscle, but never twist or wiggle the card while you're installing it! Figure 5-9 illustrates the proper alignment of card to expansion bus.

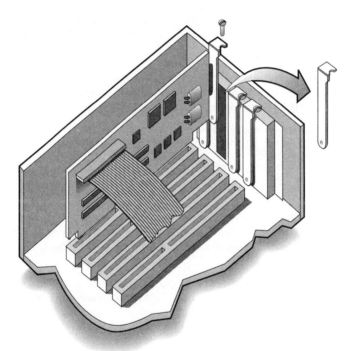

Figure 5-9: The installation of an expansion card. Make certain all points are aligned before applying force!

10. Replace the screw you removed in step 5 and tighten it to secure the card in place.

11. If you're using an internal drive, skip ahead to the next section. If you're installing an external drive, close up your computer and plug it in. Connect the recorder's cable to your external SCSI port and plug your recorder in.

12. If you're running an external CD recorder, turn it on now. As a rule, always turn on external SCSI devices first before you turn on your computer. Run your SCSI device management software — for example, the SCSISelect software that ships with Adaptec SCSI cards, shown in Figure 5-10 — or install the SCSI software that accompanied your card.

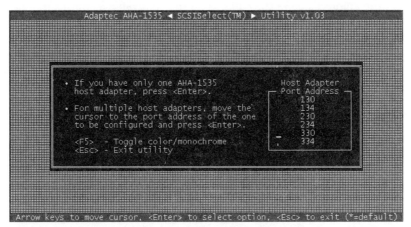

Figure 5-10: Adaptec SCSI cards ship with SCSISelect, a device manager that allows you to configure your SCSI devices.

Note that Windows 95 and Windows NT may request you to insert floppy disks with the proper drivers during the boot sequence. The software installation instructions for your SCSI card should tell you what to do if this occurs.

Good! Your card is now in place. Now let's move to the next section, where we describe the installation process for your internal drive.

Installing an Internal Drive

Follow these steps to install your internal CD recorder.

1. Determine whether your computer's device bays require device drive rails; if so, attach one rail to each side of the recorder. Most late-model computers do not require rails, so your CD recorder may simply slide into the bay.

2. Check your documentation to determine how to set your recorder's SCSI device ID, and select the ID you chose earlier.

3. Does your drive need to be terminated? Terminate your drive if you're adding just your CD recorder and there are no other SCSI devices on the chain. Follow your recorder's documentation for enabling termination.

4. If you have a sound card and it offers a CD-ROM audio connector, plug the end of the cable to your recorder's audio jack.

5. Route the cable from your SCSI adapter card through the drive bay and connect it to the recorder. Again, pin 1 on the cable must match pin 1 on the recorder's SCSI connector. Some recorders have connectors that only allow the cable to be inserted one way. Otherwise, remember this rule: as long as the colored side of the cable is on the same side as pin 1 on the recorder, your cable is correctly connected.

6. Slide the drive forward into the case, as shown in Figure 5-11. The front edge of the recorder should extend out as far as your floppy disk drive.

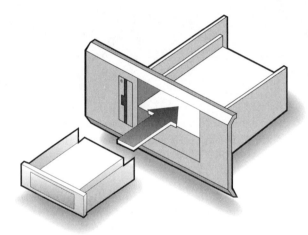

Figure 5-11: Installing a CD recorder into one of your PC's drive bays is just like installing a hard drive.

7. Align the holes in the recorder (or the rails, if your case requires them) with the holes in the walls of the device bay and secure the drive with two screws on each side.

8. Find a free power connector and plug it into the power socket on your CD recorder. These power cables are made up of four smaller wires, typically in four different colors, such as black, red, yellow, and orange; the white plastic socket on the end is keyed, so you can only connect them in the proper manner. If you can't find a spare power cable, head to your local computer or electronics store and ask for a "Y" power splitter for your PC; the trunk of the splitter connects to one of your power cables, and you can then connect two devices to your power supply on that cable instead of one.

9. Double-check **all** connections, including those to your hard drive, floppy disk drive, and ports. It's easy to accidentally dislodge a cable connection while

you're installing a device, and you'll save yourself the time required to take the case off again and reconnect that cable! Take a few moments to route the SCSI cable away from power cables and the ribbon cables leading to your hard drive and floppy disk drive; this cuts down on electrical interference that could come back to haunt you in the form of intermittent recording failures.

10. Put the cover back on your PC and check the alignment of the recorder with the front of your case. The faceplate of your recorder should be flush with the case and any other internal device you have. If the drive needs aligning, loosen all four screws — do not remove them — and slide the drive to the front or back until it's flush with the case.

11. Close up your computer.

12. Run your SCSI device management software, or install the SCSI software that accompanied your recorder.

That's it for the hardware installation. Note that Windows 95 and Windows NT may request for you to insert floppy disks with the proper drivers during the boot sequence. The software installation instructions for your recorder should tell you what to do if this occurs.

Installation Problems and Device Conflicts

In most cases, the default base address settings for your SCSI card will work correctly with your PC, especially if you're adding only a CD recorder to the device chain. According to Murphy's Law, however, if something can go wrong, it will!

BACK IT UP!

Let's face it: everyone makes mistakes, and that includes the developers of Windows and Macintosh software. Of all the timeworn pieces of advice I've given to novice computer owners, the most important (and probably the least followed) rule is **back up your system on a regular basis!** For the owners of CD recorders, this rule is more important than ever; each time you install a new program or install new drivers or system files within Windows, you run the risk of rendering your recorder unusable because of software conflicts. Once your recorder is working well and you've fine-tuned your system according to the tips I give you later, **back up your system!** If all else fails and your recorder locks your PC or continues to abort while recording, you can restore your system and reinstall new software one piece at a time (making it easy to determine which buggy new program is causing the problem). There are also a number of utilities for Windows 95 and Windows 3.1 that will restore your configuration from a "snapshot" taken of your system files. CD recorders are finicky beasts, so protect yourself by backing up often!

If you are still having problems accessing your SCSI adapter or your CD recorder after installation of all the hardware and software and rebooting of your PC, these troubleshooting questions may help you locate and fix the problem.

Your Computer Doesn't Recognize Your SCSI Adapter

✦ Is your PC's motherboard "plug and play" aware? If so, check to make sure you haven't disabled the plug and play feature available on many SCSI adapter cards. If plug and play is supported for both your motherboard and your SCSI adapter, use it and avoid device conflicts.

✦ Are you running Windows 95? If so, check the Windows Device Manager dialog to see if your SCSI card is conflicting with existing hardware. Right-click on My Computer and select Properties, then click on the Device Manager tab. There should be a plus sign next to the entry reading SCSI Controllers; click on the plus sign to display your SCSI controller's device drivers. If Windows 95 has detected a device conflict, it will display a small yellow warning sign next to the name of your SCSI adapter. Highlight the entry for the adapter and click on the Properties button, then select the Resources tab. Follow the documentation provided by your SCSI card for selecting a different set of resource settings under Windows 95.

✦ Did you insert your SCSI adapter into a 16-bit ISA slot? If you used an 8-bit slot, the adapter will not work correctly.

✦ Did you terminate your SCSI adapter? Terminate your adapter card if you're installing only a CD recorder and the only other device on the chain is the SCSI card.

Your Computer Doesn't Recognize Your Recorder

✦ Is your cabling correct? Remember, if a cable isn't connected properly or the cables are reversed (pin 1 of the cable is not plugged into pin 1 of the connector), the chain is not correct and your CD recorder cannot be identified by your SCSI controller.

✦ Is your drive assigned a unique ID? Each SCSI device is assigned a unique ID, and ID 7 is usually reserved for the SCSI adapter.

✦ Is the recorder terminated? If you're adding just your recorder and no other SCSI devices are present on the chain, you should terminate it. If you do have other SCSI devices, termination depends on the recorder's position on the SCSI cable. A termination problem usually causes all devices connected after the terminator to "disappear" — your SCSI card cannot access them.

✦ Did you install your recorder's software after the adapter card's SCSI software? Although it might seem obvious to install your recorder's SCSI software and drivers after you've installed the software for your SCSI adapter card, the order is less apparent when you're installing both pieces of hardware at the same time. Since some files required by the recorder may overwrite files installed by the adapter card — for instance, a specific vendor's ASPI device drivers — you should always install the software for your SCSI card first.

✦ Are you running Windows 95? If so, check the Windows Device Manager dialog to see if your SCSI card is conflicting with existing hardware. Right-click on My Computer and select Properties, then click on the Device Manager tab. There should be a plus sign next to the entry reading SCSI Controllers; click on the plus sign to display your SCSI controller's device drivers. If Windows 95 has detected a device conflict, it will display a small yellow warning sign next to the name of your SCSI adapter. Highlight the entry for the adapter and click on the Properties button, then select the Resources tab. Follow the documentation provided by your SCSI card for selecting a different set of resource settings under Windows 95.

✦ Is your drive plugged in to your PC's power supply? Check the front panel when you boot your PC and see if your recorder is properly connected to your computer's power supply; you should see a power or activity light when you turn on your machine.

✦ Is your SCSI cabling routed away from other cables? I know it's hard to arrange the octopus' garden of cables inside the average PC, but whenever possible try to keep your SCSI adapter ribbon cable away from power, hard drive, and floppy cables. The interference from a power cable has been known to cause intermittent problems for many SCSI devices, CD recorders included.

Tip   One possible source of trouble during the installation of an external SCSI CD recorder on a PC running Windows is a device conflict with the existing IDE drive controller. If your recorder seems to install correctly, but then sometimes "disappears" from your system — in other words, the recorder's drive letter does not appear in Windows Explorer or while browsing — contact the recorder manufacturer and the SCSI card manufacturer for help in diagnosing the conflict.

Summary

In this chapter, we covered:

✦ the hardware and software requirements for your CD recorder;

✦ the reasons for the continued popularity of the SCSI device interface;

✦ the installation process for your SCSI card;

✦ the installation process for your CD recorder;

✦ a number of possible problems you may encounter and tips on how to fix them.

In Chapter 6, we discuss the installation, configuration, and testing of Easy CD Creator.

✦   ✦   ✦

Installing Adaptec's Easy CD Creator

Now that you've successfully installed your CD recorder, it's time to focus on the recording software we use throughout most of the book: Adaptec's Easy CD Creator. Although I use other packages from time to time, depending on the situation, Easy CD Creator is my favorite for general recording, and I recommend it to both novice and experienced computer users.

In this chapter, we discuss whether you should run CD Creator 2 under 16-bit Windows 3.1 or Easy CD Creator under 32-bit Windows 95 and Windows NT 4.0. I lead you step-by-step through the installation of CD Creator under Windows 95. You learn the details behind each installation step and the various options available during installation. Finally, we round out this chapter by introducing you to the Easy CD Creator system tests and we verify that your recorder is ready for action!

Tip If you're not using Easy CD Creator, don't skip this section! You should skim through it, since we discuss configuration options that are probably included with your program. I also recommend that you read the section on the Easy CD Creator system tests.

16- or 32-Bit?

Now that the initial feeding frenzy that accompanied the highly-publicized release of Windows 95 has abated, it's become clear that a sizable percentage of Windows users didn't upgrade to Windows 95 or Windows NT — and don't plan to in the future. Why? Probably the primary reason is Windows 95's hardware requirements. If you're running a PC with an 80486DX2-66 and 8 megabytes of RAM, for example, you'll find that Windows 95 runs, but not well: it takes a considerable amount of time to boot up, and larger programs run sluggishly. In a case like this, I advise that you increase your system memory to 16 megabytes if you have to run Windows 95, which will help speed things up a bit. Take a moment, though, and consider: do you *have* to run Windows 95? Are there applications or features that you simply can't do without?

Let's look at that same PC, still with 8 megabytes of RAM, running Windows 3.11. It's lightning-fast! Applications practically jump off the screen, your PC boots up in seconds instead of minutes, and everything seems faster.

If you haven't figured out the moral of the story yet, here it is: if you're currently using Windows 3.1, there's no reason to upgrade to 32-bit platforms like Windows 95 or Windows NT just to record your own CDs. I often encounter this popular misconception when recommending recording hardware. It seems most PC owners who want to record simply assume that Windows 3.1 won't handle the job, and they'll either have to upgrade their processor, system memory, or perhaps even buy a new PC.

Don't believe it! When properly configured, Windows 3.1 is a robust, stable environment for recording your own compact discs, and as long as your system meets the minimum requirements mentioned earlier, you'll have no problem using CD Creator or any other 16-bit package.

Here's the other side of the coin: On a faster PC with memory and power to spare, Windows 95 and Windows NT are indeed better than 16-bit Windows 3.1. In my opinion, Windows 95 and NT offer much-improved interfaces. Plus both include enhancements like faster disk I/O, better memory management, and internal support for SCSI adapters and drives that make it easier to install, configure, and use your recorder.

As we continue through this chapter, then, let your current hardware and application needs determine which operating system you'll use. No matter which one you select, either CD Creator 2 or Easy CD Creator will perform well.

Installing Easy CD Creator Under Windows 95

Having said all that, Windows 95 is the most popular Windows platform today, so we'll install Easy CD Creator under it. You need the following to complete the installation:

✦ the Easy CD Creator distribution CD-ROM;

✦ one audio CD or multimedia CD with a digital audio soundtrack (for testing the digital audio capabilities of your recorder);

✦ one blank recordable disc for the system tests.

Before beginning, your CD recorder should be installed and recognized by Windows 95. You should be able to use it as a standard read-only CD-ROM, and it should appear without conflicts in the Windows 95 Device Manager as discussed in Chapter 5. Figure 6-1 illustrates the entry for a properly-installed Pinnacle Micro RCD5020 recorder in the Device Manager.

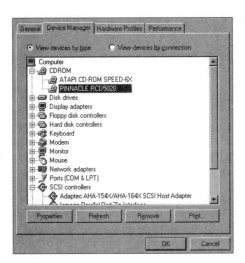

Figure 6-1: The Windows 95 Device Manager helps resolve hardware device conflicts.

Ready to begin installation? OK, here we go!

1. Insert the Easy CD Creator distribution disc into your recorder. If you happen to have a faster read-only CD-ROM drive, you can use it instead. I have a 6-speed read-only player on my system in addition to the recorder, and I use it to install software because it's much faster in transferring files from disc to my hard drive.

2. Since you've probably disabled autorun support on all of your drives as we discussed earlier, click the My Computer icon to display your drives and double-click the icon for the CD-ROM drive containing the Easy CD Creator disc. Windows 95 displays a window much like the one in Figure 6-2. Double-click the Setup program icon (which looks like a PC) to run the Easy CD Creator Setup program. It doesn't matter whether you're running Windows 95 or NT — both environments use the same Setup program.

Figure 6-2: Windows 95 displays the contents of the Adaptec Easy CD Creator disc.

3. Easy CD Creator Setup takes a few seconds to initialize, then displays the welcome screen shown in Figure 6-3. As stated in the dialog, it's always a good practice to exit other running applications while installing new software. Closing them insures that you don't lose a spreadsheet or a word processing document because of a lockup or a required Windows restart. You can switch to other programs using the Alt-Tab key combination; exit each program until Easy CD Creator Setup is the only application running. Once you've closed all other programs, click Next to continue.

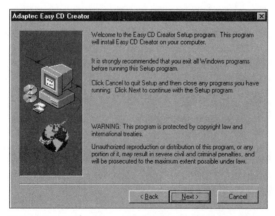

Figure 6-3: The Easy CD Creator Setup program welcome screen.

4. Next, Setup prompts you for the destination directory where all of the Easy CD Creator files will be installed, as shown in Figure 6-4. Accept the default of \Program Files\Easy CD Creator or type in another pathname. Personally, I recommend using defaults whenever possible during installations. If you're not sure of the exact pathname, click Browse to display a standard Windows directory tree and navigate to the desired path. Once you're satisfied, click Next to continue.

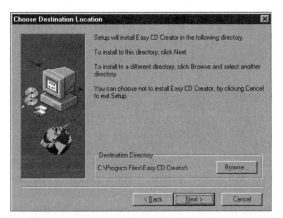

Figure 6-4: By default, Setup uses the directory path \Program Files\Easy CD Creator as the destination for Easy CD Creator files.

5. Now sit back and watch as Setup copies the Easy CD Creator files to your hard drive, creates the Start menu Program Group, and adds new keys to your Windows 95 Registry File.

6. The last dialog allows you to reboot your PC so that the changes you've made can take effect. Click Restart to reboot your computer. If you need to close a program or take care of other business, you can exit from Setup without rebooting by selecting No and clicking Finish. Remember, though, you can't use Easy CD Creator until you reboot.

That completes the installation of Easy CD Creator. Once you've rebooted your system, click the Start button to display your Programs menu and look for the new Program Group. You'll find it under Adaptec Easy CD Creator; you can also run Easy CD Creator from its directory, as in Figure 6-5.

Figure 6-5: Once you've installed CD Creator, you can run it from the Start menu group, or launch it from its directory in Windows Explorer as seen here.

Running the Easy CD Creator System Tester

Now you're ready to configure Easy CD Creator for your CD recorder's specific requirements. Sounds complicated, doesn't it? If you'd rather avoid changing settings and reading cryptic explanations, you're in luck: the Easy CD Creator System Tester will perform most of the work for us, automatically.

Note

Adaptec recommends that you run the Easy CD Creator System Tester after you make any changes to your Windows configuration, Easy CD Creator program configuration, or system hardware (including your PC's hard drive). Although I don't run it before every recording session, I do run the System Tester after making any significant change to my system.

1. To begin the tests, select the Adaptec Easy CD Creator Program Group from the Start menu and click on the Easy CD Creator item to launch the program. Click Cancel to close the Easy CD Creator Wizard, and select System Tests . . . from the Tools menu.

2. CD Creator displays the System Tester dialog within the program window, as shown in Figure 6-6. If you're familiar with Windows 95, you've seen tab dialogs like these before; to select a specific system test, click the

corresponding tab and click Do Test. First, we'll run the Transfer Rate test, which is already selected, so click Do Test.

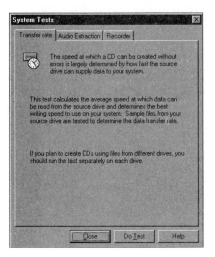

Figure 6-6: The top level of the System Tester dialog.

 Here's an important note: **Do not run the Transfer Rate test with any other Windows programs running in the background!** As you learn later, even the most powerful PC needs to devote all of its resources to recording, and the only way to determine the top transfer rate for your drive(s) is to run Easy CD Creator alone. If you're running under Windows 95 or NT, turn off any Taskbar programs that may be taking processor time, and exit all applications. If you're running CD Creator 2 under Windows 3.1, unload any TSR programs and exit all applications.

The configuration process begins with the Transfer Rate test, which determines which drives on your system are fast enough to act as the source drive during a recording session. Recording sources can include standard hard drives, CD-ROM read-only drives, removable drives (for example, the JAZ "hard drive cartridge" unit from Iomega), and network drives.

3. The System Tester displays a dialog allowing you to select a drive letter; start by testing your local hard drive (usually C:). Select C: from the drop-down list box and click Test. Once the System Tester has located suitable files for testing, you'll see a progress bar as the transfer rate of the specified drive is determined. The final statistics for the drive you chose are displayed at the end of the test, as shown in Figure 6-7. Write these totals down so that you can determine which drive on your system is the fastest (we'll use that drive later as we optimize your system for recording). You should test any drive that you could possibly use as a source drive for recording, or any drive that might store temporary files; at a minimum, I suggest all hard drives and their logical partitions. Each tested drive needs at least 6 megabytes of files ranging from 16KB to 100KB for the small files test, and at least one 6-megabyte file for the large files test. If you don't have enough files of the

proper size on the selected drive, System Tester displays an error message. If you're testing a hard drive, create a temporary directory and copy the files to it. Delete the copied files after exiting Easy CD Creator. If you're testing a CD-ROM drive, pick another disc from your computer CD-ROM collection that has a larger number of files. To select a network drive to test, click the Network . . . button. Once you've finished testing all your drives, load an audio CD into your CD recorder for the next test — don't worry, the recorder will not erase or damage your audio CD! — and then click Done.

Figure 6-7: The System Tester displays the final transfer rate figures for my C: drive.

WHY TEST SMALL AND LARGE FILES?

You may wonder why the System Tester performs two separate transfer tests on each drive you select: one for small files and another for a single large file over 6 megabytes. You may have also noticed that the transfer rate for large files is usually at least double the transfer rate for smaller files on the same drive. Why the slowdown for small files? The answer is in the file handling involved. For each file in your CD layout, Easy CD Creator must check the FAT table for its location, jump to the proper position on your hard drive, open the file, read it, and close it. A number of small files take much longer to process than a single large file, and, as we learn later, you may choose your recorder's single speed for writing a disc containing many small files if you have a slower PC!

4. The next test determines whether your recorder can "extract" (translate that as "copy") digital audio from audio CDs and multimedia CD-ROMs. Most recorders and read-only CD-ROM drives should have no problem extracting digital audio; however, just because your drive can play audio doesn't necessarily mean it can also extract it! If you have more than one drive capable of extracting digital audio, you can choose the fastest from the drop-down list box before you proceed, as shown in Figure 6-8. While the test runs, you'll see a progress bar indicating how much time remains. Finally, you should see a statistics dialog that tells you how fast the selected drive can extract digital audio.

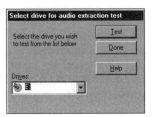

Figure 6-8: Selecting a drive for the audio extraction test.

5. The final stage of testing puts your recorder through all its paces as Easy CD Creator performs a number of separate simulated recordings. Taken together, the results of these "dry run" recordings determine the optimal recording speed for your recorder with your current system configuration. Also, this test determines whether all of your hardware and software is operating correctly and you're ready to start recording.

SIMULATED?

How can your recorder "simulate" a recording session? As you learned earlier, the organic dye layer in a blank recordable disc reacts only to a specific frequency of laser light. Because the laser write head in your recorder can toggle between different power levels, your drive can perform this test without actually making any changes to the CD-ROM. In fact, you can configure Easy CD Creator to run a simulated test each time you record a disc. This is a good practice for your first few recordings, but I recommend you skip the simulated recording step after you've fine-tuned your system and gained confidence in creating discs.

6. At the beginning of the test, your recorder will probably eject the audio CD you used for the digital audio testing stage and request that you load a blank disc, as shown in the dialog in Figure 6-9 — pretty smart! Most drives will automatically detect when you've loaded a disc (including blank media) and eject a disc when necessary. Once you've loaded your blank disc, wait a few seconds and see if your recorder will automatically recognize it; if not, click Retry.

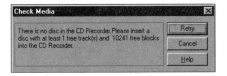

Figure 6-9: The System Tester demands a blank disc for the simulated recording tests!

7. Once your recorder has begun the simulated recording, you'll see a dialog with a progress bar and details of the test in progress, whether your drive is testing data or audio recording, and at what speed. For drives that record at double speed, the System Tester will simulate 300KB/second and

150KB/second (double and single speed, respectively). For drives that record at quad speed, the System Tester simulates 600KB/second, 300KB/second, and 150KB/second. Note that it may require more than one attempt to complete a test, so the dialog also indicates the number of attempts. The results from these simulated recordings allow the System Tester to select a default recording speed. However, you can change this default speed manually, if you like; you learn how later.

That's it! Once you've completed the simulated recording tests, the System Tester makes the minimal required changes to the configuration of Easy CD Creator to match your system. We're not quite done with configuration yet, so don't try recording now; I've got a few tips and tricks that will help speed up your PC and prepare your system for recording. Instead, select Exit from the File menu to close the program for now.

To emphasize an earlier point: if you make a major change to your PC's hardware or software configuration after this initial test, **run the System Tester again!** If the changes you've made severely impact the performance of your machine, or if you've added new hardware, running the System Tester will probably save you one or two aborted recordings (and one or two blank discs to boot). You can rerun the System Tester by selecting System Tests . . . from the Easy CD Creator Tools menu.

Summary

In this chapter, we discussed:

✦ the popular myth that "you need a 32-bit operating system to record CDs" — not true!

✦ the installation process for Easy CD Creator under Windows 95;

✦ the System Tester and the different types of tests it can perform to help configure Easy CD Creator for your computer.

Chapter 7 provides details on selecting your material, the proper recording format, and source drive for the CD-ROMs you want to create.

✦   ✦   ✦

Recording a CD-ROM

In Part II, you learn how to select the proper recording format for your material and how to organize it for easier access. We discuss tips and techniques you can use to optimize your computer for recording. Finally, you learn everything you need to know to record different types of discs with Easy CD Creator, Easy-CD Pro 95, and CD Creator.

♦ ♦ ♦ ♦

♦ ♦ ♦ ♦

CHAPTER

In This Chapter

Data, audio, and
mixed-mode

CD recordable
formats

Disc, track, packet,
and multisession
recording

Organizing files

CD-ROM legal basics

Preparing Your Material

In this chapter, you learn more about the various recording formats available and how to select the right one for each disc you create. I also discuss the importance of organizing your material logically, and give you tips on arranging material so that you can find it three years from now when you need it. Finally, I outline a few rules for avoiding copyrighted material and the legal issues involved. Throughout I refer to the different disc types, disc formats, and recording methods by both their common names and how they're used in Adaptec's Easy CD Creator. This should help in case your drive's software and recording software refer to them differently.

Data, Audio, or Mixed-Mode?

If you recall our definitions from earlier chapters, you know that there are three distinct types of compact discs that you can create with your recorder.

+ **Data.** These discs contain only computer data, without any digital audio tracks. In fact, you're likely to seriously confuse your audio CD player if you try to listen to a data CD-ROM on it. If it does recognize a track on the disc, there will be only one, and I wouldn't recommend listening to it (unless your musical tastes are very, very eclectic). You can damage an older audio CD player by trying to play a data CD-ROM! Note, however, that this does not mean you can't record digital audio in the form of .WAV or .AU files — formats that an audio CD player can't play. Figure 7-1 illustrates an Easy CD Creator layout for a data-only CD-ROM. Note that the structure closely resembles the tree structure displayed in the Windows 95 Explorer, with each directory appearing as a folder.

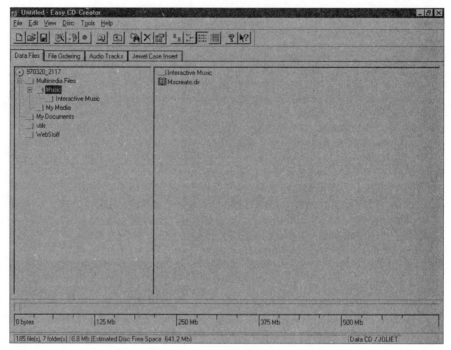

Figure 7-1: The structure of a data-only CD-ROM as it appears in Easy CD Creator.

✦ **Audio.** Digital audio is recorded according to the Red Book audio disc standard so the discs can be played on both audio CD players and computer CD-ROM drives. However, they contain no computer data. Figure 7-2 shows the layout of an audio CD in Easy CD Creator. As you can tell by comparing it to the previous figure, the program treats digital audio very differently than data.

✦ **Mixed-mode.** The third type of disc is a hybrid, often called *multimedia*. Mixed-mode discs contain both computer data and digital audio. Most mixed-mode discs have computer data on the first track and several tracks of digital audio starting with track two. Many multimedia games use this format, with the game data stored on the first track and a digital soundtrack following it that's played during the game. Note, however, that the digital audio on a mixed-mode disc should only be played on an audio CD player if it has been recorded in CD-EXTRA (also called *Plus* or *Enhanced*) format, which places all of the audio tracks before the computer data. Your audio CD player won't recognize the computer data on a CD-EXTRA disc and try to play it. Many bands and musicians are using this format to provide both an album's worth of music and an accompanying music video on the same disc! Figure 7-3 illustrates some of the extra information placeable on a CD-EXTRA disc.

Figure 7-2: The structure of an audio-only disc as it appears in Easy CD Creator.

Although many of the decisions you have to make about recording CDs lean toward the technical, the decision of which type of disc to create for a specific application is quite simple. Rather refreshing after all you've been through, isn't it? The nature of the material you're recording and the method of retrieval are the determining factors in selecting a data, audio, or multimedia disc.

DIGITAL SOUND STANDARDS

Windows sound files are stored in the WAV format, but they can vary widely when it comes to quality. The best recorded audio is sampled at 16 bits and 44KHz. If you're not an audio engineer, just remember that these files are audio CD quality, and they take up a huge amount of space on your hard drive! Other sampling rates include 22KHz, 11KHz, and 8KHz. Digital audio can also be recorded in monaural (single channel, commonly called "mono") or stereo (two channel) form. Stereo is more desirable for music, but if you're recording sound effects, speech, or other types of audio you can save space by creating mono sound files.

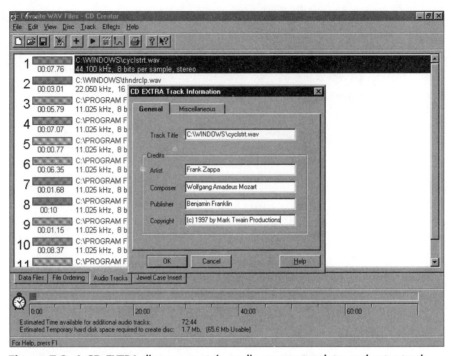

Figure 7-3: A CD-EXTRA disc can contain audio, computer data, and extra track information like that shown here.

Let's apply these two criteria. If, for example, you have only "pure" computer data or "pure" digital audio to store, you would create a data or audio disc, respectively. However, if you had a large amount of computer data and only one or two tracks of digital audio to record, you would select either a data disc (where you store the audio as data files in 44KHz WAV format) or a multimedia CD-EXTRA disc (where the audio tracks are written separately, before the computer data).

Which would you choose? It all depends on whether or not the disc must be playable on an audio CD player; if so, you would pick the CD-EXTRA disc. If you were simply storing the music and the disc will not be used in an audio player, it is easier to record a standard data-only CD-ROM. Also, not every CD-ROM drive can read a CD-EXTRA disc.

In most cases, the decision as to which type of disc to record is clear-cut. If, however, you're less certain of where the disc will be used, I recommend the simple route: the time-honored data and audio disc types may not be able to hold a mixture of material, but it's practically guaranteed that you will be able to read either one with just about any CD-ROM drive. From a compatibility standpoint, then, simpler is better.

CD Recordable Formats

Once you've decided which type of disc you'll be recording, your next task is to choose a recording format. Again, each of these recording formats is designed with certain advantages, so match the material you're recording and the method of retrieval to the format that can handle it best.

✦ **CD-ROM Mode 1.** This is the standard format for data CD-ROMs. A Mode 1 disc is usually recorded in a single *session,* which is defined as a single period of recording, no matter how much data is recorded or how long it takes. Most Mode 1 CD-ROMs are write-protected at the end of the recording session, preventing their use for re-recording. This is the only true "universal" data CD-ROM format; not every drive can read multisession discs, but you can pretty much bet that any standard CD-ROM drive around can read a Mode 1 disc. For this reason, commercial software is almost always distributed on a standard single-session Mode 1 disc.

✦ **CD-ROM/XA.** *XA* is short for Extended Architecture. The CD-ROM/XA format is a multimedia extension of the Yellow Book standard with better support for digital video. Easy CD Creator allows you to write multisession discs in CD-ROM/XA Mode 2, where your recorder can write more than one session to a blank disc. This is great for some applications, such as taking multiple CD-ROM "snapshots" of a particular directory tree on your hard drive.

✦ **CD-DA.** This is the standard format for digital audio (which is where the *DA* comes in) as specified by the Red Book. Any audio CD player or CD-ROM drive should be able to play a CD-DA disc. Easy CD Creator handles audio discs "transparently," meaning that you really don't have to set anything different for CD-DA other than specifying that you're recording a digital audio disc.

WHAT DOES "BLOCK SIZE" MEAN?

The default logical block size for Mode 1 is 2048 bytes (referred to as "2K"). This means that each file saved with this default value will occupy at least 2048 bytes on your CD-ROM, and files larger than 2048 bytes will occupy a multiple of 2048 (4096 bytes, 6144 bytes, and so on). If your material includes a large number of very small files — for example, Windows .ICO files — you can decrease this block size so that each of those tiny critters isn't taking up an entire 2K each. Common logical block sizes are 1024 bytes and 512 bytes. If you're writing files of over 2048 bytes each, the default value is fine. For more information on the different formats you can write, see the technical appendix at the end of this book.

✦ **PhotoCD Image Pac.** Discs you create in this format contain images selected from existing Corel Professional Photo and Kodak PhotoCD discs. A separate utility, called PCD Creator, records PCD Image Pac discs. As shown in Figure 7-4, PCD Creator displays the contents of the current PCD disc and the images chosen for recording. These discs cannot be used in Kodak PhotoCD players, however, since PCD Creator doesn't write all of the proprietary information required for a true PhotoCD. PCD Creator is available only with the Deluxe version of Easy CD Creator.

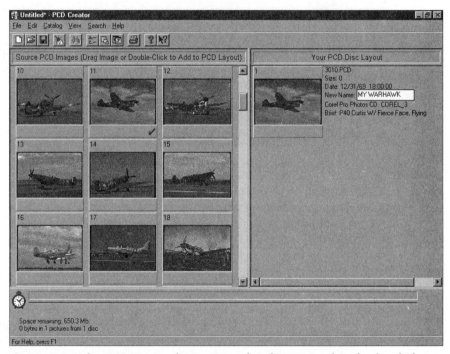

Figure 7-4: Using PCD Creator, images are taken from a Corel Professional Photo CD for recording on a CD-ROM.

✦ **Video CD.** These discs contain digital video in MPEG format and single-frame still images. Any video CD player can play them. The White Book standard defines their physical structure. A separate utility, VCD Creator, records video CDs. Figure 7-5 illustrates an AVI file that has been loaded into VCD Creator, ready to be added to the video disc layout. VCD Creator automatically converts digital video in AVI format to MPEG format before recording it. VCD Creator is available only with the Deluxe version of Easy CD Creator.

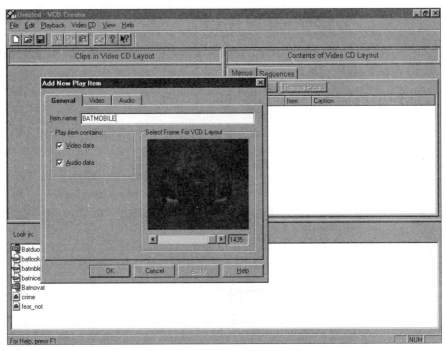

Figure 7-5: The drag-and-drop interface used in PCD Creator carries over to VCD Creator, where video files and stills can be dropped into your layout from the directory window below.

✦ **CD-EXTRA.** As mentioned earlier, you can specify CD-EXTRA format for multimedia/mixed-mode discs that are safely playable in an audio CD player, yet also contain computer data.

Easy CD Creator under Windows 95 and Windows NT 4.0 supports all these formats, but as you learned earlier your specific recorder may not support them. Later, you learn how to record each of these formats. For now, remember that you can handle just about any data storage task and just about any end-user application with one of these formats.

Disc, Track, Packet, and Multisession Recording

Now that we've discussed recording formats, it's time to introduce you to the different recording methods available for CD recorders. Once again, one of these methods is usually better suited to an application than the others, which should help you in making a decision about which to use.

✦ **Disc-at-once.** This is the most popular method of recording, although some recorders don't support it. In this method, all your data is written in a single stream, and the recorder's laser write head is never turned off between tracks. As you might expect, discs written with this method are single session, and they're write-protected so they can't be used again. Disc-at-once is the preferred method for creating audio discs. Also, if you're creating a master disc to send off to a replicator for mass-production, most shops prefer a master disc written using the disc-at-once method.

✦ **Track-at-once.** All recorders support this method, in which the recorder turns off its laser write head between tracks. Like disc-at-once recording, track-at-once is used to create single session, write-protected discs. The track-at-once method leaves link gaps between tracks that may produce an audible click on audio discs when played on certain audio CD players, but these gaps are no problem for data CD-ROMs (your computer's CD-ROM drive doesn't read anything between the tracks). A maximum of 99 tracks can be recorded on a blank disc.

✦ **Multisession.** Multisession discs can be recorded in either CD-ROM Mode 1 or CD-ROM/XA format (Easy CD Creator uses the latter). As mentioned earlier, multisession recording allows you to save more than one discrete session of data to the same CD-ROM disc, up to the total capacity of the disc. Although this sounds pretty neat, remember that multisession CD-ROMs are not recognized by every CD-ROM drive. This is fine, though, if you're creating archival backups for use only on your own computer and your drive can read multisession discs.

Easy CD Creator supports two types of multisession recording: *incremental* and *multivolume*. Incremental (sometimes called *appended*) is used when you're updating a specific dataset with changes that you've made; an incremental session contains all the data you've already written to the disc, plus any changes you want to make. To create an incremental session, you import the layout for the existing session on disc, then select the changes to be appended to the layout. You can even "delete" files by removing them from the layout. The files are not physically removed from the disc, but their entries are removed from the disc's Table of Contents, which effectively erases them from the new session. Multivolume, on the other hand, is like creating a separate partition on a hard drive; it holds a unique layout not shared among the other sessions on the disc.

A good use of incremental multisession recording is to update the contents of a specific directory. Because most of the files already exist on CD-ROM, you merely want to update those that have changed, delete one or two that are no longer required, and add any new ones to your CD-ROM archive. A good use of multivolume multisession recording is storing two different directories, each of which must be recorded separately in its own session. If you've ever used a tape backup program, incremental is very similar to an incremental tape backup of a hard drive, where only those files that have changed are saved; multivolume is more like creating a full backup on a tape with the append feature turned on.

Note   It's usually no big deal if you find that your recorder doesn't support one of these writing formats (or your recording software doesn't allow you to select which format it uses). Most novice recorder owners with typical needs probably don't know which method they use, and don't really care. For example, you can probably still create the disc you need using track-at-once instead of disc-at-once if your software doesn't allow you to select a different recording method. However, if you've specific need for packet, multisession or disc-at-once recording and you're hampered by your software or hardware, I suggest you consider selling your current software or hardware and buying the right tool for the job. There's a list of recorder hardware and software manufacturers at the back of this book that will help you buy what you need.

✦ **Packet**. The last recording method, packet recording, isn't widespread because there is no worldwide standard on its use. In effect, packet writing allows a CD recorder to save the data in a single file or on an entire hard drive, all the way up to the maximum capacity of a CD-ROM disc. For most of us, this is the ideal recording method because it doesn't require gathering 600-plus megabytes of data, arranging the data, and then creating a layout so that the disc can be created in a single session, as in disc-at-once and track-at-once. Instead, packet writing under Windows 95 is as simple as dragging a few files to your CD recorder icon, which acts exactly as a hard drive, and saving them immediately to the disc. Of course, you still can't physically erase the information — although you can later "hide" a file's location — but it is about as easy as CD-ROM recording can get!

So what's the problem? Unfortunately, most older drives don't support packet writing, and until recently there was no standard support for packet writing built into the Windows or Macintosh operating systems. A few companies released proprietary software for packet writing, but you couldn't read those discs on other machines without the software. The ISO 9660 directory structure used by standard CD-ROMs adds to the problem because you would have to completely rewrite the disc's directory each time you saved even one file! There is help on the way in 1997, though. Adaptec will be launching a new system called DirectCD that provides the software necessary for packet writing under Windows 95 (including the ability to save directly to your CD-ROM recorder from within a Windows 95 application). Besides eradicating buffer underruns, DirectCD will also support multitasking, so you can finally run more than one application while writing to CD! Adaptec will also be providing a logo for drive manufacturers so that they can identify their recorders to consumers as DirectCD compatible. Figure 7-6 shows the DirectCD compatibility logo.

HOW DOES DirectCD WORK?

You're probably saying, "Look, Mark, you just told us how difficult it's been to implement packet writing because of the directory problem. How did they do it?" It turns out that the directory problem has solved itself! DirectCD will use a new universal file system called the UDF (short for Universal Disc Format) that was recently approved by OSTA (short for Optical Storage Technology Association, if you hadn't guessed), whose members include Philips, HP, Seagate, Adaptec, and Sony. One of the criteria for the UDF design was the easy implementation of packet writing.

There are a couple of caveats to DirectCD: Initially, it will be available only for Windows 95, and you will need a newer drive that supports variable-length packet writing to use it. Discs created using DirectCD should be readable on most systems running Windows 95 or Windows NT, so they're not as standard as discs recorded using the other methods we've talked about; for example, you won't be able to read discs written with DirectCD under DOS, UNIX, Windows 3.1, or Macintosh.

Figure 7-6: The DirectCD logo that will appear on CD-ROM recorders compatible with Adaptec's new software.

Organizing Your Files

It's time to take a break from the technical side of CD-ROM recording. Instead, let's concentrate on the material itself, and how we can logically organize your files to make them easier to locate in the months (or even years) ahead. If you're creating a CD-ROM data disc, you should make it a practice to arrange your files in a separate step before you build your disc layout in Easy CD Creator.

First, let's consider the two different approaches to a directory structure for your CD-ROM illustrated in Figures 7-7 and 7-8.

You could consider these two illustrations as sort of a "before" and "after" presentation. Which arrangement seems easier to navigate, and which would make it easier to locate a specific file — an image in GIF format, for instance? Of course, the organization of Figure 7-8 into separate subdirectories is much better; unfortunately, the first discs created by many novice users look more like Figure 7-7, with all files appearing in the root directory. Unless you're recording three or four 100-megabyte files, saving everything in the root directory creates a jumbled mess that you'll have to decipher later!

Divide and conquer. If you can, group your files before you record into separate directories according to criteria such as file type, project name, financial quarter and year, or — if all else fails — by letter of the alphabet. I've yet to create a data disc that completely defied organization into at least three or four groups.

Don't be afraid to use subdirectories to arrange files. For example, suppose you've created a directory called "SOUNDS" for all of your digital sound files, but then you notice that you have several separate types of sound files; some are in WAV format, others are in SoundBlaster VOC format, and there are even a few AU files from Web pages. Now, you could add subdirectories under your SOUNDS directory for each different format of sound file, such as "WAVs," but is that the criteria you are likely to use searching this disc? If you're like me, you look for a particular sound or image by what it represents, not what format it is. For example, I would rather look for a sound byte of a golf ball being hit under the subdirectory "SPORTS" than dig through 150 WAV files to find the right one!

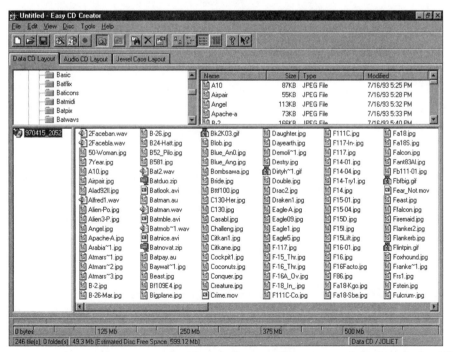

Figure 7-7: A CD-ROM created with a single root directory containing hundreds of files.

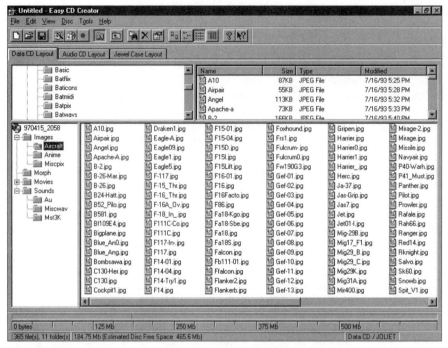

Figure 7-8: A CD-ROM created with multiple directories grouped by type.

Next, consider whether you can use long filenames on your discs. I'd recommend long filenames if

✦ you're using Windows 95 or Windows NT on your computer;

✦ your discs will be read only on your computer (or another PC that also uses Windows 95).

Using Easy CD Creator, you can enable support for long filenames by selecting the Microsoft Joliet file system. These discs are readable only on a PC running Windows 95, but filenames and directory names can be up to 64 characters, you can use multiple periods (".") in a filename, and you can use international characters. As an example, which filename would be easier to decipher after your archival disc had been stored for a year or so: the filename "APRJUNAR.DOC" or the filename "April/June Annual Report"?

Note   If you'd rather not use long filenames, consider creating a text file that contains the names and short descriptions of each file in the directory. If you're storing shareware files for a BBS or a distribution disc, most shareware ZIP files contain a standard file called "file_id.diz" that describes the contents of the ZIP. There are utilities available enabling BBS sysops to read and compile all of these descriptions into a single text file automatically!

Finally, if you're using a specific catalog program to browse through images, sounds, or video in a directory, see if that program can save its catalog data to a specific file. If it can, then record the catalog as another file in that directory. As an example, the Browse function in Paint Shop Pro creates a catalog file called "PSPBRWSE.JBF" when you browse the contents of a directory, and that file is saved within the directory when you exit Paint Shop Pro. Once you've recorded the disc, you can select that directory and Paint Shop Pro will use the PSPBRWSE.JBF file that's stored on your CD-ROM. I've found that this trick saves quite a bit of time when browsing through thumbnails of images I've stored on CD-ROM.

To summarize: the idea behind organizing files before you record is to spend a little time in preparation, saving yourself a lot of search time over the life of the disc.

CD-ROM Legal Basics

We end this chapter on preparing your material with a few guidelines on legal issues surrounding CD-ROM recording. I'm certainly no lawyer, and there may be special circumstances surrounding the material you copy, but these general rules will go a long way toward making certain that you stay on the right side of the law while recording.

✦ First and foremost, the legality of copying each program or file that you record must be determined on an individual basis. To create a collection of images on CD-ROM, for example, you must either own the copyright for each image or have permission from the copyright owner. Some shareware programs freely allow distribution on CD-ROM, while others allow only online distribution. Never assume that it's OK to copy any data — check any documentation or accompanying files first for copyright information! If you need to, don't hesitate to call the copyright owner for clarification.

✦ Most software companies do allow you to create a backup copy of their program for your own use, which is why most of us don't worry about copyrights when we back up our hard drives. Of course, you're much less likely to find yourself in legal trouble if you create discs only for your own use, and not for distribution.

✦ The phrase "royalty-free" is often misleading. If you're creating a disc with clip art, sound clips, or video that's been advertised as royalty-free, make sure you check whether you're allowed to copy those files to another medium, or add them to another collection. Often, you're only allowed to use royalty-free material in your own projects, not redistribute it.

✦ If you created the data, don't hesitate to copyright it yourself! The material must be entirely yours, however. You can't copy a MIDI file from a game or scan a picture from a magazine and copyright those files, since you didn't own the original material. For an image, program, or text file, all that's generally needed is the line:

Copyright (c) 1997 by [name], All Rights Reserved.
where you substitute your name or company name for the label "[name]'"
and change the date to the year that you created the material.

✦ If you need help in determining the copyright ownership of a file, or if you
have a legal question about copying or distributing certain material on
CD-ROM, ask your lawyer, or refer to a book covering computer intellectual
property laws. One good source of information is Stephen Fishman's *Software
Development: A Legal Guide* (Nolo Press).

Summary

In this chapter, we discussed:

✦ the different types of CD-ROMs you can create — data, audio, and mixed-
mode;

✦ common recording methods and their applications;

✦ the formats available for recording;

✦ guidelines for organizing your data for easy identification later;

✦ legal rules to follow when recording.

In Chapter 8, you learn about the general preparations you should make before
each recording session, as well as a number of specific configuration changes you
can make to optimize your Windows 3.1 or Windows 95 system.

✦   ✦   ✦

Preparing Your Computer

In Chapter 7, you learned about the different decisions you need to make about your material before creating a CD-ROM, including choosing a file organization system and selecting the correct CD-ROM type, format, and recording method for the job. In this chapter, we discuss a number of preparations you should make to your computer before you record your first CD. I consider these "fine tuning" operations more as requirements than optional steps you can ignore.

Some of these items need only be done once (or they're suggestions on additions you can make after you've gained experience recording), while others I strongly recommend you take care of before each recording session. Each of these preparations will help in configuring your computer and your operating system for the best possible performance, and they may even make the difference between a successful recording and a ruined disc.

Remember, if you perform any of the optimizing steps in this chapter, make sure you run the Easy CD Creator System Tester again before you record your first disc! Many of the changes we make here might significantly change the properties of your recorder within Easy CD Creator.

General Preparations

First, let's consider the general preparations you should perform before each recording session. I'll take you through each detail step-by-step, and I'll also explain why each of them improves the recording process.

If you're running Windows 3.1, you'll notice that some of these preparations involve exiting Windows and running programs from the DOS prompt. If you like, you can perform all of the DOS steps at the same time. For example, you can disable any TSRs (short for terminate and stay resident) and reboot, then scan your hard drives for errors, then delete any unnecessary files, and then defragment your drives before running Windows and recording. After you've gained experience with recording, you'll probably develop your own prerecording ritual, and you'll handle these preparations in the order you like the best.

Make Room, Make Room!

Whenever possible, I like to give my computer plenty of elbow room during a recording session. This isn't likely to be a problem if you've dedicated an entire drive or partition exclusively to creating CDs, but if you're moving data onto your existing drive and trying to organize it for recording, the last thing you need is to run low on hard drive space! Remember that some space must be reserved for temporary files, and if you're running Windows 95 remember that your operating system will likely try to expand its virtual memory pool (which requires more hard drive space) once you begin recording.

Having problems clearing out enough space to hold a CD image? Here's a short list of files you may be able to delete to gain back some of that hard drive territory.

✦ **Internet cache files.** If you run a Web browser like Netscape Navigator or Internet Explorer, you can usually release at least a couple of megabytes by deleting files from the browser cache.

✦ **Windows temporary files.** By default, Windows 95 stores temporary files in the \WINDOWS\TEMP directory, and sometimes these files are not erased by their programs. Typically, most temporary files end in .TMP, so if you see a number of files with that extension and older file dates in any directory, it's a good bet they can be deleted.

✦ **Unused programs.** Tired of that game demo that's taking up 30 megabytes worth of your valuable hard drive real estate? There's no better time to "clean house" by deleting or uninstalling unwanted programs than right before recording a disc! If you're using an "uninstaller" utility like Quarterdeck's Cleansweep, you can be sure that all of the associated files are deleted when you remove applications from your system, and you won't mistakenly erase a file that you actually need later!

✦ **Backup files.** Files ending in .BAK are generally backup data files, and you may be able to erase them. Check the documentation for the specific program to make sure.

Once you've deleted files from your drive, it's best to defragment your hard drive for the most efficient possible transfers from your drive to your CD-ROM recorder, so let's discuss defragmenting next.

Defragmenting Your Hard Drive

As you've already learned, the data throughput of your hard drive — how fast it can actually read and transfer data to your CD-ROM recorder — is all-important to successful recording. Any interruption or pause in the flow of data can abort the recording session, usually with a buffer underrun error.

If you're knowledgeable about computer hardware, you'll probably consider this problem solved when you buy a fast hard drive of 11 milliseconds access time or less, and connect it to a VLB or PCI hard drive controller. And you'd be right — at least for a short time! However, once you begin reading and writing to your new drive, the files you're using become fragmented.

Fragmentation occurs when you continually erase files and write new files to your hard drive; typically, new files are written to the first available empty areas on your hard drive. Now, some of those new files created by programs you run will fit in the space freed up by erased files, so there's no problem and everyone's happy. However, other files "slop over" the available empty space, and portions of those files must be saved into other areas of your hard drive. Of course, you don't have to keep track of this. DOS maintains a File Allocation Table (or FAT for short) in the first sector of your hard drive that contains the location of each portion of every file on your drive. Windows 95 has a similar area called a VFAT. Figure 8-1 illustrates the surface of a hard drive platter and how a typical file might be arranged on it.

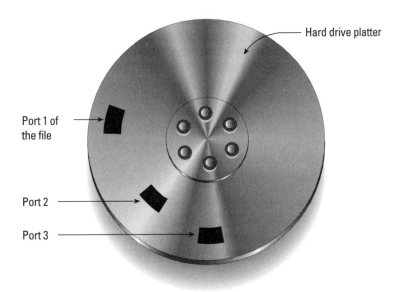

Figure 8-1: The traditional DOS file system can spread files across many clusters of your hard drive.

So what happens when one of your programs opens that file to read it? Ah, that's where the magic kicks in. Although little chunks of a file may be spread over several physical areas of your hard drive, your computer's file system "assembles" all the pieces automatically and creates a single, contiguous file for use by the program.

Unfortunately, this magic takes time, and that's what can cause problems during CD-ROM recording. After a few weeks of normal use (and even a few days of heavy use), the files on your drive are fragmented into countless pieces, and if you're trying to record one of those files to CD-ROM it will take much longer for your PC to read the data in a heavily fragmented file. The more fragmented files in your CD layout, the more processing time is required to read them. In fact, a heavily fragmented drive can significantly slow down your entire computer, making all of your programs suffer.

There's nothing that you can do to prevent fragmentation from occurring; after all, it's a result of technology that hasn't changed much in more than a decade, and every drive becomes fragmented over time. However, there are defragmenting programs available — in fact, Microsoft recognized the problem and provided defragmenting programs with DOS 6.22 and Windows 95. Defragmenting programs take the files on your disk and rewrite them in contiguous format, so that each file is readable in one operation from one specific spot on your hard drive. There are also shareware and commercial defragmenting programs available. My favorite (and probably the best known) is Speed Disk, shown in Figure 8-2, which is included with the Symantec's Norton Utilities.

Tip   If you have a defrag program that runs within Windows (such as Microsoft's Windows 95 Disk Defragmenter or Speed Disk for Windows), avoid running other programs (including screen savers) while you're defragmenting your drive. Any disk operations performed by other programs on the drive while the defrag program is working usually results in the entire process starting over. The defrag process will eventually complete, but it can take much longer if you're running other applications.

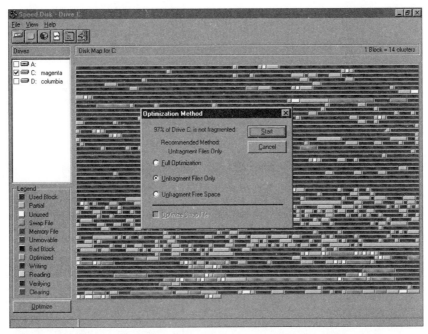

Figure 8-2: Speed Disk, which is included in Norton Utilities for Windows 95, is a popular and fast defragmenting program.

Running Defrag Under Windows 95

If you're running Windows 95, you can defragment your hard drive (or drives) before a recording session by following these steps.

1. Click the Start button on your Taskbar to display the Start menu and select Programs ➪ Accessories ➪ System Tools ➪ Disk Defragmenter.

2. Windows displays a dialog prompting you to select a drive for defragmenting. Choose a drive from the drop-down list box and click OK.

3. Next, the program runs a quick scan and reports how fragmented the selected drive actually is, as shown in Figure 8-3. If your drive needs it, click Start to begin the defrag process.

Figure 8-3: The Windows 95 Disk Defragmenter program displays how fragmented your drive is so you can decide which action to take.

4. I like to watch the full graphical status display, as shown in Figure 8-4, while the Disk Defragmenter is doing its job; if you'd like to see the process in action, click Show Details.

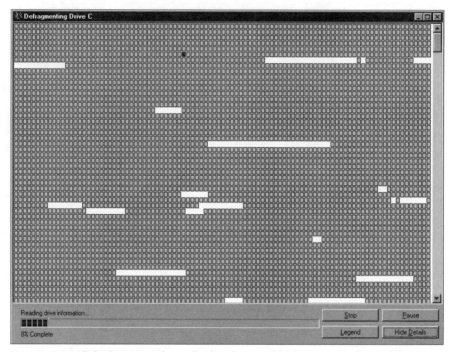

Figure 8-4: Click Show Details to display the graphical status window while Windows 95 Disk Defragmenter is running.

5. Once the defrag is complete, click <u>Y</u>es to exit the program or <u>N</u>o to select another drive for defragmenting.

Running Defrag Under Windows 3.1

If you're running DOS 6.22 and Windows 3.1, you can defragment your hard drive (or drives) before a recording session by following these steps.

1. First, shutdown Windows and exit to DOS — Microsoft Defrag will not run from within Windows (thank goodness, because you could do some serious damage to your data if it did)!

2. At the DOS prompt, type SCANDISK and press Enter. This will run ScanDisk on your current drive. There's no need to run a surface scan, so you can select NO at the prompt. If any repairs are required, they should be fixed before you run Defrag. You should run ScanDisk on each drive you will defrag — to select a drive other than the current drive, type SCANDISK X: (where X is the drive letter) and press Enter.

3. Once your drives check out OK (Figure 8-5), click Exit and you're ready to defrag. Type DEFRAG and press Enter. Defrag will prompt you to select a drive. Highlight the desired drive and press Enter.

4. After Defrag scans the drive, it displays a dialog indicating the level of fragmentation and the suggested action to take. To accept the default action, select Optimize by pressing Enter.

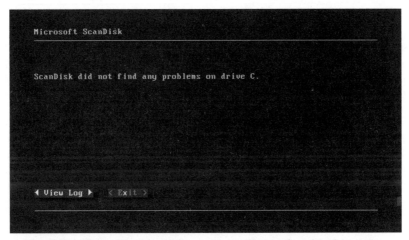

Figure 8-5: Microsoft's ScanDisk program indicates that this drive is in good shape and ready to defrag.

5. Now you can sit back and watch as Defrag reorders the files on your drive. Once the process has completed, don't forget to defragment any other drives on your system that will hold files that are being recorded or temporary files that will be created during recording. As a rule, you should also defragment the drive containing your Windows directory on a regular basis.

TSRs and Taskbar Programs

If you're like me, you take advantage of the Windows multitasking environment to run a few programs in the background — for example, a digital clock, a MIDI music player, or a system resources meter. Even if you haven't actually installed one or two of these programs, they may be there, because some "hidden" applications are installed along with programs or hardware you add to your machine. My favorite example is the scanner I bought that suddenly added about two megabytes of unwelcome extra utilities to my Startup group!

Generally, programs like this launch automatically at startup with little or no notice. You may be surprised at the number of programs running when your computer appears to be idle. For example, if your computer is running on a network, your recording session could be interrupted by a network-wide message. Another common background task is the antivirus monitor, that examines each

program you run and each disk operation to prevent damage from software
infected with a virus.

As you might expect, these programs steal part of your processor time while
running. If you've a very fast Pentium or Pentium Pro, then you might have the
power to spare, but if you're running a slower 486 or Pentium (or you've got many
background tasks running) you'll likely be taxing your PC if you try to record a disc.
Your computer needs to focus its entire "attention" on recording, so we need to
shutdown any background tasks, at least for the duration of your recording session.

Disabling Background Tasks Under Windows 3.1

If you're running DOS 6.22 and Windows 3.1, you may be running TSR programs
loaded in your AUTOEXEC.BAT file as well as background tasks within Windows.
To disable background tasks before a recording session, follow these steps:

1. First, shutdown Windows and exit to DOS. Since some programs can load
   before Windows 3.1, you will need to check your AUTOEXEC.BAT file.

2. Change to the root directory of your boot drive, which is usually C:, type
   EDIT AUTOEXEC.BAT, and press Enter. Microsoft's Editor loads and displays
   the contents of your AUTOEXEC.BAT file, as shown in Figure 8-6. Your file
   will, of course, contain different statements.

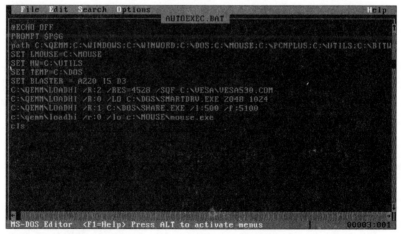

Figure 8-6: Microsoft's Editor displays my AUTOEXEC.BAT file from my
computer running Windows 3.1.

3. Check for any batch statements that may run programs you don't need in
   Windows — for example, the DOS version of SideKick, or a screen capture
   TSR. You should ignore any statements for system programs like your SCSI
   drivers, SMARTDRV, SHARE, or your mouse driver, because all of those are
   required.

Warning If you find anything in your AUTOEXEC.BAT that's so cryptic that you have no idea what it does, it's better to leave it alone than risk a crippling lockup! However, if you can at least determine what program is being loaded, you can check the documentation for that program to see whether it can safely be disabled.

4. If you find any statements that load unnecessary TSRs, you have two choices of action: disable the statements or delete them. I never delete anything from my computer's configuration files as long as disabling will have the same effect — after all, you can reenable a batch statement very easily if you suddenly discover it's required!

You can disable a statement in your AUTOEXEC.BAT file by adding the word REM (short for REMark) in front of it. For example, if you have the statement:

```
C:\SIDEKICK\SIDEKICK.EXE
```

in your file, move the cursor to the first character in the line, turn insert ON and type "REM " (don't forget the space). The disabled statement should look like this:

```
REM C:\SIDEKICK\SIDEKICK.EXE
```

5. To save the file, press Alt-F and select Exit; select Yes when prompted. Reboot and run Windows again. Once it has completed loading, you should also check your task list to make sure that no programs are running that you don't need; double-click your desktop to display the Task List dialog shown in Figure 8-7. In this case, I don't need my Klingon Klock for recording, and I can do without my trackball control program.

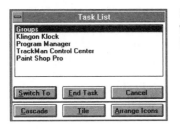

Figure 8-7: The Windows 3.1 Task List dialog, where you can switch to unnecessary background tasks and close them.

6. To close any background tasks you don't need, highlight the program's entry in the Task List and click End Task. Display the Task List dialog again and repeat this step for each task you need to close.

Warning There are some programs that can be configured to run "hidden" in the background, and they don't show in your Task List. A good example is the After Dark for Windows 3.1 family of screen savers, which can be configured to run without an icon or a Task List item. Basically, you must remember that such hidden applications are running, because you won't see any indication that they're there. Whenever possible, make certain that you disable hidden programs as well — check the program's documentation for instructions on how to temporarily disable or quit the application.

Disabling Background Tasks Under Windows 95

If you're running Windows 95, you may be loading unnecessary background tasks that can be disabled while recording. To disable background tasks before a recording session, follow these steps:

1. Display the Windows 95 Taskbar; if it's hidden, move the mouse cursor over it to display it.

2. Most Windows 95 users have at least one or two tasks running that add icons to the far end of the Taskbar — sometimes called the *System Tray* — as shown in Figure 8-8. You can usually quit these tasks directly by right-clicking their icons to display their menus and selecting Quit or Exit. Some icons display their configuration dialogs when you double-click them; you can select Quit or Close from the dialog.

Figure 8-8: The Windows 95 Taskbar, complete with a number of task icons. Close most of these tasks before you record.

3. You should also display the Windows 95 Close Program dialog by pressing CTRL-ALT-DEL. Highlight the program's entry in the list and click Εnd Task. Display the Close Program dialog again and repeat this step for each task you need to close.

Warning Do you use the Windows 95 System Agent, which automatically launches programs at scheduled times (or, even worse, when your system is "idle")? If so, you should know that System Agent could care less that you happen to be recording a disc; it will launch the program (or programs) at the scheduled time, which will probably throw a king-sized monkey wrench into your recording session! For this reason, I disable the System Agent and never use it.

Your Screen Saver Can Be Your Enemy

I know, I know, I'm talking blasphemy here — I enjoy my collection of screen savers as much as anyone, but any screen saver can ruin a recording session. Not only do most savers eat up a tremendous amount of processor power, many are also not as well-behaved as they should be. These savers actually disrupt other tasks running on your computer, or even interrupt other tasks entirely. You can imagine what havoc would occur if your screen saver made even a single appearance during a recording session!

Like other background tasks, you should disable your screen saver while you create a new disc; however, screen savers must be disabled differently from other tasks in both Windows 3.1 and Windows 95.

Disabling Your Screen Saver Under Windows 95

If you're running Windows 95, follow these steps to disable your screen saver:

1. Right-click your desktop and select the Properties item.

2. Windows opens the Display Properties dialog. Click the Screen Saver tab to display the Screen Saver properties, as shown in Figure 8-9.

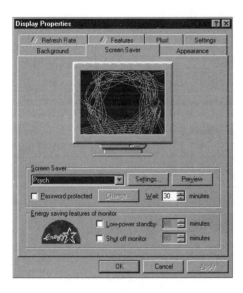

Figure 8-9: You can disable your screen saver in Windows 95 from this Display Properties dialog.

3. Click the Screen Saver drop-down list box and select (None).

4. Click OK to close the dialog and save your changes.

Disabling Your Screen Saver Under Windows 3.1

If you're running Windows 3.1, follow these steps to disable your screen saver:

1. From the Windows Program Manager, open the program group containing the Control Panel icon and click it to open the Control Panel.

2. From within the Control Panel window, click the Desktop icon. Windows displays the dialog shown in Figure 8-10.

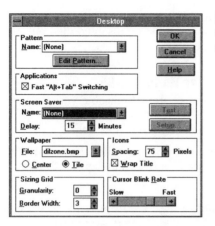

Figure 8-10: The Windows 3.1 Desktop dialog, where you can disable your screen saver before recording.

3. Click the Screen Saver drop-down list box and select (None).

4. Click OK to close the dialog and save your changes.

Hard Drive Considerations

So far, I've stressed how important a fast hard drive is to recording, and how the thermal calibration performed by all drives can interrupt the flow of data during a recording. I've also mentioned that a dedicated drive or partition reserved only for recording can be a great help. You should keep these guidelines in mind when buying new drive hardware for recording.

In this section, we save a little money! I discuss two changes you can make to your existing drive system that can fine-tune disk operations and provide that reserved space for your recording needs: cluster sizing and partitioning.

Cluster Sizing

Earlier we discussed block sizes used on CD-ROMs, but you may be more familiar with cluster sizes on hard drives. A cluster represents the minimum size that DOS reserves for a single file when you save it to disk. For example, if your hard drive is configured for 8K clusters, each file occupies at least 8K of space, no matter how short the file actually is.

Older hard drives used 8K or 16K clusters, but today's gigantic two- to three-gigabyte drives commonly use a cluster size of 32K. This poses a problem for CD recording, since the larger the cluster size the less efficient the transfer rate and the more likely your CD recorder will suffer buffer underrun errors during recording. As a rule, the source drive or partition for CD recording should be under one gigabyte, which should allow you to use 16K clusters.

If your drive was formatted with 32K clusters, however, it's not necessary to reformat the drive (although that is one solution). You can use a partition management program like Partition Magic, shown in Figure 8-11, to reconfigure your cluster size without losing any data. If you have a single drive of two gigabytes or more, it's likely you won't be able to reconfigure your cluster size until you divide your drive into at least two partitions, one of which should be less than one gigabyte in size and designated as your recording partition.

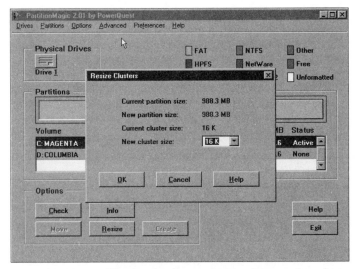

Figure 8-11: Partition Magic allows you to select another cluster size for a hard drive or partition without losing data.

Partitioning Your Hard Drive

If you can't buy a dedicated hard drive to use as a recording source, you're likely to find yourself making a solemn oath to reserve 600 megabytes or more of your existing hard drive for use with your recorder. If you already have a fast hard drive formatted with 16K clusters and it has that much room to spare — and you're not using DriveSpace or Stacker — this is certainly possible.

However, maintaining that much free space on a single drive is harder than you can imagine, especially if you love to try out new software, or you use your computer heavily in other applications. Over time, all of the excess baggage installed by other programs will collect, and the insidious crawling monster that is Windows will eventually swallow that real estate!

Here's a better idea: If you have the space, why not create a separate partition (and therefore a separate drive letter) that you can dedicate completely to recording? In effect, you are indeed "adding" a dedicated drive, and suddenly it becomes much easier to reserve space; simply avoid saving anything extraneous to that drive letter, and you'll never find yourself 100 megabytes short of space again.

Again, programs like Partition-It and Partition Magic come in very handy when creating a separate logical partition on an existing drive. No reformatting is required, and Partition Magic provides a real-time graphical display of the results before the process begins (making it easier to determine how much space will remain on your existing partition). Figure 8-12 illustrates the bar graph control used to select a size for your new partition in Partition Magic.

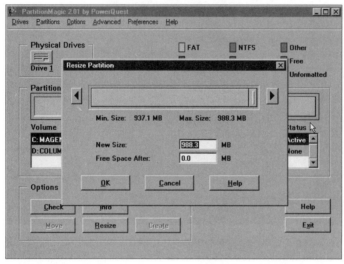

Figure 8-12: Partition Magic comes in handy again, this time in creating another partition solely for recording discs.

Optimizing Windows for Recording

Although the typical configuration that you probably selected during the installation of Windows works well with most applications, you've already learned that CD-ROM recording is very demanding on your computer. In this section, we change several settings within Windows 95 and Windows 3.1, optimizing your system for creating discs. In many cases, the changes will help all your applications run faster!

Fine-Tuning Windows 3.1

If you're running Windows 3.1, I recommend that you make these changes to your system before you try recording your first disc.

Selecting 32-Bit File I/O

You can greatly improve the file transfer rate of your system under Windows 3.1 by using 32-bit file and disc access. Faster transfer rates translate into fewer buffer underrun errors, since it's easier for your computer to maintain the flow of data to your CD-ROM recorder.

Follow these steps to enable 32-bit support:

1. From the Windows Program Manager, open the program group containing the Control Panel icon and click it to open the Control Panel.

2. From within the Control Panel window, click the Enhanced icon to display the Enhanced Properties dialog.

3. Next, click the Virtual Memory . . . button to display the current settings for your virtual memory swapfile. Windows displays the dialog shown in Figure 8-13.

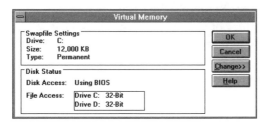

Figure 8-13: The Virtual Memory dialog allows you to change the settings for your swapfile and disk access.

4. Click the Change> button to change your disk access status, which appears at the bottom of the expanded Virtual Memory dialog, as shown in Figure 8-14.

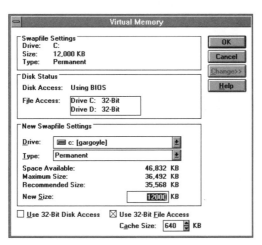

Figure 8-14: The Virtual Memory dialog allows you to change the settings for your swapfile and disk access.

5. If you have the resources, you should enable both 32-bit disk access and 32-bit file access. If you select 32-bit file access, I recommend that you also set the file cache to a minimum of 640K. Once you've made these changes, click OK to save them, and click Yes to confirm this. You'll have to reboot to apply these changes.

Adding a Hard Drive Cache

Another change you can make to your Windows 3.1 system that will dramatically speed data transfers to and from your hard drive is the addition of a hard drive cache. If you're not already using a cache, it's probably one of the most important additions you can make to your computer — without a cache, you probably won't be able to record at all!

The most popular cache program is Microsoft's SMARTDRV, which is provided as a part of DOS 6.22. Follow these steps to add SMARTDRV to your system:

1. First, shutdown Windows and exit to DOS. You need to add the command line for SMARTDRV to your AUTOEXEC.BAT file.

2. Change to the root directory of your boot drive, which is usually C:, type EDIT AUTOEXEC.BAT, and press Enter. Microsoft's Editor loads and displays the contents of your AUTOEXEC.BAT file.

3. Add the following statement near the end of your AUTOEXEC.BAT file:

    ```
    C:\DOS\SMARTDRV.EXE
    ```

    If you have 8 megabytes of RAM or more, you can increase the size of your cache by using the following statement instead:

    ```
    C:\DOS\SMARTDRV.EXE 2048 1024
    ```

    If you run Windows at the end of your AUTOEXEC.BAT file, make sure that the SMARTDRV statement appears before the statement loading Windows.

4. To save the file, press Alt-F and select Exit, then select Yes when prompted.

5. Reboot your PC to activate the cache.

Fine-Tuning Windows 95

Windows 95 allows you to change several options to fine-tune your system, especially for CD-ROM recording.

Optimizing the File System

If you have 16 megabytes or more of RAM, you'll improve file transfers for all applications under Windows 95 (and reduce the chance of buffer underrun errors during recording) by changing the settings for your file system.

Follow these steps to speed up your file system.

1. Right-click the My Computer icon and select Properties to display the System Properties dialog.

2. Click the Performance tab to display your system's performance status and click the File System . . . button under Advanced settings. Windows 95 displays the File System Properties dialog, as shown in Figure 8-15.

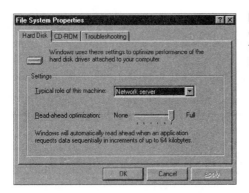

Figure 8-15: Under Windows 95, you can change the performance of your file system from the File System Properties dialog.

3. The field *Typical role of this machine:* is usually set to "Desktop computer." If you have at least 16 megabytes of RAM, change this value to "Network server," which dedicates more system resources to providing the fastest possible file transfers.

4. Next, set your *Read-ahead optimization:* sliding control to "Full." This allows Windows 95 to read more data ahead of time on larger files, increasing the efficiency of read operations. In fact, Windows 95 will have already read most of the data in larger files before your CD-ROM recording software actually needs it!

5. Now let's check your read-only CD-ROM file settings. Click the CD-ROM tab in the File System Properties dialog to display the CD-ROM file settings; the dialog changes to look like Figure 8-16.

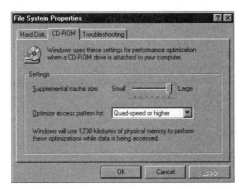

Figure 8-16: This tab in the File System Properties dialog controls CD-ROM performance.

6. Set your *Supplemental cache size:* sliding control to "Large." Just as with a hard drive, the larger the CD-ROM cache, the more efficiently your CD-ROM drive can transfer files to your system. This field is especially important if you'll be copying disc-to-disc from a read-only SCSI CD-ROM drive.

7. Typically, Windows 95 selects the proper default for read-ahead, but check to make certain that the value matches your drive's speed. If not, select the proper speed.

8. Now we're ready to exit and save our changes; click OK to save your settings and close the System Properties dialog.

Disabling Support for Auto-Insert

One of the nice features of Windows 95 is the automatic detection of an inserted CD-ROM; if the disc supports Windows 95, it can run launch programs or open a dialog automatically.

This feature is nifty, all right, unless you happen to be recording CDs! Many recording programs disable auto-insert for you, but it's always a good idea to disable the feature manually on every SCSI CD-ROM drive you have, just to be sure. Follow these steps to turn auto-insert detection off.

1. Right-click the My Computer icon and select Properties to display the System Properties dialog.

2. Click the Device Manager tab to display your system's hardware, and then click the plus sign next to the CD-ROM entry to display your CD-ROM drives. You should see an entry for each of your drives, including your CD-ROM recorder as in Figure 8-17.

Figure 8-17: The Device Manager displays all of the hardware on your system, including CD-ROM drives.

3. Next, click the first drive in the list that's connected to your SCSI adapter (for most of us, that's only the CD-ROM recorder itself) and click the Properties button to display the Properties panel for the drive.

4. Now click the Settings tab to display the options you can control for the selected drive. Your Settings panel should look something like Figure 8-18.

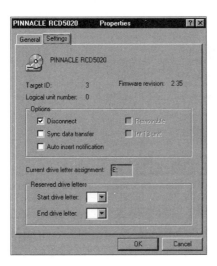

Figure 8-18: The Device Manager Settings panel for a typical CD recorder, showing the option for Auto insert notification and Disconnect.

5. Click the checkbox labeled *Auto insert notification* to clear it and disable the insert detection feature.

6. Click OK to save your changes and return to the Device Manager panel, then click OK to exit the System Properties dialog. Reboot your system as instructed by Windows 95.

Repeat these steps for each CD-ROM drive connected to your SCSI adapter.

Enabling Disconnect

Do you have a SCSI hard drive as well as a recorder? While you're rummaging around in the Device Manager, you should also check each SCSI hard drive and CD-ROM drive on your system to make sure that the SCSI disconnect option is enabled. Follow these steps.

1. Right-click the My Computer icon and select Properties to display the System Properties dialog.

2. Click the Device Manager tab to display your system's hardware, and then click the plus sign next to the CD-ROM entry to display your CD-ROM drives. You should see an entry for each of your drives, including your CD-ROM recorder.

3. Next, click the first drive in the list that's connected to your SCSI adapter (for most of us, that's only the CD-ROM recorder itself) and click the Properties button to display the Properties panel for the drive.

4. Now click the Settings tab to display the options you can control for the selected drive.

5. If the field labeled *Disconnect* isn't checked, click it to enable it, as shown in Figure 8-18.

6. Click OK to save your changes and return to the Device Manager panel, then click OK to exit the System Properties dialog. Reboot your system as instructed by Windows 95.

Repeat these steps for each hard drive and CD-ROM drive connected to your SCSI adapter.

A Word on Network Recording

We've discussed how critical file transfer speed and system resources are for successful recording, and you know that multitasking of any kind is to be avoided while you're recording to a disc. This rule doesn't apply to packet-writing recording — for example, if you're running Adaptec's DirectCD on your Windows 95 system — but for any other type of recording, you should apply every time-slice your processor can spare to your recording software.

Then what about network recording? It is possible to record CDs over a network; the source drive and CD-ROM recorder can be located on different workstations or the network server. This appears to be the ideal solution for an office-wide recording environment — every employee would have access to the company recorder, no matter where they were located in the building.

Now, let me qualify that statement: If you're using recording software designed for use on a single PC (Easy CD Creator, CD Creator, or Easy-CD Pro, for example) I advise you not to attempt network CD-ROM recording when you can record on a single computer instead! In fact, you should log off your network before recording a CD if you're recording on a workstation.

Why? Once again, the answer lies in the tremendous resource requirements for CD recording. Your network had better be fast if you're going to try transferring source data from another computer, and even in the best case, you'll probably only be able to record at single speed. Also, recording a disc through a network opens the recording computer to a host of possible network interruptions, including global network messages, electronic mail notification, and file requests from other computers on the network.

Finally, can you be sure that all the preparations we've covered in this chapter were made to every workstation that might act as the source drive? Probably not. On the other hand, though, if a single computer in your office is dedicated solely as a recording workstation, it will be much easier to maintain the proper configuration.

For most companies, then, the dedicated recording workstation is the best solution. Using the multiple boot feature of Windows 95, you can run this workstation with a standard network configuration most of the time, which allows you to transfer files over the network from any PC and store them locally for recording. Alternately, you can "premaster" your disc by storing a disc image on the local workstation hard drive; we discuss creating disc images in Chapter 10. Then, you'll reboot the recording workstation and select the recording configuration, disabling the network connection. Without the network connection, the workstation becomes a standalone PC, ready for uninterrupted recording.

This doesn't mean, however, that there are no reliable solutions for true network CD-ROM recording; it's just that the solutions that really work on a busy network are standalone recorders especially designed for network use, like the Netscribe series of CD-ROM recording servers. These devices are practically computers themselves, containing everything necessary to record discs remotely, and they are bundled with software that makes network recording as easy in Windows as sending files to a specific drive letter. As you might imagine, these dedicated network recorders are very expensive, so this is not the answer for the small office.

Summary

In this chapter, we discussed preparations you can make to optimize your Windows system for CD recording. These guidelines included:

+ making additional room on your hard drive;

+ defragmenting your source drive;

+ disabling background tasks, resident programs, network connections, and screen savers;

+ changing your hard drive's cluster and partition configuration;

+ making changes to your Windows 3.1 and Windows 95 system configuration.

In Chapter 9, we begin creating disc layouts and recording discs with Adaptec's Easy CD Creator.

✦   ✦   ✦

Using Easy CD Creator

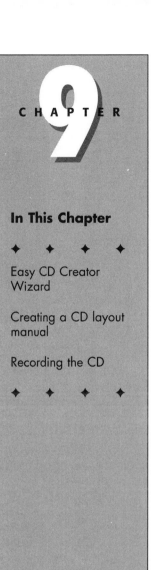

CHAPTER

9

In This Chapter

◆ ◆ ◆ ◆

Easy CD Creator Wizard

Creating a CD layout manual

Recording the CD

◆ ◆ ◆ ◆

In Chapter 6, we installed Easy CD Creator and ran the system tests, but you haven't actually recorded your first disc yet. Now that your system is fine-tuned for recording, it's time to examine all of the standard features within Easy CD Creator. In this chapter, we use the Easy CD Creator Wizard, select a file system, learn all about loading, designing, and saving CD layouts, and — brace yourself — create our first data CD-ROM!

Throughout this chapter (and actually a bit beyond it), we create and modify example layouts. If you have files ready to archive, you may wish to follow the book's examples but create a layout using those files. Later in the chapter, you can use your layout and actually record your first disc as I record the example disc.

The Easy CD Creator Wizard

One of the reasons Easy CD Creator is so popular is the Easy CD Creator Wizard, a friendly utility that guides you through the most common recording functions with step-by-step instructions. By default, the Wizard appears as soon as you run Easy CD Creator, as shown in Figure 9-1. You can run the Wizard at any time by selecting the Wizard item from the File menu, or the Wizard button from the Toolbar. To move forward to the next step of a process within the Wizard, click the Next> button; you can usually move backward to the previous step by clicking the <Back button.

In this section, we follow the Wizard step-by-step through the two most common tasks performed in Easy CD Creator: creating a data CD-ROM and creating an audio disc. I explain each step in detail, as well as describe some of what the Wizard is doing in the background.

Figure 9-1: The Easy CD Creator Wizard guides the set up of a recording session.

Creating a Data CD-ROM

1. From the opening Wizard screen, click *Data CD* and click Next> to move to the next screen.

2. The Wizard displays the Adding Data Files screen, shown in Figure 9-2, where you can select the files to add to your disc. You can select different source drives from the *Look in:* drop-down list box. Once you've highlighted the directory or files you want to add to your layout, click Add Now. You can see that the Wizard is building your layout for you behind the dialog, adding each file and directory when you press Add Now. By default, the directories and files you add will be placed in the root directory of your new disc. As you add files and subdirectories, the Wizard's Disc Info bar graph at the bottom of the screen displays how much space remains for more data.

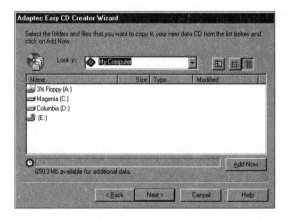

Figure 9-2: The Adding Data Files screen makes it easy to select directories and files for recording.

3. The Wizard displays the Test Before Writing screen shown in Figure 9-3, where you determine whether Easy CD Creator performs a simulated recording to test the layout and your equipment. This will not actually write any data to the disc; if the test fails, no damage is done! I suggest you perform the test for your first several recordings, and that you run the test whenever you make significant changes to your system hardware, software, or configuration settings. Choose the desired option and click Next> to continue to the next screen.

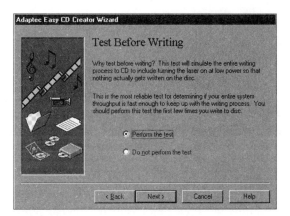

Figure 9-3: You should perform a simulated recording before you create your first few discs.

Tip   As I mentioned, you should run a test recording for your first several discs, or whenever you make changes to your system hardware or software — but you should also run a test recording the first time you create a different type of disc! For example, CD-ROM XA discs demand better performance from your system, because additional bytes are written for each sector of the disc and successfully recording audio CDs requires better hard drive throughput than a standard data CD-ROM. Avoid buffer underrun errors by testing and optimizing your system beforehand.

4. The Wizard displays the Ready to Create CD screen shown in Figure 9-4, where you can make final changes or begin the recording process. You have two choices: you can elect to create the disc now (which launches Easy CD Creator in recording mode) or make changes to the CD (which closes the Wizard and returns you to the Easy CD Creator menu system, where you can make changes to the layout). We stop here, because the rest of the process is discussed later in this chapter.

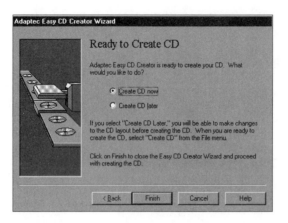

Figure 9-4: Here's your last chance to change your disc layout manually before creating a disc.

Creating an Audio Disc

1. From the opening Wizard screen, click *Audio CD* and click Next> to move to the next screen.

2. The Wizard displays the Adding Audio Tracks screen, as shown in Figure 9-5. From here, you can select which audio tracks to add to your disc. As you add tracks, the Wizard's Disc Info bar graph at the bottom of the screen displays how many minutes remain for more music. You can add tracks from existing audio CDs or WAV format sound files stored on your drive. Right now, let's copy files from another audio disc; this is the most common method of adding tracks. Insert an audio CD into your drive and double-click the drive's icon in the list to display its contents, as shown in Figure 9-6. Each track is listed by number, and the length of the track is also displayed. Pick some tracks (hold down the Ctrl key to select multiple tracks) and click Add Now to add them to your audio disc layout. To specify the name for a track, right click the track entry and select Properties.

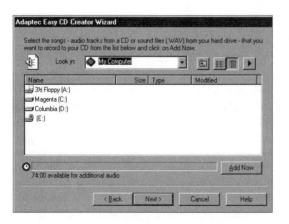

Figure 9-5: From the Adding Audio Tracks screen, you select the tracks to create an audio CD layout.

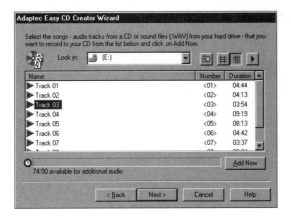

Figure 9-6: If you add items from an audio CD, Easy CD Creator allows you to select the tracks.

You can see that the Wizard is building your layout behind the dialog, adding each track when you press Add Now.

If you'd like to listen to a specific track before you add it to your layout, double-click the small "play" icon next to the track name, or click the button marked with the similar icon at the top of the dialog next to the List and Detail buttons. Easy CD Creator displays the Preview dialog shown in Figure 9-7 and begins to play the selected track directly from the disc. To stop the preview, click the button marked with a square; to pause the preview, click the button marked with the double vertical line. These buttons look just like their counterparts (the play, stop, and pause buttons) on an audio CD player.

Figure 9-7: Previewing an audio track within the Wizard.

You can also preview and add existing WAV files from your hard drive in the same manner; just navigate to the correct directory and the Wizard will automatically display any WAV files it finds there.

Once you're done adding all your audio tracks and WAV files, click Next> to continue to the next screen.

3. The Wizard displays the screen shown in Figure 9-8, where you enter the artist's name and the disc name. The names you enter here will be used when you create a jewel case insert for your new audio CD. Once you've entered the information, click Next> to continue to the next screen.

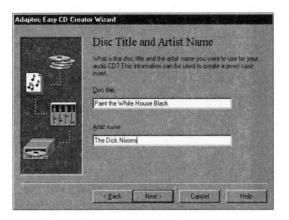

Figure 9-8: Enter the artist and disc name on this Wizard screen.

4. The Wizard displays the Close Session screen shown in Figure 9-9, where you determine whether the disc session should be "closed" (or write-protected) after the recording has completed. Since your audio CD player will not be able to play the disc until the session is closed, you should leave the session open only if you're planning on adding a few more tracks before you close the disc. Even if you don't close the disc, however, you can still listen to it on most CD recorders. Choose the desired option and click Next> to continue to the next screen.

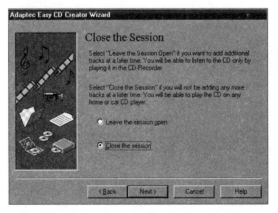

Figure 9-9: Easy CD Creator allows you to close a session or leave it open for further recording.

5. The Wizard displays the Test Before Writing screen shown in Figure 9-3. As in data CD-ROM recording, you should perform the test for your first several recordings, or if you make significant changes to your system hardware, software, or configuration settings. Choose the desired option and click Next> to continue to the next screen.

6. The Wizard displays the Ready to Create CD screen shown in Figure 9-4, where you can make final changes or begin the recording process. You can elect to create the disc now (which launches Easy CD Creator in recording mode) or make changes to the CD (which closes the Wizard and returns you to the Easy CD Creator menu system, where you can make changes to the layout). We stop here, because the rest of the process is discussed later in this chapter.

Creating a CD Layout Manually

Now that you've used the Easy CD Creator Wizard to automate the recording of data and audio discs, let's discuss how to create a CD layout manually and record without the Wizard.

Why record manually? Some of the more advanced features of Easy CD Creator are not available within the Wizard, so you have to configure them by hand. Usually, I find it's easiest to use the Wizard to prepare my CD layout, then I select the *Create CD Later* option on the last Wizard screen and make whatever changes I need to make manually.

Once you've gained experience with recording, you may decide to ignore the Wizard completely and create discs exclusively from the menu — there's a configuration item that allows you to bypass the Wizard when you launch Easy CD Creator.

In this section, we recreate the Wizard's steps manually, so you can see where to make these changes in the menu system.

Creating a New Layout

By default, Easy CD Creator always displays the Wizard when you select File ➪ New CD Layout, but you can change this. Select the Options... item on the Tools menu to display the Easy CD Creator Options dialog, shown in Figure 9-10. Click the General tab and disable the option labeled *Open Easy CD Creator Wizard at Startup*.

Now when you select New CD Layout . . . from the File menu, you'll get a new, blank layout window. In the example in Figure 9-11, I added four bitmap images to my layout in a new folder, appropriately titled "Images." The top two panels display the directories and files on my system, while the bottom two panels display my data CD layout in a similar fashion: directory tree in the left panel, and a file display on the right.

This layout is the template for a complete disc, including all data items, audio tracks, their arrangement on the disc, and even the information to be printed on the jewel case insert. Remember, changes you make to the current layout affect only the disc recorded with that layout. Another layout represents another disc, and it may use completely different settings, which are stored as a part of the layout when you save it to your hard drive.

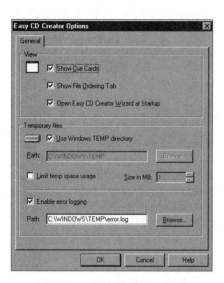

Figure 9-10: You can make a number of changes in the operation of Easy CD Creator from the Options dialog.

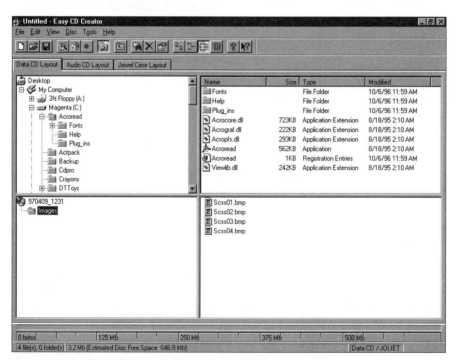

Figure 9-11: If you don't use the Wizard, every disc you create starts from a blank layout window.

Below the menu system, you'll see the *Toolbar*; most Windows applications have a Toolbar these days. The buttons provide the same functionality as most of the common menu items; for example, you can click the New button on the Toolbar (which looks like a document page with a corner turned down) to open a new blank layout. To display the function of a button, move your mouse cursor over the button and leave it motionless for a few seconds. The Toolbar changes to reflect the type of disc, so the data Toolbar looks different from the audio Toolbar.

Loading, Saving, and Printing Layouts

You can also load existing layouts from the File menu. Select the Open CD Layout... item on the File menu to display a standard Windows Open File dialog, as shown in Figure 9-12, or click the Open button on the Toolbar, which looks like a folder being opened. By default, any layouts saved with Easy CD Creator have the extension .CL3, and the Open File dialog displays only these files; however, you can view all files regardless of extension by clicking the Files of type drop-down list box and selecting All Files (*.*). Once you've found the layout file you want to load, double-click it, or highlight it and click the Open button.

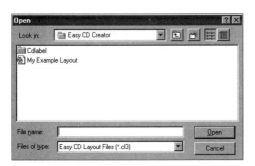

Figure 9-12: This File Open dialog allows you to browse your system and locate Easy CD Creator layout files to load.

If you want to work on a layout later or record it some time in the future, you need to save it to disk before you exit Easy CD Creator.

If this is the first time you've worked with this layout, select the Save item on the File menu to display a standard Windows Save As dialog, as shown in Figure 9-13, or click the Save button on the Toolbar, which looks like a floppy disk. Enter a name in the File Name field, and click Save. Easy CD Creator automatically adds the extension .CL3 to the filename you entered.

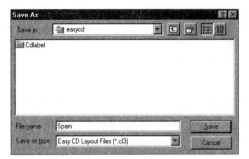

Figure 9-13: This Save As dialog allows you to browse your system and save the current layout in any directory.

If you loaded this layout file from disk, selecting the Save item on the File menu automatically updates the existing file on your disk.

If you want to save an existing layout file under a new name, select the Save As... item from the File menu. Easy CD Creator allows you to rename the file before saving it to disk — this is a good way of creating a copy of an existing layout as a starting point for a new layout.

Need a hard copy of an audio disc layout? You can print the layout directly from the Toolbar by clicking the Print button, which looks like a printer, or you can select Print... from the File menu. To display a preview image of the printed page before you print it, select Print Preview from the File menu. Note that layout printing is available only from the Audio CD layout; you can't print a data layout.

Selecting a File System Manually

When you're manually creating a disc, you should always specify which file system should be used on your new CD-ROM. You can choose between the ISO 9660 system, which offers the most compatibility between different operating systems, and the Microsoft Joliet system, which allows you to use long filenames and directory names but can only be read on computers running Windows 95 or Windows NT 4.0. The default is Joliet. Easy CD Creator always displays the file system on the far right side of the status bar at the bottom of the window. To change this, double-click the file system name on the status bar. Alternately, pull down the File menu, select CD Layout Properties, and click the Data Settings tab. Either method displays the dialog shown in Figure 9-14.

To select ISO 9660, click the File System drop-down list box and click ISO 9660. The *Bootable* and *CD EXTRA* options are only available for ISO 9660 discs.

Note the Properties... button next to the list box. It lets you configure certain file system features. Click the button to display the Properties dialog for the file system you've selected; Figure 9-15 shows the Joliet Properties dialog. Both the ISO 9660 and the Joliet Properties dialogs are similar, except the Joliet properties dialog doesn't need the file name characteristics section.

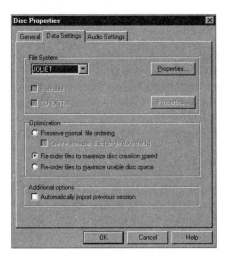

Figure 9-14: Manually selecting a file system.

Note Easy CD Creator can record "bootable" CD-ROMs — these are very specialized discs that can be used as boot drives on some machines. We cover this setting later; for now, **do not** check the *Bootable* option!

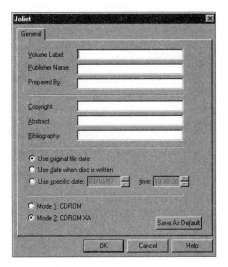

Figure 9-15: This dialog allows you to specify a number of items specific to the Joliet file system.

First, you'll see a number of optional text fields that some applications can automatically read; they are often included on reference CDs. You do not need to complete any of these fields (including the Volume Label) to record a disc. With the exception of the Volume Label, each of these fields specifies the name of a text file that exists in the root directory of the disc. These are text that you create and add to the layout manually.

✦ **Volume Label.** This is the only field on this panel that I usually use. Easy CD Creator automatically assigns a default label. DOS recognizes a maximum of 11 characters, which you can use to identify the disc. For compatibility, I do not use spaces.

✦ **Publisher Name.** This text file identifies the disc's publisher. The filename must begin with an underscore ("_") character, such as _PUBLISH.TXT.

✦ **Prepared By.** This text file identifies the disc's author or preparer. The filename must begin with an underscore ("_") character, such as _PREPARE.TXT.

✦ **Copyright.** This text file contains the disc's copyright information.

✦ **Abstract.** This text file contains the disc's abstract copy.

✦ **Bibliography.** This text file contains the disc's Bibliography.

Depending on which file system you've chosen, the fields on the General tab can also include:

✦ **File Dates.** Here you can specify which date stamp is applied to the files you're recording. Select *Use original file date* to save files with their current time/date stamp, just as they appear on your hard drive. This is the default, and there are times when you need to refer to file dates, so I suggest you use it. Select *Use date when disc is written* to change the time/date stamp on all files to the date you record the disc. Finally, you can also choose *Use specific date* and enter a date and time for use on all files.

✦ **Valid File Names.** We cover these settings in the next section.

✦ **Data Sector Format.** You can select either Mode 1 (CD-ROM) or Mode 2 (CD-ROM XA). The default is Mode 2, which I recommend for most recordings. If you select Mode 1, you can specify a sector size other than 2048 bytes, but all multisession discs must be Mode 2.

To save your changes and exit the dialog, click OK. To save the current disc properties as the default for future layouts, click Save as Default. Click OK again to exit back to the menu system.

Selecting a Filename Convention Manually

If you're creating an ISO 9660 disc, your next step in manually creating a disc is to select a filename convention. Once again, click the File menu, select CD Layout Properties and click the Data Settings tab. Now that you've selected your file system, click the Properties... button to display the Properties dialog for the file system you've selected. You have three choices. The first is the restrictive ISO 8.3 character filename convention. ISO filenames can contain only alphanumeric characters and the underscore ("_") symbol, and they can only be up to eight characters long with extensions of up to three characters. The ISO convention allows your new disc to be read on *any* computer that supports the ISO 9660 standard.

The second is the default convention MS-DOS 8.3 character filename, which allows a filename to include any legal DOS filename character. However, filenames can still only be up to eight characters long with extensions of up to three characters. This is the best choice for DOS and Windows systems, as well as most other computers, and I usually don't change it.

The third filename convention choice, long filenames, is suitable only for computers running Windows 95 and Windows NT, but you can use a maximum of 30 characters for a filename or a directory name.

Once you've selected the right convention, click OK to save your changes and OK again to return to the menu system.

Adding Data Items Manually

At this point, if we were using the Wizard it would prompt you to add data files or audio tracks to your layout. The type of disc you're creating depends on which tab you've selected at the top of the layout window. For example, if you select the Data Files tab, you're adding data to a CD-ROM. If you select the Audio Tracks tab, you're adding audio to a CD-ROM. Of course, you can have both and create a mixed-mode (or multimedia) CD-ROM. In this section, we manually add data items to your layout.

Tip   The upper half of the data layout window should be familiar to you if you've used Windows Explorer; in fact, it's a "built-in" copy of Explorer! If a directory contains subdirectories, a small plus sign ("+") appears next to it — you can click this plus sign to expand the view to see the subdirectories. To collapse the view and hide the subdirectories, click the minus sign ("-") next to the parent directory. You can also expand and collapse the view of the highlighted directory from the Item menu.

To add data items manually to the current layout, simply drag and drop files and entire directories just as you would in Windows Explorer! If you drag items to the layout directory tree in the lower left portion of the window, Easy CD Creator adds them to the target directory; if you drag a folder to the lower right portion of the window, you'll add it as a subdirectory of the current folder.

If your layout is particularly large or complex, or if you'd rather use the actual Windows Explorer instead of the default screen arrangement, select Hide Windows Explorer from the View menu and launch Explorer as you normally would. The Easy CD Creator window now looks like Figure 9-16, with only the disc layout showing; if you're familiar with version 2 of CD Creator, this looks much like the layout window in that program. Now you can drag and drop from the Explorer window in the same manner as before, but you have additional space to display your layout. Pretty slick, eh?

Figure 9-16: You can choose to hide the built-in Windows Explorer interface, showing only the disc layout.

Either method creates the same layout; the method you use depends on your personal preference. As with the Wizard, the layout window displays a bar graph at the bottom to let you know how much space remains empty.

Oh, by the way, you can also create a new directory on your disc. From the Edit menu, select New Folder to add a new directory below the currently highlighted location. Type the name of the new directory and click OK, and the new directory is added to your layout.

Adding Audio Tracks Manually

Adding audio tracks manually is very similar to the data side of things! First, however, you must select the Audio Tracks tab at the top of the window to switch to the audio portion of the layout. To add a track from an existing audio CD, insert the disc into your drive and select that drive in the Explorer portion of the window. Pick one or more tracks (hold down the Ctrl key to select multiple tracks) and drag them to the layout. To add WAV files, navigate to the directory where you've saved them, select the desired files, and drag them to the layout. If you're not sure which sound to pick, you can preview the sound from Explorer by clicking the small play icon next to the WAV filename. Easy CD Creator loads the program you've associated with the WAV format, so you can play or edit the file.

Figure 9-17 shows a typical audio layout after adding tracks from a source disc and WAV files from a hard drive.

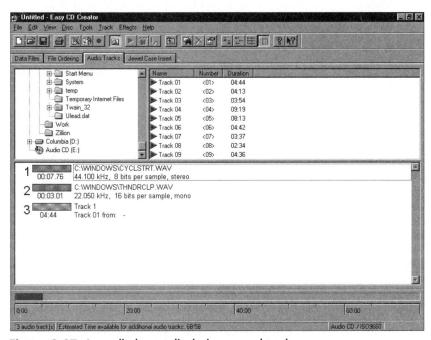

Figure 9-17: An audio layout displaying several tracks.

 Unless you're creating a data archive of WAV format sound files, avoid adding WAV files from your hard drive into a data CD layout! The result is a data disc with audio files, which your audio CD player will definitely *not* be able to play.

Adding Mixed-Mode Items Manually

Manually creating a mixed-mode disc is as simple as combining the previous two sections! To add data to the layout, select the Data Files tab at the top of the layout window and follow the instructions in the section "Adding Data Items Manually." Once you've added all the data items, select the Audio Tracks tab from the layout window and follow the instructions in the section "Adding Audio Tracks Manually." Easy CD Creator automatically recognizes that you're now creating a mixed-mode CD-ROM.

Editing a Data CD-ROM Layout

Here's a common scenario: you've loaded an existing data CD-ROM layout that you started yesterday so that you can add a few more files before you record the disc. Unfortunately, you discover that you've added several files that you don't need and some of the files need to be moved to other directories before you record. How do you make changes to an existing layout?

In this section, we discuss each of the data CD-ROM editing tools provided by Easy CD Creator for such occasions! Remember, to use the data layout editing tools you must switch to the Data Files tab of the layout window. Most of these commands are disabled until you add data items to the layout or highlight a specific data item.

Moving Files and Directories

You can use your mouse to move items by dragging and dropping them. To move a directory, click its icon in the directory tree display and drag it onto the target directory's icon; the highlighted directory will become a subdirectory of the existing directory. To move one or more files, click their icons in the right portion of the layout window and drag them onto the target directory's icon. You can also right-click an item and use the familiar Cut and Paste commands.

Copying Files and Directories

To copy data items, use your mouse to drag and drop them. To copy or move items, click their icons in the right portion of the layout window, hold down the CTRL key, and drag them onto the target directory's icon. Hold down the Shift key to select multiple contiguous files. Easy CD Creator prompts you for permission to overwrite existing items that have the same names.

Renaming Files and Directories

To rename files and directories within your data layout, click the item once to highlight it and again to display the edit box around the item name. Type the new name and press Enter to complete the process. You can also rename an item by right-clicking it and selecting Rename from the resulting menu. This does not affect the original files and directories on your hard drive — only the data items used in the layout are changed.

Deleting Files and Directories

To delete a file or a directory, highlight it and press your Delete key, or right-click the item and select Remove. You can delete multiple files at once by selecting them with the CTRL key. You can also hold down the Shift key to select multiple contiguous files. If you delete a directory, you also delete any subdirectories under it in the directory tree display. You can delete the root directory of your disc layout, but it will delete everything, so use caution!

Also, remember that deleting an item from your data layout within Easy CD Creator does **not** delete the file from your hard drive!

Editing Item Properties

Easy CD Creator also allows you to change certain properties for individual files and directories. First, highlight the desired item, then select Properties from the File menu; alternately, you can simply right-click directly on the item and select Properties. Easy CD Creator will either display the Directory Properties (Figure

9-18) or File Properties (Figure 9-19) dialog, whichever is appropriate. You can hide a file or directory from the Properties dialog; hidden items won't show up when you display the contents of the completed CD-ROM, so they're similar to hidden files on a hard drive. If you're changing the File Properties on an individual file, you can also change its priority, which we discuss in more detail later. Click OK to save your changes.

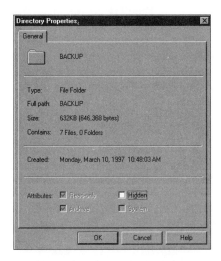

Figure 9-18: The Directory Properties dialog.

Figure 9-19: The File Properties dialog.

Editing an Audio Disc Layout

Let's turn to the audio side of Easy CD Creator again. In this section, we discuss the audio editing tools, which I consider much more fun than the mundane data editing features we discussed in the previous section! Remember, to use the audio layout editing tools you must switch to the Audio Tracks tab of the layout window. Most of these commands are disabled until you add tracks to the layout or highlight an audio track.

Playing an Audio Track

Need to play one of the tracks you've added to your audio disc layout? No problem! Highlight the track name and select the Play item from the Track menu, or click the Play button on the Toolbar (it looks like the Play button on an audio CD player). Easy CD Creator displays the Preview dialog and plays the track. If you're previewing an audio track you added from an existing audio CD, Easy CD Creator prompts you to load the source CD so that it can be played. If the track is longer than a few seconds, you can pause or stop the track before it's finished with the controls on the Preview dialog. Again, these buttons look like their counterparts on an audio CD player.

Editing a WAV File

If you've added WAV files to your layout, you can edit them directly from the menu. Highlight the WAV file you'd like to modify and select Edit WAV File from the Track menu, or click the Edit Audio button on the Toolbar (which looks like a pencil). You can also use this command if you right-click directly on the track. Easy CD Creator launches the editor program associated with WAV files within Windows. Unless you've changed the association, you see the Adaptec Sound Editor, as shown in Figure 9-20, which was installed with Easy CD Creator. Once the changes to the WAV file are saved, Sound Editor returns you to Easy CD Creator. We discuss both Sound Editor and Cool Edit 96 in the Chapter 10.

Renaming Tracks

If you intend to create a jewel case insert for an audio disc, you may want to make changes to the song titles in your audio layout. There are two methods you can use to rename tracks within your audio layout.

✦ You can use the menu system. To rename a track, highlight it and select the Rename command from the Track menu. Easy CD Creator displays an edit box around the track name, and you can type the new name. Press Enter to complete the process. You can also use this command if you right-click directly on the track.

✦ You can use your mouse. Click the track name once to highlight it and again to display the edit box around the name. Type the new name and press Enter to complete the process.

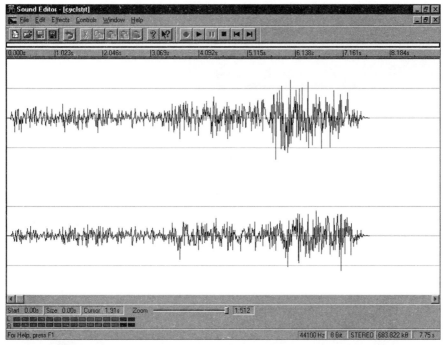

Figure 9-20: Making changes to a WAV file within the Adaptec Sound Editor.

Deleting Tracks

To delete audio tracks from your layout, highlight them and select the Remove command from the Track menu, or press your Delete key. You can also use this command if you right-click directly on a track. You can delete multiple tracks by selecting them while holding down the CTRL key. Easy CD Creator prompts you for confirmation before deleting the tracks. As with data items, remember that deleting a WAV file or audio track from your audio layout within Easy CD Creator does not delete the file from your hard drive!

Moving Tracks

There are two methods of changing the order of audio tracks.

✦ You can use the menu system. To move a track, highlight it and select the Properties command from the Track menu, or right-click directly on the track and select Properties. Easy CD Creator displays the dialog shown in Figure 9-21. Type the new track number in the Track Number field. When you click OK, the track is inserted at that number and all tracks after it are automatically renumbered.

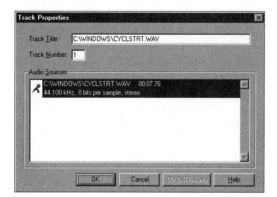

Figure 9-21: Displaying a track's properties.

Tip   Need information on how a track was recorded? Highlight the track and click the Properties item under the Track menu. You can change the name of the track, view its source, change the track number, and view its characteristics from the Properties dialog.

✦ You can use your mouse to move tracks by dragging and dropping them. To move a track, click its entry in the layout window and drag it to the desired slot; a dotted line indicates where the track will be inserted when you release the mouse button.

Combining and Splitting Tracks

From time to time, you may need to combine two or more tracks into a seamless single track. This avoids a pause between them, and an audio CD player will read them as a single track. To combine tracks from two different sources, click each track to be included and select Merge Tracks from the Effects menu. The tracks will be combined in order, with the first track to be combined in the layout appearing first in the merged track. If it is necessary to rearrange the combined track, repeat the merge operation. You can also right-click directly on the combined track and select Merge Tracks.

To split a combined track back into individual tracks, select the combined track with your mouse and select Split Tracks from the Effects menu. You can also right-click directly on the combined track and select Split Tracks.

Validating a Data CD-ROM Layout

That's it! Our manual layout is ready, we've arranged all the files and audio tracks, and we've configured all the necessary settings — it's time to record, right?

Wrong! Hang on there a second: What if some of the data files you added have changed since the last time you saved that layout? If you're using the Wizard, this isn't a concern, since all of those files and audio tracks are copied and readied right before recording. But if you've saved and loaded a layout several times, file locations and filenames may have changed, and Easy CD Creator would be unable to find them.

As a final step before recording a data CD-ROM, I always validate the disc layout. Validating a layout ensures that each data item and audio track on your hard drive is still available for recording in the path stored within the layout. If you're using a removable drive (like a JAZ drive) or a remote drive (like a network drive) as the source for some of your files, Easy CD Creator will prompt you to load them as necessary.

To validate your data items, select Validate Layout... from the File menu. Easy CD Creator displays a status screen to let you know which files are currently being validated. If your layout includes only data items from your hard drive, the validation should be fast, even with a full disc's worth of data.

Recording the CD

Yes! Finally, it is time to record your layout. In this final section, we follow the status of a recording, as well as discuss simulated recording and how to write-protect your completed disc.

Once you've validated your layout and everything checks out OK, follow these steps to start the recording process:

1. Select Create CD... from the File menu, or click the Create CD button on the Toolbar.

2. Easy CD Creator displays the Disc Creation Setup dialog shown in Figure 9-22. This is where you can make changes to the recording process itself.

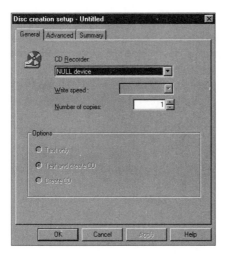

Figure 9-22: The Disc Creation Setup dialog appears at the beginning of the actual disc recording process.

3. If you have more than one CD-ROM recorder on your computer — you lucky technowizard! — click the drop-down list box to select the recorder to use. For the rest of us who have only a single recorder, leave this list box alone.

4. If your source files are stored on a fast hard drive and you've performed a System Test on your hardware, you should be able to use the default recording speed. If you like, however, you can select another speed from the *Write Speed:* drop-down list box. If you want to record at single (or 1x) speed, for example, this is the place to select it.

5. Next, select the test option for this recording session. As I mentioned earlier, if you choose to simulate the recording your drive will first run a low-power test of your entire layout. This is a good way to insure that everything will run smoothly, but it does take as long as the actual recording. I recommend that you simulate your first few discs by checking the *Test and create CD* option — especially if you're creating a new type of disc — but once you've gained experience you can skip this step.

6. If you're creating more than one copy of the same layout, enter that number in the *Number of copies:* field. Easy CD Creator will prompt you to load another blank disc for each copy. If you're creating multiple copies of a multisession disc, each disc you load afterwards must be identical to the first disc, including any data and sessions that should already exist.

7. Next, click the Advanced tab to specify Track at Once or Disc at Once recording, as shown in Figure 9-23. You can elect to leave an audio session open, close the session but not the disc (for multisession recording), or close the entire disc (preventing its use for rerecording). Of course, you should not close multisession discs until you're adding the last session. Closing a disc usually decreases the amount of time it takes for your PC to load its contents.

If you select the Disc at Once option, the disc is automatically closed and write-protected — this operation requires a new, blank disc.

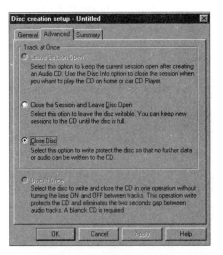

Figure 9-23: The Advanced section of the Disc Creation Setup dialog.

8. If you'd like to check the statistics for the layout, click the Summary tab, illustrated in Figure 9-24, to display the information for this disc.

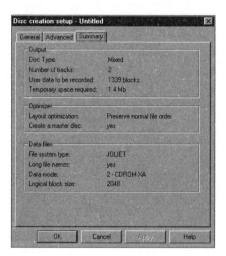

Figure 9-24: All of the important information for the current layout is available on the Summary tab of the Disc Creation Setup dialog.

9. Is everything correct on the Disc Creation Setup dialog? If so, click OK! If you haven't loaded a blank disc yet, Easy CD Creator prompts you for one. Load a blank and click Retry if your recorder doesn't recognize the new disc.

10. Easy CD Creator displays the Creating Disc from Layout dialog. To display more information than the default progress bar, click the Details button. If you've specified a simulated recording, you'll see the word "Simulation" appear at the bottom right corner of the dialog, and this first pass will not make any changes to the disc.

11. Once the actual recording begins, you can monitor the progress of the session from the detailed dialog, which displays the total number of tracks and files remaining to record. Easy CD Creator displays how many copies you're creating and the number of the current disc. The disc icon and percentage amount indicate how much of the disc has been recorded. If you're creating a disc with only one track (for example, most data-only CD-ROMs have only one track), however, these indicators will not be updated until the recording is complete. I've found that the progress bar at the bottom displays your recording progress more accurately in most cases.

12. Keep in mind that you can abort the recording process by clicking the Stop button, but I've found that results are somewhat unpredictable, and naturally the remaining data is not recorded. In fact, you may never actually use the Stop button, since any error will generally abort the recording automatically. In general, *never interrupt the recording process* until the disc is ejected and/or the dialog reports that recording has completed!

WATCH THAT BUFFER LEVEL!

Of all the indicators on the detailed Creating Disc from Layout dialog, the only two I really watch are the progress bar and the buffer percentage at the bottom of the dialog. If you're encountering buffer underrun errors, pay close attention to the buffer percentage; it indicates whether your computer is supplying that all-important constant, steady flow of data to your CD-ROM recorder. As each track is recorded, the buffer percentage should start at 0 percent and then hold at 95 to 100 percent for most of the track. Near the end of the track, the percentage should slowly drop to 0 percent again. If the buffer percentage does not follow this pattern, you should rerun the System Tester to check your hardware again.

13. Once the recording has successfully completed, Easy CD Creator also records the disc Table of Contents (or TOC for short) if you're closing the session. The TOC provides the directory information needed by DOS or Windows to access the disc. This generally takes a minute or two. Once the TOC has been written, a disc appears with a big red check mark next to the progress bar, and the dialog indicates that recording successfully completed, as in Figure 9-25. *Truly one of the most beautiful sights in the world (at least to us)!* If you're making multiple copies, Easy CD Creator prompts you to insert another disc. On the other hand, if errors are reported or the recording process aborts, click the View Errors button that appears and access the online help for each different error entry. Fortunately, I've found that the error code summaries provided in Easy CD Creator's online help system are excellent, and they provide possible solutions that helped me many times in the past.

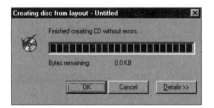

Figure 9-25: A time for rejoicing! You've successfully recorded your first disc!

Tip   As you record your first few discs, keep a notebook handy to record notes about the creation process for future reference. Did you change a setting somewhere that wasn't set by the Wizard? What was that error number and the solution from the last time? Are you using a specific naming structure for your files, such as starting all of them with a department prefix? These notes make valuable reading each time you sit down to record, especially until you get the process down pat.

Summary

You survived — great job! In this chapter, we discussed how to create standard data, audio, and mixed-mode discs. The topics included:

✦ using the automated Easy CD Creator Wizard to perform typical tasks;

✦ creating, saving, and loading layouts;

✦ manually configuring settings like the file system and filename conventions for a disc;

✦ adding and editing data items and audio tracks;

✦ arranging data items and tracks in your layout;

✦ validating your layout before recording;

✦ the status displays available during the recording process.

In Chapter 10, we move on to advanced recording topics — writing disc images, creating multisession discs, setting file priorities, optimizing your discs, and the special programs included with Easy CD Creator for editing audio and creating discs in different formats.

✦   ✦   ✦

Advanced Easy CD Creator Features

CHAPTER

10

The techniques you learned in Chapter 9 are likely to be all you need to produce the majority of your CD-ROMs. Standard data, audio, and mixed-mode discs are compatible with any read-only CD-ROM drive, created easily with the Wizard, and great for most of the applications we've discussed.

In this chapter, however, we unlock some of the more advanced features of your CD-ROM recorder and Easy CD Creator. First, you learn how to use some of the advanced features offered by Easy CD Creator to reconfigure your drive, alter the program to fit your preferences, and optimize the discs you record.

Next, we record a number of specialized formats that you learned about, like Picture CD and Video CD discs. You learn to create multiple sessions on a single disc, write disc images to your hard drive, record CD-EXTRA CD-ROMs, and much more!

I also review some of the shareware applications that I've used that have proven indispensable in recording, like Paint Shop Pro, Media Center, and Cool Edit 96.

Finally, we end the chapter by creating professional jewel case inserts for your discs using the powerful design features in Easy CD Creator.

Advanced Recording Options

Let's begin by discussing a number of advanced features within Easy CD Creator that you can use before and after a recording session. You may not need or use each of these each time you create a CD-ROM, but they come in handy when you're fine-tuning a disc layout or having problems with your hardware.

Reconfiguring Your CD-ROM Recorder

The System Tester automates most of the settings required to configure Easy CD Creator for your system's hardware. However, occasionally you may experience problems while recording, and the likely solution to many of these problems lies in reconfiguring your CD recorder. Easy CD Creator's online help may instruct you to change these settings, or you might find your specific system hardware or software mentioned in the README file as requiring these changes. In this section, you learn the details of changing your recorder's settings.

First, let's display the CD Recorder Setup dialog. Pull down the Tools menu and select the CD-Recorder Properties item. Easy CD Creator displays the dialog shown in Figure 10-1. If you're lucky enough to have more than one recorder, you can select which one we configure by clicking the correct entry within the *CD Recorder:* drop-down list box.

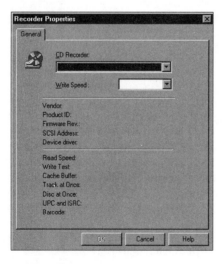

Figure 10-1: If you need to change your CD recorder configuration, start from the Recorder Properties dialog.

Default Write Setting

As you know, just about any recorder available today can record at different speeds. For most of us, the choices are single (1x)- and double (2x)-speed, and more and more drives available today can also write at quad (4x)-speed.

Although the default write setting is selected by the System Tester, you may decide to change it depending on the success you're having at recording with your current speed. For example, if you've been experiencing a number of buffer underrun errors and you can't seem to track them, one trick that can help ensure a successful recording is to select the next lower recording speed. The slower the recording speed, the less trouble your system will have in providing a constant, uninterrupted flow of data to your recorder. On the other hand, if you've never experienced any problems with recording and you find that you can use the next higher speed, you can change the default here so that recording always takes place at a faster clip!

To change the default recording speed, click the *Write Speed:* drop-down list box and click the desired speed.

Technical Information

The other items on the Recorder Properties dialog are display-only, so you can't change them; however, they're important if you have to call technical support for help with your recorder or its device driver. For example, the *Firmware version:* field displays the version number of the on-board electronics within your recorder, much like the BIOS version displayed when you run the SETUP program that accompanies your PC's motherboard. Some recorders are upgradable with new firmware that supplies new features or bug fixes. The *SCSI Address:* field displays the SCSI chain information for the current device. The *Device driver:* indicates the full pathname for the CD-ROM recorder device driver recognized by Easy CD Creator. The other fields show the read-only speed for this device, as well as indicating whether your drive can perform special functions like disc-at-once recording and barcodes.

Once you've made all the changes you need to make within the Recorder Properties dialog, click OK to save your changes and return to the layout window menu.

Selecting Preferences Within Easy CD Creator

Next, let's set some of the preferences within Easy CD Creator. General preferences include:

- ✦ enabling or disabling certain interface items;
- ✦ determining what Easy CD Creator will do when you run it.

Disc creation preferences include:

- ✦ the location of temporary files;
- ✦ enabling or disabling the error log file.

To begin, display the Easy CD Creator Preferences dialog by selecting Options . . . from the Tools menu, as shown in Figure 10-2.

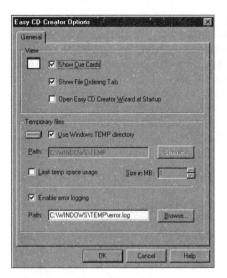

Figure 10-2: Easy CD Creator allows you to change a number of preferences that control the look and feel of the program.

The first section of the General tab, View, allows you to disable two features of the user interface that are meant for novices — they're great when you're just getting started, but once you're familiar with the program you can remove them to streamline the layout window. You can turn off the Cue Cards which appear in the corner of each editor window by disabling the *Show Cue Cards* checkbox. Cue Cards tell you what you can do from the current window and how you can perform a function like adding items. You can also hide the File Ordering Tab by disabling the *Show File Ordering Tab* checkbox, which we cover later; most discs you create will not require special file ordering.

As we discussed earlier, Easy CD Creator also launches the Wizard automatically on startup, but you can prevent this by disabling the *Open Easy CD Creator Wizard at Startup* checkbox. You can still access the Wizard from the menu system and the Toolbar.

Next is the Temporary Files options. Here you can specify where you would like Easy CD Creator to store temporary files during recording. To use the default location assigned for Windows temporary files, enable the *Use Windows TEMP directory* checkbox. If you disable this checkbox, you can select the location yourself by typing the full pathname into the *Path:* field, or you can select an existing directory by clicking the Browse . . . button to navigate through your system.

Warning As I've already mentioned, you should avoid recording from a source drive that's been compressed using programs like DriveSpace or Stacker, and this limitation also applies to your temporary files. For example, if your Windows directory is located on drive C: and that drive is compressed, you should not use the default Windows TEMP directory, because that directory is probably C:\WINDOWS\TEMP, and it's actually compressed! Instead, you would disable the *Use Windows TEMP directory* checkbox and click the Browse . . . button to select a directory on your uncompressed source drive, for example, the root of drive D:.

No matter where you decide to send temporary files, you can limit the amount of space that Easy CD Creator uses to store them by enabling the *Limit temp space usage* checkbox and entering the maximum number of megabytes usable in the *Size in MB:* field. This may be necessary if you're low on space on the drive you'll be using for temporary storage. This field does not apply to audio tracks that you've copied to your hard drive for recording.

Next, the Log file preferences control whether Easy CD Creator writes a log file to disc containing information about the recording session. This is especially helpful if you're trying to track intermittent problems with your recorder, since the log file will contain a list of any errors. If you're using a recorder on a network workstation, a log file is also good for keeping track of what was recorded and when. Click the *Enable error logging* checkbox to turn error logging on or off. ERROR.LOG is the default log file. Click the Browse . . . button to select a different location or name for your log file. To read the log file, I use any text editor that's handy.

Once you have finished making changes to the settings on the Easy CD Creator Options dialog, click OK to save them to disk and return to the layout window.

Selecting and Editing File Priorities

Typically, all files you add to a data CD-ROM are equally important; you don't usually know which file will be accessed first, or how often it will be used. However, it is possible to physically arrange a number of files on a data CD-ROM so that they're accessed faster than other files. Writing them closer to the center of the disc, as shown in Figure 10-3, does this. Files that are written farther away from the spindle hole take more time to access. Of course, we're talking a very small time savings here per file, but if your CD-ROM fits one or more of these criteria, those time savings can add up!

✦ Will it contain a large number of files? If so, it pays to place the files you know will be accessed most often towards the center of the disc.

✦ Will it contain a group of files that typically are accessed in order, such as a series of screens in a presentation? If so, you'll speed up your application by assigning those files a better spot.

✦ Will it be accessed frequently by a program on your PC to load data? If your CD-ROM is acting as a database archive, for example, placing the database files closer to the center should speed up the retrieval of information.

Also, if you do know that certain files will be used only once or twice — for example, a set of drivers or an installation program — those files can be placed toward the edge of the disc.

Easy CD Creator includes a system of file priorities that make it easy to indicate which files should be written first for faster access. You can assign three different priority levels: normal (the default), faster access, and fastest access. Files using the normal priority are recorded on your disc in the order you added them to the layout.

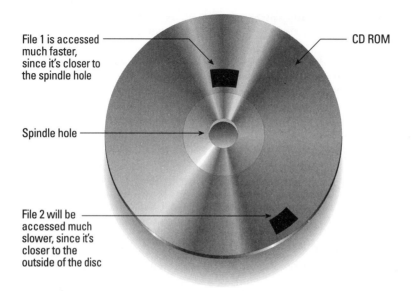

File 1 is accessed much faster, since it's closer to the spindle hole

CD ROM

Spindle hole

File 2 will be accessed much slower, since it's closer to the outside of the disc

Figure 10-3: The closer a file is written to the spindle hole on a data CD-ROM, the faster it can be accessed.

Note

Before we jump into all the advanced features offered by Easy CD Creator for prioritizing your files, let me again assure you that assigning any file priority at all is strictly **optional**! If you decide not to assign special priorities, all your files will be labeled as normal, and you can get on with your life. Besides, the measurement of "fastest access" is a relative value, so you're not going to speed up the entire disc by tagging all the files in the layout! I use this feature only when a disc I'm recording fits one of the three criteria listed in this section; otherwise, I skip this step entirely, since I usually don't know which files will be accessed more than others. The faster the CD-ROM drive that will read the files, the less important it is to prioritize your layout — and don't forget, file priorities are relative, so you can't choose "fastest access" for all your files and magically speed up your finished CD!

Editing File Priorities From the Data Layout Window

To assign file priorities from the data layout window, follow these steps:

1. Highlight one or more files in the lower right panel of the layout window and select Change Priority . . . from the Edit menu.

2. Easy CD Creator displays the File Priority dialog, as shown in Figure 10-4. Click the *File Priority* drop-down list box and choose the desired priority for the selected files. Click OK to confirm the change.

3. A small colored spot appears next to the files indicating their new priority: blue indicates a file with faster priority, while green indicates a file with fastest priority. Files with normal priority have no colored spot next to their names.

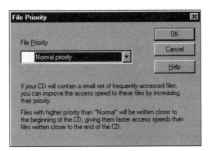

Figure 10-4: The File Priority dialog makes it easy to change the access priority for any file in your layout.

You can also change the priority on a single file from its File Properties dialog by following these steps:

1. Highlight a single file in the right side of the layout window and select Properties from the File menu.

2. Easy CD Creator displays the File Properties dialog, as shown in Figure 10-5. Click the *Priority:* drop-down list box and choose the desired priority for the selected file. Click OK to confirm the change.

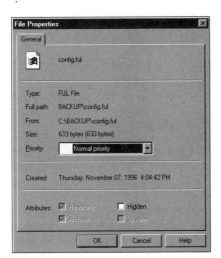

Figure 10-5: You can also change the priority for a file from its File Properties dialog.

Editing Priorities From the File Ordering Editor

Easy CD Creator also provides a graphical method of arranging file priorities and displaying the physical location of data items. From the data layout window, click the File Ordering tab to display the File Ordering editing window shown in Figure 10-6.

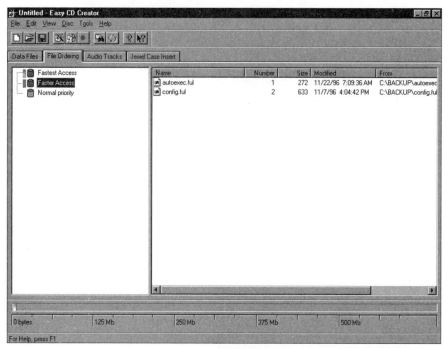

Figure 10-6: If you prefer a graphical method of setting file priorities, the File Ordering editor is just what the doctor ordered.

The File Ordering editing window replaces the standard tree directory listing on the left with a separate branch for each one of the three priorities, with the folder icon replaced by a clipboard icon. Just like the branches in the Data Files window, you can expand or collapse these branches from the menu, or you can click the plus and minus characters next to their names.

Easy CD Creator will create and remove subgroups automatically as needed under a priority; subgroups are really only an easy way for the program to organize files for display, and they do not represent directories in the data layout. To display the contents of a file subgroup, click its icon in the tree window.

The right portion of the File Ordering editing window displays an entry with basic information for each file in the selected subgroup. The most important element in the file display is the number to the right of the name, which indicates the order in which the file will be written to disc. This display makes it easy to arrange sequentially read files together, as in our example of a series of screens in a presentation.

Assigning Priorities
To change a file's priority, follow these steps:

1. Select the icon for the file's current priority in the tree window. This displays the file subgroups, if any were required; search them manually to locate your file, or use the Find File command, which we discuss shortly.

2. Once you've located the file you'd like to reassign, highlight it in the right side of the window.

3. Click and drag the highlighted file to the icon for the new priority in the tree display in the left portion of the window.

You can also right-click directly on the icon for a file and select Change Priority . . . from the menu that appears.

If Easy CD Creator needs to create another subgroup for the files you just assigned, you'll see the tree display update immediately.

Reordering Files

There are two methods of reordering the physical arrangement of files from the File Ordering editor:

✦ You can click and drag one or more files to a new slot in the right side of the window; or

✦ To reorder one or more files by their properties, highlight them in the right side of the window and select Re-order Files from the Edit menu (or click the Toolbar icon, which looks like a circle made from two arrows). Easy CD Creator will prompt you for the reorder criteria — for example, the file date, size, or name. Select one and click OK.

Adding Priority Levels

You can even add new priority levels of your own to the current layout within the File Ordering editor. This is one feature I don't think most of us will ever use, because three levels of file priorities seem like all anyone needs! If you do need an extra priority level or two, though, follow these steps:

1. From the File Ordering editor window, select New Priority . . . from the Edit menu. Easy CD Creator displays the New Priority dialog shown in Figure 10-7.

2. Type in a name for the new priority and select a color to indicate files assigned to the new level.

3. Now click the Move Up and Move Down buttons to position the new level within your existing levels. The closer to the top of the list, the higher the priority.

4. Once the new level is in place, click OK to add the new level to the current layout, or click Save as Defaults to add the new priority to all future layouts.

Figure 10-7: Adding a new priority level to our current disc layout.

Deleting Priority Levels

You can also delete a priority level. If there are files currently assigned to that level, Easy CD Creator automatically reassigns them as normal priority. To delete a file priority, click its icon in the tree display to highlight it and press your Delete key, or select Delete Priority from the Edit menu.

Finding Files

Looking for a single file in the tree display can feel like searching for a needle in a haystack! Fortunately, Easy CD Creator makes it easy to find one or more files within the File Ordering editor by using wildcards. Follow these steps:

1. From the File Ordering editor window, select Find . . . from the Tools menu, or click the Toolbar button that resembles a pair of binoculars. Easy CD Creator displays the Find Files dialog shown in Figure 10-8.

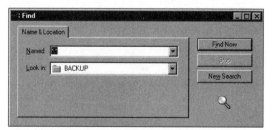

Figure 10-8: From the Find Files dialog you can locate a file anywhere in your layout.

2. Next, type a full filename or a DOS wildcard in the *Named:* field; for example, FINDME.EXE or *.EXE are both valid. You can narrow the search by selecting any specific priority level in the *Look in:* field, or use the default of the entire layout.

3. Click Find Now to begin the search. If the file you're looking for turns up before the search process completes, you can click the Stop button to abort the rest of the search.

4. Once the search process is complete, Easy CD Creator displays any matches in the list. To change the priority of a file, right click it and select Change Priority; as usual, you can use the Shift and Ctrl keys to select multiple files.

Displaying and Changing Priority Properties

Finally, you can always modify the properties sheet for any priority level. To display the properties for a priority, highlight its icon in the File Ordering editor tree display and select Properties from the File menu. Easy CD Creator displays the Priority Properties dialog shown in Figure 10-9.

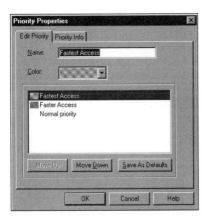

Figure 10-9: The Priority Properties dialog allows you to modify characteristics for an existing priority.

From the Edit Priority tab, you can change the name, color, and level of an existing priority. The Priority Info tab displays information regarding all of the files currently assigned to this priority, as well as those files assigned higher and lower priority levels. If you make any changes on the Priority tab, click OK to save them and return to the editing window.

Optimizing Your Layouts

Have you noticed the word "Optimizing . . ." that sometimes appears in the lower right corner of the layout window? This status message indicates that a hidden friend of yours is working on arranging your layout: the automatic Disc Optimizer! The Disc Optimizer works behind the scenes while you work, calculating important information such as how much space is used in a layout and how much remains; how much temporary space is needed for recording; and how many tracks are required to record your layout.

Depending on the speed of your PC, the size of your layout and its complexity, Disc Optimizer usually finishes within a few seconds. Easy CD Creator runs it whenever you make just about any change to your layout, so it runs quite often. In fact, if you click the Create CD button on the Toolbar before the Disc Optimizer has finished, Easy CD Creator delays the display of the disc creation setup dialog until the optimization step is complete.

Although Disc Optimizer runs automatically, you can configure it to some extent from the Disc Properties dialog. To display the dialog shown in Figure 10-10, select CD Layout Properties from the File menu and click the Data Settings tab.

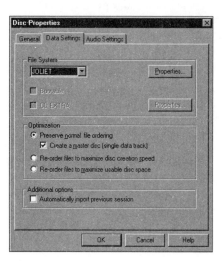

Figure 10-10: You can control how the Disc Optimizer works from this tab of the Disc Properties dialog.

Through the Optimization options group, you can specify whether the Disc Optimizer uses the file ordering you've assigned, or whether it arranges files to conserve space or reduce recording time.

✦ Select *Preserve normal file ordering* to use the order you've arranged within the File Ordering editing window; in effect, this disables any automatic file ordering by the Disc Optimizer. Enable the *Create a master disc (single data track)* checkbox if you're creating a master disc to send for duplication. This is the Easy CD Creator term for disc-at-once recording, which ensures that the finished disc will have only one track. Most replication facilities require a master disc to be a single-session disc recorded in disc-at-once mode.

✦ Select *Re-order files to maximize disc creation speed* to save time during the recording process. The Disc Optimizer modifies the file order so that your layout records in the smallest amount of time possible. Any file priorities you've set are followed, but files within each priority may be reordered.

✦ Select *Re-order files to maximize usable disc space* to leave the maximum amount of free space possible on the disc after you've recorded your layout. If you plan on recording additional sessions on this disc, this is definitely the option you should choose! Once again, Disc Optimizer respects any file priorities you've set, but files within each priority may be rearranged.

Advanced Recording Methods

In Chapter 9, we created a standard single-session CD-ROM that could contain data, audio, or a mixture of the two. However, as I've mentioned, Easy CD Creator offers a wide range of recording formats and methods usable to create specialized discs.

Some of the discs we discuss in this section require extra work to create, and we may have to use other programs that are supplied with the Deluxe Edition of Easy CD Creator. For example, the Deluxe Edition of Easy CD Creator comes with Video CD Creator, which is used to create a video CD layout. Easy CD Creator automates as much of the process as possible, so you shouldn't encounter any problems creating one of these discs. However, there are two important points to remember about these specialized formats:

✦ Not every CD-ROM drive can read some of the discs we create in this chapter. If you're looking for a disc that can be universally read on just about any PC, you should consider a standard CD-ROM (after all, the lowest common denominator is still the most compatible)!

✦ Not every CD recorder can create some of the discs I describe in this chapter. If you're using an older recorder, check its documentation for details on what formats it supports.

With that said, let's get to work!

Recording with a Disc Image

One of the advanced recording techniques that I use often is a disc image. In effect, a disc image is the complete contents of a CD-ROM you wish to create — only it's stored on your hard drive instead of recorded on a blank disc.

Why would you need to do this? As an example, let's use a series of disc images I've recorded for my shareware business. The final CD-ROM disc I create contains a copy of each of my shareware games, all the documentation, and a generous supply of public domain source code, as shown in Figure 10-11. As you can tell by the space remaining, it contains less than 250 megabytes, but it's still enough information that you wouldn't even consider sending the contents of this disc on floppy disks. I send this disc to customers who decide to buy all of my programs as a package deal.

I could save this layout to my hard drive, and simply reload it and record it each time I need to send a copy to a customer. That's not quite as simple as it sounds, though, because I would have to maintain those files in the same place, and I would have to make sure that the files weren't altered or changed in any way between recordings. That's harder for a software developer to do than you might think! Also, I'd end up reloading all those files and revalidating the disc each time I needed a copy.

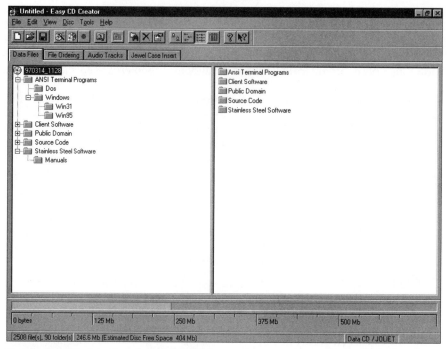

Figure 10-11: A typical data CD-ROM layout I use to create distribution discs from a disc image file I've stored on my hard drive.

I could make multiple copies of the disc at one recording session, but I have no idea how many customers will order all of my programs at once. Blank discs are still too expensive to waste, and if I must make a change to one of the programs to correct a bug or add a feature, my stockpile of discs is suddenly worthless.

Disc image to the rescue! Instead of recording directly to a CD-ROM, I record the data on my hard drive as an image file, which has these advantages:

✦ This single image file contains all of the data, so I don't need to worry about inadvertently altering the contents of one of my source files.

✦ I only collect and verify the data once, including any data stored on removable or network drives. Once the disc image is complete, I never have to load files or audio tracks again — the only step involved is the actual recording.

✦ If I must change a file in the layout, I simply erase the disc image and create a new one; or, if I'm archiving versions of these discs, I backup the old image and create a new disc from it at any future time.

Also, disc images are ideal if you have a slow hard drive. As you learned, a slow source drive can cause problems like buffer underrun errors, particularly if you're trying to record a layout containing a large number of smaller files; for example, if you're trying to record a layout containing several hundred image files of less than 100K each. Remember that the transfer rates for larger files were much faster than for smaller files? That's why recording a disc image to a blank disc usually succeeds where recording the individual files does not; the disc image is stored on your hard drive as a single huge file, so your PC's hard drive doesn't have to jump through hoops to locate and load all of the individual files. Instead, your system need only open a single file and send its contents to the recorder. Disc images stored by Easy CD Creator have the extension .CIF.

If you share an external CD-ROM recorder with others in your office, there's one more advantage to using a disc image: you can actually "record" a disc to an image file even if someone else is using the drive! It's much more convenient to build the layout and read the files when you have the time; then, once you've reattached the recorder to your computer, you can simply record directly to a blank disc from the disc image.

Of course, there is a downside — isn't there always? Writing a disc image to your hard drive requires as much space as the actual CD-ROM will store, so if you're creating a full CD-ROM disc image, look forward to losing almost 700 megabytes of hard drive space for as long as you keep the disc image.

Creating a Disc Image

To create a disc image from the current layout, follow these steps:

1. Select Create Disc Image . . . from the File menu. Easy CD Creator displays the Select image file dialog shown in Figure 10-12.

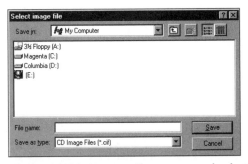

Figure 10-12: You specify a name and select a destination directory for your disc image file from this dialog.

2. Navigate to the destination directory where you want to store the .CIF file and enter a name into the *Filename:* field. Click <u>S</u>ave to create the disc image.

3. Easy CD Creator will display the Creating image from Layout dialog shown in Figure 10-13, which — no surprise here — resembles the Creating Disc from

Layout dialog you saw in Chapter 9. In fact, you are actually writing an ISO 9660 image file, just as it would be sent to the recorder if the destination was a blank disc. You see the same status bar and information on the total number of files to be stored, as well as how many files remain to be processed, but the entire session takes only a fraction of the time required to record the same data on a blank disc.

Figure 10-13: This dialog displays status information while writing your disc image file to the hard drive.

4. Once the entire disc image is created on your hard drive, you should see that same disc with the bold red check mark, indicating that the process completed without errors. Click OK to return to the layout window.

Using a Disc Image

You can record a CD-ROM from a disc image file by using the menu system. Follow these steps:

1. Select Create CD from Disc image . . . from the File menu. Easy CD Creator displays the Select image file dialog.

2. Navigate to the directory where you originally stored the .CIF file and double-click it to load the file.

Easy CD Creator displays the Disc creation setup dialog, and from this point recording from a disc image is just like recording from a layout.

Recording Multiple Copies

If you don't need to create copies of a CD-ROM over an extended time and you know how many copies you need, there's no reason to create a disc image file. As you learned in Chapter 9, you can specify creation of multiple copies of a CD-ROM before you start recording. To create multiple copies, follow these steps:

1. Design your layout and begin the recording process as usual.

2. Easy CD Creator displays the Disc Creation Setup dialog shown in Figure 10-14. Enter the number of copies you wish to make in the *Number of copies:* field.

3. If everything is correct on the Disc Creation Setup dialog, click OK.

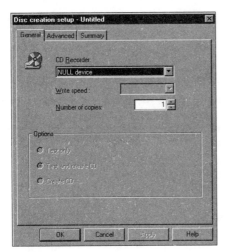

Figure 10-14: You can specify creation of multiple copies of the same disc from the Disc Creation Setup dialog.

4. The recording continues as usual, but once you've successfully created the first disc, Easy CD Creator ejects it automatically and prompts you to insert another disc.

Easy CD Creator repeats step 4 for each copy.

When creating multiple copies of the same disc, the general rule is always reach for a blank disc for each copy; even if a disc has plenty of room remaining and it's not write-protected, Easy CD Creator rejects it. This is because Easy CD Creator requires that each disc you load for the copies be identical to the first disc, and the easiest way to keep track of this is to use blanks. There is one exception to this rule: if you're creating multiple copies of a multisession disc, each disc must already contain exactly the same data as the first disc you loaded. Why? Because files are accessed according to their physical locations on the disc, which are recorded in the file system; if a file is written to a different location, your CD-ROM drive can't locate it.

Recording Disc-to-Disc

All of our recording to this point uses the hard drive as a source. We've recorded files stored on the hard drive and written a disc image file and recorded it. Easy CD Creator also uses the hard drive to store temporary files during the recording process.

Although you can record from a removable or network source drive, I recommend that you copy the files temporarily onto your hard drive for recording unless the source drive's transfer rate is as least as fast as your hard drive.

In this section, however, I describe two methods of making an exact copy of an existing CD-ROM or audio disc: one procedure for those who have more than one

SCSI CD-ROM device (which can be either a read-only drive or another recorder), and one procedure for those who want to make a disc-to-disc copy with only the CD-ROM recorder itself.

Recording Disc-to-Disc with Another Drive

There is another source for recording that can be a wonderful convenience if you need to make duplicates of existing CD-ROMs. In Chapter 5, I discussed using a read-only CD-ROM as an option for disc-to-disc recording. If you have one, and you've run the Transfer Rate portion of the System Tester on it, you can exactly duplicate an existing CD-ROM without even building a layout! There's another advantage, too: direct disc-to-disc copying requires only a minute fraction of the hard drive space required to duplicate the same disc from a layout or a disc image.

To record disc-to-disc with two CD-ROM devices, follow these steps:

1. Click the Start button and select the Adaptec Easy CD Creator group from the Programs menu. There is an entry for the Adaptec CD Copier; click it to run the Copier. The Copier is a separate program; it's also available from the Tools menu if you select CD Copier . . ., or click the Toolbar Duplicate CD button. The Standard version of Easy CD Creator has a "lite" version of the Copier, while the Deluxe Edition Copier has several additional features.

2. From the CD Copier Source and Destination tab, select the correct source and destination devices from the drop-down list boxes, as shown in Figure 10-15.

3. Click the Advanced tab, as shown in Figure 10-16, to select a writing speed for your recorder. Depending on the transfer rate of the source drive and the speed of your system, dropping to the next lower recording speed may make the difference between success and failure. If you're making multiple copies, you may want to enable the *Copy source CD to the hard disk first* checkbox; to select a temporary path for the data, click the Select Location . . . button.

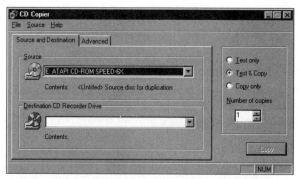

Figure 10-15: Selecting source and destination drives within CD Copier.

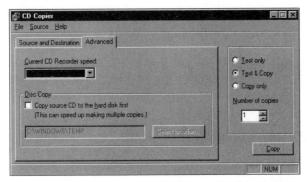

Figure 10-16: The advanced options available in CD Copier.

4. Now select one of the three options for simulated recording: you can elect to run only the test recording, copy after a successful test, or copy without a test recording.

5. If you'll be creating more than one copy, specify how many in the *Number of copies:* field.

6. Finally, click *C*opy to begin the duplication process.

From this point, the process is just like making multiple copies of a disc, except that data is read and transferred directly from the source disc to the blank disc.

Recording Disc-to-Disc with a Single Drive

Are you lamenting that you only have one CD-ROM device? Cheer up! It's not necessary to have two SCSI CD-ROM devices to use the CD Copier. If all you have is your CD-ROM recorder, you can still create an exact duplicate of another disc. However, the Copier must rely on your hard disk drive to store the information while you "swap" between the source disc and your blank CD-ROM. If you've ever used the DOS command DISKCOPY with a single floppy drive, you know that swapping involves unloading one disk and loading another.

To record disc-to-disc with just your CD-ROM recorder, follow these steps:

1. Select the Adaptec CD Copier from the Programs menu; as I said earlier, it's also available from the Easy CD Creator menu system and Toolbar.

2. From the CD Copier Source and Destination tab, select your recorder as both the source and destination devices from the drop-down list boxes.

3. If you need to make any changes to the Advanced options, click the Advanced tab and set them as we discussed in the previous section.

4. Select one of the three options for simulated recording: you can elect to run only the test recording, copy after a successful test, or copy without a test recording.

5. Specify how many copies to create in the *Number of copies:* field.

6. Finally, click Copy to begin the duplication process.

From this point, the process is just like making multiple copies of a disc, except that data is read and transferred from the source disc to the hard drive, and then to the blank disc.

Recording Multisession CD-ROMs

Multisession recording is probably the most popular of all the specialized formats available with recordable CD-ROMs. Unlike standard single-session CD-ROMs, where all of the data is written to the disc at once and write-protected, multi-session discs can be recorded, used, and recorded again and again up to the total amount of space on the disc.

Warning   When I say that you can record additional sessions on a disc up to the total amount of space on the disc, I'm actually leaving out the 14 megabytes or so of space that separates each track. In fact, the first session you close takes nearly 30 megabytes of space to separate itself from the next track; thereafter, each time you write another session to a multisession CD-ROM you lose another 14 to 15 megabytes of space. For this reason, avoid recording multisession tracks for small amounts of data, because you may be losing more space on the disc than you use to record!

As I mentioned earlier, Easy CD Creator allows you to write two different types of multisession discs:

✦ **Incremental.** If you need to add data to an existing session, incremental (sometimes called *linked multisession*) recording is your ticket. It includes all the accumulated data from the previous session that's stored on the disc, and you can add to and delete files from the layout. To create a multivolume incremental disc, you must import the last session recorded on the disc before making changes to it. This allows Easy CD Creator to display the existing file layout so that you can make changes to it. Any files that remain in the new session are not actually re-recorded; instead, Easy CD Creator merely includes their location in the directory for the new session. When the final session is added to an incremental disc, it's write-protected, and most CD-ROM drives that support multisession recording are able to read the final session. Figure 10-17 gives you an idea of how an incremental multisession disc is created.

HOW CAN I DELETE FILES FROM A CD-ROM?

Although I say you can delete files in an incremental backup, those files are not actually removed from the disc. After all, we are working with "write-once" media, and you can't actually erase files or format a recordable CD-ROM as you can a floppy or hard drive. However, if you indicate that a file that exists in the last session should not be included in the new incremental session, Easy CD Creator will not add it to the new directory that is written to the disc, as shown in Figure 10-18. This prevents your computer from reading the location of that file, so the file can't be read without a utility such as Session Selector!

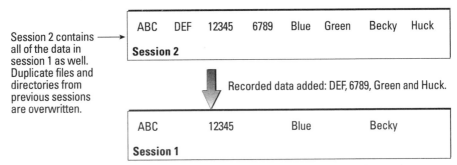

Session 2 contains all of the data in session 1 as well. Duplicate files and directories from previous sessions are overwritten.

Figure 10-17: An incremental disc contains data from the last session and new data that you add; you can also delete existing data items.

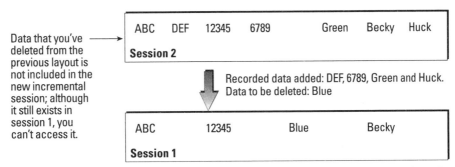

Data that you've deleted from the previous layout is not included in the new incremental session; although it still exists in session 1, you can't access it.

Figure 10-18: A deleted data item is deleted and "masked" in the new session of an incremental disc.

✦ **Multivolume.** Multivolume discs are simpler to create than incremental multisession discs, but you can't modify a previous session. Instead of appending data, Easy CD Creator records another discrete session (or "volume"), and each session is accessed separately, much like separate drive letters on your PC. You can only read one session at a time, but all sessions recorded on the disc are available, and the Deluxe Edition of Easy CD Creator includes a Session Selector usable to view the contents of each session. These discs are more suited to full archival backups or the storage of different types of files on the same disc. For example, if you're creating 3D graphics, you might have a collection of texture images in one session and a collection of 3D wireframe models in another. Figure 10-19 illustrates how a multivolume multisession disc is created.

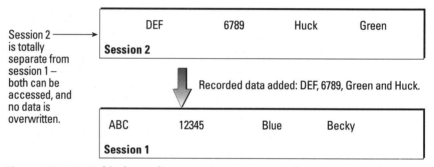

Figure 10-19: Multivolume discs contain separate sessions that are independent from one another.

Most recorded multisession discs are incremental. Although both types of multisession discs require running special software to switch between sessions, because some older CD-ROM drives are limited to reading the first or last session of a multivolume disc, multivolume discs are often only for personal use. I'm assuming, of course, that your recorder is able to read the multivolume discs it creates!

One very important rule to remember: if you are planning to create a multisession disc, do not close (or write-protect) it! Once you have write-protected a CD-ROM disc, you can never record to it again, and it cannot become a multisession disc. You can still read and use a disc you've recorded without write-protection, but a CD-ROM drive takes a little longer to locate and load files.

As for other multisession requirements, you need a CD-ROM you've recorded with:

✦ at least one existing session;

✦ at least one available track for recording;

✦ enough free space for any new files that you're going to add.

Both types of multisession discs begin with a disc that meets these requirements; you determine which type you're creating by how you create the disc layout before recording.

Creating an Incremental Session

To keep most of the data you recorded in the previous session and simply add or delete data items, you should create an incremental multisession disc. Follow these steps:

1. Load the target CD-ROM into your recorder and run Easy CD Creator.

2. Select Import Session . . . from the data layout Disc menu.

3. Easy CD Creator displays a list of the recorded sessions on the disc. Easy CD Creator uses one of these existing sessions as the basis for your new session; typically, you'll pick the last session you recorded on this disc. Click a session entry to select it, and click OK to load the layout for the session.

Additionally, from the Data Settings tab of the Disc Properties dialog you can set Easy CD Creator to import automatically a previous session for the current disc. To display this dialog, select the Properties item from the File menu, and click the Data Settings tab. Enable the *Automatically import previous session* checkbox to turn this feature on.

From this point, you can add and delete data items just as if you were creating a layout for a single-session CD-ROM. The recording procedure is also the same; simply click the Create CD Toolbar icon, or select Create CD . . . from the File menu.

Creating a Multivolume Session

If you wish to record a completely separate session that's not connected to existing sessions on a disc, you should create a multivolume multisession disc.

No special steps are required to record a multivolume session; simply create a new layout from scratch. However, remember that Easy CD Creator doesn't know you're building the layout for a multisession disc that already contains data, so the amount of remaining space it shows at the bottom of the layout window is not accurate! Instead, you should subtract the space required for the layout from the actual space remaining on your target disc.

To record the session, simply click the Create CD Toolbar icon, or select Create CD . . . from the File menu. Make certain that you load the proper disc for recording!

Switching Between Sessions

The Deluxe Edition of Easy CD Creator ships with a stand-alone utility, Session Selector, that can switch between different sessions on a multisession disc. To switch between sessions, follow these steps:

1. Load the multisession CD-ROM into your recorder or read-only CD-ROM drive.

2. Click the Start button and select the Adaptec Easy CD Creator group from the Programs menu. Select the Advanced Features submenu. Click the Adaptec Session Selector entry to run the utility.

3. The Selector displays the dialog shown in Figure 10-20, which looks similar to the Windows Explorer. Click the drive letter to display the contents in the right pane, which shows you all of the detectable sessions on the disc you loaded, along with their creation date and time.

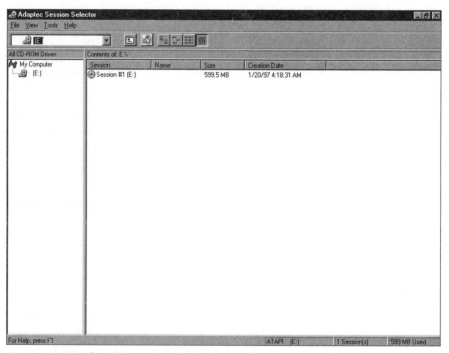

Figure 10-20: The Adaptec Session Selector allows you to switch to another session on drives that support multisession discs.

4. Once the sessions are displayed, highlight the desired session entry in the list and select Activate Session from the Tools menu, or double-click directly on the desired entry to switch to it.

5. If you have the Deluxe Edition, you can also launch, if necessary, Explorer or the Windows File Finder utility from the Tools menu.

Your CD-ROM device now displays the directory contents for the session you selected.

Tip

By the way, under Windows 95, once you've installed Easy CD Creator, you can also select a different session on a disc from Explorer! Double-click the My Computer icon to display your drives and right click the CD-ROM device that's using the multisession disc, as shown in Figure 10-21. From the pop-up menu, choose Select Session and pick the desired session from the submenu.

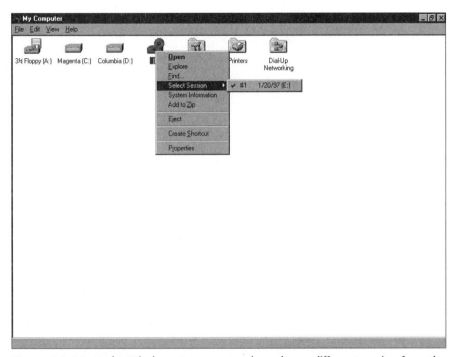

Figure 10-21: Under Windows 95, you can also select a different session from the drive icon in Explorer.

Recording Picture CDs

As we discussed earlier, one of the most popular applications for recordable CDs is the archival storage of today's gigantic multimedia audio, video, and image files. For example, let's consider stock digital images that you use for professional desktop publishing. These files are usually saved in .BMP, .PCD, .TIF, or .PCX format at high resolutions to preserve their detail and make them easier to reduce to different sizes. However, at these resolutions it's not unusual for these image files to each occupy anywhere from 5 megabytes to 25 megabytes of hard drive territory. Obviously, you're not going to keep your prized collection of rhinoceros and elephant images that you snapped in the wilds of Africa on your hard drive for very long!

For this reason, companies such as Corel Corporation have been distributing their stock images on CD-ROM for many years. I have several of the CD-ROMs from the Corel Professional Photos series, each of which includes 100 stock images of a particular subject in PCD format. Plus, if you have a Kodak Photo CD player, you're likely to have several CD-ROMs full of your own snapshots in high-resolution digital form. These snapshots are developed from a standard roll of film — no need for an expensive flatbed scanner.

If you're using the Deluxe Edition of Easy CD Creator, you can use Adaptec's PCD Creator to compile your own picture CD-ROMs with images from Corel Professional Photo discs and Kodak PhotoCDs. PCD Creator is actually a sophisticated "front-end" interface for the Deluxe Edition of Easy CD Creator; you design your Picture CD layout and read in the source files using PCD Creator, but it automatically launches Easy CD Creator when you're ready to record the disc.

Warning Kodak's Photo CDs are written in a proprietary format, so the Picture CDs you create cannot be used in a Kodak PhotoCD player. However, you can add images to your Picture CDs from an existing Photo CD using PCD Creator.

Using the PCD Creator Layout Window

First, let's launch PCD Creator and introduce you to its layout window. Click the Start button on the Windows 95 Taskbar and select the Adaptec Easy CD Creator group from the Programs menu. Select the Advanced Features submenu. Click the entry for the Adaptec PCD Creator to run the program.

When you run PCD Creator, it immediately opens its layout window, shown in Figure 10-22. A movable vertical bar divides this windows into two sections. On the left will appear the thumbnails for all of your source images from the Corel or Kodak disc in the drive, while the thumbnails representing the images you choose to record will appear in the right section. I usually move the bar to the middle of the window, so that I can see more of my layout on the right.

Along the top there is a menu system and a Toolbar very similar to their Easy CD Creator counterparts; however, there is an additional drop-down list box at the end of the Toolbar. This list box displays the text description of each image on the source disc, and you can jump directly to a specific image by selecting it from this list box. At the bottom of the window is the familiar bar graph indicating how much space remains for additional items, and the status line that displays a single line of help for each menu command or Toolbar button.

Loading and Saving PCD Layouts

Just like Easy CD Creator, existing layouts can be loaded from the File menu. Select the Open . . . item on the File menu to display a standard Windows Open File dialog. By default, any layouts saved with PCD Creator have the extension .PCL, and the Open File dialog displays only these files. However, you can view all files regardless of extension by clicking the *Files of type:* drop-down list box and selecting All Files (*.*). Once you've found the PCD layout file you want to load, double-click it, or highlight it and click the Open button.

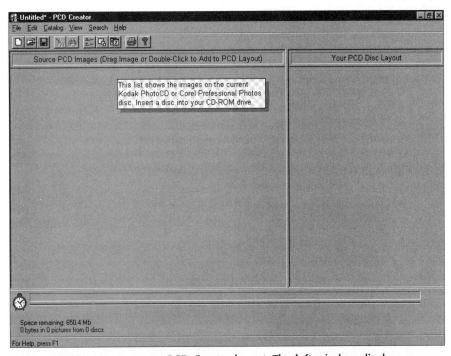

Figure 10-22: A new, empty PCD Creator layout. The left window displays source images, while the right window displays the images you want to record.

If you need to work on a layout later or record the layout in the future, you'll need to save it to disk before you exit PCD Creator.

If this is the first time you've worked with this layout, select the Save item on the File menu to display a standard Windows Save File dialog. Enter a name in the *File Name* field, and click Save. The .PCL extension is added automatically.

If you loaded this layout file from disk, selecting the Save item on the File menu automatically updates the existing file on your disk.

If you want to save an existing layout file under a new name, select the Save As . . . item from the File menu. PCD Creator allows you to rename the file before saving it to disc; this is a good way to create a copy of an existing layout as a starting point for a new layout.

Adding Images to Your Layout

Although there's no Wizard to help automate the task of adding images to your PCD Creator layout, it's still a very simple process! You can add a total of 100 images to a single Picture CD. Follow these steps to add an image:

1. Load a Kodak PhotoCD or Corel Professional Photo disc into the fastest CD-ROM device on your system. Although you can read images into PCD Creator from your CD recorder, it's much faster to load them from your read-only drive!

2. Now run PCD Creator to display a new blank layout window. Pull down the Catalog menu and click the Select CD-ROM Drive . . . item. PCD Creator displays a small dialog prompting you to specify the drive that contains the source image disc, as shown in Figure 10-23. Select the desired drive from the *Source CD-ROM Drive:* drop-down list box. If you'd like to display shared network CD-ROM drives in the list, enable the *Include Network Drives* checkbox. Click OK to close the dialog and load the images. Your screen should now look something like Figure 10-24.

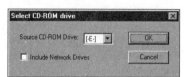

Figure 10-23: The Select CD-ROM drive dialog allows you to load source images from the fastest CD-ROM device on your system.

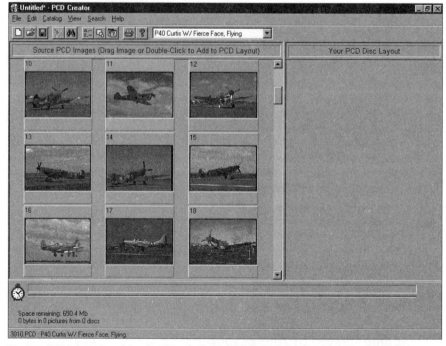

Figure 10-24: A Corel Professional Photo disc has been loaded into PCD Creator, and we're ready to begin selecting images for our layout.

3. There are three ways to add images to the right side of the PCD Creator window:

✦ Add a single image by dragging its thumbnail to the right side of the screen, or by double-clicking directly on the thumbnail.

✦ Add multiple images by holding down the Shift key while clicking each image you want to add and dragging them to the right side of the window. You can also select multiple files with the Shift key and either press the Insert hotkey or use the Add Selected item from the Edit menu to add them to the layout.

✦ Finally, you can select all of the images on the source disc and add them all to your layout with the Edit menu Add All command.

Each source image added to your layout is marked with a check mark in the left side of the window to indicate that it was added. PCD Creator also displays information next to each thumbnail image in your layout, including the filename, date and time stamp, source disc, and size.

If you need to change directories on the source disc to locate the images you need, select the Show PCD Files . . . item from the Catalog menu. PCD Creator displays the dialog shown in Figure 10-25. You can type the full directory path where the source files are stored, or you can click the B̲rowse . . . button and navigate with your mouse. Once you've found the directory containing the source files, highlight the files and click V̲iew to add them to the left side of your PCD Creator window.

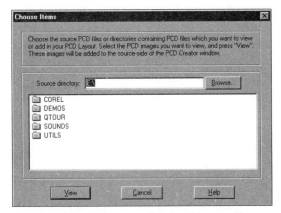

Figure 10-25: If you need to load image files from a directory on the source disc, you can specify the directory or the individual files from this dialog.

Deleting Images

"Whoops, I didn't mean to add that!" Luckily, PCD Creator allows you to remove one or more images from your layout. Use one of these methods:

✦ Delete a single image by clicking the thumbnail and pressing the Delete key, or select the Remove Selected item from the Edit menu.

✦ Delete multiple images by holding down the Shift key while clicking each image you want to delete, and then press the Delete key, or select the Remove Selected item from the Edit menu.

✦ Finally, you can remove all of the images in your PCD layout with the Edit menu Remove All command.

Note that PCD Creator will not prompt you for confirmation, so be careful when deleting images! Of course, you won't be deleting them from the source disc, so you can always add an image again if you delete it by mistake.

Renaming Images

Because you may add images from different discs, and because Picture CDs do not have directories like a data disc, PCD Creator allows renaming of one or all of the files in your layout for easier recognition.

There are two methods of naming images in PCD Creator:

✦ Standard 8.3 MS-DOS filenames. If you elect to use MS-DOS filenames, PCD Creator reserves the last three characters of each filename for a number that's automatically generated, like "BATMN001" through "BATMN300". The three-character extension is always .PCD, for Photo CD.

✦ Long filenames. You can select long filenames from the Options dialog, but they must still use the .PCD extension. We cover this dialog later.

If PCD Creator is displaying catalog information, you can rename an individual image. Simply click in the New Name edit field and type the new prefix.

Tip   By default, PCD Creator displays information next to each image in your layout; this information contains an edit field where you can rename individual images. If you don't see any text next to the images in your layout, you can toggle catalog information on from the View menu Options dialog, which we discuss later.

You can also rename all of the images you've added already to your layout with the same prefix. From the Edit menu, select Rename All. PCD Creator displays the Rename All Images dialog, as shown in Figure 10-26. Enter the prefix you want and click OK to begin the process.

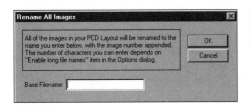

Figure 10-26: You can give all of the image files in your layout the same prefix from this dialog.

Viewing Images

PCD Creator includes a convenient "slide show" mode where you can display one or more of the images on your source disc. Are the images on your source disc very similar? Or perhaps it's been some time since you've looked at these images? If the thumbnails don't show enough detail for you to determine which images you want to copy, use the slide show mode to display them full-screen. You can configure the delay, display size, and mode for slide shows from the View menu Options dialog, which we discuss later.

There are two methods of starting a slide show:

✦ If you only want to display one or two images, hold down the Shift key and select them, then pull down the View menu and click Selected Image. You can also use the Ctrl-I hotkey sequence.

✦ If you want to display all of the images on the source disc, select All Images from the View menu.

By default, PCD Creator displays each image for two seconds and then moves to the next one; however, if you selected manual mode, you can continue to the next image at any time by clicking the left mouse button. To exit the slide show, press Esc.

Sorting Images

Another easy way of organizing the images you added to your layout is to sort the layout display. PCD Creator gives you three sort criteria: filename, date, and source disc.

✦ To sort your layout by filename, select Sort from the Edit menu and then click Name. You can also click the Name Toolbar button, which looks like a list with entries marked "A" and "Z."

✦ To sort your layout by the source disc(s) you used, select Sort from the Edit menu and then click Source. Alternately, click the Source Toolbar button, which looks like three cascading squares.

✦ To sort your layout by the image date stamps, select Sort from the Edit menu and then click Date. You can also click the Date Toolbar button, which looks like two calendar pages.

Searching for an Image

As you might imagine, manually searching through a hundred source images for a specific shot to add to your layout can be a task! However, PCD Creator offers a Search feature that can help; you can search for a specific string within the descriptive text that accompanies each image on your source disc. To find an image, follow these steps:

1. If you haven't yet specified a search string, select the Find item from the Search menu. PCD Creator displays the Find dialog shown in Figure 10-27.

Figure 10-27: Use the Find dialog to locate a picture by a string in its text description.

2. Enter the target string in the *Find What:* field and indicate whether PCD Creator should search above or below the image that's currently selected. Click the Find Next Toolbar button (it looks like a pair of binoculars) to jump to the next image with a description that contains your target string.

3. To continue the search using the same target string, click Find Next again, or press F3, or click the Find Next Toolbar button.

Also, remember that the Find feature built into Windows 95 can locate an image on your source disc by its filename.

Printing Your Layout

A jewel case insert for your Picture CD will only display a thumbnail for each image. However, you can print the contents of your layout at any time, which includes both thumbnails and text information. Instead of an insert, I always print a copy of my PCD layout before I record it and store it in the jewel case along with the disc. If you save this printout, you can quickly determine the contents of each Picture CD in your collection. Either method saves a tremendous amount of time you'd otherwise spend loading and viewing the contents of each disc. It's even faster than searching for an image from the Find dialog!

To print a layout, select Print . . . from the File menu, or click the Print icon on the Toolbar. PCD Creator displays a standard Windows Print dialog, allowing you to select a system printer and specify copies or a page range; click OK to send the pages to your printer.

PCD Creator also offers a Print Preview function, so you can see what the printed pages will look like before you actually send them to your printer. To display the pages, select Print Preview from the File menu; PCD Creator displays the preview window, as shown in Figure 10-28.

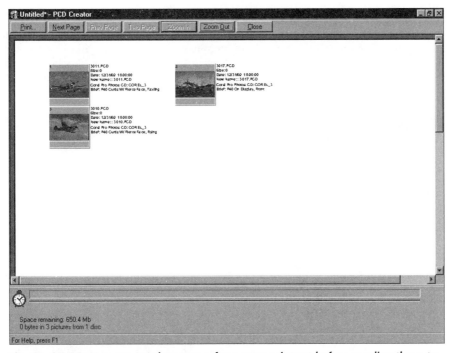

Figure 10-28: You can preview pages from your printout before sending them to your printer with the Print Preview function.

To display the next page in your printout, click the Next Page button, and you can move backwards through your printout by clicking the Previous Page button. If you'd like to see more real estate on a single screen, toggle the Print Preview display between one and two pages by clicking the Two Page button. To magnify or reduce the display, click Zoom In and Zoom Out, respectively. If the contents of the printout are acceptable, you can print directly from the preview window by clicking the Print . . . button.

To exit the Print Preview window, click the Close button.

Creating a Jewel Insert

Although I prefer to print the layout because the printout includes the text descriptions, you can create a jewel case insert for your new disc that looks very professional. You use Easy CD Creator to design your insert; you can switch to the Easy CD Creator layout window at any time. We discuss how to create jewel case inserts later, but you can display the Insert editor by following these steps:

1. Select Create CD Jewel Case . . . from the File menu.

2. Select the Show Easy CD Creator command on the View menu to display the Insert editor. Your images will appear in this layout.

Changing Options Within PCD Creator

If you're like me, the larger the thumbnail display the better, especially if you have a 17-inch or 21-inch monitor! You can configure the size of the thumbnail images and other display options within PCD Creator from the Options dialog. From the View menu, select the Options . . . item to display the dialog shown in Figure 10-29.

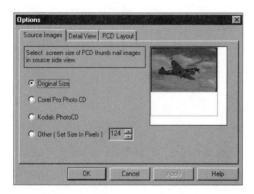

Figure 10-29: The Options dialog allows you to configure some functions within PCD Creator.

The Options dialog is divided into three tabs:

✦ On the **Source Images** tab, you can specify the size of the thumbnail images on the source side of your layout. The default choice is Original Size. Click Corel Pro Photo CD or Kodak PhotoCD to select a thumbnail size that matches the aspect ratio for the type of source disc you're using. In general, the Kodak display option allows you to fit more thumbnails in the same space. Finally, if you'd like to specify a custom thumbnail size, click the Other option and set a size in pixels.

✦ On the **Detail View** tab, you can configure the PCD Creator's slide show. The View Size option specifies the size of the slide show images; you can select one of three window sizes, or you can choose Fit to Window to display each image within the current slide show window size. If you would rather have the slide show advance automatically, enable the *Automatic Mode* checkbox and set the amount of time that PCD Creator should delay before displaying the next image. If you disable automatic mode, each image displays until you click the left mouse button to continue.

✦ The options on the **PCD Layout** tab allow you to customize the appearance of the layout window. Under View PCD Layout, you can elect to display text information and the New Name edit box next to each image by selecting the *Image List with Text Information* option. If you'd rather display only the thumbnail, click *Image Catalog*. Under Show Text Information, you can choose which text information fields you would like to appear; naturally, these fields are automatically turned off if you've selected to display only an image catalog. To remove a text field from the layout display, disable the corresponding checkbox. Finally, you can use long filenames as prefixes for your images by clicking the *Enable Long File Names* checkbox — remember, though, that PCD Creator still appends numbers to the prefix.

To save your changes and exit the Options dialog, click OK.

Recording with PCD Creator

Ready to record your PCD layout? As I mentioned earlier, PCD Creator launches Easy CD Creator to record the disc. Follow these steps:

1. Select Create CD from Layout . . . from the File menu, or click the Create CD button on the Toolbar. PCD Creator displays the dialog shown in Figure 10-30.

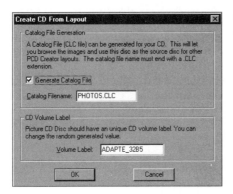

Figure 10-30: This dialog allows you to add a catalog file and specify a volume label for your Photo CD.

2. PCD Creator can optionally generate a catalog file that allows you to browse and select images using your new disc as a source in the future. If you disable this field, you will save a small amount of room on your new disc, but you will not be able to access these images from within PCD Creator; in effect, you are storing the image instead of creating a Photo CD readable by other applications. I always generate a catalog file, and I recommend that you do, too; you never know when you may have to create another disc using these images! You can specify the filename for your catalog file in the *Catalog Filename:* field; it should be eight characters or less, and the .CLC extension is required. By default, the program uses the name PHOTOS.CLC.

3. Because PCD Creator displays the source CD in the text information for each image (and sorts by it as well), you should also specify a unique volume label for your new Photo CD. The program generates one randomly, but I always type a more friendly, descriptive name in the *Volume Label:* field that will help me remember the contents of the disc.

4. Once you've specified the catalog and volume name, click OK to begin the recording process. Control now passes to Easy CD Creator, which displays the familiar Disc creation setup dialog.

From this point, the recording process is the same as it is for a data CD-ROM.

Recording Video CDs

Another form of multimedia file that requires hundreds of megabytes to store is digital video. The expensive computer hardware once required to create digital video has suddenly become affordable for everyone, and multimedia editing software for digital video is rapidly dropping in price. At the same time, home PCs with MMX technology are now powerful enough to provide the high frame rate needed for good quality digital video, and Windows 95 has finally brought seamless support for PC video to the operating system itself. Of course, if you're using a Macintosh, you've been enjoying digital video for years.

Everywhere you look these days you'll see applications for digital video, including multimedia entertainment and "edutainment" titles, raytraced animation and morphing, Internet content, videoconferencing, and even full-length feature films on disc. I have a few of these video CD-ROMs in my collection — my favorite is GODZILLA vs. MEGALON, which is just as enjoyable on a computer monitor as on a television!

Digital video is usually stored on compact disc in .MOV (Quicktime), .MPG (MPEG) or .AVI (Windows Video) format. In this section, we use Adaptec's VCD Creator, which is included only in the Deluxe Edition of Easy CD Creator, to record digital video in .MPG format. You can read these discs using computer CD-ROM drives, Video CD players, and — with the proper application — CD-I players.

Just like PCD Creator, you create your VCD layout using VCD Creator, but Easy CD Creator does all of the actual recording.

Using the VCD Creator Layout Window

To launch VCD Creator, click the Start button on the Windows 95 Taskbar and select the Adaptec Easy CD Creator group from the Programs menu. Select the Advanced Features submenu. Click the entry for the Adaptec VCD Creator to run the program.

We create a disc using the VCD Wizard in the next section; for now, click Cancel and let's have a look at the VCD Creator layout window. As Figure 10-31 shows, this window is actually composed of two smaller windows, each displaying a different view. The left window displays the clips you've added to your VCD layout, much like the right side of the PCD Creator window. The right window displays the branches of your layout's menu system and the sequence list.

The vertical bar can be adjusted anywhere you like to change the window sizes, just like the PCD Creator layout window. However, the Toolbar contains only a set of standard buttons for file and editing functions like opening and closing files, cut/copy/paste, and print, so you're using the menu system more often.

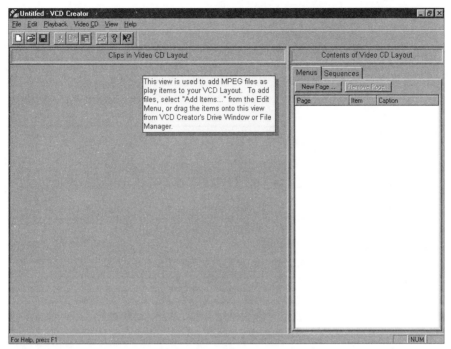

Figure 10-31: A new, empty VCD Creator layout. The layout window is divided into two major sections, each containing a different view.

Loading and Saving VCD Layouts

You can load existing VCD Creator layouts that you've saved to disk from the File menu. Select the Open VCD Layout . . . item on the File menu to display a standard Windows Open File dialog. By default, any layouts you've saved with VCD Creator have the extension .VCL, and the Open File dialog displays only these files; however, you can view all files regardless of extension by clicking the *Files of type* drop-down list box and selecting All Files (*.*). Once you've found the VCD Creator layout file you want to load, double-click it, or highlight it and click the Open button.

If your layout design is interrupted or you want to record the layout in the future, you need to save it to disk before you exit VCD Creator. If this is the first time you've worked with this layout, select the Save item on the File menu to display a standard Windows Save File dialog. Enter a name in the File Name field, and click Save. The .VCL extension is added automatically. If you loaded this layout file from disk, selecting the Save item on the File menu automatically updates the existing file on your disk.

If you want to save an existing layout file under a new name, select the Save As . . . item from the File menu. VCD Creator will allow you to rename the file before saving it to disk.

Using the VCD Wizard

By default, VCD Creator displays the Video CD Creator Wizard welcome screen shown in Figure 10-32. You can prevent the VCD Wizard from running each time you start the program by enabling the *Do not run Wizard at startup* checkbox. The VCD Wizard operates similarly to the Easy CD Creator Wizard; you also navigate the VCD Wizard with the Next> and <Back buttons.

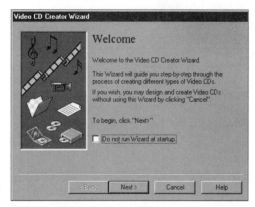

Figure 10-32: The opening screen for the Video Easy CD Creator Wizard.

Creating a Sequential Video CD

To create a simple sequential Video CD using the Wizard, follow these steps:

1. From the VCD Wizard welcome screen, click Next> to continue. The VCD Wizard displays the screen shown in Figure 10-33. Select the *Simple Video Sequence* option and click Next>.

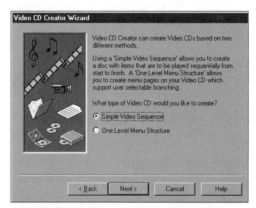

Figure 10-33: You determine the structure of your Video CD from this VCD Wizard screen.

VIDEO CD STRUCTURES

So what exactly are these two structures I have to choose from, anyway? Well, the Simple Video Sequence structure (often called *sequential* or *linear* display) is designed to show your video clips and still images one after another, from beginning to end, with no control necessary from the viewer (except to move backwards and forwards through the video that's currently playing). Think of simple sequence as a standard video tape, where you can rewind and fast forward, but you can't jump to another section of the tape or choose an alternate path through the tape. On the other hand, a one-level menu structure is much more complex (as you'll see from the extra steps in our VCD Wizard tutorial), and it offers the viewer onscreen menus controllable through the numeric keypad on the Video CD player's remote. When you design a layout using a menu structure, you're actually linking a separate sequence of digital video clips to each menu choice.

2. Next, the VCD Wizard displays the Adding Play Items screen shown in Figure 10-34. VCD Wizard calls its video clips "*play items.*" You add video play items to your layout using one of two methods:

   ✦ You can simply click the Add . . . button to display a standard Windows Open File dialog, where you can navigate through your system and select video clips. Once you've highlighted the file you want to add to your layout, click Open.

   ✦ You can also drag and drop play items to the Adding Play Items screen from the Windows Explorer; open an Explorer window, drag the file over to the VCD Wizard screen, and release the mouse button.

Figure 10-34: You can add play items to your Video CD layout from this VCD Wizard window.

3. For each video file play item you add, VCD Creator displays the Add New Play Item dialog shown in Figure 10-35.

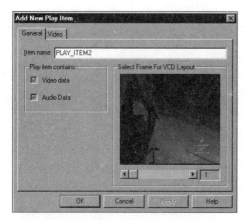

Figure 10-35: The Add New Play Item dialog allows you to set several options for recording a specific play item while you're adding it to your layout.

✦ On the General tab, you should enter a unique name for the play item. I recommend that you leave a number somewhere in the name, though, so that you can quickly tell where the video falls in the sequence. You can select an individual frame from the video that will appear in your layout by scrolling through the video with the sliding bar. The *Video Data* and *Audio Data* checkboxes allow you to enable and disable the video and audio for the play item. I often use this to drop the audio portion of a video file that will be accompanied by a different music source.

✦ On the Video tab, VCD Creator displays a wealth of basic information regarding the video you've selected, including the format, frame rate, frame size, movie size in frames, and the total run time. On the right, you may have multiple choices for the output data format, depending on the source file. If you are offered choices, click the desired format.

✦ Once all the information is correct, click OK. These same properties are displayable from the menu system by highlighting the play item and selecting Properties from the Edit menu. VCD Creator will update the left portion of the layout window with your play item, and you can add additional items. To remove a play item from your layout, click Remove . . . to display the dialog shown in Figure 10-36. Highlight the entry you wish to remove and click the Remove button, or click Cancel to exit the dialog.

Figure 10-36: You can remove play items from your VCD layout from the Remove Play Items dialog.

4. Once you've added all your play items, VCD Creator requires you to arrange them in a play sequence. You determine this order from the next VCD Wizard screen, shown in Figure 10-37. In the left column of the screen, is a thumbnail representing each video clip you've selected. To add a clip to the next slot in the sequence in the right column, click the thumbnail to select the play item and click Add> (or simply double-click the item). As you add items in order to the sequence, they appear in the right side of the layout window. To remove a play item that you've added to the sequence column, click the thumbnail to select the play item and click <Remove (or simply double-click the item). You can also add new play items from this screen: click the Add File . . . button and the VCD Wizard will take you through the process described in the last step. When all of your play items are added in the order you like, click Next> to continue.

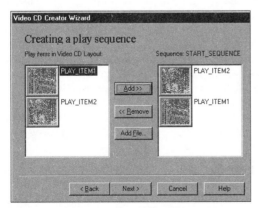

Figure 10-37: The VCD Wizard allows you to change the order of your video clips in the sequence from this dialog.

5. As a final step to confirm your layout before recording, the VCD Wizard allows you to play back the entire layout sequence. To view your layout, click the Playback . . . button; the VCD Wizard displays a set of standard VCR controls that allow you to pause, stop, or fast forward and rewind through the sequence. When you're ready to record your handiwork, click Next>.

From this point, the recording process is the same as a data CD-ROM.

Creating a One-Level Menu Video CD

As I mentioned earlier, building the menu structure for a Video CD is much more complex than for a simple sequential disc, and it requires a certain amount of preparation. For example, you should plan the branching structure on paper before you actually run VCD Creator. When designing the menu structure for your disc, remember that a menu with more than 9 or 10 choices is unwieldy! The simpler, the better.

Warning

If you've just picked up your Video CD player or you're new to recording, I strongly suggest you read through this tutorial section before you try to create a disc with a one-level menu structure! Remember, it's not necessary to build a menu if you're simply storing a number of clips for sequential viewing; the sequential structure is much simpler and requires far less preparation.

To create a Video CD with a one-level menu structure using the Wizard, follow these steps:

1. From the VCD Wizard welcome screen, click Next> to continue. The VCD Wizard displays the screen shown in Figure 10-33. Select the *One Level Menu Structure* option and click Next>.

2. Next, the VCD Wizard displays the Adding Play Items screen shown in Figure 10-34. As in Step 2 of the previous section, video play items can be added to your layout using one of two methods: click the A̲dd . . . button to display a standard Windows Open File dialog, or drag and drop play items to the Adding Play Items screen from the Windows Explorer. For each play item you add, you can make the changes I described in Step 3 of the previous section from the Add New Play Item dialog. These same properties are displayable from the menu system by highlighting the play item and selecting Properties from the Edit menu. You can also remove play items from your layout by clicking the Remove . . . button. When you are finished adding play items, click Next> to continue.

3. Once you've added all your play items, VCD Creator requires you to arrange them in a play sequence called START_SEQUENCE. This is the first sequence that appears when you load your new disc into your Video CD player. You determine this order from the next VCD Wizard screen. The process is the same as Step 4 of the previous tutorial on creating a sequential disc. Once you've created your sequence and all of your clips are in the desired order, click Next> to continue.

4. To this point, the VCD Wizard steps for a simple sequential structure and a one-level menu structure are almost identical, but now we need to perform some additional steps to create our menu. The VCD Wizard displays the screen shown in Figure 10-38. The background for your Video CD menu should contain a list of the viewer's menu choices. The viewer will select one from the Video CD player's remote control. However, it's been my experience that you never have a video clip that actually starts with a still image of those choices; therefore, I always click the Add from file . . . button and select an image I've already prepared with Paint Shop Pro. However, if you do wish to use a frame you specified earlier for one of your video clips as your background, you can select it from the *Play item:* drop-down list box. Click Next> to continue.

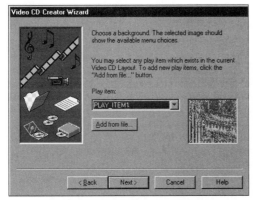

Figure 10-38: Selecting the background for a Video CD with a one-level menu structure.

5. Next, as shown in Figure 10-39, the VCD Wizard asks how many menu choices will be on your layout. Generally, one menu choice is required for each separate sequence you add to the disc. Highlight the value in the *Number of menu choices:* field and enter the correct number, or use the up and down arrows for the field to select the number you want. Click Next> to continue.

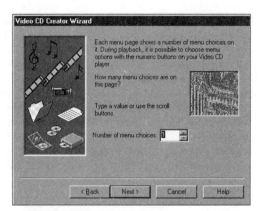

Figure 10-39: On this VCD Wizard screen, you specify the number of menu choices that will be available to the viewer.

6. On the next VCD Wizard screen, each of your menu choices is linked to a separate sequence. By default, VCD Wizard creates a corresponding sequence name for each menu choice, as in "PLAY_SEQUENCE1" for menu choice 1, and so on. To edit these defaults, highlight the menu number to change and click the Edit button to display the Edit Sequence Name dialog shown in Figure 10-40. You can specify a new name for the play sequence in the _Name:_ field, or link the menu choice number to another sequence from the _Available play sequences:_ drop-down list box. Once everything is satisfactory, click OK to continue.

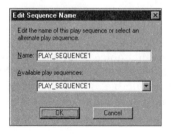

Figure 10-40: This dialog allows you to edit the name and link for any menu item or play sequence.

7. At this point, you've added a single menu page to your layout (at least one is required for the one-level menu structure). However, you can create additional menu pages with their own menu choices from this VCD Wizard screen; the viewer can jump between menu pages with the "Next >" and "<< Previous" buttons on the Video CD player remote control. Sounds familiar, doesn't it? To add a new menu page to your layout, click the Add Page button; the VCD Wizard returns to Step 4 of this procedure, and returns to this Adding Pages to Menu screen after each page. Once you've added all the menu pages you need, click Next> to continue.

8. Now it's time to build each of the play sequences that you created. VCD Creator displays the same dialog you saw in Step 3, when you were building the START_SEQUENCE; however, now you're creating the sequences linked to your menu choices. Click Next> after each sequence; VCD Wizard allows you to edit each sequence in turn.

Tip   Here are a few tips for making this process a little easier! First, keep a sketch of your menu pages, their menu choices, and each linked sequence handy so that you can refer to it. To avoid getting sequences mixed up, give each sequence a distinct name in Step 6. Finally, always check the *Sequence:* field above the right column on the Creating a play sequence screen; it displays the name of the current sequence you're working on. When you're working on a layout with multiple pages, it's easy to lose track of which sequence you **thought** you were editing!

9. You made it! As with the simple sequence procedure, the VCD Wizard gives you a chance to play back your layout before you begin the recording process. To watch your layout, click the Playback . . . button; the VCD Wizard displays a set of standard VCR controls that allow you to pause, stop, or fast forward and rewind through the sequence. Unlike a sequential layout, you can use the numbered keys under the VCR controls to select a menu choice, just as the viewer will do with the remote control. When you're ready to launch Easy CD Creator, click Next>.

From this point, the recording process is the same as a data CD-ROM.

Adding Play Items Manually to a VCD Layout

There are two ways to add play items to the left side of the VCD Creator window:

✦ Add a play item by selecting Add Item . . . from the Edit menu. VCD Creator displays a standard Windows File Open dialog, allowing you to navigate through your system to find the source file. Double-click the item to add it.

✦ Drag and drop a play item directly from Windows Explorer into your VCD layout.

Editing Menus and Sequences Manually

Although the VCD Wizard is definitely the easiest way to create a Video CD, you can edit menus and sequences manually from the right portion of the VCD layout window. The displayed fields are identical to those displayed by the Wizard — in fact, VCD Creator actually runs portions of the Wizard when you add a new page or link a sequence, so I won't repeat the steps here!

You can switch between the Menu and Sequence tabs by clicking the desired tab. To move a play item within the Sequences tab, drag and drop the thumbnail image to the desired position. When displaying the sequences you've created, you can switch between them by clicking the drop-down list box at the top of the tab and selecting the desired sequence to view from the list.

Validating a VCD Layout

Because of the complexity of a Video CD layout, proper validation before recording is even more important than it is within Easy CD Creator. To validate your VCD Creator layout, select Validate Layout . . . from the Video CD menu. VCD Creator displays the dialog shown in Figure 10-41.

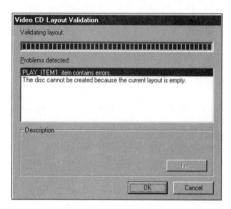

Figure 10-41: Validating a Video CD is recommended before you record it.

If no problems are found, VCD Creator displays the message "No errors detected." If VCD Creator does encounter problems in your layout, you can click the Fix . . . button to delete any play items from your layout that can no longer be found.

Selecting VCD Creator Preferences

There are a number of configuration settings you can change in VCD Creator to alter the look and feel of the program. Some of them are similar to their counterparts within Easy CD Creator.

To begin, display the Adaptec VCD Creator Preferences dialog by selecting Preferences . . . from the File menu.

✦ On the General tab, the Startup fields determine what actions VCD Creator takes when you run it. By default, *Show Startup Window* is enabled, so the program will display its welcome banner and copyright information; you can turn the display off by disabling this checkbox. VCD Creator also launches the VCD Wizard automatically on startup, but you can prevent this by disabling the *Open Disc Wizard* checkbox. The New CD Layout option group specifies what will happen when you select New CD Layout . . . from the File menu. By default, VCD Creator opens the VCD Wizard, but you can display only the blank layout window by selecting *Create an empty CD layout* instead.

✦ On the Disc Creation tab, you can specify where you would like VCD Creator to store temporary files during recording. Due to the huge size of most digital video clips, VCD Creator uses multiple directories on several drives to store temporary files (unlike Easy CD Creator, which uses only a single temporary file location). To use the default location assigned for Windows temporary files, enable the *Use Windows TEMP directory* checkbox. If you disable this checkbox, you can select one or more locations yourself by clicking the Add . . . button, which displays the Add Temporary Files Directory dialog shown in Figure 10-42. Either type the full pathname in the *Path:* field, or select an existing directory by clicking the Browse . . . button to navigate through your system. To limit the amount of temporary space allocated to this directory, enable the *Limit disk space usage* checkbox and enter a maximum size in megabytes. I recommend that you do **not** limit your temporary space if you have several hundred megabytes free; the more temporary space available, the faster the recording process will be. If you must limit your disk space, I recommend a minimum of at least 100 megabytes and a maximum of three-fourths of the available space on your drive. Click OK to accept the new location. You can also remove a temporary directory assignment by highlighting the path entry and clicking the Remove . . . button.

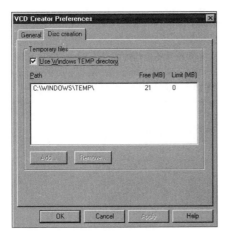

Figure 10-42: This dialog allows you to select temporary directories for VCD Creator, as well as limit the usable space.

Modifying Video CD Properties

You can also make a number of changes to the properties for your new Video CD disc from the Video CD Properties dialog, just as you can change some of the properties for a data CD-ROM. To begin, display the Properties dialog, shown in Figure 10-43, by selecting Properties . . . from the Video CD menu.

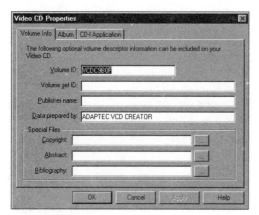

Figure 10-43: The Video CD Properties dialog.

✦ On the Volume Info tab, you specify the Volume ID, Volume set ID (for multidisc sets), a publisher name, and a preparation ID. All of these fields are optional except for the Volume ID (and possibly the Volume set ID), and VCD Creator supplies a default Volume ID and preparation ID for you. Under Special Files, you find the same optional *Copyright*, *Abstract*, and *Bibliography* fields we saw in Easy CD Creator; they identify three text files that exist in the root directory of the disc. The three files contain the disc's copyright information, abstract copy, and bibliography, respectively. If you decide to use these fields, you must create the files manually on your hard drive; you then select them by clicking the File Browser buttons next to each field, which carry the rather cryptic ellipsis label (". . .").

✦ On the Album tab, you define the characteristics of a multivolume album set. The same *Album identification:* field value must be used on each volume in the set, and you must specify in advance how many volumes the album set will contain in the *Number of volumes in album:* field. Set the *Ordinal number of the volume:* field to the volume number for the disc you're currently creating. If you feel that the material should be rated for parents, select one of three rating categories in the *Viewing restriction:* drop-down list box. If no rating is required, leave the field set to the default value of None.

✦ On the CD-I Application tab, you enable or disable Video CD support for CD-I players. If you are certain that your Video CD will not be played on a CD-I player, you can disable this field. The CD-I application does not interfere with the operation of your Video CD player; I leave it enabled by default. For CD-I, your CD-ROM recorder must be able to write mixed Form 1 and Form 2 sectors on a Mode 2 CD-ROM; most drive manufacturers simply state that their recorders support CD-I recording as another format.

Tip

If you're not certain whether your drive can handle mixed sectors in Mode 2 and there's no mention of CD-I support for Video CDs in the list of formats supported by your recorder, you can still determine whether to use it without ruining a disc! Create a Video CD layout with the *Include CD-I player application on Video CDs* checkbox enabled and try a simulated recording; if it completes successfully without reporting errors due to sector recording problems, then your drive supports this feature.

Once you've made all the changes to the properties for your Video CD, don't forget to click OK to save your changes!

Modifying Display Properties

Need more screen area to work with a really complex VCD layout? VCD Creator allows you to toggle off the display of the Toolbar and Status Bar. Pull down the View menu and click the desired item to toggle it; if the display item is on, a check mark appears next to it.

Click the Options . . . item from the View menu to specify the thumbnail image size you prefer; you can select one of three image sizes, or you can choose Custom to enter your own size.

Recording with VCD Creator

Once your VCD layout is ready to go, VCD Creator will launch Easy CD Creator for the actual recording. Follow these steps:

1. Select Create CD from Layout . . . from the Video CD menu. You can also create a disc image from the same menu if you prefer. You'll see VCD Creator launch Easy CD Creator and build the data layout automatically — it's fun and doesn't cost anything, so sit back and relax while you watch it!

2. Easy CD Creator displays — you guessed it — our old friend, the Disc creation setup dialog! From this point, the recording process is the same as it is for a data CD-ROM.

Recording CD-EXTRA Discs

Now that we've discussed PCD Creator and VCD Creator in detail, let's return to some of the advanced recording formats available within Easy CD Creator itself: for example, the CD-EXTRA disc. As you learned earlier, a CD-EXTRA disc is much like a standard mixed-mode CD-ROM, but the data and audio tracks are recorded in separate sessions. The audio tracks are recorded first, so a standard audio CD player can read them; this prevents your CD player from attempting to play a data track intended for your computer's CD-ROM drive. CD-EXTRA discs can also carry additional text information describing each track, so they're often used to carry both music and digital video clips.

Note

This all sounds great, but once again, the specter of compatibility raises its ugly head! As I've mentioned before, not every CD-ROM drive can correctly read a CD-EXTRA multisession disc, so the data session may not be accessible on many computers. If you're more concerned with the audio portion, this isn't a problem; any audio CD player or CD-ROM drive should be able to play the audio tracks on a CD-EXTRA disc. Also, if you already know that the computer that will use the disc supports the CD-EXTRA format, there's no problem; otherwise, I suggest that you use a CD-EXTRA disc only when you require a separate data session or you must have the special CD-EXTRA information. If you don't require either of these features, then create a standard audio disc (and a separate standard data CD-ROM if you need it). You may end up with two discs, but you can guarantee that **any** computer CD-ROM drive **can read all** of the information.

To record a CD-EXTRA disc, follow these steps:

1. First, run Easy CD Creator and display a new blank layout.

2. Select the CD Layout Properties item from the File menu to display the Disc Properties dialog, and choose the Data Settings panel.

3. Select the ISO 9660 file system and click the *CD EXTRA* checkbox; notice that the Properties . . . button is no longer grayed out.

4. While we're in this dialog, click Properties . . . and add the general disc data. Easy CD Creator displays the dialog shown in Figure 10-44.

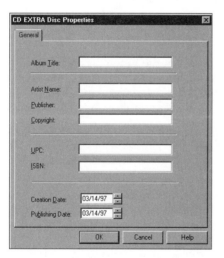

Figure 10-44: The CD EXTRA Disc Properties dialog allows you to specify general identifying data for your CD-EXTRA disc.

5. Enter an album title, artist, publisher name, and the copyright date. These fields are optional, but I recommend that you enter at least the album title and artist name. If you need more exotic information like UPC and ISBN product codes or creation and publishing dates on the disc, enter them here. Both dates must fall between January 1, 1980, and January 18, 2038. Once again, these fields are optional. Click OK to save your changes and return to the Disc Properties dialog, then click OK again to return to the menu system. At this point, Easy CD Creator now knows you're creating a disc in the CD-EXTRA format, and it automatically creates the separate sessions and makes the necessary changes for recording.

HEY, WHERE DID THOSE FILES COME FROM?

If you explore the data layout for a CD-EXTRA disc, you'll see that a directory named CDPLUS was automatically created, and that this directory contains files that are grayed out. You can't modify or delete these files from your layout because they contain the information specific to this CD-EXTRA disc, including the text you've added for audio tracks and the general information you added in step 5 of the CD-EXTRA tutorial. You can safely ignore this entire directory . . . now, go about your business, there's nothing more to see here!

6. The next step is to add audio tracks to your layout. Use the procedures you learned in Chapter 9 to add tracks until the audio portion of the layout is complete.

7. Now we add the CD-EXTRA information for each audio track. From the Audio CD Layout tab of the layout window, highlight the first track in your layout and select the CD-EXTRA Info item from the Track menu. Easy CD Creator displays the CD-EXTRA Track Information dialog, which is very similar to the CD-EXTRA Disc Information dialog we saw earlier — but this time all of the fields pertain only to the highlighted track. On the General tab, you can change the track title and enter an artist, composer, publisher name, and the copyright date. You can also specify the ISRC number, creation and publishing dates, the genre, and the musical key for this track. These fields are optional and do not default to the same values you entered in the CD-EXTRA Disc Information dialog. If you do change the track name, the CD-EXTRA information is saved with the new name, but the track name in the layout window is not changed. Once all the information you need has been entered, click OK to save the data and return to the layout window.

8. Repeat step 7 with each audio track in your layout.

9. Once you've added all the track-specific information, you're done with the audio portion of your disc. Next, click the Data Files tab to display the data portion of your layout. Use the procedures you learned in Chapter 9 to add data items until the data portion of the layout is complete. To avoid conflicts with the CD-EXTRA files, do not add any data items within the \CDPLUS directory.

10. Done with the data layout? Then you're ready to record! Click the Create CD Toolbar button or select Create CD . . . from the File menu. From this point, everything is standard operating procedure for recording a mixed-mode disc. CD-EXTRA discs are automatically write-protected, so make certain that your layout is correct before you actually record!

Recording Bootable CD-ROMs

Let's turn our attention to recording a truly specialized disc: the "bootable" CD-ROM, which can actually contain the operating system and all the required system files for certain computers! Essentially, a bootable CD-ROM contains the same system information and system files as a bootable floppy, as well as programs and data files. The system BIOS and drive controller in most PC's don't support booting from a CD-ROM, so don't expect your home system to be able to do this, but many "diskless" workstations used on networks have this feature built-in to their motherboards or drive controllers. The operating system boots off the CD-ROM just like it was booting from a floppy drive. Of course, the big difference is that the boot procedure cannot write any data to the disc. For example, if you're creating an MS-DOS bootable disc, you must make certain that your AUTOEXEC.BAT file doesn't contain any statements or programs that would write data to the A: drive during the boot process.

Note   The "El Torito" specification is the official standard for bootable CD-ROMs, and it provides the ability for some computers to boot from any one of several separate floppy or hard drive images stored on a single CD-ROM. Now there's a fun fact to share with others, right?

Before you start, you need a to create a bootable 1.2, 1.4, or 2.88 megabyte floppy. Easy CD Creator will copy the boot information from this disk as a disc image to a special file on the CD-ROM named BOOTIMG.BIN. To create a bootable floppy under MS-DOS 6.22, insert a blank floppy disk into your A: drive and from the DOS prompt type the command:

FORMAT A: /S

If you booted your PC from the A: drive, format the disk in your B: drive instead with the command:

FORMAT B: /S

At the end of the formatting process, DOS adds the required system files to the disk to make it bootable. You should also add whatever special files will be needed during the boot process; in other words, you should be able to boot your computer correctly using only this floppy, so make certain that you add mouse drivers, DOS programs, and whatever else is needed.

Now follow these steps to create the CD-ROM:

1. Run Easy CD Creator and open a new CD layout by selecting New CD Layout from the File menu.

2. Insert the bootable floppy in your A: drive.

3. Click the Data Files tab of the layout window to display your data layout, then select the CD Layout Properties item under the File menu.

4. Select the ISO 9660 file system from the drop-down list box. Note that you can't create a bootable CD-ROM with the Joliet file system.

5. Enable the *Bootable* checkbox and click OK to return to the menu system.

6. Easy CD Creator immediately begins reading the contents of the boot floppy disk you loaded; it's creating a disc image that will be read by the special BIOS I mentioned earlier.

7. Once Easy CD Creator is finished reading the disk, you'll see that two special read-only files have been added to the root of your layout: BOOTCAT.BIN and BOOTIMG.BIN.

From this point, the rest of the process is the same as building a standard data CD-ROM.

Recording a Master Disc for Duplication

If you need several hundred copies of a single CD-ROM, it's probably not practical to duplicate them by yourself on your PC. Although the prices for blank discs have dropped dramatically, a commercial replication center is still your best bet. You'll save money, headaches, and a heck of a lot of your time!

However, you still have to supply the replication company with a master disc that they can use for duplication, and most companies have requirements for a recordable CD-ROM master disc. Typically, these shops request a write-protected, single-session disc created using the disc-at-once method.

A good rule is to check with the replication company before creating your master disc to find out their requirements. In most cases, these rules will insure that your master disc is acceptable:

✦ First, if a single data track is required (disc-at-once), select CD Layout Properties from the Easy CD Creator File menu to display the Disc Properties dialog and click the Data Settings tab. Click the *Preserve normal file ordering* option and then enable the *Create a master disc (single data track)* checkbox. Click OK to close the dialog and save your changes.

✦ Do not create a multisession master!

✦ Make sure your master disc is write-protected by enabling the *Close Disc* option on the Advanced tab of the Disc Creation Setup dialog.

Recording From Removable or Remote Drives

As I mentioned earlier, it's good practice to avoid recording a CD-ROM disc directly from a network drive or a removable drive. If at all possible, copy the data to your local hard drive and use that as the source drive instead. Easy CD Creator attempts to do this automatically by copying the data to a temporary buffer area it creates on your hard drive. However, if you don't have enough space to record locally and the data cannot be staged, remember these tips:

✦ Use the System Tester to determine the transfer rate for the drive you plan to use as the source.

✦ Make recording from a removable drive easier on yourself by minimizing the number of swaps you'll have to perform — combine as much data on a single piece of media as possible.

✦ Finally, consider writing a disc image to the network or removable drive instead of attempting to record a disc layout with a large number of small files. Of course, you have to have enough room to hold the image on the removable or network drive, but if you use a disc image you eliminate the delays your system would otherwise incur as each file is opened, read, and closed. Remember, it's faster to open and transfer a single large file than dozens of smaller files!

Prerecording Tracks to WAV Files

You can prerecord tracks you've added to an audio layout to your hard drive; this step saves time during the actual recording process, because you won't have to load and read the source disc. For example, if you have one or two sound files that you use on almost every recording, you can prerecord them as WAV files. Once Easy CD Creator has converted the source tracks to WAV files, you add them to your layout in the normal manner.

By the way, this is also a handy way of creating WAV files from any source disc; for example, if you have a sound effects audio CD, you can record each track as a separate WAV file for use in Windows! Follow these steps:

1. Run Easy CD Creator and add an audio track from a source CD in the normal manner.

2. Click the track entry in the layout and select the Pre-record to WAV File . . . item from the Track menu.

3. If the track will fit, you'll see a dialog displaying a progress bar and general information about the track as the digital audio is converted into a WAV file for storage on your hard drive.

"Must-Have" Utilities

In this section, I introduce you to several programs that I find helpful when creating a layout; except for the one supplied with Easy CD Creator, the programs are inexpensive shareware. These programs are just what you need to edit and catalog images, WAV files, and audio tracks!

Although we can't exhaustively describe each program, I cover the most common functions to give you a good idea of the features. Also, the shareware programs in this section are included on the companion CD-ROM, so you can evaluate them yourself.

Using Paint Shop Pro

Of all the shareware programs I've registered and use on a daily basis, I'd have to say that Paint Shop Pro from JASC Incorporated is the best. It's a rock-solid image editor, scanning package, paint program, screen capture utility, and image thumbnail browser that supports just about every image format ever encountered. Plus, it converts images between all of them! Paint Shop Pro has been the leading shareware image utility distributed on bulletin board systems and the Internet for years, and because of its success it's also sold in retail stores in its registered form. The program is available in 16-bit and 32-bit versions, and you can always find the latest version on the Web at www.jasc.com (or use FTP at ftp.jasc.com).

Let's look at the interface and the main editing window. Install the program and run it, and you'll see the window shown in Figure 10-45. Paint Shop Pro offers both a standard menu system and a customizable Toolbar, and it supports Adobe plug-ins and Aldus import filters, so you can expand the functionality of the program with external modules. On the right is a complete color palette — changing colors while painting or editing is as simple as clicking the eyedropper cursor on the desired color. Paint Shop Pro can also be configured with "floating" Toolbars.

Figure 10-45: The Paint Shop Pro main editing window.

Loading Files

To load files within Paint Shop Pro, select the Open . . . item from the File menu or click the Open Toolbar button. You have a wide range of image types to pick from, so I usually leave the *File type*: set to All Files. If you highlight an image, Paint Shop Pro provides its size and color depth, or you can click the Details . . . button to see the dialog shown in Figure 10-46.

Figure 10-46: Need to see a complete description of an image before you load it? Click the Details . . . button within the Paint Shop Pro Open File dialog.

Once you've selected an image and opened it, Paint Shop Pro displays it within the editing window. Now you're ready to work your magic! Like any well-designed Windows program, Paint Shop Pro remembers where you last opened files and what type you were displaying, so it's easy to load more than one file in succession from the same directory.

Converting Between Image Formats

Converting files within Paint Shop Pro from one image format to another is as easy as using the Save As . . . command from the File menu. From the Save As dialog, select the new image format in the *Save as type*: drop-down list box; depending on the new format, you may have to select a format subtype as well (for example, GIF 87a or 89a). You can overwrite the existing filename, or select another to keep the original intact. Paint Shop Pro also offers a batch conversion feature for converting entire directories of images from one format to another automatically; select the Batch Conversion . . . item from the File menu.

Capturing Screen Images

Paint Shop Pro offers a number of different screen capture methods. As you can see from the Capture Setup dialog shown in Figure 10-47, you can capture a window, the entire screen, or a specific area or object. The capture can be triggered from the keyboard, the mouse, or a delay timer. Paint Shop Pro is my favorite screen capture program; it produced all the screen shots in this book.

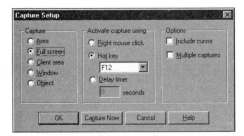

Figure 10-47: The screen capture support within Paint Shop Pro is excellent.

Image Editing

Whether you're looking to change a single pixel or an entire area of an image, Paint Shop Pro provides a good selection of standard paint tools: a variety of brushes, an airbrush, flood fill, line and shape drawing, text objects, and a color replacement tool. You can zoom the image to the pixel level for close editing, or reduce even the largest TIF format images to fit within the window. The program also includes a number of methods to outline various screen areas for editing, including a neat Magic Wand feature you can use to selectively crop or alter parts of the image according to color. Paint Shop Pro comes with a number of image editing filters, and you can easily add your favorite plug-ins.

Modifying Image Color and Size

Another range of common tasks that Paint Shop Pro performs well is altering the color characteristics of an image: changing the color depth, adjusting brightness, contrast and gamma correction, posterizing, and creating a negative image are all available from the Colors menu. For example, when I convert images for use on a Web site, I change their color depth because a 256-color image is still the standard for Internet graphics. Most of these features allow you to preview the change before you make it, so you can avoid the Undo button unless you really need it.

"All this is great, but what if I just want to resize or add a border?" No problem, Paint Shop Pro includes a complete range of sizing features under the Image menu. You can resize (with the same aspect ratio or not), crop, mirror, rotate, flip, and add borders.

Without a doubt, Paint Shop Pro is the "Swiss Army Knife" of image editors, and it performs all of its functions as well as better-known commercial packages costing many hundreds of dollars more!

Using Media Center

Our second "must-have" program is also from JASC Incorporated. Media Center is a superb image catalog program — or at least that's its primary function, because I've found it useful in other applications as well! Like Paint Shop Pro, Media Center can convert images, and it can also perform batch manipulation; plus, it's a good slide show engine, and it even prints professional-looking catalogs of all of your multimedia files!

Yes, you read right: Media Center isn't just for images, it also catalogs WAV clips, MIDI music, AVI video, and FLI animation! All of these different formats can be arranged in albums, making it the ideal cataloging system for anyone with an ever-growing library of multimedia files. The program is currently available in a 16-bit version at www.jasc.com (or use FTP at ftp.jasc.com).

Catalog Those Files!

Media Center's primary job is to logically organize your multimedia files. This is done by arranging the files into albums, like the one shown in Figure 10-48. Of course, if that were all it did, I would be less impressed, but all the features Media Center provides work within this album environment, so you feel you're working with a tangible book. For example, you can

✦ keep your album current by adding and deleting thumbnails;

✦ arrange the images any way you like using drag and drop;

✦ sort the contents of an album by one of several criteria;

✦ print any image, or the entire album with filenames;

✦ add keywords and descriptions to help locate any file with the Search option;

✦ use a removable drive or a recordable CD-ROM to store your images, because Media Center keeps track of disk and CD-ROM volume labels.

In fact, you can merge albums together, making it a good tool for any office that routinely handles business graphics and clipart.

Slide Show Features

Need a good slide show program for running a demo or displaying your image collection? How about a multimedia slide show? With the Media Center slide show engine, you can link WAV files to your show or pipe in background music directly from an audio CD. If you like, the show will repeat a specified number of times, or run continuously. You can configure Media Center to move to the next image with the space bar, the mouse, or automatically after a certain delay. Are some of your images larger than the screen resolution? Media Center can automatically scale only those images that need altering for full-screen display.

After using Media Center, you'll wonder how you ever located a particular sound file, video clip, or image file without it!

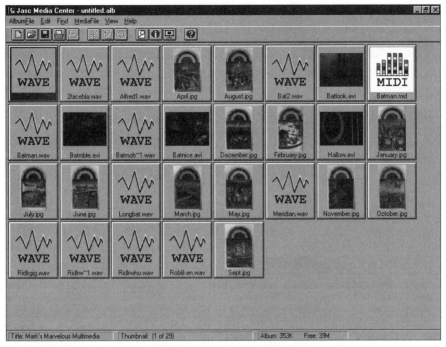

Figure 10-48: A typical multimedia album created with Media Center.

Using the Adaptec Sound Editor

We cover two sound editors in this section, either of which can perform basic editing of WAV files before you record them on an audio disc. The first editor is supplied free with the Deluxe Edition of Easy CD Creator — it's the Adaptec Sound Editor.

Sound Editor's main window, displayed in Figure 10-49, features a basic Toolbar very similar to its cousin Easy CD Creator; however, note the addition of standard audio deck controls such as you see on a cassette deck. These include Play, Record, Fast Forward and Rewind, Stop and Pause. There's also a level meter at the bottom of the window that displays the volume of both the left and right channels.

Standard Editing Features

Like any Windows sound editor worth launching, the Adaptec editor allows cutting and pasting of any portion of a WAV file. It even provides a luxury or two, such as convenient Toolbar controls for replacing a portion of the file with the Clipboard contents (Paste Over), mixing the Clipboard contents with a highlighted portion of the file (Mix Paste), and playing the contents of the Clipboard. You can also enable an Undo feature if you have sufficient disk space.

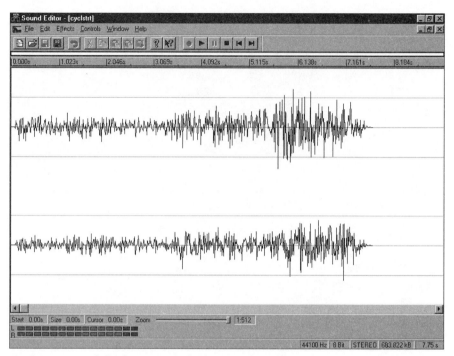

Figure 10-49: The Adaptec Sound Editor window with a stereo WAV file loaded.

Recording and Effects

The Adaptec Sound Editor can record directly from your sound card in 8 or 16 bits, mono or stereo, and in four standard rates: 8,000, 11,025, 22,050 and 44,100Hz. You can also select a specific rate other than the standard choices. There's a 10-band graphic equalizer (one feature that Cool Edit 96 doesn't have), and the program can convert a WAV file to another sample rate or sample size. You can also switch a file between stereo and mono.

The Adaptec editor offers a healthy selection of effects as well — not as many as Cool Edit 96, but more than I expect in a utility that ships with CD recording software! It includes support for amplify, echo and fade, flange, inversion, pop removal, and pitch shift; each of these effects is controllable from its own panel, including a number of preset effects. Figure 10-50, for example, shows the Flange settings panel.

The Adaptec Sound Editor should provide more than enough features for anyone but an audio professional, and it works well as a WAV editing tool.

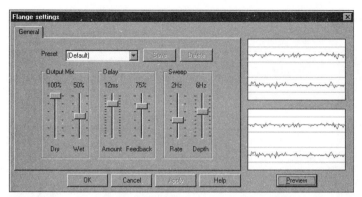

Figure 10-50: Adding a robotic flange effect to a WAV file with the Adaptec Sound Editor.

Using Cool Edit 96

Although the Adaptec Sound Editor is a fine utility, Syntrillium Software's Cool Edit is my sound editing program of choice. Like Paint Shop Pro, it's a shareware success story that has grown up on bulletin boards and through the Internet. I think of the Adaptec editor as vanilla ice cream and Cool Edit 96 as Fudge Chocolate Chip — either will do the job, but Cool Edit 96 offers a lot more! The program is available in 16-bit and 32-bit versions, and you can download the latest version from www.syntrillium.com. Figure 10-51 shows the Cool Edit 96 window.

Cool Edit 96 Extras

Cool Edit 96 provides almost all of the same features as the Adaptec Sound Editor, so I'll discuss here only the additional features provided by Cool Edit 96.

First, the interface: You can configure the entire color scheme within Cool Edit 96, as well as customize the Toolbar to your liking. The program includes a very interesting and colorful spectral view, as well as the standard waveform display, or you can choose a frequency analysis. If you're interested in raw data, Cool Edit 96 can display a waveform statistics screen.

Both Adaptec Sound Editor and Cool Edit 96 provide basic conversion between sampling rates — but unlike the Adaptec program, which was designed for use only with WAV format files, Cool Edit 96 allows you to load and save files in completely different formats! For example, you can load a SoundBlaster VOC format sound file, edit it, and save it as a WAV file for recording with Easy CD Creator. Other file formats supported by Cool Edit are AIF, AU, SND, and VOX, so you can even edit files you pick up on the Internet that are meant for other operating systems. There's also a built-in macro scripting language that allows you to perform multiple functions on one or more files automatically.

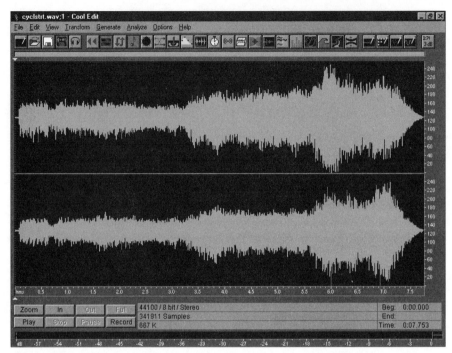

Figure 10-51: The Cool Edit 96 editing window with a stereo WAV file loaded.

Cool Edit 96 Luxuries

Cool Edit 96 offers all the effects I mentioned with the Adaptec Sound Editor, and adds noise reduction, custom filters, and an honest-to-goodness brainwave synchronizer for creating your own relaxation sounds! You can put a sound file to music, harmonize a sound using a particular chord, or generate the same DTMF tones as your telephone and modem. A favorite effect of mine is the distortion feature; try the "Bad FM reception" preset for a nifty effect. Cool Edit 96 can also generate brown, pink, or white noise (I didn't even know there was a "brown noise").

Cool Edit 96 also provides a full set of CD-ROM controls, so you can use the program to play audio CDs. The program saves disc titles and song titles for display, and you can mark and return to a specific point on the audio disc.

In short, Cool Edit 96 is a professional tool for both the novice and advanced user, and it includes a number of unique features that you'll find in no other package. I recommend you give it a try!

Creating Jewel Case Inserts

Our final section deals with another Easy CD Creator advanced feature. You will either love or ignore this feature, depending on whether you need a professional appearance for your finished data and audio discs. The feature is the Jewel Case Editor, which creates paper inserts that fit in the front and back of a standard CD-ROM jewel case.

If you have a standard CD-ROM jewel case with inserts handy, you can see how the front insert slides into the front of the case in front of the four tabs, while you must pry off the plastic square that holds the disc to reach the back insert. Normally this isn't too hard, and you can do it in a few seconds without a tool. If the case is a bit stubborn, I sometimes use a screwdriver with a flat blade to carefully pry open the back cover.

Tip

The editor provides support for a Disc Printer that can print a label directly on the top of a recordable disc; however, Easy CD Creator requires a professional CD-ROM disc printer, which you and I aren't likely to have! I would recommend the NEATO labeling system we talked about earlier for creating a disc label with a standard inkjet or laser printer.

If you're making archival backups of your hard drive or simply recording a video clip to take with you on a business trip, there's probably no need to print a jewel case insert. On the other hand, if you're recording an audio CD of harpsichord music, or your rare live recording of your harmonica tunes to give as a gift, you probably need an insert. After all, a standard audio CD player can only display the track number, and most of us like to know whether we are listening to Chopin or George Thorogood and the Destroyers! If you're distributing data CD-ROMs to beta testers or shareware customers, you should also consider the presentation of your work. To make a good first impression, I would both create an insert and use a disc labeler like the NEATO system, or buy a number of blanks that have been screen-printed.

The Jewel Case Editor Window

To use the Jewel Case Editor, run Easy CD Creator and load a layout or create the layout from scratch. When your layout is complete, click the Jewel Case Layout tab at the top of the window to display the editor, as shown in Figure 10-52. Any changes you make to the default insert are saved along with the current layout.

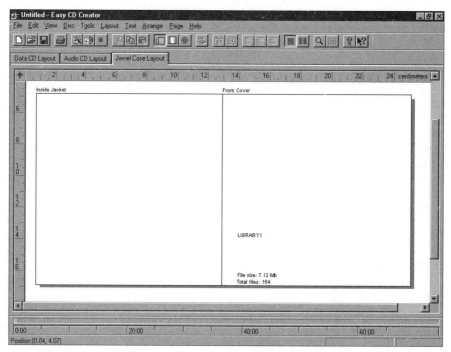

Figure 10-52: The Jewel Case Layout window displaying a simple data CD insert.

The editor Toolbar includes standard icons for cutting and pasting, as well as icons for switching between the three modes (front cover, back cover, and disc label), column and paragraph formatting, and moving text and graphic objects to the front or back of the design. Along the top and left side of the window are handy rulers that indicate your horizontal and vertical positioning; these rulers move to follow your cursor.

What's missing? Well, you've probably noticed that the Jewel Case Editor does not provide drawing tools for creating graphics; instead, it relies on other Windows drawing applications with OLE support to provide graphics. It can also acquire images directly from a scanner. You can, however, alter the font and layout characteristics from inside the editor.

Building a Simple Insert

First, let's build a simple insert with a title on the front cover and a version number on the back. We use only text objects in this example. Notice that Easy CD Creator automatically added two text items to the front cover: the file size and total number of files automatically appear at the bottom left corner of the front cover for data layouts. To build a simple insert, follow these steps:

1. Select Insert text . . . from the Edit menu, or simply press your Insert key. Easy CD Creator displays the dialog shown in Figure 10-53, where you can configure the font, size, color, and orientation of the text. For this tutorial, let's create a front and back insert for my shareware distribution disc.

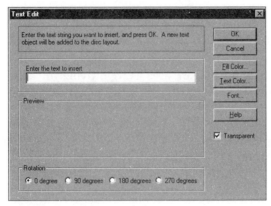

Figure 10-53: The Text Edit dialog contains all the controls you need to add text objects to your inserts.

2. Click the Font . . . button to display the Font selection dialog shown in Figure 10-54. Let's make the title large, bold, and unique, so pick Stencil Sans from the *Font:* drop-down list box, Bold from the *Font Style:* list and 36 points from the *Size:* list. Once you've made your selections, click OK to return to the Text Edit dialog.

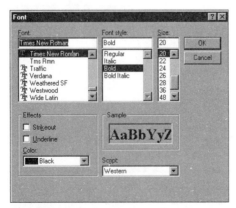

Figure 10-54: It's easy to select font characteristics from this dialog.

3. Next, let's specify a fill color for the background behind each character and a text color for the outline of each character by clicking the Fill Color and Text Color buttons, respectively. Each button displays a standard Windows color selection dialog where you can click a color to select it or define a custom color. Let's use black as a text color, but because we want to see the background behind the text, we need to enable the *Transparent* checkbox.

4. Next, we specify the rotation to be applied to this text. Because we want this text to appear with no rotation, let's leave it at 0 degrees.

5. Now we're ready to specify the text itself. Enter "Stainless Steel" into the edit field; the text appears in the Preview area as well, giving you an idea of what the chosen font and text characteristics will look like. When everything is correct, click OK!

6. We've returned to the editor window, and the text now appears on the page — but wait, this was supposed to be a title, and it's not where we want it! Don't panic; remember, these are text objects, and they can be selected, moved, or modified just like objects in a paint program. When we click the text, *handles* appear around the object border, as shown in Figure 10-55, and we can drag the object to the front cover. Plus, while a text object is selected we can left justify it, right justify it, or center it using the Toolbar buttons. Let's center it. Now it looks better! If you need to remove the selected object, just press your Delete key.

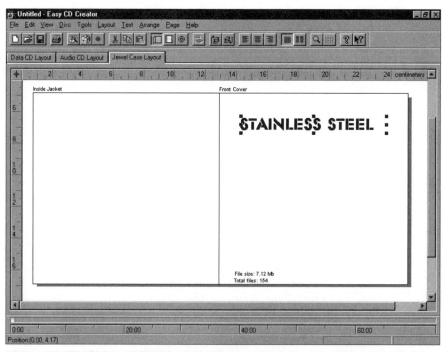

Figure 10-55: The small squares that appear around the text object are called handles, and indicate that you've selected this text object.

Note If you've never used a drawing package, you might not know that handles are more than just indicators. If you click a specific handle with your mouse and drag it, you can change that dimension of the text object. For example, if I activate a text object and drag the bottom middle handle down, the text object expands to fill the new space; if I click the middle handle on the right side, I can make the text object longer or shorter.

7. For the rest of the title, let's do something a little special. Repeat steps 1 through 5, but select 270-degree rotation instead and enter the string "oftware" in the edit field. Click OK, move the result to the front of the existing title, and voila! You have an interesting title treatment for your front cover, as shown in Figure 10-56.

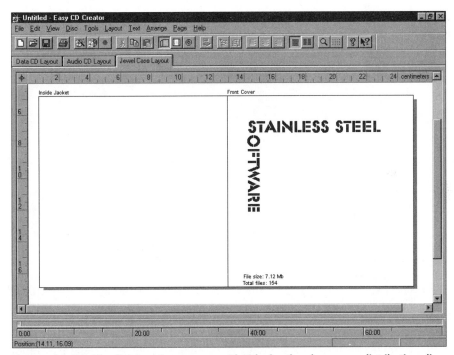

Figure 10-56: The finished front cover with title for the shareware distribution disc.

8. Now we need to switch to the back cover. Select Jewel Back from the Page menu, or click the Back Cover Toolbar button. The editor window changes to display the back insert, as in Figure 10-57. To add the version number, repeat steps 1 through 5, click the text object to select it, and move it wherever you like. Remember to save your layout to disc once your inserts are completed!

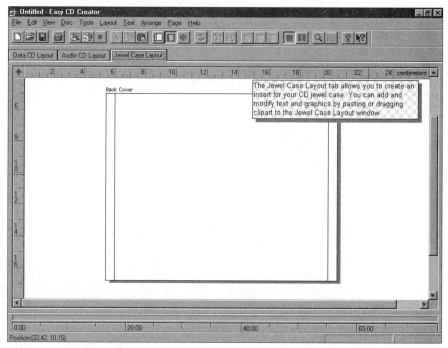

Figure 10-57: The Jewel Case Layout tab displays this layout screen for the back insert.

Building an Audio Insert

Easy CD Creator adds enough information to an audio CD jewel case insert that you might not need to add any custom text! As Figure 10-58 shows, the front cover lists the Disc Title and Artist Name you entered in the Disc Properties dialog. If you decide to change these, select Properties from the Disc menu and enter the new text. Easy CD Creator automatically updates the display. On the inside jacket, Easy CD Creator lists each track and its length; this information is repeated on the back cover.

If you do decide to make changes, though, you can add, delete, or modify the text on an audio CD insert in the same manner as the simple insert we created in the previous tutorial.

Using Custom Graphics

Since the Jewel Case Editor supports OLE (Object Linking and Embedding), you can pick just about any existing image to add to your inserts, or even draw your own! There are five methods to add graphic objects:

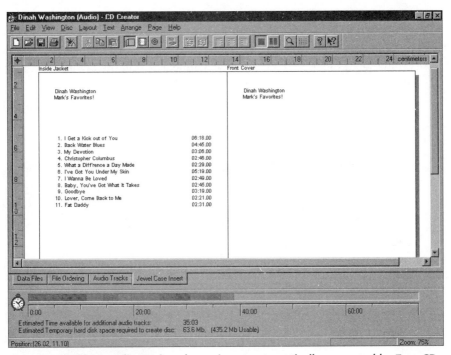

Figure 10-58: An audio CD jewel case insert automatically generated by Easy CD Creator for one of my discs.

✦ Create an OLE object in another application and insert it. Select Insert New Object . . . from the Edit menu, choose the Create New option, pick your application, and Easy CD Creator launches it automatically.

✦ Insert an existing OLE object. Select Insert New Object . . . from the Edit menu, choose the Create from File option, and click the Browse . . . button to navigate through your system and open the file.

✦ Add objects using drag and drop from another application.

✦ Cut them from another application and paste them into your layout.

✦ Scan an image directly into your layout. When the scanner is ready, select Acquire Image from the File menu and click Select Source to pick a scanning device. Select Acquire from the same submenu to display your scanner's control dialog and begin the scanning process.

I tend to use either drag and drop or cut and paste, since they're the easiest methods. As an example, let's use a clipart image from my collection and add it to the front cover of a MIDI music disc, as shown in Figure 10-59. Follow these steps:

1. Open your graphics application and load the image. For me, that means loading Paint Shop Pro.

2. Select the Copy command from the application's Edit menu to copy the graphic into your Windows Clipboard.

3. Click the Easy CD Creator window to activate it and select the Paste item from the Edit menu. The graphic will appear within the layout window, but it usually requires you to drag it to the proper location.

4. Resize the graphic if necessary by dragging the handles at the edges of the object.

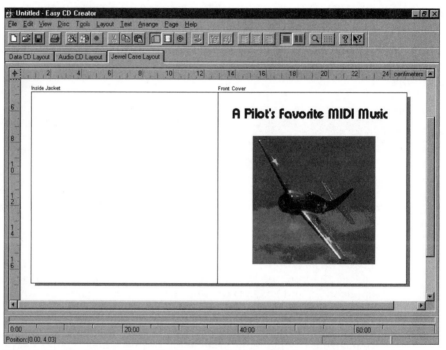

Figure 10-59: A cover for a disc featuring both text and a graphic I pasted from Paint Shop Pro.

Printing and Cutting Your Inserts

Finally, you're ready to print the insert pages and cut them out. Switch to the Jewel Case Editor, load the layout if it isn't already loaded, and select Print . . . from the File menu. If you don't have a good quality printer, I suggest you visit a friend who does — producing these inserts is not a task for a dot matrix printer!

When cutting your inserts, I get the best results with either an office cutting board or a modeler's knife and a ruler. Try to cut just inside the lines, or use an existing insert set from a factory-made disc as your cutting guide. A ruler comes in handy when making the creases for the back cover.

Summary

We covered quite a bit of ground in this chapter!

✦ First, you learned about the advanced features and recording methods within Easy CD Creator, PCD Creator, and VCD Creator.

✦ You were introduced to a number of utilities that will prove indispensable during the preparation of your discs.

✦ Finally, we created custom jewel case inserts for those discs that deserve special treatment!

In Chapter 11 we'll troubleshoot potential recording problems.

✦   ✦   ✦

Troubleshooting

If you enjoy chatting about computer hardware (and who doesn't?), you've probably heard a horror story or two about a computer owner who positively could not get a particular piece of equipment to work on their system. I'll admit this does happen, but it's also true that many computer owners simply give up and return a piece of hardware without trying to figure out what's really wrong with it.

CD recorders are prime candidates for trouble. Even the latest recorders are complex, finicky devices that require a finely-tuned environment to work properly, and mistakes can cost you $10 each! It pays to learn how to read the symptoms of the problem as well as the error code. This process is called *troubleshooting*, and it applies to any computer hardware.

In this chapter, we address some of the solutions for common CD recorder problems (no matter what software you're using), and we outline a simple troubleshooting method to help track down a problem with your drive.

Using Error Logs

As we mentioned in the last chapter, you can specify that Easy CD Creator create a log file during each recording session. Probably the most important part of the log file (and the data you'll likely use the most) is the section devoted to error messages returned during a recording session.

If errors do occur during the recording of a CD, you'll be able to view them from the Creating Disc from Layout dialog with the View Errors button. The text of the error message itself might not mean a great deal — in fact, some of them, such as "Invalid Bits in Identify Message (Sense Code 0x3D)," don't seem to belong to the English language — but you can double-click the error message in the list box to display the complete description. Most of the error descriptions also indicate where the problem is, as well as at least one or two possible solutions.

A separate section within the Easy CD Creator online help system lists all of these error messages divided into groups. Let's cover the problem area for each of these groups.

✦ **ASPI Manager errors.** These errors indicate a problem reported by your SCSI drivers somewhere in your SCSI device chain; they are also related to improper configuration of your SCSI card.

✦ **Host Adapter errors.** Your SCSI adapter itself reports this group of errors, usually because of improper cabling or termination.

✦ **Disc Preparation errors.** Errors caused by file open or temporary file problems, especially over a network. Other culprits could be a lack of disk space or memory.

✦ **Sense Code errors.** These are the really troublesome errors that you're likely to encounter the most, and they are caused by an entire cavalcade of problems! Your recorder uses sense codes to report errors, and these codes include everything from diagnostic failure (your drive has an internal hardware problem) to the caddy not being present in the recorder. One of the most common sense code errors is the buffer underrun error. Figure 11-1 illustrates just the first page of the sense code error list from Easy CD Creator's online help system.

✦ **DOS errors.** Of all the errors you can receive when using Easy CD Creator, DOS errors are probably the most familiar and easiest to deal with. They're caused by file open and file access problems that you might also have encountered in other DOS applications.

✦ **Sense Key errors.** This group is a general set of error codes returned by your drive, and one or more sense code errors typically accompanies them. For example, you might receive a Blank Check sense key error and a Disk Write-Protected sense code error in combination. The sense key error indicates that your drive is encountering a problem with the disc you're using, while the sense code error narrows the problem down to indicate that you're attempting to record to a write-protected disc.

✦ **General errors.** These are nonspecific error codes returned during the recording process. Insufficient memory, flawed or dirty media, and problems with the source hard drive can cause them. If CD Creator encounters one of these errors, it might be able to continue recording or it might abort the disc.

✦ **Target Status errors.** The drive reports this group of errors during recording. They are usually due to improper cabling, incorrect termination, or a problem with another SCSI device connected to the same adapter. If one of these errors occurs, it usually aborts the entire disc.

Figure 11-1: The formidable list of sense code errors displayed within Easy CD Creator's online help system.

DISPLAYING ERROR CODES

You may be wondering why Easy CD Creator doesn't display many of these sense key and sense code errors for common problems. For example, why didn't it display an error code yesterday when you mistakenly loaded an audio CD into your recorder instead of a blank disc? That's because Easy CD Creator recognizes and intercepts many of these error codes, and displays a dialog to prompt you for the required action. In the case of our example, Easy CD Creator identified the error sent by your recorder when it determined that the disc you loaded wasn't a blank, and displayed a dialog prompting you to load a blank disc. In general, CD-ROM recording software will only display an error code when it can't recover from or recognize the error.

✦ **Track Writer errors.** Another group of errors reported by a recorder while it's writing data in track-at-once mode. Some of these errors can result in a particular track not being written to the disc, while all of the other tracks are successfully recorded.

If you're using another program for recording, make sure that it has well-documented error codes, including possible solutions — they're your first line of defense!

Another good resource for determining the meaning of a recording error is the Adaptec Web site at www.adaptec.com, where many of the messages that can appear within Easy CD Creator are explained in detail. There are also a number of FAQs (short for *Frequently Asked Questions*) text files that cover recording problems.

The General Checklist — First Level Troubleshooting

Starting with this section, I introduce you to the troubleshooting method used in many computer repair shops to track and solve problems. The first level is a general checklist of items that helps insure that your recorder is correctly hooked up and your recording software has the system resources it needs to perform its job.

Note If you encounter an isolated file error in one recording session, there's probably no need to start a bug hunt — don't grab your flame thrower and automatic rifle! Because of the endless variety of data items and audio tracks you can throw at a CD recorder and the precise requirements for a successful recording, it's very likely that you'll lose a disc or two for each hundred that you create. Typically reasons for these sporadic errors include electrical brownouts, a large number of short files in your layout that may result in a buffer underrun error, or even a system slowdown caused by a badly-behaved application that you closed. The troubleshooting model is meant for a recorder that consistently returns errors, recording software that constantly locks up, and so on.

As I said earlier when we installed your SCSI card and recorder, many computer owners are uneasy about getting "down and dirty" with their computer; this troubleshooting method may involve removing the cover and changing settings on hardware. As long as you unplug your computer before removing the cover and ground yourself by touching the metal frame of the computer's case, you can perform these troubleshooting steps without fear of damaging your machine. However, if you'd rather have someone else perform these steps, bring your computer to your local PC repair shop and have a technician check out your computer for you — and if you have an external recorder, don't forget to bring it, too!

Whoops! Almost forgot — have you checked the contents of the README files that accompanied your recorder and SCSI card software? The answer you're looking for might be there, so take a few moments to look through these files for any information that pertains to your system.

The General Checklist — Hardware

To perform the general hardware checklist, follow these steps.

1. If you have an external recorder, check the SCSI cable connecting it to the card's external port. The cable should be free of kinks, less than three feet long, and firmly attached at both ends.

2. If you have an external recorder, make sure that it's plugged in, turned on, and is receiving power.

3. If you have an internal recorder, make sure that it's receiving power; is the front panel light blinking? Does it activate when you load a CD-ROM? If not, the power cable running from the computer's power supply to your recorder may have been inadvertently pulled off.

4. Next, remove the case from your computer and check the SCSI adapter. Is it firmly seated in the slot and are all of the SCSI ribbon cables firmly attached? Remember, the cables must be oriented correctly, so that pin 1 of the cable links to pin 1 of the connector. Don't forget to check the cables running to any SCSI devices other than your recorder, like a SCSI hard drive. If you've recently moved your PC any distance at all, a loose cable is often to blame for device errors.

5. Now check the termination on all of your SCSI devices on the same adapter. If your CD-ROM recorder is the only SCSI device in your system, then both your recorder and the SCSI card should be terminated; if your system includes other SCSI devices attached to the same card, make sure that the correct devices are terminated.

6. Finally, double-check that each device on your SCSI chain has a unique ID number. You may also be able to do this through your SCSI device management software.

This checklist is often helpful if your system is reporting problems with your SCSI cabling, termination, or the SCSI adapter itself. I always use this hardware checklist and perform these steps after I add or change any components within my system, because I almost always have to temporarily move or detach cables.

The General Checklist — Software

Now follow these steps to check your system environment and software.

1. First, drop to DOS (or a DOS box) and check your remaining free disk space with the DIR command. Although the amount of temporary hard drive space required differs for each disc you record, I would never use a drive for temporary files that has less than 50 megabytes of free space remaining — and remember, no compressed drives, please! Running out of hard drive space for temporary files and disc images is a leading cause of errors.

2. Next, check for free memory and system resources under Windows. If you're using Windows 95, you can check on this from the System Properties dialog; right-click the My Computer icon and select Properties from the menu, and then click the Performance tab to display the information shown in Figure 11-2. This tab displays both the total system memory and the percentage of free system resources. From Windows 3.1, pull down the Help menu in the Program Manager and select About Program Manager . . . to display the same information. Your computer is not going to be able to successfully record discs if it's "bogged down" with other applications, so make sure that you've disabled any background programs as discussed in Chapter 8.

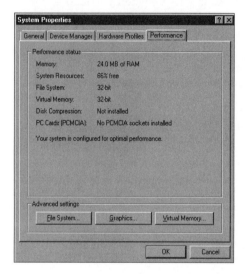

Figure 11-2: The Performance panel of the My Computer Properties dialog displays your total system memory and the percentage of free resources.

3. If you're running Windows 95, the next step is to check for a device conflict; this is a common occurrence if you've added a new piece of hardware. Right-click the My Computer icon and select Properties from the menu, and then click the Device Manager tab. Double-click the CDROM device entry, highlight the name of your recorder, and click the Properties button. If everything is set correctly, Windows 95 tells you that the device is working properly. You can perform the same check on your SCSI adapter card.

4. Our next step is to check on the software drivers required by your CD recorder and your SCSI card. Have you recently upgraded either of these driver sets? If so, re-install the latest upgrade — if not, re-install the drivers from the discs included with your SCSI card and recorder. If your drivers have been altered (or even erased!) by the installation of another application, this should restore your recorder to working condition.

5. Does your recording software immediately return an error when you launch it, or does your computer lock up soon after you run it? If the problem is this noticeable and severe, it's possible that someone has inadvertently erased some of the files required by the program. If so, you should uninstall your

recording software and re-install it. Another possibility, although slim, is the infection of your PC by a computer virus. If you don't already have a good virus detection program, I recommend you visit the McAfee web site (`www.mcafee.com`) or support bulletin board system (408-988-4004) and download the latest version of Viruscan for your system.

6. Finally, consider any settings you might recently have changed within Windows — for example, the Virtual Memory settings. Although a small change to the Windows 95 Registry or the Windows 3.1 SYSTEM.INI and WIN.INI files might seem inconsequential, the calls made to technical support departments around the world say different! This is where a configuration tracking program or a commercial uninstall program can come in handy, but you can always restore your system from a backup if your drive was functioning well at the time you made that backup.

Second Level Troubleshooting

OK, so you've performed both the software and hardware general checklists, and nothing that's obviously wrong has surfaced. At this point, we turn to the second level of our troubleshooting procedure: a logical method that will help you narrow the problem, which may help your diagnosis. Follow these steps:

1. We start with your CD recorder. Will it play audio discs without trouble? Can you successfully record using different recording software? Can you run all tests within the Easy CD Creator System Tester successfully? If your drive came with a diagnostic program, run it and check the operation of your recorder — did your drive check out OK? Do not depend on error messages to indicate whether your drive is causing the trouble. Many errors returned by your software may mention the recorder or even sound like they're pointing to your recorder, but they're actually caused by something else. If your drive passes these tests, it's likely that it's working properly; if not, contact the manufacturer's technical support department and seek their help.

2. If your drive passed with a clean bill of health, follow the "chain of command" to your recording software. Is it exhibiting problems with specific menu commands or complaining of low system resources? The acid test for most software (including Easy CD Creator) is the recording process itself, and, of course, you want to avoid this — however, you *can* attempt to record a disc image to your hard drive! If your software successfully writes a disc image, the problem is likely not with the program. Another good test is to run another CD recording program; even if it's only a demonstration version, it should still exhibit errors if your problem lies outside the software.

THE CLASSIC ERROR CODE

If there could ever be such a thing as an Oscar award for "Best CD Recording Error," the winner would most certainly be that archenemy of all recorders, *Buffer Under Run (Sense Code 0xAD)*. I know we've talked about it several times before in this book, but it bears repeating in this instance for this reason: If you receive this error code during successive recording sessions, you probably don't need to tear your system apart or follow our troubleshooting checklist to fix it unless it continues to occur over many sessions. That's because this error is usually due to a number of things in combination: the speed of your hard drive and whether it's fragmented, the size and number of the files you're recording, the location of the temporary and source files, older device drivers, incompatible blank media, and many other considerations. In most cases, you can kiss the buffer underrun errors goodbye if you rerun the System Tester and set the read and write buffer sizes within your recording software to the largest size possible. Also, if a particular layout proves too troublesome, you can drop your recording speed or record a disc image first.

3. If you've reached this point, we can assume that your recorder and your software have both checked out; it's time to check your SCSI adapter and the other SCSI devices in your PC. An incorrect SCSI configuration can result in particularly nasty and intermittent errors. It's possible, for example, to doom a recording to failure by simply switching source or temporary file locations between an IDE hard drive and an improperly connected SCSI hard drive. One moment a layout records perfectly, and the next your CD recorder aborts as soon as it begins a simulated recording! If you have a SCSI manager or benchmark utility, run it and check to insure that each device has a unique ID, and that no errors are reported in termination. If a SCSI device doesn't appear in the list and it should, then it's likely that your termination or cabling are incorrect. As an example, Figure 11-3 illustrates the excellent SCSI Explorer program from Adaptec that's included in their EZ-SCSI 4.0 utility set. Note that it displays the SCSI ID number for each device on my SCSI chain.

Do you have two SCSI adapters in your PC? If so, you might be experiencing compatibility or configuration problems. It is certainly possible to use more than one SCSI card in the same machine, but if you consistently have problems recording from a SCSI hard drive or removable drive on the second card, it could be a clue. If the problems persist, try removing the second adapter and attaching the orphan SCSI devices to the same card as your CD recorder. Again, don't forget to modify your termination and device IDs as necessary!

That concludes our quick-and-dirty troubleshooting method! If you find no obvious problem and everything checks out, it is time to visit your local PC repair shop and ask a technician to diagnose your computer, or call the technical support number for the manufacturer of your recorder. If you visit a local shop, make sure that you bring the documentation and all software for both your recorder and your SCSI adapter. If you call the manufacturer's technical support line, you should have the serial number and model number of your recorder or adapter card handy, as well as the version numbers of the software and drivers you're using. Whenever possible I call while sitting at my computer, because I may be asked to run the program while on the telephone. Other resources for troubleshooting tips include the technical support area on the manufacturer's web site and the CD recording newsgroups I mentioned earlier.

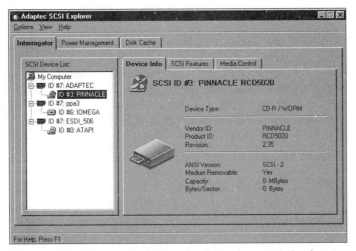

Figure 11-3: It's easy to display the drive characteristics for my CD recorder with Adaptec's SCSI Explorer.

Summary

In this chapter, you learned:

✦ how to display additional information about error messages you receive while recording;

✦ the different categories of error messages you can receive within CD Creator;

✦ the general and specific troubleshooting methods for tracking down the source of recording errors.

In Chapter 12, I introduce you to Easy-CD Pro 95, another product in the Adaptec line of CD-ROM mastering software!

Using Easy-CD Pro 95

Easy-CD Pro is famous for its ease-of-use and simple menu structure. It's a "no-nonsense" program that creates all the formats we've discussed, with the exception of Video CDs and Photo CDs. Easy-CD Pro is a favorite of recorder manufacturers and is often bundled with recording kits.

In this chapter, we discuss version 2.0 of the program, which offers a number of significant improvements over version 1, including a Wizard system and jewel case printing.

The Easy-CD Pro Wizard

As with Easy CD Creator, I tend to use the Wizard for most of my recording with Easy-CD Pro. The Wizard appears as soon as you click the Easy-CD Wizard button on the welcome screen shown in Figure 12-1. To move to the next step of a process within the Wizard, click the Next> button; you can usually move to the previous step by clicking the <Back button. For example, click Next> to advance to the next screen, which is shown in Figure 12-2.

The Wizard can create standard single-session audio and data CD-ROMs. We follow the procedures for creating both types of CD-ROMs.

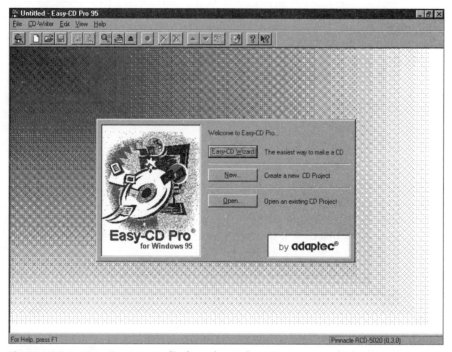

Figure 12-1: Easy-CD Pro 95 displays the welcome screen each time you launch it.

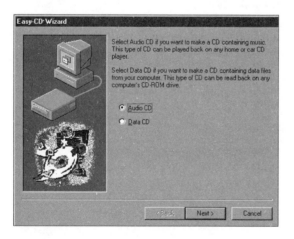

Figure 12-2: From this Wizard screen, you can select whether to create a data or audio disc.

Creating a Data CD-ROM

1. To record a data disc, click *Data CD* and click Next> to move to the next screen.

2. The Wizard displays the Selection screen, shown in Figure 12-3, where you choose which files to add to your disc. Because the Easy-CD Wizard does not allow you to create new directories, it places the directories and files you add in the root directory of your new disc. As you add items, the program displays the total number of files, the number of directories, and the total space used by the items you've already added. There are two methods for selecting files:

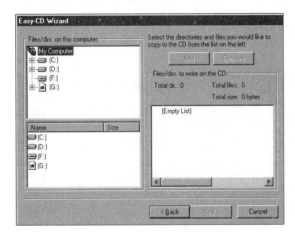

Figure 12-3: You add data items to your project from the Easy-CD Wizard Selection screen.

✦ Within the Selection screen, highlight the files or directories you'd like to select and click the Add button. You'll see the data items appear in the right column. To select contiguous items, hold down the Shift key while you click them; to select noncontiguous files, hold down the Ctrl key while you click them.

✦ If you're a fan of drag and drop, you can also copy files and entire directories to your layout from the Windows Explorer. Simply open an Explorer window, select and drag the items you want to the Selection screen, and release the mouse button. The Easy-CD Wizard takes a few seconds to add your data to the CD project, and then updates the project status data to indicate how much total space is used.

Warning Copying a directory also copies all of its contents and subdirectories. You can't double-click a folder icon to display its contents, so you can't remove individual items; instead, you should exclude them on the File Names pane within the project window.

You can also remove files and directories from the Selection screen — note that you're only removing entries from your layout, not deleting the actual directories or files themselves. To remove a file from the root directory, highlight the filename in the right column and click Remove. To remove a directory and all the files it contains, highlight the directory entry and click Remove.

Once you're done adding all your data files, click Next> to continue to the next screen.

3. The Wizard displays the Test screen shown in Figure 12-4, where you determine whether Easy-CD Pro performs a simulated recording to test the project and your equipment. Since the recorder's laser write head will be set to a lower power level, this will not actually write any data to the disc — if the test fails, no damage is done! I suggest that you perform the test for your first several recordings, and that you run the test whenever you make significant changes to your system hardware, software, or configuration settings. Choose the desired option and click Next> to continue to the next screen.

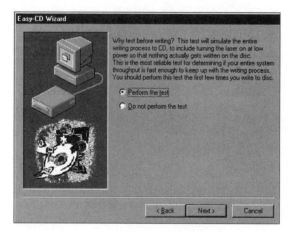

Figure 12-4: With Easy-CD Pro 95, you can choose to run a simulated test recording before you actually create the disc.

4. On the final Wizard screen, shown in Figure 12-5, you can save your project or begin the recording process. You have three choices: You can elect to create the disc now without saving your project file (which begins the recording process), create the disc now and save the project file to your hard drive (you can specify a full path or click the Browse button), or make changes to the CD project (which closes the Easy-CD Wizard and returns you to the menu system, where you can make changes to the project). If you elect to save your project file, Easy-CD automatically adds the extension .ECD to the project name.

5. Click Finish to exit the Wizard and perform the actions you specified.

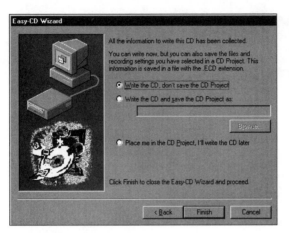

Figure 12-5: From this Easy-CD Wizard screen, you can specify whether to save the project file before creating the disc.

Creating an Audio CD

1. To record an audio disc, click *Audio CD* on the first Wizard screen and click Next> to move to the next screen.

2. The Wizard displays the Track Selection screen, shown in Figure 12-6, where you pick the audio tracks to add to your disc. You can select tracks from existing audio CDs and WAV format sound files. As you add tracks, the program displays the total playing time available on the disc and the playing time currently used by your project. There are two methods for selecting files:

   ✦ Click Add Wave . . . to add a WAV file as an audio track. The Wizard displays a standard Windows File Open dialog, allowing you to navigate through your system and select the desired file.

   ✦ Click CD Deck . . . to display the Easy-CD Deck shown in Figure 12-7, where you can play audio CDs. If your audio disc is already cataloged, the Easy-CD Deck automatically recognizes it. If the audio disc is not already cataloged, you can add the Artist, Title, and Track information to your catalog if you load a new disc. To add a specific track to your audio CD project, select the desired track from the *Track:* drop-down list box and click the Add Track button. You can also read the track directly to your hard drive as a WAV file by clicking the Read Track to Hard Disk . . . button. The Wizard displays a standard Windows Save As dialog, so you can specify the location for the file.

   Once you've added all of the tracks for this project, click Next> to continue.

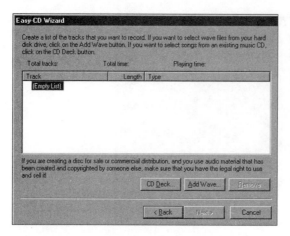

Figure 12-6: From this Easy-CD Wizard screen, you can add audio tracks from audio CDs or WAV files on your hard drive.

Figure 12-7: The convenient Easy-CD Deck allows you to load and play different audio CDs to locate the tracks for your project.

3. The Wizard displays the Close Session screen shown in Figure 12-8. Here you must specify whether Easy-CD Pro is to close the session after the recording is complete. Since your audio CD player cannot play the disc until the session is closed, you should leave the session open only if you're planning on adding a few more tracks. Even if you don't close the session, however, you can still listen to the disc in a computer CD-ROM drive. Choose the desired option and click Next> to continue to the next screen.

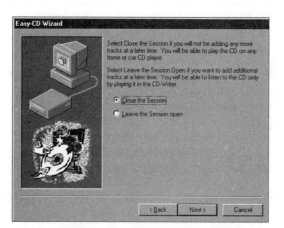

Figure 12-8: In most cases, you'll want to close the session on your audio CD so that you can listen to it using any standard audio disc player.

4. The final screen in the audio portion of the Easy-CD Wizard is identical to the last screen of the data portion. You have three choices: You can elect to create the disc now without saving your project file (which begins the recording process), create the disc now and save the project file to your hard drive (you can specify a full path or click the Browse button), or make changes to the CD project (which closes the Easy-CD Wizard and returns you to the menu system, where you can make changes to the project). If you elect to save your project file, Easy-CD automatically adds the extension .ECD to the project name.

5. Click Finish to exit the Wizard and perform the actions you specified.

Creating and Loading Projects

Easy-CD Pro 95 displays its welcome screen each time you run it, or when you select New from the File menu. If you click the New . . . button on the welcome screen to create a new CD project, you can specify which type of CD-ROM you would like to record from the dialog shown in Figure 12-9. This is the starting point for the more advanced recording methods and formats we've discussed. For example, you'd click New . . . to create a mixed-mode disc, add a session to a multisession disc, create a disc copy using another SCSI CD-ROM device, create a disc image, or create a CD-EXTRA disc.

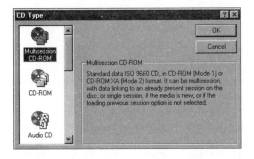

Figure 12-9: From this dialog you can select which type of disc you'd like to create with your new project.

If you click the Load . . . button, you can load a project file that you saved to disk in an earlier session. Easy-CD Pro displays a standard Windows File Open dialog, and you can browse for the .ECD file throughout your system.

After you select which type of disc you'd like to create, you'll get a new, blank project window like the one in Figure 12-10. This project is the template for a complete disc, including all data items and audio tracks.

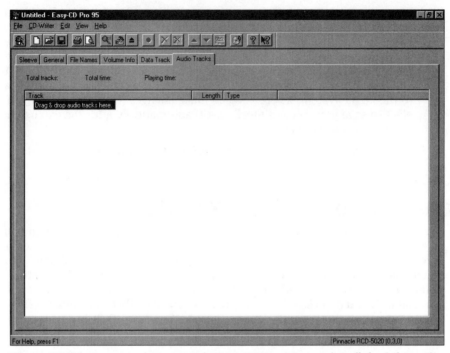

Figure 12-10: A new project screen in Easy-CD Pro 95 contains all the information needed to create a disc or a disc image.

Below the menu system is the familiar Toolbar; to display the function of a button, move your mouse cursor over the button and leave it motionless for a few seconds. The status line at the bottom of the screen will display help for each menu command and Toolbar button.

The rest of the project window is taken up by a number of panels, each of which is displayed when you click the corresponding tab. The number of panels varies, depending on what type of disc you select; for example, a mixed-mode disc project will have panes for both Data Tracks and Audio Tracks. These tabs are:

✦ **Sleeve.** You can create jewel case inserts from this pane. We discuss how to use these controls later in a separate section.

✦ **General.** The General tab contains a number of configuration settings that are saved from disc to disc, as shown in Figure 12-11. At the top right, you see the type of disc created with this project. In the *Writing Parameters* group, you can select the directory for temporary files in the *Temporary directory:* field; unless you change it, this is set to the default directory used by Windows 95 for temporary files (typically \WINDOWS\TEMP). You can write a disc image instead of recording directly to a blank disc by enabling the *Write real ISO image only to:* field — click the ISO File button to specify a filename and location. The next field, *Writing speed:*, determines the recording speed for this disc. If you've changed source drives, you can test the transfer rate for your new source drive by clicking the Speed Test . . . button. Also, you can run a simulated recording test before you actually record the disc by enabling the *Test before writing* checkbox. If the test is successful, you can select whether Easy-CD Pro 95 should start recording automatically or delay for a predetermined time in the drop-down list box. If the test is not successful, the program attempts to record at the next slowest speed. In the *CD Format* group, you should specify the session type in the drop-down list box. You can also indicate whether the disc should be closed (or write-protected) after recording with the *Close disc* checkbox; all sessions on the disc must be closed before you can close the entire disc. Finally, enable the *Disc at once* checkbox to specify that Easy-CD Pro 95 should use disc-at-once recording. If this checkbox is disabled, the program will use track-at-once recording. Easy-CD supports disc-at-once only for audio discs, and it requires that all of your tracks come from the hard drive. You can't record in disc-at-once mode if you combine tracks from a disc and WAV files on your hard drive.

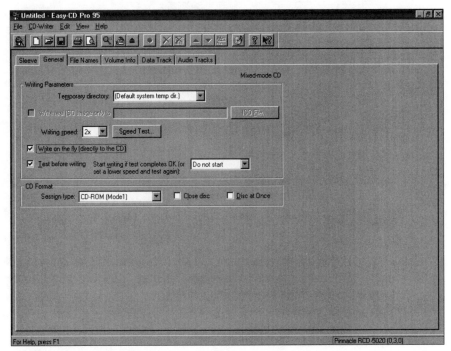

Figure 12-11: The General tab of the project window allows you to set a number of important recording options for this disc.

✦ **File Names.** From the File Names tab shown in Figure 12-12, you can select a naming convention and exclude one or more files from being recorded. Under the *Data Structure* group, you can pick from one of four convention options: strict 8.3 ISO 9660 filenames, standard DOS 8.3 filenames, Joliet filenames (including both 8.3 and long filenames up to 64 characters, with Unicode character support) or Romeo (long filenames of up to 128 characters that can be read only under Windows 95). Under the *Files to Exclude* group, you can specify directories, individual filenames, and DOS wildcard templates for files that should not be included in the finished disc. This feature comes in handy if you've added a folder to your project from the Windows Explorer, but there are two or three files within that folder that shouldn't be copied. Each exclusion entry should appear on a line by itself, so press Ctrl-Enter after each entry to start a new line. Each exclusion line can include full or partial paths, and you can specify a particular file by prefacing it with the full pathname.

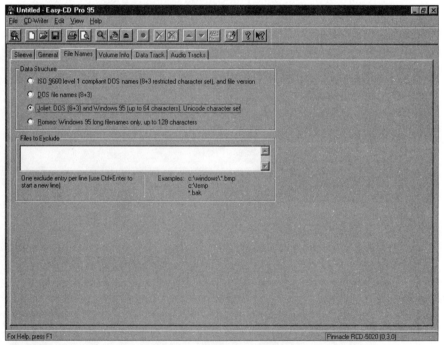

Figure 12-12: The File Names tab allows you to select a particular filename convention or to exclude files or directories from your recording.

✦ **Volume Info.** As shown in Figure 12-13, this tab allows you to specify a number of identifying fields that some applications use. All of these fields are optional, and you don't need to complete them unless you're creating a disc that requires this special information. Under the <u>V</u>olume names group, the most important field is the Volume name label; DOS recognizes a maximum of 11 characters, which you can use to identify the disc; Easy-CD Pro adds a random volume name by default. For compatibility I do not use spaces. You can also specify a System name and Volume Set name for multivolume sets that span more than one disc. The fields in the Information file <u>n</u>ames on disc group specify the names of the Copyright, Abstract, and Bibliography files. These filenames must be added to the root directory of the project manually. The fields in the C<u>o</u>pyright Identifiers group specify the names of the Publisher, Preparer, and Application, such as "PUBLISH.TXT." You must create these files and add them to the root directory of the project manually. Finally, the four values you enter in the <u>D</u>ates group specify the Creation, Modification, Expiration, and Effective dates for this disc.

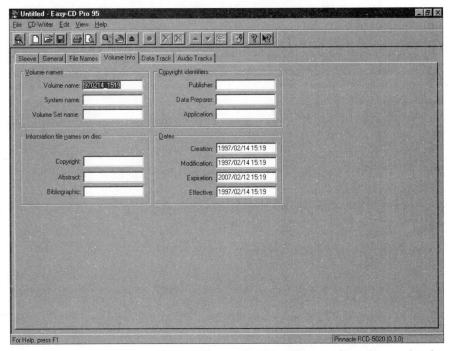

Figure 12-13: You can specify a number of disc identifiers on the Volume Info tab.

✦ **Data Track.** Easy-CD Pro displays all of the files and directories added to your project on this tab, as shown in Figure 12-14. Its size, type, last modification date, and its destination path follow each data item on the finished disc. At the top of the tab, you'll see the total number of data items and the space they'll occupy on the finished disc. You also use this display to manually add data items to your project; we cover this procedure in the next section. Note that you will not have a Data Track tab in your project if you're creating an audio disc.

✦ **Audio Tracks.** Easy-CD Pro displays all of the audio tracks you've added to your project on this tab, as shown in Figure 12-15; each track entry is followed by its length and type. At the top, the total number of tracks, the total time, and the playing time for the audio portion of your project are listed. You also use this display to manually add audio tracks to your project; we'll cover this procedure in the next section. Note that you will not have an Audio Tracks tab in your project if you're creating a CD that contains only computer data.

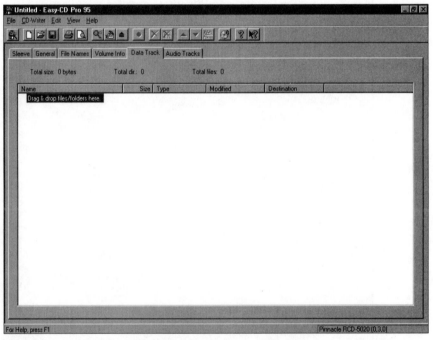

Figure 12-14: The Data Track tab allows you to add data items manually to your project.

Easy-CD Pro 95 automatically sets the proper configuration options for the type of disc you selected from the New . . . dialog, so you need only add data items and audio tracks, and click the Record Toolbar button (which looks like the red dot on an audio cassette deck record button).

To save a project to disk for later recording, select Save from the File menu. Easy-CD Pro displays a standard Windows File Save dialog. Any sleeve design you've worked on for the current project is saved as well.

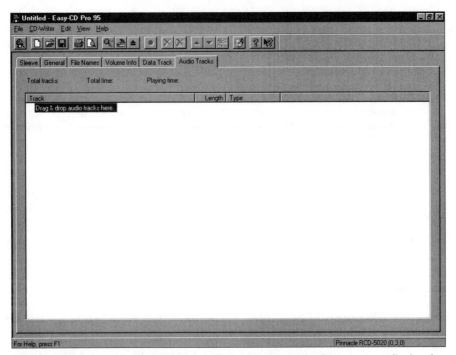

Figure 12-15: If you're creating an audio or mixed-mode disc, you can display the audio content of your project using the Audio Tracks tab.

Adding Items to a Project

Easy-CD Pro 95 has been known for years now as a "drag and drop" program, first using File Manager and now using Windows Explorer. In fact, it's the only method available for manually adding data items to your project!

Adding Data Items

To add one or more directories or files to the root directory of your new CD-ROM, follow these steps:

1. Click the Data Track tab.

2. Open an Explorer window and click the desired data item to select it. You can use the Shift and Ctrl keys to select multiple files in the standard Windows fashion.

3. Drag the files or directories over to the Data Track window and release the mouse button.

Tip If you add two directories with the same name to the data track of your CD-ROM from two different sources, Easy-CD Pro 95 will merge the contents of both directories.

Adding Audio Tracks

There are two methods of adding audio tracks to your project. First, you can use drag and drop to add WAV format sound files stored on your hard drive. Follow these steps:

1. Click the Audio Tracks tab.

2. Open an Explorer window and click the desired sound file to select it. You can use the Shift and Ctrl keys to select multiple WAV files in the standard Windows fashion.

3. Drag the files over to the Audio Tracks window and release the mouse button.

You can also add tracks using the CD Deck. Follow these steps:

1. Click the CD Deck button on the Toolbar; it looks like a compact disc with a musical note. Easy-CD Pro displays the CD Deck.

2. Load your source disc and select the correct letter for that drive.

3. If your audio disc is already cataloged, the Easy-CD Deck automatically recognizes it; otherwise, add the Artist, Title, and Track information to your catalog.

4. Select the desired track from the *Track:* drop-down list box and click the Add Track button.

Recording Your Project

Once you're ready to record your project, you can select the Write! item from the CD-Writer menu to begin the process, or you can click the Record button on the Toolbar. If you've enabled the *Test before writing* checkbox in the General tab of your project window, Easy-CD Pro 95 runs a simulated recording first.

Rearranging and Reparenting Data Items

When you add a file or folder to a project within Easy-CD Pro 95, it's inserted before the data item you've highlighted. Usually, this insertion point falls at the end of the list, so each item you add appears at the end of the project list. However, you can use the Up and Down Arrow buttons on the ToolBar to move the highlighted data or audio item up or down in the recording sequence.

Note, however, that rearranging items in the recording sequence does not affect their destination path on the disc. Files and directories are saved to your new CD-ROM using the path displayed in the *Name:* field in the Data Track tab. Unless you edit the path, it's the same as the source drive. If you'd like to change the path for one or more data items on the finished disc, you must use *reparenting*.

Follow these steps:

1. Click the Data Tracks tab.

2. Select those files and folders that you'd like to move to a different directory using the Shift and Ctrl keys.

3. Select Reparenting from the Edit menu. Easy-CD Pro displays the dialog shown in Figure 12-16.

4. Type the new destination path. If you leave the edit field blank or type a single backslash character ("\"), the program places the items in the root directory of your new disc.

Figure 12-16: From this dialog, you can specify a new path for data items added to your project.

Verifying Your Recorded Discs

If you've created a CD from an ISO 9660 disc image saved on your hard drive, Easy-CD Pro 95 allows you to verify the contents of your completed disc to make sure that it exactly matches the source disc image. This is a valuable feature for those of us who create multiple copies of a disc image stored on a hard drive. We discussed how you create disc images in Chapter 10.

Follow these steps:

1. Load the disc to be verified into your recorder.

2. Select the Disc Info and Tools item from the CD-Writer menu, or click the Tools button on the Toolbar — it looks like a hammer in front of a document.

3. Click the Disc Info and Tools tab to display the dialog shown in Figure 12-17. If you've been working with other discs during this recording session, you may need to click the Refresh button to force your recorder to read the disc you just loaded.

4. Highlight the track entry that you want verified and click the Compare Track button. Easy-CD Pro displays the Compare Track dialog, where you can select a disc image on your hard drive to compare with the disc and verify the track.

5. Click Browse . . . to navigate through your system and select the source disc image. Once you've found it, Easy-CD Pro displays the characteristics of both the track on the disc you've loaded and the disc image file, including the content, volume label, and size. If you've selected the correct track on the disc and the correct disc image, these characteristics should match. If the two sets of characteristics don't match, there's no reason to continue with the comparison, since they obviously are not the same!

To verify the data, click the Compare button. A progress bar appears as the data is compared. Easy-CD Pro 95 displays a success or failure message once the comparison is complete. If the verification failed, the program will display the sector number where the data differed.

Figure 12-17: The Disc Info and Tools dialog displays information about the currently loaded disc and provides a number of utility functions.

Selecting a Recorder

If you're fortunate enough to have more than one CD-ROM recorder installed in your computer, you can specify a recorder using the Select CD-Writer . . . item from the CD-Writer menu. Alternately, you can click the Select CD-Writer button on the Toolbar; it shows a magnifying glass studying the word SCSI. Easy-CD Pro 95 uses the device you select as the recorder until you use this menu command again to select another recorder.

Displaying a File History

As you learned earlier, you can effectively "delete" files from an incremental multisession disc; however, Easy-CD Pro 95 includes a neat feature that allows you to access previous versions of a specific file stored on older sessions!

Follow these steps:

1. Load the disc containing the files into your recorder.

2. Select the CD File History item from the CD-Writer menu. Easy-CD Pro 95 displays a standard File Open dialog, allowing you to navigate through your system. Locate and select the file you wish to find.

3. Easy-CD Pro 95 will search the disc and locate all occurrences of the file you specified that have the same path. Each match is displayed, along with its time and date stamp and the session number on the disc where the file was found.

   You can choose to copy one of the files found in the scan; highlight the desired file and click Copy to display a standard Windows Save As dialog.

Closing an Open Session

It is possible to leave an audio session open with Easy-CD Pro, but you should close the session before attempting to read the disc in a standard CD-ROM drive or an audio CD player. If you don't close the session, only your CD recorder can correctly read the disc, because the session's contents are not yet included in the disc's Table of Contents. This is different from closing a disc, which write-protects the disc and prevents you from recording additional data to it later.

Follow these steps to close a session:

1. Load the disc with the open session into your CD-ROM recorder.

2. Select the Disc Info and Tools item from the CD-Writer menu.

3. Click the Disc Info and Tools tab.

4. Click the Close Session button.

To close a disc and write-protect it, the final session must be closed.

Reading Data and Audio Tracks

You can create an ISO 9660 disc image file on your hard drive by reading the contents of a data track from a source CD-ROM; or, on the audio side, you can copy an audio track from an audio disc to a WAV format file on your hard drive. Follow these steps to read a track:

1. Load the source disc into your CD-ROM recorder.

2. Select the Disc Info and Tools item from the CD-Writer menu.

3. Click the Disc Info and Tools tab. If you've been working with other discs during this recording session, it may be necessary to click the Refresh button to force your recorder to read the disc you just loaded.

4. Highlight the track entry that you want to read and click the Read Track button.

Note that disc image files are saved to your hard drive with the extension .ISO.

Creating Jewel Case Inserts

The latest version of Easy-CD Pro 95 allows you to create colorful jewel case inserts, with support for fonts, graphics, and predesigned layout styles that you can choose from, including background colors and tiled designs! Let's create an insert, and you'll see how these elements work together. If you like, substitute your own text and graphics as you follow along.

1. From the project window, click the Sleeve tab to display the window shown in Figure 12-18.

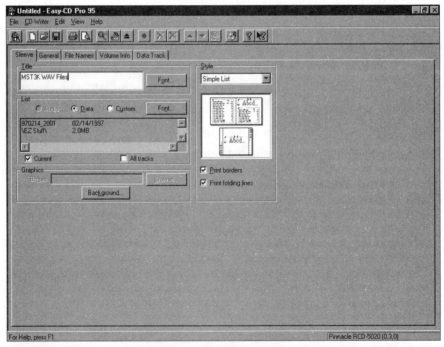

Figure 12-18: The Sleeve tab of the Easy-CD Pro 95 project window, where you can create professional-looking front and back sleeves for your jewel cases.

2. First, let's select our font for the title and the track listing. Click the Font . . . button to display a standard Font Selection dialog. For our example, pick Cartoon Hollow and set it to bold and italic at 20 points.

3. Next, enter the title for your CD in the _Title:_ field. Remember, if your title is too long in the current font size, you can specify a smaller font size. It's easy to check length by using the Print Preview function, which I describe shortly. For our example, let's use "The Gargoyles — Rockin' at Notre Dame."

4. Now we should configure our track listing. Easy-CD Pro allows you to select from three types of listings: data, audio, and custom. Your choices for the type of listing depend on the type of disc you're recording with this project. If you create an audio listing, you can optionally include the artist name and source CD title for each track. If you create a data listing, you can choose to list only the files and directories in the current session, or you can list all data items on all sessions. Finally, the custom listing opens a text editing window, and you can type whatever you wish. For our example, let's choose the audio list.

5. How about a bitmap graphic? The size and position of the image depends upon the style we choose in the next step, but you can choose the bitmap by clicking the Browse . . . button to navigate through your system and select an image.

6. For a really nice touch, add a background! If you have a color printer, this is a great option; you can specify a solid color background from a Windows Color Selection dialog. Even if you're limited to black and white, a tiled bitmap background can look very professional; click the Browse . . . button to select a tile image, just as you would for your Windows background. I recommend a simple, light design for a tiled background, since it should never interfere with the text and graphics in the foreground.

7. Finally, select a layout style. Although it's optional to print borders and folding lines, I always do — it makes it much easier to cut and fold your finished sleeves! If you need to see the effect of a particular style, select Print Preview from the File menu, as shown in Figure 12-19.

Ready to print your sleeve? Then select the Print item from the File menu, or click the Print button on the Toolbar.

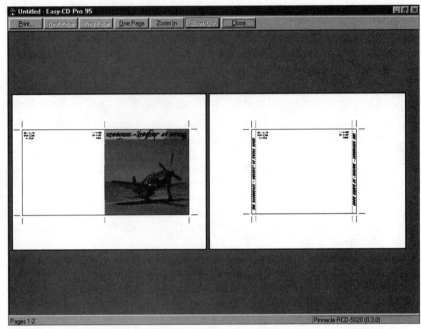

Figure 12-19: Why waste paper? If you'd like to see how your sleeve set will look, use the Print Preview command.

Summary

In this chapter, we discussed the latest version of Adaptec's Easy-CD Pro 95 recording software. You learned:

✦ how to use the Easy-CD Wizard to create standard audio and data CD-ROMs;

✦ how to manually add audio tracks and data items to a project;

✦ how to verify your finished discs to check whether they match an ISO 9660 disc image source file;

✦ how to create an attractive sleeve design for the front and back cover of the jewel case.

Coming up in Chapter 13, we take a detailed look at Easy-CD Pro 95's partner in the Adaptec line of CD-ROM recording software – CD Creator 2.0!

✦   ✦   ✦

Using CD Creator

CD Creator works under both Windows 95 and Windows 3.1, so it's a natural choice for those who want to record CDs in a 16-bit environment. In this chapter, we discuss all of the standard features in version 2 of CD Creator, including the CD Creator Disc Wizard. You also learn how to manually create CD layouts and record data, audio, and mixed-mode discs.

Throughout this chapter, we create and modify example layouts. If you have files ready to archive, you may wish to follow the book's examples by creating a layout with those files instead of using our example files. Later in the chapter, you can use your layout and actually record your first disc as I record our example disc.

Our discussion of CD Creator focuses on version 2 for Windows 95 (the most popular configuration). Almost all of the functions we discuss, however, are available in version 1 for Windows 3.1.

The CD Creator Disc Wizard

Like the Easy CD Creator Wizard, the CD Creator Disc Wizard leads you through the most common recording functions. By default, the CD Creator Disc Wizard, shown in Figure 13-1, appears as soon as you run CD Creator. To move to the next step of a process within the Disc Wizard, click the Next> button; you can usually return to the previous step by clicking the <Back button. For example, click Next> now to advance to the next screen, shown in Figure 13-2, where you select the task you want Disc Wizard to perform.

Figure 13-1: The CD Creator Disc Wizard provides an easy way to set up a recording session in CD Creator 2.

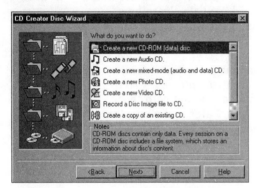

Figure 13-2: Each entry in this list is a job that the CD Creator Disc Wizard can help you perform.

In this section, we follow the CD Creator Disc Wizard through the three most common tasks performed in CD Creator: creating a data CD-ROM, creating an audio disc, and creating a mixed/multimedia disc. I explain each step in detail, including what the Disc Wizard is doing behind the scenes.

Creating a Data CD-ROM

1. From the list of CD Creator Disc Wizard tasks, click *Create a new CD-ROM (data) disc* and click Next> to move to the next screen.

2. The Disc Wizard displays the screen shown in Figure 13-3, where you specify which file system to use on your new CD-ROM. You have two choices: the ISO 9660 system, which offers the most compatibility between different operating systems, and the Microsoft Joliet system, which allows you to use long filenames and directory names but is readable only by computers running Windows 95 or Windows NT 4.0. Unless you have a need for long filenames, stick with the ISO 9660 default, which allows your new disc to be read on as many computers as possible, and click Next> to move to the next screen.

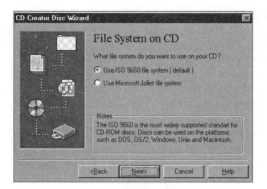

Figure 13-3: Unless you're specifically creating a disc only for Windows 95 or Windows NT 4.0, do not use the Joliet file system.

3. Next, the Disc Wizard asks you to select a filename convention to use on each file recorded on your new disc, as shown in Figure 13-4. There are three choices: first is the restrictive ISO 8.3 character filename convention. ISO filenames can contain only alphanumeric characters and the underscore ("_") symbol, and they can only be up to eight characters long with extensions of up to three characters. The ISO convention allows your new disc to be read by any computer that supports the ISO 9660 standard. The second choice, and default convention, is MS-DOS 8.3 character filenames, which allows filenames to include any legal DOS filename character. However, filenames can still only be up to eight characters long with extensions of up to three characters. This is the best choice for discs that only need be readable on DOS and Windows systems. The final filename convention choice, long filenames, is suitable only for computers running Windows 95 and Windows NT. If you're creating a disc for Windows or DOS, leave this setting as it is and click Next> to move to the next screen.

Figure 13-4: This CD Creator Disc Wizard screen allows you to specify a filename convention applicable to all files you add to your disc.

Note CD Creator will alert you if you try to later add files with names that are not supported by the convention you've chosen. However, I recommend you use the MS-DOS 8.3 character option unless you absolutely must have ISO 9660 compatibility. Most of us are creating discs for use on Windows and DOS machines, so this convention should be fine. The prospect of renaming hundreds of files because they have a tilde "~" or an exclamation point "!" character in their filename may make you deathly ill if you try forcing ISO 9660 character filenames on a layout full of DOS or Windows files!

4. On the next screen, Other Disc Properties, the Disc Wizard prompts you for the volume label for your new disc. Since only the first 11 characters are displayable under DOS, I like to keep volume labels fairly short, and you should avoid using spaces; let's enter POSTERS, as in Figure 13-5. There's no need to click the Advanced Properties button, because all of the ISO 9660 defaults are fine for just about any application; just remember that by clicking Advanced Properties you can select Mode 1 recording and specify a different block size, as well as create "bootable" CD-ROMs and alter file dates. We cover these advanced features in more detail later. Click <u>N</u>ext> to advance to the next step.

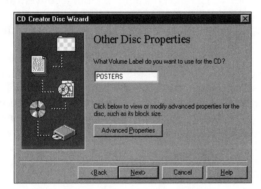

Figure 13-5: For most applications, you'll just enter a volume label for your new disc here, and then move on to the next screen.

5. Now we're cooking! The CD Creator Disc Wizard displays the Adding Data Files screen shown in Figure 13-6. At last, you can select the files you'd like to add to your disc. By default, the directories and files you add are placed in the root directory of your new disc, but you can specify a target directory (or "folder") that already exists in the layout by selecting the Folder option button. If you select the Folder option, click the Browse button next to it (which is marked with three periods) to pick the destination folder in the layout. As you add files and subdirectories, the Disc Wizard's Disc Info bar graph at the bottom of the screen displays how much space remains for more data. There are two methods for selecting files:

   ✦ First, you can simply click the <u>A</u>dd . . . button to display the dialog shown in Figure 13-7, where you can browse and tag files. If you've arranged the files you want to record in separate directories before running the CD Creator Disc Wizard, this is the simplest method. Once you've highlighted the directory or files you want to add to your layout, click <u>A</u>dd Now. Disc Wizard builds your layout for you behind the dialog, adding each file and directory when you press <u>A</u>dd Now. If you use the Add Data Items dialog, don't change the priority of any files right now —

normal priority is fine for most applications. As you can see from Figure 13-7, I've created a simple example layout for a disc that will hold hundreds of movie posters in JPEG format.

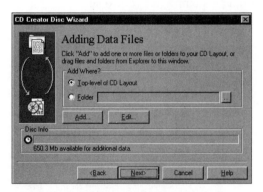

Figure 13-6: From the CD Creator Disc Wizard's Adding Data Files screen, you automatically build a layout for your new disc by selecting files.

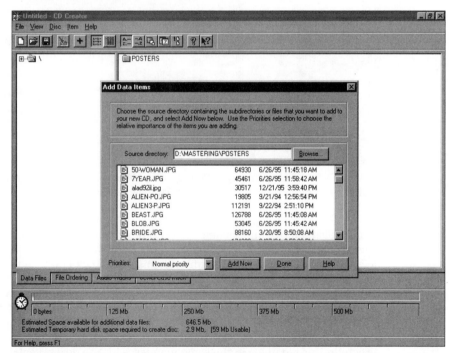

Figure 13-7: If you decide to select files with the <u>A</u>dd button, Disc Wizard displays this dialog. The layout window in the background updates automatically.

✦ If you're a fan of drag and drop, you can also copy files and entire directories to your layout from the Windows Explorer (or the Windows 3.1

File Manager)! Simply open an Explorer window, as in Figure 13-8, drag the files or directories to the Adding Data Files screen, and release the mouse button. The Disc Wizard takes a few seconds to add your data to the CD layout, and then you'll see the Disc Info bar updated to indicate how much space remains empty on your disc.

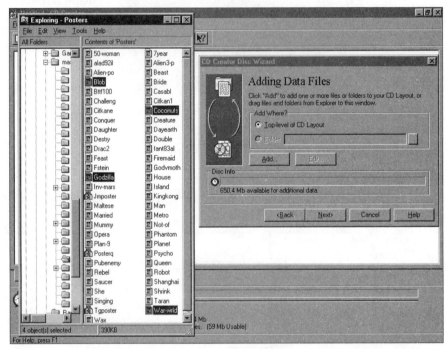

Figure 13-8: It's easy to drag files and entire directories from the Windows Explorer and drop them on the Adding Data Files screen.

You can also remove and rename files and directories from the Adding Data Files screen — note that you're only removing entries from your layout, not deleting the actual directories or files themselves. Click Edit . . . to display the Remove Data Items dialog, which contains a list of all the directories and files that have been added to your layout (Figure 13-9). To remove a directory and all the files it contains, highlight the directory entry and click Remove. To remove an individual file inside a folder, double-click the folder to open it, highlight the file and then click Remove. You can select existing files and directories for renaming in the same manner; with the desired entry highlighted, click Properties to display the Directory Properties (Figure 13-10) or File Properties (Figure 13-11) dialog. Note that you can hide both files and directories, which means they won't show when you display the contents of the completed CD-ROM; they're similar to hidden files on a hard drive. If you're changing the File Properties on an individual file, you can also change its priority. We discuss changing priorities in more detail later. Click OK to save your changes, and click Close to return to the Adding Data Files screen.

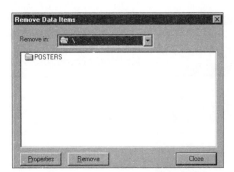

Figure 13-9: You can remove files or directories that you've already added to your layout from the Remove Data Items dialog.

Figure 13-10: If you display the properties on an individual directory from your layout, you can mark it as hidden or rename it.

Figure 13-11: If you display the properties on an individual file from your layout, you can change its priority, mark it as hidden, or rename it.

Once you're done adding all your data files, click Next> to continue to the next screen; the CD Creator Disc Wizard prompts you for confirmation that you've added everything you need to the CD layout. Click Yes to confirm that you've finished adding files.

6. The CD Creator Disc Wizard displays the Ready to Create CD screen shown in Figure 13-12. Here you can make final changes or begin the recording process. You have three choices: you can elect to create the disc now (which launches CD Creator in recording mode), create a disc image (which builds an image of the CD's contents on your hard drive for multiple copies or recording at a later time), or make changes to the CD (which closes the Disc Wizard and returns you to the CD Creator menu system, where you can make

changes to the layout). At this point let's stop; we discuss the rest of the process later. Click Cancel to back out of the process.

Figure 13-12: Here's your last chance to change your disc layout manually before creating a disc or a disc image for later recording.

Creating an Audio Disc

Next, let's use the CD Creator Disc Wizard to create an audio disc with your favorite music! Select New CD Layout . . . from the File menu, and restart the Disc Wizard with a new layout.

1. From the list of CD Creator Disc Wizard tasks, click *Create a new Audio CD* and click <u>N</u>ext> to move to the next screen.

2. The Disc Wizard displays the screen shown in Figure 13-13, where you enter the artist's name and the disc name. The values you enter here will be used when you create a jewel case insert for your new audio CD in Chapter 14.

Figure 13-13: Even if you're creating a compilation audio disc, always enter an artist name and disc name here since you may create a disc jewel case insert later.

3. As you can see, a standard Red Book audio disc requires very little preparation as compared to a data disc! The Disc Wizard displays the Adding Audio Tracks screen shown in Figure 13-14. From here, you select the audio

tracks to add to your disc. As you add tracks, the Disc Wizard's Disc Info bar graph at the bottom of the screen displays how many minutes remain for more music.

Figure 13-14: The Disc Wizard displays the Adding Audio Tracks screen, making it easy to create an audio CD layout.

There are two methods for selecting files:

✦ First, you can simply click the Add . . . button to display the dialog shown in Figure 13-15. From here you can add tracks from existing audio CDs, WAV format sound files stored on your drive, or your music cache. Right now, we'll simply copy files from another audio disc; this is the most common method of adding tracks, and we cover WAV files and the music cache later. Insert an audio CD into your drive to display the song list; if this is a disc you've already added to your music database, the CD Creator Disc Wizard will display the disc title and each track's title. Pick one or more tracks (hold down the Ctrl key to select multiple tracks) and click Add Now to add them to your audio disc layout.

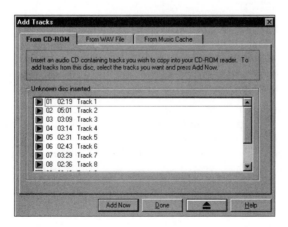

Figure 13-15: If you use the Add . . . button to select files for your audio CD, the Disc Wizard displays this dialog.

Note If the source disc isn't in your music database, the CD Creator Disc Wizard displays the dialog shown in Figure 13-16, and you must enter the artist and disc name. Further, the Disc Wizard prompts for each track name with the dialog in Figure 13-17, and adds those to the database. If you really don't need to worry about creating a jewel box insert or adding these track titles to your music database, check the box labeled *Do not prompt for additional track names* to enable it. You won't see this dialog for each track.

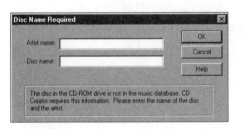

Figure 13-16: The Disc Wizard prompts you for the disc and artist name if it doesn't find the source disc in its music database.

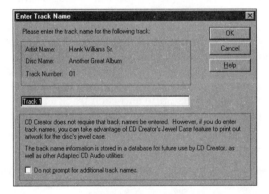

Figure 13-17: Each track name you enter is auto-matically added to the audio CD database, or you can choose not to enter any more track names at this time.

You can see that the CD Creator Disc Wizard is building your layout for you behind the dialog, adding each track when you press Add Now.

✦ Just like with a data CD, you can also drag and drop WAV files stored on your hard drive to your audio CD layout from the Windows Explorer (or the Windows 3.1 File Manager). Open an Explorer window, drag one or more WAV files over to the Adding Audio Tracks screen, and release the mouse button. The Disc Wizard takes a few seconds to add your data to the CD layout, and updates the Disc Info bar to indicate how much recording time remains on your disc.

You can also remove, rename, and reorder audio tracks from the Adding Audio Tracks dialog much as you can change the properties of files and directories in your data CD-ROM layout. Click Edit . . . to display the Edit

Audio CD Layout dialog, which contains a list of all the audio tracks that have been added to your layout (Figure 13-18). To remove a track, highlight the entry and click Remove. You can also change the title of a track or move it to another slot. Highlight the desired entry and click Properties to display the Track Properties dialog (Figure 13-19). To change the title, highlight it in the Track Title field and enter the new title. To move the track to a different slot in the layout, highlight the Track Number field and enter the new slot where the track should appear (all tracks following the inserted track are automatically renumbered). If you're creating a CD-EXTRA format disc, click CD EXTRA Info to enter the text for this track; if you haven't enabled CD-EXTRA support for this disc, this button is disabled. Click OK to save your changes, and click Close to return to the Adding Audio Tracks screen.

Figure 13-18: You can remove tracks from your audio layout from the Edit Audio CD Layout dialog.

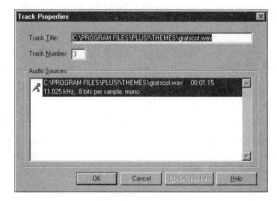

Figure 13-19: The Track Properties dialog allows you to rename or renumber individual tracks on your audio CD layout.

Once all your audio tracks are added, click Next> to continue to the next screen; the Disc Wizard prompts you for confirmation that you've added everything you need to the CD layout. Click Yes to confirm that you've finished adding files.

4. The CD Creator Disc Wizard displays the Ready to Create CD screen shown earlier in Figure 13-12, where you can make final changes or begin the recording process. You have three choices: you can elect to create the disc now (which launches CD Creator in recording mode), create a disc image (which builds an image of the CD's contents on your hard drive for multiple copies or recording at a later time), or make changes to the CD (which closes the Disc Wizard and returns you to the CD Creator menu system, where you can make changes to the layout). At this point let's stop. We discuss the rest of the process later.

Creating a Mixed-Mode CD-ROM

Finally, let's use the CD Creator Disc Wizard to create a mixed-mode disc with both data and audio tracks. Select New CD Layout ... . from the File menu, and restart the Disc Wizard with a new layout.

1. From the list of CD Creator Disc Wizard tasks, click *Create a new mixed-mode (audio and data) CD* and click <u>N</u>ext> to move to the next screen.

2. From this point, creating a mixed-mode disc is exactly like the process for creating a data disc immediately followed by the process for creating an audio disc, so I won't elaborate on each step again. For additional help on each step, follow the section "Creating a Data CD-ROM," and then continue with the section "Creating an Audio Disc."

Creating a CD Layout Manually

Now that you've used the CD Creator Disc Wizard to automate the recording of data, audio, and mixed-mode discs, let's discuss how to create a CD layout manually and record without the Disc Wizard.

Why record manually? Some of the more advanced features of CD Creator are not available within the Disc Wizard; you have to configure them by hand. I find it easiest to use Disc Wizard to prepare my CD layout, then I select the Make changes to the CD option on the last screen and make whatever changes I need to make manually.

Once you've gained experience with recording, you may decide to ignore the CD Creator Disc Wizard completely and create discs exclusively from the menu — there's a configuration item that allows you to bypass the Disc Wizard when you launch CD Creator.

In this section, we recreate the Disc Wizard's steps manually, so you can see where to make these changes in the menu system.

Creating a New Layout

By default, CD Creator always displays the CD Creator Disc Wizard when you select New CD Layout . . . from the File menu, but you can change this. Select the Preferences . . . item on the File menu to display the CD Creator Preferences dialog, as shown in Figure 13-20. Click the General tab and select the option button labeled Create an empty CD layout.

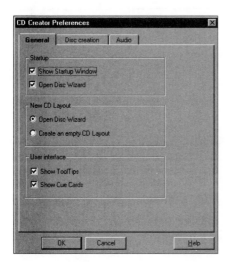

Figure 13-20: The Preferences dialog allows you to make a number of changes in the operation of CD Creator.

Now when you select New CD Layout . . . , you get a new, blank layout window like the one in Figure 13-21. This layout is the template for a complete disc, including all data items, audio tracks, their arrangement on the disc, and even the information to be printed on the jewel case insert. Remember, changes made to the current layout affect only the disc recorded with that layout. Another layout represents another disc, and it may use completely different settings, which were stored as a part of the layout when you saved it to your hard drive.

Below the menu system, you'll see the Toolbar; most Windows applications have a Toolbar these days. The buttons provide the same functionality as most of the common menu items; for example, you can click the New button on the Toolbar (which looks like a document page with a corner turned down) to open a new blank layout. To display the function of a button, move your mouse cursor over the button and leave it motionless for a few seconds. The Toolbar changes to reflect the type of disc; the data Toolbar looks different from the audio Toolbar.

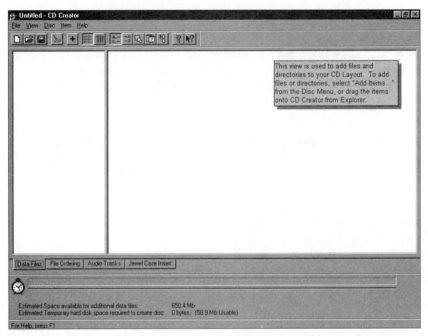

Figure 13-21: If you don't use the CD Creator Disc Wizard, every disc you create starts from a blank layout window like this one.

Loading, Saving, and Printing Layouts

You can also load existing layouts from the File menu. Select the Open CD Layout . . . item on the File menu to display a standard Windows Open File dialog, as shown in Figure 13-22, or click the Open button on the Toolbar, which looks like a folder being opened. By default, any layouts saved with CD Creator 2 have the extension .CL2, and the Open File dialog displays only these files; however, you can view all files regardless of extension by clicking the Files of type: drop-down list box and selecting All Files (*.*). Once you've found the layout file you want to load, double-click it, or highlight it and click the Open button.

Figure 13-22: This File Open dialog allows you to browse your system and locate CD Creator layout files to load.

If you need to work on a layout later or record the layout in the future, you'll need to save it to disk before exiting CD Creator.

If this is the first time you've worked with this layout, select the Save item on the File menu to display a standard Windows Save File dialog, as shown in Figure 13-23, or click the Save button on the Toolbar, which looks like a floppy disk. Enter a name in the File Name field, and click Save. CD Creator 2 automatically adds the extension .CL2 to the filename you entered.

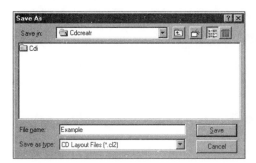

Figure 13-23: This File Save dialog allows you to browse your system and save the current layout in any directory.

If you loaded this layout file from disc, selecting the Save item on the File menu automatically updates the existing file on your disc.

If you want to save an existing layout file under a new name, select the Save As . . . item from the File menu. CD Creator allows you to rename the file before saving it to disk — this is a good way of creating a copy of an existing layout as a starting point for a new layout.

Need a hard copy of an audio disc layout? You can print the layout directly from the Toolbar by clicking the Print button, which looks like a printer, or you can select Print . . . from the File menu. To display a preview image of the printed page before you print it, select Print Preview from the File menu. Layout printing is available only from the Audio Tracks pane within the layout window; you can't print a data layout.

Selecting a File System Manually

Because we're manually performing the steps performed by the CD Creator Disc Wizard, our next step is to specify which file system to use on your new CD-ROM. You can choose between the ISO 9660 system, which offers the most compatibility between different operating systems, and the Microsoft Joliet system, which allows you to use long filenames and directory names but is readable only by computers running Windows 95 or Windows NT 4.0. The default, of course, is ISO 9660, which allows your new disc to be read by as many computers as possible. To change this, click the Disc menu and select Properties to display the dialog shown in Figure 13-24.

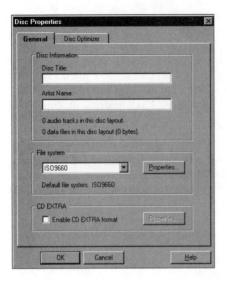

Figure 13-24: Selecting a file system for use on our new disc from the Disc Properties dialog.

To select Joliet, click the File System drop-down list box and click Joliet.

You'll also notice a Properties . . . button next to the list box. It lets you configure certain file system features. Click the button to display the Properties dialog for the file system you've selected; Figure 13-25 shows the ISO Properties dialog. Both the ISO 9660 and the Joliet Properties dialogs are very similar, except that Joliet doesn't support bootable CD-ROMs and doesn't need the file name characteristics section.

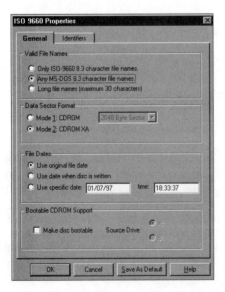

Figure 13-25: The File System Properties dialog allows you to specify a number of items specific to the ISO 9660 or Joliet file system.

The ISO 9660 Properties on the General tab include:

✦ **Valid File Names.** We cover these settings in the next section.

✦ **Data Sector Format.** You can select either Mode 1 (CD-ROM) or Mode 2 (CD-ROM XA). The default is Mode 2, which I recommend for most recordings. If you select Mode 1, you can specify a sector size other than 2048 bytes, but all multisession discs must be Mode 2.

✦ **File Dates**. Here you can specify which date stamp will be applied to the files you're recording. Select *Use original file date* to save files with their current time/date stamp, just as they appear on your hard drive. This is the default, and you'll probably need to refer to file dates from time to time, so I suggest you use it. Select *Use date when disc is written* to change the time/date stamp on all files to the date you recorded the disc. Finally, you can also choose *Use specific date* and enter a date and time for use on all files.

✦ **Bootable CD-ROM support.** This is a very specialized disc that is usable as a "bootable floppy" on some machines. We discuss it later; for now, *do not* check *Make disc bootable!*

The ISO 9660 Properties on the Identifiers tab are optional text fields that can be automatically read by some applications; they are often included on reference CDs. You do not need to complete any of these fields (including the Volume Label) to record a disc.

✦ **Volume Label.** This is the only field on this panel that I use. DOS recognizes a maximum of 11 characters, which you can use to identify the disc. For compatibility I do not use spaces.

✦ **Publisher Name.** This field specifies the name of a text file that exists in the root directory of the disc that identifies the disc's publisher. The filename must begin with an underscore ("_") character, such as _PUBLISH.TXT.

✦ **Prepared By.** This field specifies the name of a text file that exists in the root directory of the disc that identifies the disc's author or preparer. The filename must begin with an underscore ("_") character, such as _PREPARE.TXT.

✦ **Copyright.** This field specifies the name of a text file that exists in the root directory of the disc that contains the disc's copyright information.

✦ **Abstract.** This field specifies the name of a text file that exists in the root directory of the disc that contains the disc's abstract copy; the abstract typically summarizes the contents of the disc as a convenience for research.

✦ **Bibliography.** This field specifies the name of a text file that exists in the root directory of the disc that contains the disc's Bibliography. Like the bibliography for a printed book, this file usually contains a listing of the sources for the material included on the disc.

Note If you use any of the fields on the Identifiers tab except for the Volume Label field, you must create any files you specify with a text editor and manually add them to your disc layout.

To save your changes and exit the dialog, click OK. To save the current disc properties as the default for future layouts, click Save as Default. Click OK again to exit back to the menu system.

Selecting a Filename Convention Manually

The next step in creating a disc manually is to select a filename convention. Once again, click the Disc menu and select Properties, then click the File System Properties . . . button to display the Properties dialog for the file system you've selected. You have three choices under Valid File Names: the ISO 8.3 character filename convention, MS-DOS 8.3 character filenames, or long filenames.

For more information on what these choices involve, see Step 3 in the section "Creating a Data CD-ROM" in this chapter.

Once you've selected the right convention, click OK to save your changes and OK again to return to the menu system.

Adding Data Items Manually

At this point, the CD Creator Disc Wizard would prompt you to add data files or audio tracks to your layout. The type of disc you're creating depends upon which tab you've selected at the bottom of the layout window. For example, if you select the Data Files pane, you're adding data to a CD-ROM. If you select the Audio Tracks pane, you're adding audio to a CD-ROM. Of course, you can have both, creating a mixed-mode (or multimedia) CD-ROM. In this section, we manually add data items to your layout.

Note The left portion of the data layout window is called the directory tree display, and it should be familiar to you if you've used Windows Explorer. If a directory contains subdirectories, a small plus sign ("+") appears next to it — you can click this plus sign to expand the view so that you can see the subdirectories. To collapse the view and hide the subdirectories, click the minus sign ("-") next to the parent directory. You can also expand and collapse the view of the highlighted directory from the Item menu.

There are two methods of manually adding data items to the current layout:

✦ From the Disc menu, select Add Items . . . to display the dialog shown in Figure 13-7, where you can browse and tag files. If you've arranged the files you want to record in separate directories before running CD Creator, this is the simplest method. You can also click the Add Items button on the Toolbar, which looks like a plus sign. Once you've highlighted the directory or files you want to add to your layout, click Add Now to update the layout display with the new items. Don't change the priority of any files right now — normal priority is fine for most applications, and we cover priorities later. When you've finished adding data items, click Done to return to the menu. For example, Figure 13-26 shows a data CD-ROM layout I built with separate directories for Batman images, movie poster images, my morphing projects, pinball sound bites, and my collection of Web graphics. Remember, this disc is for archival purposes only, and not for distribution; if you don't own the copyright on each and every file or audio track you record, don't give the disc to others — you'll be breaking the law!

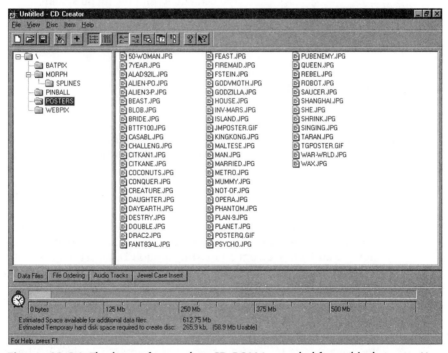

Figure 13-26: The layout from a data CD-ROM I recorded for archival storage. You can see how the files are logically grouped into separate directories.

✦ You can also drag and drop files and entire directories to your layout from the Windows Explorer (or the Windows 3.1 File Manager)! Simply open an Explorer window, as in Figure 13-8, drag the files or directories to the Adding Data Files screen, and release the mouse button.

Either method creates the same layout; the method you use depends on your personal preference. As with the CD Creator Disc Wizard, the layout window displays a bar graph at the bottom of the window to let you know how much space remains empty.

By the way, you can also create a new directory on your disc without selecting it through the Add Items . . . menu item. From the Disc menu, select Create Directory . . . to display the Create CD Directory dialog shown in Figure 13-27. Type the name of the new directory and click OK, and see the new directory added to your layout.

Figure 13-27: Need a new directory in your layout? You can add it from the menu system.

Adding Audio Tracks Manually

Just like the data side of things, there are two methods of manually adding audio tracks — but there are also three locations that can serve as the source! First, you must display the Add Tracks dialog. From the layout window, select the Audio Tracks pane at the bottom to switch to the audio portion of the layout, and then select Add Tracks . . . from the Disc menu.

✦ You can click the Add . . . button to display the dialog shown in Figure 13-15, where you can add tracks from existing audio CDs, WAV format sound files stored on your drive, or your music cache. From the Toolbar, you can display this dialog by clicking the Add Tracks button, which looks like a plus sign. To add a track from an existing audio CD, insert the disc into your drive to display the track list. If this is a disc you've already added to your music database, CD Creator displays the disc title and the title for each track. Pick one or more tracks (hold down the Ctrl key to select multiple individual tracks, or the Shift key to select contiguous tracks) and click Add Now to add them to your audio disc layout.

We can also add tracks from two other sources. To select WAV files for your layout from the Add Tracks dialog, click the *From WAV File* tab to display the pane shown in Figure 13-28. You can type the directory where the WAV files are located directly into the field, or click Browse to locate them on your system. If you're not sure which sound to pick, you can preview the sound by clicking the small play icon next to the WAV filename; CD Creator displays the Preview dialog, plays the WAV file, and returns to the Add Tracks dialog. Pretty slick, eh? Pick one or more WAV files (hold down the Ctrl key to select multiple files) and click Add Now to add them to your audio disc layout.

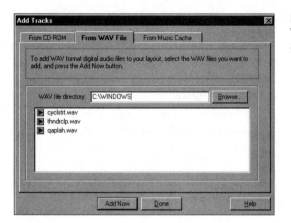

Figure 13-28: Selecting a WAV file from my Windows directory to add to the layout.

The third Add Tracks source is a new one — the *music cache* — which is useful for those who record a single track multiple times or prerecord a considerable number of audio tracks ahead of time to collect them for a single disc. Since the cache can occupy a huge chunk of hard drive space, it's typically used only by audiophiles and audio professionals, such as musicians and radio stations. The music cache must already be enabled if you're going to use it as a source for adding files. We discuss the music cache in detail in the Chapter 14; for now, let's discuss how to add tracks to your layout from the cache. Click the *From Music Cache* tab to display the pane shown in Figure 13-29. If you're not sure which sound to pick from the cache, you can preview the sound by clicking the small play icon next to the entry; CD Creator displays the Preview dialog, plays the sound, and returns to the Add Tracks dialog. Pick one or more sound files (hold down the Ctrl key to select multiple individual files, or the Shift key to select contiguous files) and click A̲dd Now to add them to your audio disc layout.

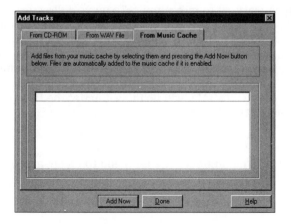

Figure 13-29: If you have the hard drive territory, the music cache is a great way to store audio for later use.

✦ Just like with a data CD, you can also drag and drop WAV files stored on your hard drive to your audio CD layout from the Windows Explorer (or the Windows 3.1 File Manager). Open an Explorer window, drag one or more WAV files over to the Adding Audio Tracks screen, and release the mouse button.

Adding Mixed-Mode Items Manually

As I said earlier, manually creating a mixed-mode disc is as simple as combining the previous two sections! To add data to the layout, select the Data Files pane at the bottom of the layout window and follow the instructions in the section "Adding Data Items Manually." Once you've added all the data items, select the Audio Tracks pane from the layout window and follow the instructions in the section "Adding Audio Tracks Manually." CD Creator automatically recognizes that you're now creating a mixed-mode CD-ROM.

Editing a Data CD-ROM Layout

Here's a common scenario: You load an existing data CD-ROM layout so that you can add a few more files before you record the disc. Unfortunately, you discover that you just added several files you don't need to your layout, and some of the files need to be moved to other directories before you record. How do you make changes to an existing layout?

In this section, we discuss each of the data CD-ROM editing tools provided by CD Creator for such occasions. Remember, to use the data layout editing tools you must switch to the Data Files pane of the layout window. Also, most of these commands are disabled until you have added data items to the layout or highlighted a specific data item.

Moving Files and Directories

There are two methods of moving files and directories from one location within your data layout to another:

✦ You can use the menu system to move items. To move a directory, highlight the directory and select the Move . . . command from the Item menu. CD Creator displays the dialog shown in Figure 13-30, with the directory to be moved already added. Type the name of an existing directory (or use the character "\" to indicate the root directory of your disc), and the highlighted directory becomes a subdirectory of the existing directory. For example, in Figure 13-30 the directory PINBALL will be moved under the POSTERS directory and become POSTERS\PINBALL.

Note   CD Creator will not create a new directory automatically, so you can't move or copy items under a new directory name that doesn't exist. You must use the Create Directory . . . item under the Disc menu to create a new directory.

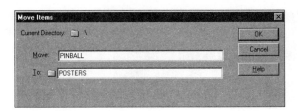

Figure 13-30: CD Creator displays this dialog when you move a directory manually using the menu system.

To move files from the menu system, highlight them and select the Move . . . command from the Item menu — remember, you can display the contents of a directory within the directory tree display by double-clicking it. You can select multiple individual files by holding down the Ctrl key, or the Shift key to select contiguous files. CD Creator displays the dialog shown in Figure 13-31, with the filenames you've selected already filled in. Type the name of an existing directory (or use the "\" character to indicate the root directory of your disc), and the highlighted files will be moved there.

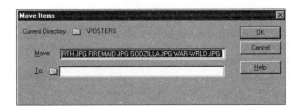

Figure 13-31: You can move selected files from one directory to another from this dialog.

✦ You can use your mouse to move items by dragging and dropping them. To move a directory, click its icon in the directory tree display and drag it onto the target directory's icon; the highlighted directory becomes a subdirectory of the existing directory. To move one or more files, click their icons in the right portion of the layout window and drag them onto the target directory's icon.

Copying Files
There are two methods of copying files from one location within your data layout to another:

✦ You can use the menu system. To copy one or more files from the menu system, highlight them and select the Copy . . . command from the Item menu. You can display the contents of a directory within the directory tree display by double-clicking it. You can select multiple individual files by holding down the Ctrl key, or the Shift key to select contiguous tracks. CD Creator displays the dialog shown in Figure 13-32, with the filenames you've selected already filled in. Type the name of an existing directory (or use the "\" character to indicate the root directory of your disc), and the highlighted files will be copied there. If there are existing files with the same name in the target directory, CD Creator will ask for permission to overwrite them with the new files.

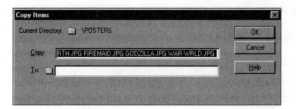

Figure 13-32: This dialog allows you to copy files from one directory to another.

✦ You can use your mouse to copy items by dragging and dropping them. To copy one or more files, click their icons in the right portion of the layout window and drag them onto the target directory's icon. As with the menu method, CD Creator asks for permission to overwrite existing files that have the same names.

Renaming Files and Directories

There are two methods you can use to rename files and directories within your data layout:

✦ You can use the menu system. To rename a file or directory, highlight it and select the Rename command from the Item menu. CD Creator displays an edit box around the item name, and you can type the new name. Press Enter to complete the process.

✦ You can use your mouse to rename items. Click the item once to highlight it and again to display the edit box around the item name. Type the new name and press Enter to complete the process.

You cannot rename the root directory of your disc layout — it is always designated by the "\" character.

Deleting Files and Directories

To delete a file or a directory, highlight it and select the Delete command from the Item menu, or press your Delete key. You can delete multiple files at once by selecting them while holding down the Ctrl key. If you delete a directory, you also delete any subdirectories under it in the directory tree display. You can delete the root directory of your disc layout, but it will delete everything, so use caution!

Also, remember that deleting an item from your data layout within CD Creator does **not** delete the file from your hard drive!

Editing Item Properties

CD Creator allows you to change certain properties for individual files and directories. First, highlight the desired item, then select Properties from the Item menu. CD Creator either displays the Directory Properties (Figure 13-10) or File

Properties (Figure 13-11) dialog, whichever is appropriate. You can rename a file or directory from the Properties dialog, and you can hide files and directories as well. Hidden items won't show when you display the contents of the completed CD-ROM; they're similar to hidden files on a hard drive. If you're changing the File Properties on an individual file, you can also change its priority, which we discuss in more detail later. Click OK to save your changes.

Editing an Audio Disc Layout

Now let's turn to the audio side of CD Creator again. In this section, we discuss the audio editing tools, which I consider much more fun than the mundane data editing features we discussed in the previous section. Remember, to use the audio layout editing tools you must switch to the Audio Tracks pane of the layout window. Also, most of these commands are disabled until you have added tracks to the layout or highlighted an audio track.

Playing an Audio Track

Need to play one of the tracks you've added to your audio disc layout? No problem! Highlight the track name and select the Play item from the Track menu, or click the Play button on the Toolbar (it looks like the Play button on an audio CD player). CD Creator displays the Preview dialog and plays the track, as shown in Figure 13-33. If you're previewing an audio track you added from an existing audio CD and you're not using the music cache, CD Creator prompts you to load the source CD so that it can be played. If the track is longer than a few seconds, you can pause or stop the track before it's finished, with the controls on the Preview dialog. Again, these buttons look like their counterparts on an audio CD player.

Figure 13-33: Playing an audio track with the Preview dialog.

Editing a WAV File

If you've added WAV files to your layout, you can edit them directly from the menu. Highlight the WAV file you want to modify and select Edit WAV File from the Track menu, or click the Edit Audio button on the Toolbar (it looks like a pencil). CD Creator launches the editor program associated with WAV files within Windows; unless you've changed the association, you'll see the Adaptec Sound Editor, shown in Figure 13-34, which is installed with CD Creator 2. Once you've saved your changes to the WAV file, you're returned to CD Creator. We discuss both Sound Editor and Cool Edit 96 in Chapter 14.

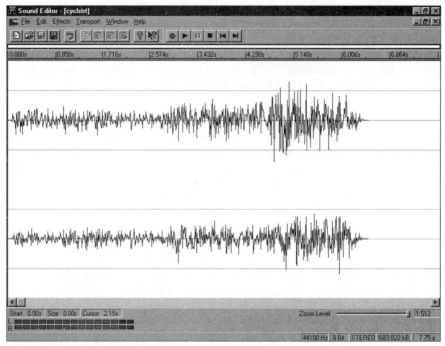

Figure 13-34: Making changes to a WAV file within the Adaptec Sound Editor.

Renaming Tracks

There are two methods you can use to rename tracks within your audio layout:

- ✦ You can use the menu system. To rename a track, highlight it and select the Rename command from the Track menu. CD Creator displays an edit box around the track name, and you can type the new name. Press Enter to complete the process.

- ✦ You can use your mouse to rename audio tracks. Click the track name once to highlight it and again to display the edit box around the name. Type the new name and press Enter to complete the process.

Deleting Tracks

To delete audio tracks from your layout, highlight the tracks and select the Delete command from the Track menu, or press your Delete key. You can delete multiple tracks at once by selecting them while holding down the Ctrl key. CD Creator asks for confirmation before deleting the tracks. As with data items, remember that deleting a WAV file or audio track from your audio layout within CD Creator does not delete the file from your hard drive!

Moving Tracks

There are two methods of changing the order of audio tracks:

✦ You can use the menu system. To move a track, highlight it and select the Properties command from the Track menu. Type the new track number in the Track Number field. When you click OK, the track is inserted at that number and all tracks after it are automatically renumbered.

Tip   Need information on how a track was recorded? Highlight the track and click the Properties item under the Track menu. You can change the name of the track, view its source, change the track number, and view its characteristics from the Properties dialog shown in Figure 13-19.

✦ You can use your mouse to move tracks by dragging and dropping them. To move a track, click its entry in the layout window and drag it to the desired slot; a dotted line indicates where the track will be inserted when you release the mouse button.

Combining and Splitting Tracks

From time to time, you may need to combine two or more tracks into a seamless single track; this avoids a pause between them, and an audio CD player will read them as a single track. To combine tracks from two different sources, click each track to be included and select Merge Tracks from the Effects menu. The tracks will be combined in order, with the first track to be combined in the layout appearing first in the merged track. You can repeat a merge operation if necessary to arrange the combined track as needed.

To split a combined track into individual tracks, select the combined track with your mouse and select Split Tracks from the Effects menu.

Validating a Data CD-ROM Layout

That's it! Our manual layout is ready, we've arranged all the files and audio tracks, and we've configured all the necessary settings — it's time to record, right?

Wrong! What if some of the data files you've added have changed since the last time you saved that layout? If you're using the CD Creator Disc Wizard, this isn't a concern, because all of those files and audio tracks are copied and readied right before recording; but if you've saved and loaded a layout several times, file locations and filenames may have changed, and CD Creator may not find them.

As a final step before recording a data CD-ROM, I always validate the disc layout. Validating a layout ensures that each data item and audio track on your hard drive is indeed still available for recording in the path stored within the layout. If you're using a removable drive (like a JAZ drive) or a remote drive (like a network drive) as the source for some of your files, CD Creator prompts you to load them as necessary.

To validate your data items, select Validate Layout . . . from the Disc menu. CD Creator displays a status screen to let you know which files are being validated. If your layout includes only data items from your hard drive, the validation should be fast, even with a full disc's worth of data.

Let's Record!

In this final section, we follow the status of a recording, as well as discuss simulated recording and how to write-protect your completed disc.

Starting the Recording

Once you've validated your layout and everything checks out OK, follow these steps to start the recording process:

1. Select Create CD From Layout from the File menu, or click the Create CD button on the Toolbar.

2. CD Creator displays the Disc Creation Setup dialog shown in Figure 13-35. From here you can make changes to the recording process itself.

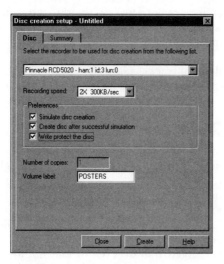

Figure 13-35: The Disc Creation Setup dialog appears at the beginning of the actual disc recording process.

3. If you have more than one CD-ROM recorder on your computer — you lucky technowizard! — click the drop-down list box to select which recorder to use. For those of us who have only a single recorder, leave this list box alone.

4. If your source files are stored on a fast hard drive and you've performed a System Test on your hardware, use the default recording speed; however, if you like, you can select another speed from the *Recording Speed:* drop-down

list box. If you decide to record at single (or 1x) speed, for example, this is the spot to select it.

5. Next, select the preferences for this recording session. As I mentioned earlier, if you choose to simulate the recording, your drive will first run a low-power test of your entire layout. This is a good way to insure that everything will run smoothly, but it does take as long as the actual recording. I recommend that you simulate your first few discs by checking the *Simulate disc creation* box, but once you've gained experience you can skip this step.

If you do elect to run a simulated recording, CD Creator enables the *Create disc after successful simulation* checkbox; this option specifies whether CD Creator automatically runs an actual recording if the simulation completes successfully. If you don't check this box, you have to manually start the real recording, so I always leave it checked if I'm running a simulation first.

Finally, you should enable the *Write protect the disc* option for most discs. This prevents the disc from being recorded again. Of course, you should not write-protect multisession discs until you're adding the last session. Write-protection usually decreases the amount of time it takes for your PC to load the contents of the disc. Audio discs are automatically write-protected.

6. If you're creating more than one copy of the same layout, enter that number in the *Number of copies:* field. CD Creator prompts you to load another blank disc for each copy. If you're creating multiple copies of a multisession disc, each disc you load after the first disc must be identical to the first disc.

7. You can also change the disc's Volume label right before recording. If you specified a label before you started the recording process, this field defaults to that label.

8. Is everything correct on the Disc Creation Setup dialog? If so, click Create! If you haven't loaded a blank disc yet, CD Creator prompts you for one. Load a blank and click Retry if your recorder doesn't recognize the new disc.

9. CD Creator displays the Creating Disc from Layout dialog. If you've specified a simulated recording, you'll see "Simulation" appear at the bottom right corner of the dialog, and this first pass makes no changes to the disc.

10. Once the actual recording begins, you can monitor the progress of the session from the dialog, which displays the total number of tracks and files remaining to record. At the top of the dialog, CD Creator displays how many copies you're creating and the number of the current disc. The disc icon and percentage amount indicate how much of the disc has been recorded. However, if you're creating a disc with only one track (for example, most data-only CD-ROMs have only one track), these indicators are not updated until recording completes. I've found that the bar graph at the bottom generally displays recording progress more accurately — plus, you can display details on the file or track that's currently being recorded by clicking the right mouse button on the progress bar.

Warning Of all the indicators on the Creating Disc from Layout dialog, the only two I really watch are the progress bar and the buffer percentage at the bottom of the dialog. If you're encountering buffer underrun errors, pay close attention to the buffer percentage; it indicates whether your computer is supplying that all-important constant, steady flow of data to your CD-ROM recorder. As each track records, the buffer percentage should start at 0% and then hold at 95 to 100% for most of the track. Near the end of the track, the percentage should slowly drop to 0% again. If the buffer percentage does not follow this pattern, you should run the System Tester to check your hardware.

11. Remember that you can abort the recording process by clicking the Stop button, but I've found that results are somewhat unpredictable, and the remaining data will not be recorded. In fact, you may never actually use the Stop button, since any error usually aborts the recording automatically. In general, *never interrupt the recording process* until the disc is ejected and/or the dialog reports that recording is complete!

12. Once the recording has successfully completed, CD Creator records the disc Table of Contents (TOC for short), which provides the directory information needed by DOS or Windows to access the disc. This generally takes a minute or two. Once the TOC is written, a disc appears with a big red check next to the progress bar and the dialog indicates that recording successfully completed — *truly one of the most beautiful sights in the world (at least to us)!* If you're making multiple copies, CD Creator prompts you to insert another disc. On the other hand, if errors were reported or the recording process aborted, click the View Errors button that appears and access the online help for each different error entry. Fortunately, I've found that the error code summaries provided in CD Creator's online help system are excellent, and they provide possible solutions that have helped me many times.

Note While recording your first few discs, keep a notebook handy to record notes about the creation process for future reference. Did you have to change a setting somewhere that the wasn't set by the CD Creator Disc Wizard? What was that error number and the solution from the last time? Are you using a specific naming structure for your files, like starting all of them with a department prefix? You'll find these notes make valuable reading each time you sit down to record, especially in the first few sessions until you get the process down pat.

Summary

In this chapter, you learned how to create standard data, audio, and mixed-mode discs using CD Creator. The topics we discussed include:

✦ using the automated CD Creator Disc Wizard to perform typical tasks;

✦ creating, saving, and loading layouts;

✦ manually configuring settings like the file system and filename conventions for a disc;

✦ adding and editing data items and audio tracks;

✦ arranging data items and tracks in your layout;

✦ validating your layout before recording;

✦ the status displays available during the recording process.

In Chapter 14, we move on to advanced recording topics, including writing disc images, creating multisession discs, setting file priorities, optimizing your discs, and the special programs included with CD Creator for editing audio and creating discs in different formats.

✦   ✦   ✦

Advanced CD Creator Features

The techniques you learned in Chapter 13 are likely to be all you need to produce the large majority of your CDs. Standard data, audio, and mixed-mode discs are compatible with any read-only CD-ROM drive, are easily created with the Wizard, and are great for most of the applications we've discussed.

In this chapter, however, we unlock some of the more advanced features of your CD recorder and CD Creator. First, you learn how to use some of the advanced features offered by CD Creator to reconfigure your drive, alter the program to fit your preferences, and optimize the discs you record.

Next, we record a number of specialized formats that you've learned about already, like Photo CD and Video CD discs. You create multiple sessions on a single disc, write disc images to your hard drive, record CD-EXTRA CDs, and much more!

Finally, we end the chapter with a full discussion for your artistic side: we create professional jewel case inserts for your discs using the powerful design features within CD Creator!

Advanced Recording Options

Let's begin by discussing a number of advanced features within CD Creator that you can use before and after a recording session. You may not need or use each of these each time you create a CD, but they come in handy when you're fine-tuning a disc layout or having problems with your hardware.

Reconfiguring Your CD Recorder

Like Easy CD Creator, System Tester automates most of the settings required to configure CD Creator for your system's hardware. However, from time to time you may experience problems while recording, and the likely solution to many of these problems lies in reconfiguring your CD recorder. CD Creator's online help may instruct you to change these settings, or you might find your specific system hardware or software mentioned in the README file as requiring these changes. In this section, you learn the details of changing your recorder's settings.

First, let's display the CD Recorder Setup dialog. Pull down the File menu and select the CD Recorder Setup . . . item. CD Creator displays the dialog shown in Figure 14-1. If you're lucky enough to have more than one recorder, you can select which one to configure by clicking the correct entry. To choose a default recorder, double-click the entry, and CD Creator will display it as the default recorder at the bottom of the dialog; remember to click OK to save your default when we're done with this dialog.

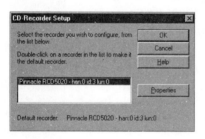

Figure 14-1: If you need to change your CD recorder configuration, start from the CD Recorder Setup dialog.

Once you've highlighted the recorder you need to configure, click the Properties button to display the Recorder Properties dialog shown in Figure 14-2. We discuss each of these settings in detail.

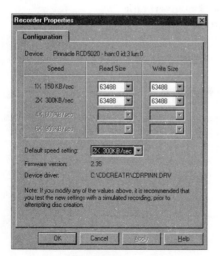

Figure 14-2: CD Creator displays the Recorder Properties dialog for my Pinnacle Micro RCD5020 recorder.

Speed, Read Size, and Write Size

As you know, just about any recorder available today can record at different speeds. For most of us, the choices are single (1x) and double (2x) speed, and more and more available drives can write at quad (4x) speed. The group of eight drop-down list boxes shown in Figure 14-2 allows you to specify both the read and write sizes in bytes for each recording speed supported by your drive.

Respectively, these read and write buffer values determine

✦ how much data CD Creator reads and stores from your hard drive while it waits for the recorder's buffer to empty;

✦ how much data the program sends to your CD recorder at a time.

Since CD Creator reads data and sends it to the recorder simultaneously, the size of these buffers has a dramatic effect on your system's efficiency. If they're improperly set, you may experience intermittent buffer underrun errors, or even find it impossible to record successfully.

Note

Are you wondering how CD Creator picks the right read and write buffer sizes for your particular drive? Remember the System Tests we covered in Chapter 6 that checked the transfer rate of your source drive and simulated recording at each speed? The results of those tests were used to determine the default values you see for these fields, so you can consider them "tailor-made" for your system!

If an error log message or the README file recommends increasing or decreasing one of these values, find the speed at which your recorder was operating when the error occurred and then increase or decrease the read and write sizes as indicated. In most cases, you increase these values.

Default Speed Setting

Although the System Tester selects the default speed setting, you may decide to change it depending upon the success you're having at recording with your current speed. As you learned in Chapter 13, you can always change the speed right before you begin recording, since it's on the Disc Creation Setup dialog; however, if you find yourself constantly lowering or raising the recording speed, why not make it a default? It's one less setting you'll have to change during the recording process.

For example, if you've been experiencing a number of buffer underrun errors and you can't seem to track them down, one trick that can help insure a successful recording is selecting the next lower recording speed. The slower the recording speed, the less trouble your system has providing a constant, uninterrupted flow of data to your recorder. On the other hand, if you've never experienced any problems with recording and you find that you can use the next higher speed, you can change the default here so that recording always takes place at a faster clip!

To change the default recording speed, click the *Default speed setting:* drop-down list box and click the desired speed.

Firmware and Device Driver

The other two items on the Recorder Properties dialog are display-only, so you can't change them; however, they are important if you have to call technical support for help with your recorder or its device driver. The *Firmware version:* field displays the version number of the on-board electronics within your recorder, much like the BIOS version displayed when you run the SETUP program that accompanies your PC's motherboard. Some recorders are upgradable with new firmware that supplies new features or bug fixes.

The other field, *Device driver:*, indicates the full pathname for the CD recorder device driver recognized by CD Creator. Typically, this driver is located within the CDCREATR directory.

Once you've made all the changes you need to make within the Recorder Properties dialog, click OK to exit the dialog, and OK again to save your changes and return to the layout window menu.

Selecting Preferences within CD Creator

Next, let's set some of the preferences within CD Creator. General preferences include:

- ✦ enabling or disabling certain interface items;
- ✦ determining what CD Creator will do when you run it.

Disc creation preferences include:

- ✦ the location of temporary files;
- ✦ enabling or disabling the error log file;
- ✦ remote and removable drive assignments.

Audio preferences include:

- ✦ the location of your music database file;
- ✦ the location and size of your music cache;
- ✦ the default drive to use for audio extraction.

To begin, display the CD Creator Preferences dialog by selecting Preferences . . . from the File menu, as shown in Figure 14-3.

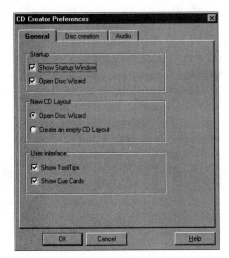

Figure 14-3: CD Creator allows you to change a number of preferences that control the look and feel of the program.

General Preferences

The Startup fields determine what actions CD Creator takes when it runs. By default, Show Startup Window is enabled, so the program will display the welcome banner and copyright information. This takes a second or two to load, however, and some people dislike these banners, so you can turn the display off by disabling this checkbox. As we discussed earlier, CD Creator also launches the Wizard automatically upon startup, but you can prevent this by disabling the *Open Disc Wizard* checkbox.

The New CD Layout option group specifies what happens when you select New CD Layout . . . from the File menu. By default, CD Creator opens the Wizard, but you can elect to display only the blank layout window by selecting Create an empty CD Layout instead.

Tip So you've been using CD Creator for months now, and you can create discs better than anyone else in the world . . . but that doggone Wizard is driving you out of your mind. As I said earlier, the Wizard is great for your first few sessions, but after you've gained experience you may find yourself clicking Cancel the moment it appears. Here's a tip on how to banish the Wizard forever: from the General tab of the CD Creator Preferences dialog, disable the *Open Disc Wizard* checkbox and select the *Create an empty CD Layout* option button. There! You've disabled the Wizard entirely, and it won't return unless you change these settings.

The final section of the General tab, User Interface, allows you to disable two features meant for novices. Once again, they're great when you're just getting started, but once you're familiar with the program you can disable them to streamline the layout window. You turn off ToolTips — those helpful little signs which pop up when you leave your mouse cursor on top of a Toolbar button for a few seconds — by disabling the *Show ToolTips* checkbox. Likewise, you turn off the Cue Cards, which appear in the corner of each editor window, by disabling the *Show Cue Cards* checkbox. Cue Cards tell you what you can do from the current window and how you can perform a function such as adding items. I generally leave the ToolTips enabled, because there are so many Toolbar buttons throughout the different Adaptec programs that I occasionally need a reminder of their functions.

Disc Creation Preferences

As shown in Figure 14-4, the first field on this tab determines whether CD Creator performs a simulated recording by default. This is a great way to check for errors and make sure your hardware and software are working correctly before recording a disc, but it takes as long as the actual recording process itself, so after you've worked with CD Creator for a while you may decide to skip a simulated recording. You should also simulate a recording if you're creating a new type of disc for the first time, such as an audio CD, which is more demanding on your hardware than a data CD.

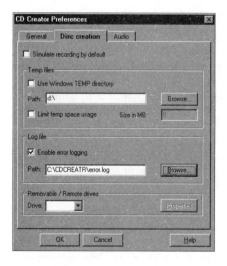

Figure 14-4: The Disc Creation tab of the Preferences dialog, where you can set several values that affect the recording process.

Note that if this field is checked, CD Creator will not automatically record a disc; instead, you must select the *Create disc after successful simulation* checkbox on the Disc creation setup dialog, as discussed in Chapter 13. On the other hand, if this field is disabled, CD Creator automatically assumes you wish to record a disc if you click Create on the Disc creation setup dialog.

Under Temp files, you can specify where you would like CD Creator to store temporary files during recording. To use the default location assigned for Windows temporary files, enable the *Use Windows TEMP directory* checkbox. If you disable this checkbox, you can select the location yourself by typing the full pathname into the *Path:* field, or you can select an existing directory by clicking the Browse . . . button to navigate through your system.

Warning As mentioned earlier, you should avoid recording from a source drive that's been compressed using programs like DriveSpace or Stacker, and this limitation also applies to your temporary files. For example, if your Windows directory is located on drive C: and that drive is compressed, you should not use the default Windows TEMP directory, since that directory is probably C:\WINDOWS\TEMP, and it's compressed! Instead, disable the *Use Windows TEMP directory* checkbox and click the Browse . . . button to select a directory on your uncompressed source drive — for example, the root of drive D: — as shown in Figure 14-4.

No matter where you decide to send temporary files, you can limit the amount of space CD Creator uses to store them by enabling the Limit temp space usage checkbox and entering the maximum number of usable megabytes in the *Size in MB:* field. This may be necessary if you're low on space on the drive used for temporary storage. This field does not apply to audio tracks that you've copied to your hard drive for recording.

The Log file preferences control whether CD Creator writes a log file to disk containing information about the recording session. This is especially helpful if you're trying to track down intermittent problems with your recorder, because the log file will contain a list of any errors. If you're using a recorder on a network workstation, a log file is also good for keeping track of what was recorded and when. Click the *Enable error log* checkbox to turn error logging on or off. The default log file is ERROR.LOG, and it's located in the CD Creator home directory. Click the Browse . . . button to select a different location or name for your log file. To read the log file, I use any text editor that's handy.

The final set of preferences on the Disc Creation tab deals with removable and remote drives. As you learned earlier, it's generally not a good idea to record directly from a network, but if your network is indeed fast enough (or you're using one of the new generation of fast removable hard drives like the Iomega JAZ drive), you can select one of those drives as a source drive here. You must check a network or removable drive for Transfer Rate with the System Tester, or it will not show in this drop-down list box. This insures that CD Creator will have some idea of the drive's performance before you use it as a recording source. You can display the properties dialog for the selected drive by clicking the Properties button.

Audio Preferences

Click the Audio tab to display the tab shown in Figure 14-5. The Music database *Path:* field allows you to specify the location of your music database files. This database holds the artist name, disc title, and track names for all of the audio discs you use as source discs for audio recording. You can add, delete, print, and edit entries in your Music database with the Adaptec Music Database Browser, a separate utility which we discuss later. To specify a different directory for the database files, click the Browse . . . button to navigate through your system and click the desired directory.

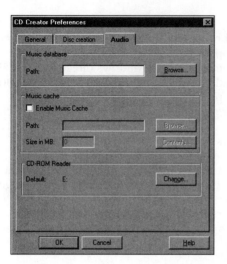

Figure 14-5: You can enable the Music Cache from the Audio tab of the Preferences dialog.

If you do a great deal of audio recording with CD Creator and you have the hard drive space to spare, you'll appreciate the Music Cache feature. The cache can store audio tracks from source discs on your hard drive for later use, making it easy to use the same track in more than one audio layout. Each 10 minutes of audio you store in the cache is equal to about 100 megabytes of hard drive space, so this feature isn't for everyone!

You'll learn more about using the cache later; for now, remember that this tab is where you can set all of your preferences for it. The *Enable Music Cache* checkbox is the "master switch" that enables and disables the cache. If the cache is enabled and currently empty, you can specify the location where it will be created; click the Browse . . . button to navigate through your system and click the desired directory. You can specify the amount of hard drive space that will be reserved for the music cache in the *Size in MB:* field. To display the contents of the cache, click the Contents . . . button; CD Creator opens the Music Cache Control dialog, which we discuss later when we cover the cache in detail.

Finally, the CD-ROM reader section of the Audio tab displays the default CD-ROM drive to be used for audio extraction as you add tracks to an audio layout from existing audio discs. This field is automatically assigned to the lowest CD-ROM drive letter on your system, but you can click the Change . . . button to specify another CD-ROM drive. Check this drive with the CD-ROM portion of the System Tester before you select it here, because the drive must be capable of digital audio extraction.

Once you finish making changes to the settings on the CD Creator Preferences dialog, click OK to save them to disk and return to the layout window.

Selecting and Editing File Priorities

Typically, all files you add to a data CD-ROM are equally important; you don't usually know which file will be accessed first, or how often it will be used. However, it is possible to physically arrange a number of files on a data CD-ROM so that they're accessed faster than other files. Writing them closer to the center of the disc, as shown in Figure 14-6, speeds access. Files written farther away from the spindle hole take more time to access. Of course, we're talking a very small time savings per file, but if your CD-ROM fits one or more of these criteria, those time savings can add up!

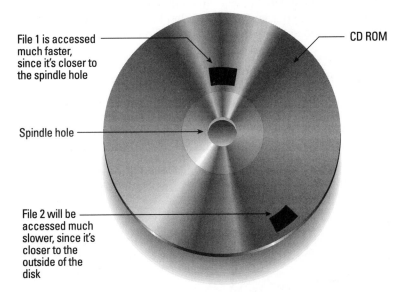

File 1 is accessed much faster, since it's closer to the spindle hole

CD ROM

Spindle hole

File 2 will be accessed much slower, since it's closer to the outside of the disk

Figure 14-6: The closer a file is written to the spindle hole on a data CD-ROM, the faster it is accessed.

✦ Will it contain a large number of files? If so, place the files you know will be accessed most often towards the center of the disc.

✦ Will it contain a group of files that are typically accessed in order, such as a series of screens in a presentation? If so, speed up your application by assigning those files a better spot.

✦ Will it be accessed frequently by a program on your PC to load data? If your CD-ROM is acting as a database archive, for example, placing the database files closer to the center should speed up the retrieval of information.

Also, if you know that certain files will be used only once or twice — for example, a set of drivers or an installation program — place those files towards the edge of the disc.

CD Creator includes a system of file priorities that makes it easy to indicate which files are to be written first for faster access. You can assign three different priority levels: normal (the default), faster access, and fastest access. Normal priority files are recorded in the order you added them to the layout.

Note

Before we jump into all the advanced features offered by CD Creator for prioritizing your files, let me again assure you that assigning any file priority at all is strictly **optional**! If you decide not to assign special priorities, all your files will be labeled as normal and you can get on with your life. I use this feature only when a disc I'm recording fits one of the three criteria listed in this section; otherwise, I skip this step entirely, since I usually don't know which files will be accessed more than others. The faster the CD-ROM drive that will read the files, the less important it is to prioritize your layout — and don't forget, file priorities are relative, so you can't choose "fastest access" for all your files and magically speed up your finished CD!

Editing File Priorities from the Data Layout Window

To assign file priorities from the Data layout window, follow these steps:

1. Highlight one or more files in the right side of the layout window and select Change Priority . . . from the Item menu.

2. CD Creator displays the File Priority dialog shown in Figure 14-7. Click the *File Priority* drop-down list box and choose the desired priority for the selected files. Click OK to confirm the change.

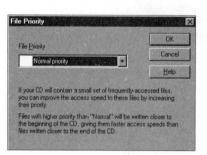

Figure 14-7: The File Priority dialog makes it easy to change the access priority on multiple files at once.

3. A small colored spot appears next to the files indicating their new priority: blue indicates a file with faster priority, while green indicates a file with fastest priority. Files with normal priority have no colored spot next to their names.

You can also change the priority on a single file from its File Properties dialog by following these steps:

1. Highlight a single file in the right side of the layout window and select Properties from the Item menu.

2. CD Creator displays the File Properties dialog shown in Figure 14-8. Click the *Priority* drop-down list box and choose the desired priority for the selected file. Click OK to confirm the change.

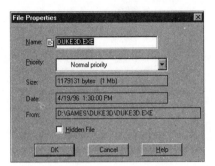

Figure 14-8: You can also change a file's priority for from its File Properties dialog.

If you like, you can change the priority of a file or the contents of an entire directory while you're adding items to your data layout. At the bottom of the Add Data Items dialog, you'll find a *Priorities:* drop-down list box, as shown in Figure 14-9. Once you've highlighted files or directories in the normal way, change their priority before you click the Add Now button.

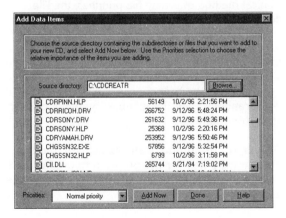

Figure 14-9: CD Creator allows you to change the priority of files or directories as they're added to your layout.

Editing Priorities from the File Ordering Editor

CD Creator also provides a graphical method of arranging file priorities and displaying the physical location of data items. From the Data layout window, click the File Ordering tab to display the File Ordering editing window shown in Figure 14-10.

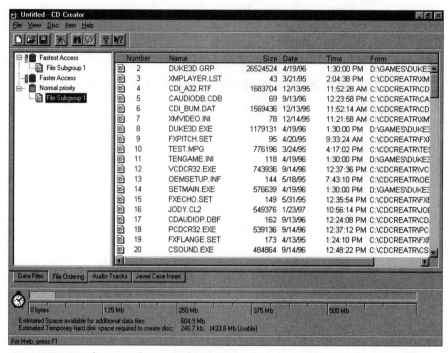

Figure 14-10: If you prefer a graphical method of setting file priorities, the File Ordering editor is just what the doctor ordered.

The File Ordering editing window replaces the standard tree directory listing on the left with a separate branch for each of the three priorities, and with the folder icon replaced by a clipboard icon. Just like the branches in the Data Files window, you can expand or collapse these branches from the menu, or you can click the plus and minus characters next to their names.

CD Creator creates and removes subgroups automatically as needed under a priority. Subgroups are really only an easy way for the program to organize files for display; they do not represent directories in the data layout. To display the contents of a file subgroup, click its icon in the tree window.

The right portion of the File Ordering editing window displays an entry with basic information for each file in the selected subgroup. The most important element in the file display is the number to the left of the name, which indicates the order in which the file will be written to disc. This display makes it easy to arrange files together that are read sequentially, as in our example of a series of screens in a presentation.

Assigning Priorities

To change the file priority on a file, follow these steps:

1. Select the icon for the file's current priority in the tree window. This displays the file subgroups. Search through them manually to locate your file, or use the Find File command, which we discuss shortly.

2. Once you've located the files you'd like to reassign, highlight them in the right side of the window.

3. Click and drag the highlighted files to the icon for the new priority in the tree display in the left portion of the window.

If CD Creator needs to create another subgroup for the files you just assigned, you'll see the tree display update immediately.

Reordering Files

There are two methods of reordering the physical arrangement of files from the File Ordering editor:

✦ You can click and drag one or more files to a new slot in the right side of the window.

✦ To reorder one or more files by their properties, highlight them in the right side of the window and select Re-order Files from the Disc menu (or click the Toolbar icon, which looks like a circle made from two arrows). CD Creator prompts you for the reorder criteria — for example, the file date, size, or name. Select one and click OK.

Adding Priority Levels

You can even add new priority levels of your own to the current layout within the File Ordering editor. This is one feature I don't think most of us will ever use, since three levels of file priorities seems like all anyone needs! If you do need an extra priority level or two, though, follow these steps:

1. From the File Ordering editor window, select New Priority from the Item menu. CD Creator displays the New Priority dialog shown in Figure 14-11.

Figure 14-11: Adding a new priority level to our current disc layout.

2. Type in a name for the new priority and select a color to indicate files assigned to the new level.

3. Now click the Move Up and Move Down buttons to position the new level within your existing levels. The closer to the top of the list, the higher the priority.

4. Once the new level is in place, click OK to add the new level to the current layout, or click Save as Defaults to add the new priority to all future layouts.

Deleting Priority Levels

You can also delete a priority level. If there are files currently assigned to that level, CD Creator automatically reassigns them as normal priority. To delete a file priority, click its icon in the tree display to highlight it and press your Delete key, or select Delete Priority from the Item menu.

Finding Files

Looking for a single file within five or six subgroups in the tree display can feel like searching for a needle in a haystack! Fortunately, CD Creator makes it easy to find files within the File Ordering editor by using wildcards. Follow these steps:

1. From the File Ordering editor window, select Find Files from the Disc menu, or click the Toolbar button that resembles a pair of binoculars. CD Creator displays the Find Files dialog shown in Figure 14-12.

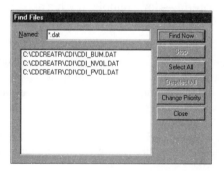

Figure 14-12: From the Find Files dialog, you can locate a file anywhere in your layout.

2. Next, type a full filename or a DOS wildcard in the *Named:* field — for example, FINDME.EXE or *.EXE are both valid.

3. Click Find Now to begin the search. If the file you're looking for turns up before the search process completes, you can click the Stop button to abort the rest of the search.

4. Once the search process is complete, CD Creator displays any matches in the list. To change the priority of a file, highlight it and click Change Priority. As usual, you can use the Ctrl key to select multiple files, or you can click Select All or Deselect All to select or deselect all the files in the list at once.

5. CD Creator displays the dialog shown in Figure 14-13. Click the desired priority, then select one of the files within the priority and specify whether to add the new files before or after that file. Click OK to confirm your changes.

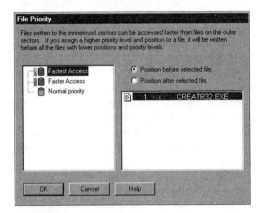

Figure 14-13: From this dialog, you can change the priority for files located with the Find Files command.

Displaying and Changing Priority Properties

Finally, you can always modify the properties sheet for any priority level. To display the properties for a priority, highlight its icon in the File Ordering editor tree display and select Properties from the Item menu. CD Creator displays the Priority Properties dialog shown in Figure 14-14.

Figure 14-14: The Priority Properties dialog allows you to modify characteristics for an existing priority.

From the Priority tab, you can change the name, color, and level of an existing priority. The Files tab displays information regarding all of the files currently assigned to this priority, as well as those files assigned higher and lower priority levels. If you make any changes on the Priority tab, click OK to save them and return to the editing window.

Optimizing Your Layouts

Have you noticed the word "Optimizing . . . " that appears from time to time in the lower right corner of the layout window? This status message indicates that a hidden friend of yours is working on arranging your layout: the automatic Disc Optimizer! Disc Optimizer works behind the scenes while you work, calculating important information such as how much space is used in a layout and how much remains; how much temporary space is needed for recording; and how many tracks are required to record your layout.

Depending on the speed of your PC, the size of your layout, and its complexity, Disc Optimizer usually finishes within a few seconds, but CD Creator runs it whenever you make just about any change to your layout, so it runs often. In fact, if you click the Create CD button on the Toolbar before the Disc Optimizer has had a chance to finish, CD Creator will delay the display of the Disc creation setup dialog until optimization is complete.

Although Disc Optimizer runs automatically, you can configure it to some extent from the Disc Properties dialog. To display the dialog shown in Figure 14-15, select Properties from the Disc menu and click the Disc Optimizer tab.

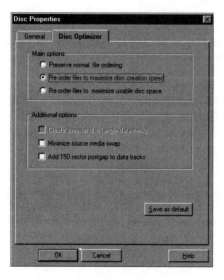

Figure 14-15: You can control how Disc Optimizer works from this tab of the Disc Properties dialog.

Through the Main options group, you can specify whether Disc Optimizer uses the file ordering you've assigned, or whether it arranges files to conserve space or reduce recording time.

✦ Select *Preserve normal file ordering* to use the order you've arranged within the File Ordering editing window. In effect, this disables any automatic file ordering by the Disc Optimizer.

✦ Select *Re-order files to maximize disc creation speed* to save time during the recording process. Disc Optimizer modifies the file order so that your layout is recorded in the smallest amount of time possible. Any file priorities you've set are still followed, but files within each priority may be reordered.

✦ Select *Re-order files to maximize usable disc space* to leave the maximum amount of free space possible on the disc after you've recorded your layout. If you plan on recording additional sessions on this disc, this is definitely the option you should choose! Once again, Disc Optimizer will respect any file priorities you've set, but files within each priority may be rearranged.

Under Additional options, are three more configuration settings for the Disc Optimizer:

✦ Enable the *Create a master disc (single data track)* checkbox if you're creating a master disc to send for duplication. This is the CD Creator term for disc-at-once recording, which insures that the finished disc will have only one track. Most replication facilities require a master disc to be a single-session disc recorded in disc-at-once mode.

✦ Are you using removable media disks as your recording source? If so, I recommend you enable the *Minimize source media swap* checkbox. This allows Disc Optimizer to rearrange the order of your files to reduce the inevitable swapping needed to a minimum (if you've ever made several copies of a floppy disk using only a single drive, you know what I mean)!

✦ The final checkbox, *Add 150 sector postgap to data tracks*, is another highly specialized field that's of interest only to those creating a master disc for replication. If you need to add 150 blank sectors to the end of each data track, enable this checkbox; if you don't know what that means, leave the field disabled and forget that it exists! Standard CD-ROMs don't require this feature, and, unless it's specifically needed, there's no good reason to lose 150 sectors of space for each data track.

Advanced Recording Methods

In Chapter 13, we created a standard single-session CD-ROM that could contain data, audio, or a mixture of the two. However, as I've mentioned, CD Creator offers a wide range of recording formats and methods that you can use to create specialized discs.

Some of the discs we discuss in this section require extra work to create, and we may have to use other programs that are supplied with CD Creator; for example, we'll use VCD Creator to create a video CD layout. CD Creator automates as much of the process as possible, so you shouldn't encounter any problems creating one of these discs. However, there are two important points to remember about these specialized formats:

✦ Not every CD-ROM drive can read some of the discs we create in this chapter. If you're looking for a disc that can be universally read on just about any PC, you should consider a standard CD-ROM (after all, the lowest common denominator is still the most compatible)!

✦ Not every CD recorder can create some of the discs described in this chapter. If you're using an older recorder, check its documentation for details on what formats it supports.

With that said, let's get to work!

Recording with a Disk Image

Disc image is one of the advanced recording techniques that I use often. In effect, a disc image is the complete contents of a CD you wish to create, stored on your hard drive instead of recorded on a blank disc.

Why would you need to do this? As an example, let's use a series of disc images I recorded for my shareware business. The final disc that I create contains a copy of each of my shareware games, all the documentation, and a generous supply of public domain source code, as shown in the layout in Figure 14-16. As you can tell by the space remaining, it contains less than 250 megabytes, but it's still enough information that you wouldn't even consider sending the contents of this disc on floppy disks. I send this disc to customers who decide to buy all of my programs as a package deal.

I could save this layout to my hard drive, and simply reload it and record it each time I need to send a copy to a customer. That's not quite as simple as it sounds, though, since I would have to maintain those files in the same place, and I would have to make sure that the files weren't altered or changed in any way between recordings. That's harder for a software developer to do than you might think! Also, I'd end up reloading all those files and revalidating the disc each time I needed a copy.

I could make multiple copies of the disc at one recording session, but I have no idea how many customers will order all of my programs at once. Blank discs are still too expensive to waste, and if I make a change to one of the programs to correct a bug or add a feature, my stockpile of discs is suddenly worthless.

Disc image to the rescue! Instead of recording directly to a CD, I record the data on my hard drive as an image file, which gives me these advantages:

✦ This single image file contains all of the data, so I don't need to worry about inadvertently altering the contents of one of my source files.

✦ I only collect and verify the data once, including any data stored on removable or network drives. Once the disc image is complete, I never have to load files or audio tracks again — the only step involved is the actual recording.

✦ If I must change a file in the layout, I simply erase the disc image and create a new one; or, if I'm archiving versions of these discs, I can backup the old image and create a new disc from it at any future time.

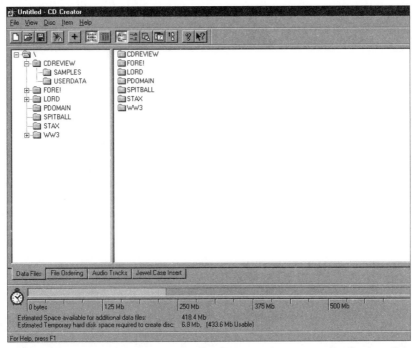

Figure 14-16: A typical data CD-ROM layout used to create distribution discs from a disc image file stored on my hard drive.

Disc images are ideal if you have a slower hard drive on your computer. As you learned earlier, a slow source drive can cause problems such as buffer underrun errors, particularly if you're trying to record a layout containing a large number of smaller files; for example, if you're trying to record a layout containing several hundred image files of less than 100K each. Remember how the transfer rates for larger files were much faster than for smaller files? That's why recording a disc image to a blank disc usually succeeds where recording the individual files does not — the disc image is stored on your hard drive as a single huge file, so your PC's hard drive doesn't have to jump through hoops to locate and load all of those individual files. Instead, your system need only open a single file and send its contents to the recorder. Disc images stored by CD Creator have the extension .CIF.

If you share an external CD recorder with others in your office, there's one more advantage to using a disc image: you can actually "record" a disc to an image file even if someone else is using the drive! It's much more convenient to build the layout and read the files when you have the time; then, once you've reattached the recorder to your computer, you can simply record directly to a blank disc from the disc image.

Of course, there is a downside — isn't there always? Much like the CD Creator music cache, writing a disc image to your hard drive requires as much space as the actual CD will store, so if you're creating a full CD disc image, look forward to losing 650 to 670 megabytes of hard drive space for as long as you keep the disc image.

Creating a Disc Image

To create a disc image, follow these steps:

1. Select Create Disc image from Layout . . . from the File menu. CD Creator displays the Select image file dialog shown in Figure 14-17.

Figure 14-17: You specify a name and select a destination directory for your disc image file from this dialog.

2. Navigate to the destination directory where you want to store the .CIF file and enter a name into the *Filename:* field. Click Save to create the disc image.

3. CD Creator will display the Creating image from Layout dialog shown in Figure 14-18, which — no surprise here — resembles the Creating Disc from Layout dialog you saw in the last chapter. In fact, you are actually writing an ISO 9660 image file, just as it would be sent to the recorder if the destination was a blank disc. The same status bar and information on the total number of files to be stored, as well as how many files remain to be processed, are displayed, but the entire session will take only a fraction of the time required to record the same data on a blank disc.

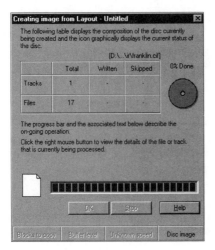

Figure 14-18: This dialog displays status information while writing your disc image file to the hard drive.

4. Once the entire disc image is created on your hard drive, that same disc with the bold red check mark is displayed, indicating that the process completed without errors. Click OK to return to the layout window.

Using a Disc Image with the Wizard

A disc image gives you the freedom to create a CD whenever you like; you no longer need to have the individual files handy, and you don't have to load the layout you used! If you like, you can automate the creation of a CD from a disc image within the CD Creator Wizard by following these steps:

1. Run CD Creator and display the Wizard; if you've turned it off, enable it as we discussed at the beginning of this chapter.

2. From the Wizard task list, click the *Record a Disc Image file to CD* entry to highlight it and click Next>.

3. The Wizard displays the screen shown in Figure 14-19. Click the Select . . . button to display a standard Windows Open File dialog, where you can navigate to the directory where you stored the .CIF file. Select the desired disc image and click Open to load it. Alternately, you can drag the .CIF file to the Wizard's Disc Image File screen. When you've selected a file by either method, click Next> to move the next screen.

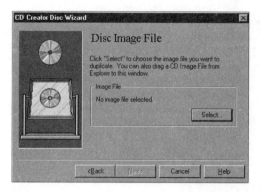

Figure 14-19: When recording a disc image to CD, the Wizard prompts you to specify an existing image file.

4. The Wizard displays a confirmation screen before the recording process begins. Click Finish to start recording, or click <Back to back up and select another disc image file.

CD Creator displays the Disc creation setup dialog, and from this point recording from a disc image is just like recording from a layout.

Using a Disc Image Manually

You can also manually record a CD from a disc image file by using the menu system. Follow these steps:

1. Select Create CD from Disc image . . . from the File menu. CD Creator displays the Select image file dialog shown in Figure 14-17.

2. Navigate to the directory where you originally stored the .CIF file and double-click it to load the file.

CD Creator displays the Disc creation setup dialog, and from this point recording from a disc image is just like recording from a layout.

Recording Multiple Copies

If you don't need to create copies of a CD over an extended time and you know how many copies you need, there's no reason to create a disc image file. As you learned in Chapter 13, you can specify more than one copy of a CD before you start recording. To create multiple copies, follow these steps:

1. Design your layout and begin the recording process as usual.

2. CD Creator displays the Disc Creation Setup dialog shown in Figure 14-20. Enter the number of copies you wish to make in the *Number of copies:* field.

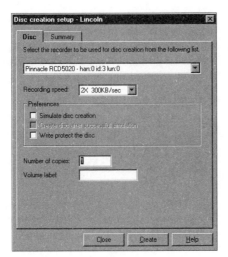

Figure 14-20: You can specify recording of multiple copies of the same disc in the Disc Creation Setup dialog.

3. If everything is correct on the Disc Creation Setup dialog, click Create — remember to check the *Create disc after successful simulation* checkbox if you're simulating the recording.

4. The recording continues as usual, but once you've successfully created the first disc, CD Creator will eject it automatically and prompt you to insert another disc.

CD Creator repeats step 4 for each copy.

Tip   When you're creating multiple copies of the same disc, the general rule is always reach for a blank disc for each copy; even if a disc has plenty of room remaining and you didn't write-protect it, CD Creator will reject it. CD Creator requires that each disc you load for the copies be identical to the first disc, and the easiest way to keep track of this is to use blanks. There is one exception to this rule: If you're creating multiple copies of a multisession disc, each disc must already contain exactly the same data as the first disc you loaded. Why? Because the files are accessed according to their physical location on the disc and which locations are recorded in the file system; if the files are written to a different location, your CD-ROM drive is unable to locate them.

Recording Disc-to-Disc

All of our recording to this point uses the hard drive as a source. We've recorded files stored on the hard drive, written a disc image file, and recorded it, and later we use the music cache to hold audio tracks. CD Creator also uses the hard drive to store temporary files used during the recording process.

You can record from a removable or network source drive, but even then I recommend that you copy the files temporarily onto your hard drive for recording unless the source drive's transfer rate is as least as fast as your hard drive.

In this section, however, I describe two methods of making an exact copy of an existing CD-ROM or audio disc: one procedure for those who have a second SCSI CD-ROM device (either a read-only drive or another recorder), and one procedure for those who want to make a disc-to-disc copy using only the CD recorder.

Recording Disc-to-Disc with Another Drive

There is another source for recording that can be a wonderful convenience if you need to make duplicates of existing CD-ROMs. In Chapter 5, we discussed adding a SCSI read-only CD-ROM to your system as an option for disc-to-disc recording. If you have one, and you've run the Transfer Rate portion of the System Tester on it, you can exactly duplicate an existing CD without even building a layout! There's another advantage, too: direct disc-to-disc copying requires only a minute fraction of the hard drive space required to duplicate the same disc from a layout or a disc image.

To record disc-to-disc with two SCSI CD-ROM devices, follow these steps:

1. Click the Start button and select the Adaptec Multimedia group from the Programs menu. You should see an entry for the Adaptec CD Duplicator; click it to run Duplicator. Duplicator is a separate program; it's also available from the Wizard if you select the *Create a copy of an existing CD* entry from the task list.

2. From Duplicator's opening screen, click <u>N</u>ext>.

3. Duplicator displays the screen shown in Figure 14-21. Select the *Copy from CD to CD* option and click <u>N</u>ext>.

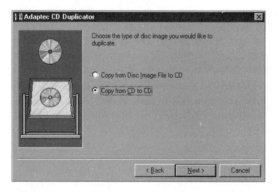

Figure 14-21: Adaptec CD Duplicator's disc image selection screen.

4. Duplicator displays the screen shown in Figure 14-22, prompting you to select a SCSI CD-ROM device on your system to use as the source. After you load the source disc into your second SCSI CD-ROM device, click the *CD-ROM Reader:* drop-down list box and select it from the list. Duplicator scans the

source disc and displays the name of the disc (if it's an audio disc that you've already added to your music database), as well as the maximum read speed for the drive for the source disc. If you'd like to retest the speed of the drive and disc, click the Retest Speed button. When you're ready to continue, click the Next> button.

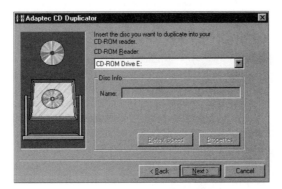

Figure 14-22: If you have more than one SCSI CD-ROM device on your system, you can select which to use as the source from this Duplicator dialog.

 Tip No label on your source disc? You don't even have to leave CD Creator! You can display information about your source disc by clicking the Properties button, which displays the Disc Properties dialog shown in Figure 14-23. This dialog displays the disc name, as well as the number of existing sessions and tracks stored on it; to display details on each track, click the Tracks tab.

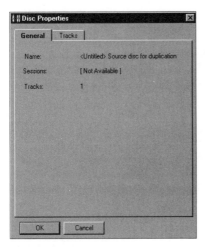

Figure 14-23: Duplicator's Disc Properties dialog shows you information on the disc you've selected as your source.

5. The next screen displayed by Duplicator, shown in Figure 14-24, allows you to select a recorder, a recording speed, and whether you need hard drive

staging. Because you have more than one SCSI CD-ROM device, you can select your recorder as the target drive. Duplicator displays a default recording speed; however, depending on the transfer rate of the source drive and the speed of your system, dropping to the next lower recording speed may make the difference between success and failure. I recommend recording disc-to-disc at single speed for the best results. Since you're using two devices, select the *Direct disc-to-disc* option. Click <u>N</u>ext> when you're ready to continue.

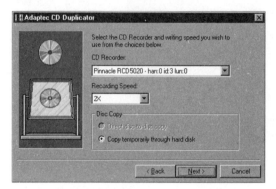

Figure 14-24: This Duplicator screen allows you to select the target recorder and the recording speed. It also indicates whether you need hard drive staging.

6. Figure 14-25 illustrates the next Duplicator screen, where you can choose whether you'd like to perform a simulation, create the disc, or both. You can also specify how many copies of the source disc you'd like to make. Click Finish to start the recording process.

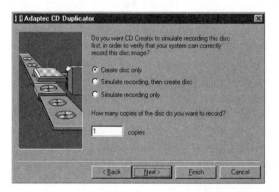

Figure 14-25: Like CD Creator, Duplicator allows you to run a simulated recording before you actually duplicate a disc.

From this point, the process is just like making multiple copies of a disc, except that data is read and transferred directly from the source disc to the blank disc.

Recording Disc-to-Disc with a Single Drive

Are you lamenting that you only have one SCSI CD-ROM device? Cheer up! It's not necessary to have two SCSI CD-ROM devices to use the Adaptec CD Duplicator. If all you have is your CD-ROM recorder, you can still create an exact duplicate of another disc. However, the Duplicator must once again rely on your hard disk to store the information while you "swap" between the source disc and your blank CD-ROM. If you've ever used the DOS command DISKCOPY with a single floppy drive, you know that swapping involves unloading one disc and loading another.

To record disc-to-disc with just your CD-ROM recorder, follow these steps:

1. Select the Adaptec CD Duplicator from the Programs menu; it's also available from the Wizard if you select the *Create a copy of an existing CD* entry from the Wizard's task list.

2. From Duplicator's opening screen, click Next>.

3. Duplicator displays the screen shown in Figure 14-21. Select the *Copy from CD to CD* option and click Next>.

4. Duplicator displays the screen shown in Figure 14-22, prompting you to select a SCSI CD-ROM device on your system to use as the source. After you've loaded the source disc into your recorder, Duplicator scans it and displays the name of the disc (if it's an audio disc that you've already added to your music database), as well as the maximum read speed for the drive for the source disc. If you'd like to retest the speed of the drive and disc, click the Retest Speed button. When you're ready to continue, click the Next> button.

5. The next screen displayed by Duplicator, shown in Figure 14-24, allows you to select a recorder and a recording speed, and indicates whether you need hard drive staging. Your recorder is selected by default. The Duplicator displays a default recording speed; because you're staging the data temporarily to your hard drive, you record at the default speed. Because you're using just your recorder, Duplicator disables the *Direct disc-to-disc* option and automatically selects *Copy temporarily through hard disk*. Click Next> when you're ready to continue.

6. Figure 14-25 illustrates the next Duplicator screen, where you can choose whether you'd like to perform a simulation, create the disc, or both. You can also specify how many copies of the source disc you'd like to make. Click Finish to start the recording process.

From this point, the process is just like making multiple copies of a disc, except that data is read and transferred from the source disc to the hard drive, and then to the blank disc.

Recording Multisession CDs

Of all the specialized formats available with recordable CDs, multisession recording is probably the most popular. Unlike standard single-session CDs, where all the data is written to disc-at-once and write-protected, multisession discs can be recorded, used, and recorded again and again up to the total amount of space on the disc.

Warning

When I say that you can record additional sessions on a disc up to the total amount of space on the disc, I'm actually leaving out the 14 megabytes or so of space that separates each track. In fact, the first session you close takes nearly 30 megabytes of space to separate itself from the next track; thereafter, each time you write another session to a multisession CD you lose another 14 to 15 megabytes of space. For this reason, avoid recording multisession tracks for small amounts of data, since you may be losing more space on the disc than you use to record!

CD Creator allows you to write two different types of multisession discs:

✦ **Incremental.** If you need to add data to an existing session, incremental (sometimes called *linked multisession*) recording is your ticket. It includes all the accumulated data from the previous session that you've stored on the disc, and you can add to and "delete" files from the layout. To create a multivolume incremental disc, you must import the last session recorded on the disc before making your changes to it; this allows CD Creator to display the existing file layout so that you can make changes to it. Any files that remain in the new session are not actually re-recorded; instead, CD Creator merely includes their location in the directory for the new session. When the final session is added to an incremental disc, it's write-protected, and most CD-ROM drives that support multisession recording are able to read the final session. Figure 14-26 gives you an idea of how an incremental multisession disc is created.

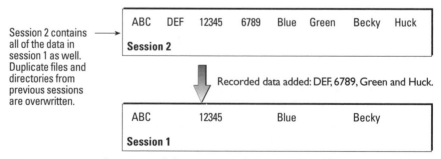

Figure 14-26: An incremental disc contains data from the last session and new data that you add. You can also delete existing data items.

HOW CAN I DELETE FILES FROM A CD-ROM?

Although I say you can delete files in an incremental backup, those files are not actually removed from the disc. After all, we are working with "write-once" media, and you can't actually erase files or format a recordable CD as you can a floppy or hard drive. However, if you indicate that a file that exists in the last session should not be included in the new incremental session, CD Creator will not add it to the new directory it writes to the disc, as shown in Figure 14-27. This prevents your computer from reading the location of that file, so it can no longer be read without a utility like Session Selector!

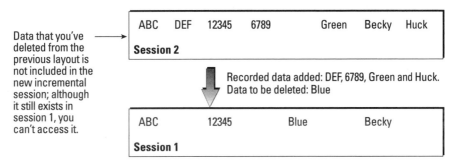

Figure 14-27: A deleted data item is deleted and "masked" in the new session of an incremental disc.

✦ **Multivolume.** Multivolume discs are simpler to create than incremental multisession discs, but you can't modify a previous session. Instead of appending data, CD Creator records another discrete session (or "volume"), and each session is accessed separately, much like separate drive letters on your PC. You can only read one session at a time, but all sessions recorded on the disc are available. These discs are suited for full archival backups or the storage of different types of files on the same disc. For example, if you're creating 3D graphics, you might have a collection of texture images in one session and a collection of 3D wireframe models in another. Figure 14-28 illustrates how a multivolume disc is created.

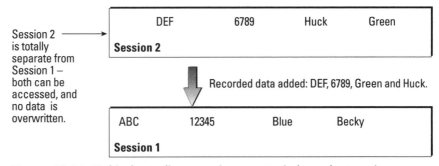

Figure 14-28: Multivolume discs contain separate, independent sessions.

Most multisession discs recorded these days are incremental. Although both types of multisession discs require you to run special software to switch between sessions, some older CD-ROM drives are limited to reading only the first or last session of a multivolume disc, so they're often only for your personal use. I'm assuming, of course, that your recorder is able to read the multivolume discs it creates!

One very important rule to remember: If you are planning to create a multisession disc, do not write-protect it! Once you have write-protected a disc, you can never record to it again, and it cannot be made into a multisession disc. You can still read and use a disc you've recorded without write-protection, but a CD-ROM drive takes a little longer to locate and load files.

As for other multisession requirements, you need a CD-ROM you've recorded with:

✦ at least one existing session;

✦ at least one available track for recording;

✦ enough free space for any new files that you're going to add, plus the extra space necessary to close the session and start a new session.

Both types of multisession discs begin with a disc that meets these requirements. You determine which type you're creating by how you create the disc layout before recording.

Creating an Incremental Session

If you want to keep most of the data you recorded in the previous session and simply add or delete data items, you should create an incremental multisession disc following these steps:

1. Load the target CD into your recorder and run CD Creator.

2. Select Import Session . . . from the data layout Disc menu.

3. CD Creator displays a list of sessions recorded on the disc. CD Creator uses one of these existing sessions as the basis for your new session; typically, you'll pick the last session you recorded on this disc. Click a session entry to select it, and click OK to load the layout for the session.

From this point, you can add and delete data items just as if you were creating a layout for a single-session CD-ROM. The recording procedure is also the same; simply click the Create CD Toolbar icon, or select Create CD from Layout . . . from the File menu.

Creating a Multivolume Session

If you wish to record a completely separate session that's not connected in any way to existing sessions on a disc, you should create an multivolume multisession disc.

No special steps are required to record a multivolume session; simply create a new layout from scratch. However, remember that CD Creator doesn't know that you're building the layout for a multisession disc that already contains data, so the amount of remaining space it shows at the bottom of the layout window is not accurate! Instead, you should subtract the space required for the layout from the actual space remaining on your target disc.

To record the session, simply click the Create CD Toolbar icon, or select Create CD from Layout . . . from the File menu. Make certain you load the proper disc for recording!

Switching Between Sessions

CD Creator 2 ships with a standalone utility, Session Selector, that can switch between different sessions on a multisession disc. To switch between sessions, follow these steps:

1. Load the multisession CD-ROM into your recorder or read-only CD-ROM drive.

2. Click the Start button and select the Adaptec Multimedia group from the Programs menu. Select the Advanced Features submenu. Click the entry for the Adaptec Session Selector to run the utility.

3. The Selector displays the dialog shown in Figure 14-29. The *Sessions on the CD:* list displays all of the detectable sessions on the disc you loaded, along with their creation date and time. If the Selector cannot locate any sessions on the loaded disc, try an alternate method by clicking the *Perform track-based search* checkbox and then the Refresh List button. You can also select another CD-ROM drive on your system that supports multisession discs. Click the *Available CD-ROM drives:* drop-down list box and pick the drive, then click the Refresh List button to display the sessions on the new disc.

Figure 14-29: The Adaptec Session Selector allows you to switch to another session on drives that support multisession discs.

4. Once the sessions are displayed, highlight the desired session entry in the list and click the Change button, or double-click directly on the desired entry to switch to it.

5. Finally, click Done to exit the Selector and return to Windows.

Your CD-ROM device should now display the directory contents for the session you selected.

Tip   By the way, once you've installed CD Creator 2 under Windows 95 you can also select a different session on a disc from Explorer! Double-click the My Computer icon to display your drives and right click the CD-ROM device that's using the multisession disc, as shown in Figure 14-30. From the pop-up menu, choose Select Session, and Windows 95 automatically loads Selector.

Figure 14-30: Under Windows 95, you can select a different session from the drive icon in Windows Explorer.

Recording Photo CDs

One of the most popular applications for recordable CDs is the archival storage of gigantic multimedia audio, video, and image files. Consider, for example, stock digital images that you use for professional desktop publishing. These files are usually saved in .BMP, .PCD, .TIF, or .PCX format at very large resolutions, which preserves their detail and makes them easier to reduce to different sizes. However, at these resolutions it's not unusual for these image files to occupy anywhere from 5 to 25 megabytes of hard drive space each. Obviously you're not going to keep your prized collection of rhinoceros and elephant images that you snapped in the wilds of Africa on your hard drive for very long!

For this reason, companies like Corel Corporation have been distributing their stock images on CD-ROM for many years. I have several of the CD-ROMs from the Corel Professional Photos series, each of which includes 100 stock images of a particular subject in PCD format. Plus, if you have a Kodak PhotoCD player, you're likely to have several CD-ROMs full of your own snapshots in high-resolution digital form, which are developed from a standard roll of film — no need for an expensive flatbed scanner.

In this section, we use Adaptec's PCD Creator to compile our own Photo CDs with images from Corel Professional Photo discs and Kodak PhotoCDs. PCD Creator is actually a sophisticated "front-end" interface for CD Creator. You design your Photo CD layout and read in the source files using PCD Creator, but PCD Creator automatically launches CD Creator when it's time to actually record the disc.

Actually, Kodak's PhotoCDs are written in a proprietary format, so the Photo CDs you create cannot be used in a Kodak PhotoCD player. However, you can add images to your Photo CDs from an existing Photo CD using PCD Creator.

Using the PCD Creator Layout Window

Let's launch PCD Creator and introduce you to its layout window. Click the Start button on the Windows 95 Taskbar and select the Adaptec Multimedia group from the Programs menu. Select the Advanced Features submenu. Click the entry for the Adaptec PCD Creator to run the program.

When you run PCD Creator, it immediately opens its layout window, as shown in Figure 14-31. This window is divided into two sections by a movable vertical bar. On the left will appear the thumbnails for all of your source images from the Corel or Kodak disc in the drive, while the thumbnails representing the images you choose to record appear in the right section. I usually move the bar to the middle of the window, so that I can see more of my layout on the right.

Along the top is a menu system and a Toolbar very similar to their CD Creator counterparts; however, there is an additional drop-down list box at the end of the Toolbar. This list box displays the text description of each image on the source disc, and you can jump directly to a specific image by selecting it from this list box. At the bottom of the window is the familiar bar graph indicating how much space remains for additional items, and the status line that displays a single line of help for each menu command or Toolbar button.

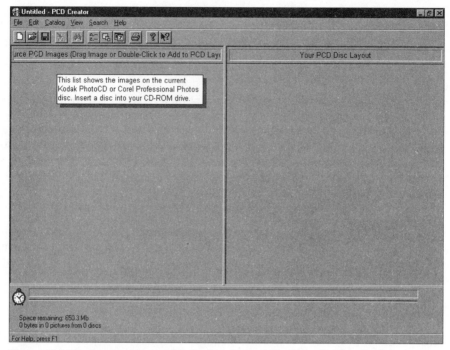

Figure 14-31: A new, empty PCD Creator layout. The left window displays source images, while the right window displays the images you want to record.

Loading and Saving PCD Layouts

Just like CD Creator, existing layouts can be loaded from the File menu. Select the Open . . . item on the File menu to display a standard Windows Open File dialog. By default, any layouts you've saved with PCD Creator have the extension .PCL, and the Open File dialog displays only these files; however, you can view all files regardless of extension by clicking the *Files of type* drop-down list box and selecting All Files (*.*). Once you've found the PCD layout file you want to load, double-click it, or highlight it and click the Open button.

If you need to work on a layout later or record the layout in the future, you need to save the layout to disk before exiting PCD Creator.

If this is the first time you've worked with this layout, select the Save item on the File menu to display a standard Windows Save File dialog. Enter a name in the *File Name* field, and click Save. The .PCL extension is added automatically.

If you loaded this layout file from disk, selecting the Save item on the File menu automatically updates the existing file on your disk.

If you want to save an existing layout file under a new name, select the Save As . . . item from the File menu. PCD Creator allows you to rename the file before saving it to disk — this is a good way of creating a copy of an existing layout as a starting point for a new layout.

Adding Images to Your Layout

Although there's no Wizard to help automate the task of adding images to your PCD Creator layout, it's still a very simple process! You can add a total of 100 images to a single Photo CD. Follow these steps to add an image:

1. Load a Kodak PhotoCD or Corel Professional Photo disc into the fastest CD-ROM device on your system. Although you can read images into PCD Creator from your CD recorder, it's much faster to load them from a read-only drive!

2. Now run PCD Creator to display a new blank layout window, pull down the Catalog menu, and click the Select CD-ROM Drive . . . item. PCD Creator displays a small dialog prompting you to specify the drive that contains the source image disc, as shown in Figure 14-32. Select the desired drive from the *Source CD-ROM drive:* drop-down list box. If you'd like to display shared network CD-ROM drives in the list, enable the *Include Network Drives* checkbox. Click OK to close the dialog and load the images. Your screen should now look something like Figure 14-33.

Figure 14-32: The Select CD-ROM drive dialog allows you to load source images from the fastest CD-ROM device on your system.

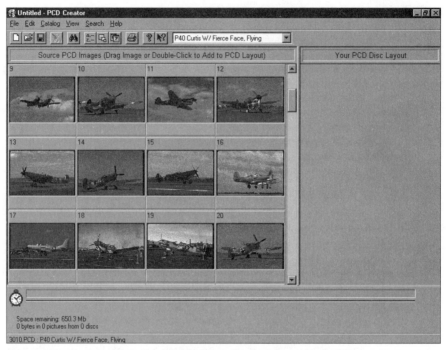

Figure 14-33: A Corel Professional Photo disc has been loaded into PCD Creator, and we're ready to begin selecting images for our layout.

3. There are three ways to add images to the right side of the PCD Creator window:

✦ Add a single image by dragging its thumbnail to the right side of the screen, or by double-clicking directly on the thumbnail.

✦ Add multiple images by holding down the Ctrl key while clicking each image you want to add, and dragging them to the right side of the window. You can also select multiple files using the Ctrl key and use the Add Selected item from the Edit menu to add them to the layout.

✦ Finally, you can select all of the images on the source disc and add them all to your layout with the Edit menu Add All command.

Each source image added to your layout is marked with a check mark in the left side of the window to indicate that it has been added. PCD Creator also displays information next to each thumbnail image in your layout, including the filename, date and time stamp, source disc, and size.

If you need to change directories on the source disc to locate the images you need, select the Show PCD Files . . . item from the Catalog menu. PCD Creator displays the dialog shown in Figure 14-34. You can type the full directory path where the source files are stored, or you can click the Browse . . . button and navigate with your mouse. Once you've found the directory containing the source files, highlight the files and click View to add them to the left side of your PCD Creator window.

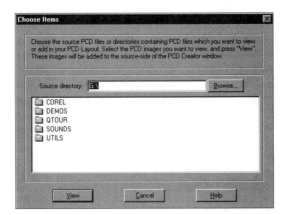

Figure 14-34: If you need to load image files from a directory on the source disc, you can specify the directory or the individual files from this dialog.

Deleting Images

"Whoops, I didn't mean to add that!" Luckily, PCD Creator allows you to remove one or more images from your layout. Use one of these methods:

✦ Delete a single image by clicking the thumbnail and pressing the Delete key, or select the Remove Selected item from the Edit menu.

✦ Delete multiple images by holding down the Ctrl key while clicking each image you want to remove, and then press the Delete key, or select the Remove Selected item from the Edit menu.

✦ Finally, you can remove all of the images in your PCD layout with the Edit menu Remove All command.

PCD Creator does not prompt you for confirmation, so be careful when deleting images! Of course, you aren't deleting them from the source disc, so you can always re-add an image if you delete it by mistake.

Renaming Images

Because you may add images from several different discs and Photo CDs do not have directories like a data disc, PCD Creator allows you to rename one or all of the files in your layout so that you can more easily recognize them.

There are two methods of naming images in PCD Creator:

✦ Standard 8.3 MS-DOS filenames. If you elect to use MS-DOS filenames, PCD Creator reserves the last three characters of each filename for a number that's automatically generated, like "BATMN001" through "BATMN300." The three-character extension is always .PCD, for Photo CD.

✦ Long filenames. You can select long filenames from the Options dialog, but they must still use the .PCD extension.

If PCD Creator is displaying catalog information, you can rename an individual image. Simply click in the New Name edit field and type the new prefix.

Tip By default, PCD Creator displays information next to each image in your layout; this information contains an edit field where you can rename individual images. If you don't see any text next to the images in your layout, you can toggle catalog information on from the View menu Options dialog, which we discuss later.

You can also rename all of the images you've already added to your layout with the same prefix. From the Edit menu, select Rename All. PCD Creator displays the Rename All Images dialog shown in Figure 14-35. Enter the prefix you want and click OK to begin the process.

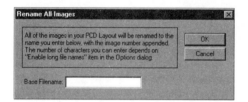

Figure 14-35: You can give all of the image files in your layout the same prefix from this dialog.

Viewing Images

PCD Creator includes a convenient "slide show" mode to display one or more of the images on your source disc. Are the images on your source disc very similar? Or perhaps it's been some time since you looked at these images? If the thumbnails don't show enough detail for you to determine which images you want to copy, use the slide show mode to display them full-screen. You can configure the delay, display size, and mode for slide shows from the View menu Options dialog, which we discuss later.

There are two methods of starting a slide show:

✦ If you only want to display one or two images, hold down the Shift key and select them, then pull down the View menu and click Selected Image. You can also use the Ctrl-I hotkey sequence.

✦ If you want to display all of the images on the source disc, select All Images from the View menu.

By default, PCD Creator displays each image for two seconds and then automatically moves to the next one; however, if you've selected manual mode, you can continue to the next image at any time by clicking the left mouse button. To exit the slide show, press Escape.

Sorting Images

Another easy way of organizing the images you've added to your layout is to sort the layout display, and PCD Creator gives you three sort criteria: name, date, and source disc.

✦ To sort your layout by filename, select Sort from the Edit menu and then click Name. You can also click the Name Toolbar button, which looks like a list with entries marked "A" and "Z".

✦ To sort your layout by the source disc(s) you've used, select Sort from the Edit menu and then click Source. Alternately, click the Source Toolbar button, which looks like three cascading squares.

✦ To sort your layout by the image date stamps, select Sort from the Edit menu and then click Date. You can also click the Date Toolbar button, which looks like two calendar pages.

Searching for an Image

As you might imagine, manually searching through a hundred source images for a specific shot to add to your layout can be a task! However, PCD Creator offers a Search feature that can help; you can search for a specific string within the descriptive text that accompanies each image on your source disc. To find an image, follow these steps:

1. If you haven't yet specified a search string, select the Find item from the Search menu, or click the Toolbar Find Next button (it looks like a pair of binoculars). PCD Creator displays the Find dialog shown in Figure 14-36.

Figure 14-36: Use the Find dialog to locate a picture by a string in its text description.

2. Enter the target string in the *Find What:* field and indicate whether PCD Creator should search above or below the image that's currently selected. Click F̲ind Next to jump to the next image with a description that contains your target string.

3. To continue the search using the same target string, click F̲ind Next again, or click the Find Next Toolbar button.

If you're running Windows 95, remember that its Find feature can locate an image on your source disc by its filename.

Printing Your Layout

You can create a jewel case insert for your Photo CD, but it only displays a thumbnail and number for each image. On the other hand, you can print the contents of your layout, which includes both thumbnails and text information, at any time. Instead of an insert, I print a copy of my PCD layout before I record it and store it in the jewel case along with the disc. If you save this printout, you can quickly determine the contents of each Photo CD in your collection and find a specific image. Either method saves a tremendous amount of time you'd otherwise spend loading and viewing the contents of each disc. It's even faster than searching for an image from the Find dialog!

To print a layout, select Print . . . from the File menu, or click the Print icon on the Toolbar. PCD Creator displays a standard Windows Print dialog, allowing you to select a system printer and specify copies or a page range; click OK on this dialog to send the pages to your printer.

PCD Creator also offers a Print Preview function, so you can see what the printed pages will look like before you actually send them to your printer. To display the pages, select Print Preview from the File menu; PCD Creator displays the preview window, as shown in Figure 14-37.

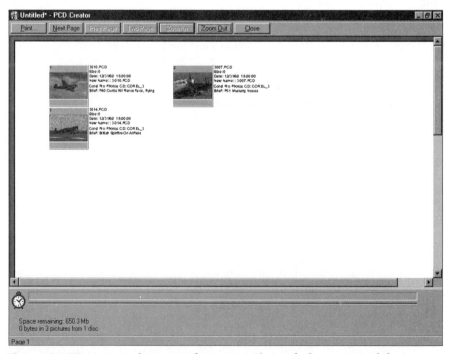

Figure 14-37: You can view pages from your printout before you send them to your printer with Print Preview.

To display the next page in your printout, click the Next Page button; to display the previous page in your printout, click the Prev Page button. If you'd like to see more real estate on a single screen, toggle the Print Preview display between one and two pages by clicking the Two Page button. To magnify or reduce the display, click Zoom In and Zoom Out, respectively. If the contents of the printout are acceptable, you can print directly from the preview window by clicking the Print . . . button.

To exit the Print Preview window, click the Close button.

Creating a Jewel Insert

Although I prefer to print the layout because it includes the text descriptions, you can also create a very professional looking jewel case insert for your new disc. You use CD Creator to design your insert; in fact, you can switch to the CD Creator layout window at any time. We discuss how to create jewel case inserts later, but you can display the Insert editor by following these steps:

1. Select Create CD Jewel Case . . . from the File menu.

2. Select the Show CD Creator command on the View menu to display the Insert editor. Your images appear in this layout.

Changing Options Within PCD Creator

If you're like me, the larger the thumbnail display the better, especially if you have a 17- or 21-inch monitor! You can configure the size of the thumbnail images and other display options within PCD Creator from the Options dialog. From the View menu, select the Options . . . item to display the dialog shown in Figure 14-38.

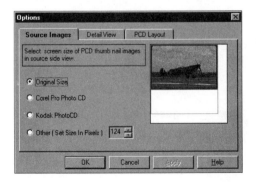

Figure 14-38: The Options dialog allows you to configure some functions in PCD Creator.

The Options dialog is divided into three tabs:

✦ On the **Source Images** tab, you can specify the size of the thumbnail images on the source side of your layout. The default choice is Original Size. Click Corel Pro Photo CD or Kodak PhotoCD to select a thumbnail size that matches the aspect ratio for the type of source disc you're using. In general, the Kodak display option allows you to fit more thumbnails in the same space. Finally, if you'd like to specify a custom thumbnail size, click the Other option and set a size in pixels.

✦ On the **Detail View** tab, you can configure PCD Creator's slide show. The View Size option specifies the size of the slide show images; you can select one of three window sizes, or you can choose Fit to Window to display each image within the current slide show window size. If you would rather have the slide show advance automatically, enable the *Automatic Mode* checkbox and set the amount of time that PCD Creator should delay before displaying the next image. If you disable automatic mode, each image is displayed until you click the left mouse button to continue.

✦ The options on the **PCD Layout** tab allow you to customize the appearance of the layout window. Under View PCD Layout, you can elect to display text information and the New Name edit box next to each image by selecting the *Image List with Text Information* option. If you'd rather display only the thumbnail, click *Image Catalog*. Under Show Text Information, you can choose which text information fields are to appear; displaying only an image catalog turns these fields off automatically. To remove a text field from the layout display, disable the corresponding checkbox. Finally, you can use long filenames as prefixes for your images by clicking the *Enable Long File Names* checkbox — remember, though, that PCD Creator still appends numbers to the prefix.

To save your changes and exit the Options dialog, click OK.

Recording with PCD Creator

Ready to record your PCD layout? As I mentioned before, PCD Creator launches CD Creator to record the disc. Follow these steps to record:

1. Select Create CD from Layout . . . from the File menu, or click the Create CD from Layout button on the Toolbar. PCD Creator displays the dialog shown in Figure 14-39.

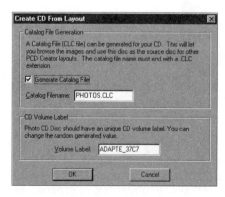

Figure 14-39: This dialog allows you to add a catalog file and specify a volume label for your Photo CD.

2. PCD Creator can optionally generate a catalog file that will allow you to browse and select images using your new disc as a source in the future. If you disable this field, you will save a small amount of room on your new disc, but you will not be able to access these images from within PCD Creator; in effect, you are storing the image instead of creating a Photo CD readable by other applications. I always generate a catalog file, and I recommend that you do, too; you never know when you may have to create another disc using these images! You can specify the filename for your catalog file in the *Catalog Filename:* field; it should be eight characters or less, and the .CLC extension is required. By default, the program uses the name PHOTOS.CLC.

3. Because PCD Creator displays the source CD in the text information for each image (and sorts by it as well), you should specify a unique volume label for your new Photo CD. The program generates one randomly, but I always type a more friendly, descriptive name in the *Volume Label:* field to help me remember the contents of the disc.

4. Once you've specified the catalog and volume name, click OK to begin the recording process. Control now passes to CD Creator, which displays the familiar Disc creation setup dialog.

From this point, the recording process is the same as it is for a data CD-ROM.

Recording Video CDs

Another form of multimedia file that requires hundreds of megabytes to store is digital video. The expensive computer hardware once required to create digital video has suddenly become affordable for everyone, and multimedia editing software for digital video is rapidly dropping in price. At the same time, home PCs are now powerful enough to provide the high frame rate needed for good quality digital video, and Windows 95 has brought seamless support for PC video to the operating system itself. Of course, if you're using a Macintosh, you've been enjoying digital video for years.

Everywhere you look these days you see applications for digital video, including multimedia entertainment and "edutainment" titles, raytraced animation and morphing, Internet content, videoconferencing, and even full-length feature films on disc.

Digital video is usually stored on compact disc in .MOV (Quicktime), .MPG (MPEG), or .AVI (Windows Video) format. In this section, we use Adaptec's VCD Creator to record digital video in .MPG and .AVI format, as well as still images in .BMP, .GIF, .JPG, .PCX, .TIF, and .TGA formats. You can read these discs using computer CD-ROM drives, Video CD players and — with the proper application — CD-I players.

Just like PCD Creator, you create your VCD layout using VCD Creator, but CD Creator does all of the actual recording.

Using the VCD Creator Layout Window

To launch VCD Creator, click the Start button on the Windows 95 Taskbar and select the Adaptec Multimedia group from the Programs menu. Select the Advanced Features submenu. Click the entry for the Adaptec VCD Creator to run the program.

Let's create a disc using the VCD Wizard in the next section; for now, click Cancel and look at the VCD Creator layout window. As you can see from Figure 14-40, this window is actually composed of three smaller windows, each of which displays a different view. The left window displays the clips you've added to your VCD layout, much like the right side of the PCD Creator window. The right window displays the branches of your layout's menu system and the sequence list. Finally, at the bottom of the screen is the Drive window that displays the source items you'll add from your hard drive.

Both the horizontal and vertical bars can be adjusted to change the window sizes, just like the PCD Creator layout window. However, the Toolbar contains only a set of standard buttons for file and editing functions like opening and closing files, cut/copy/paste, and print, so you use the menu system more often.

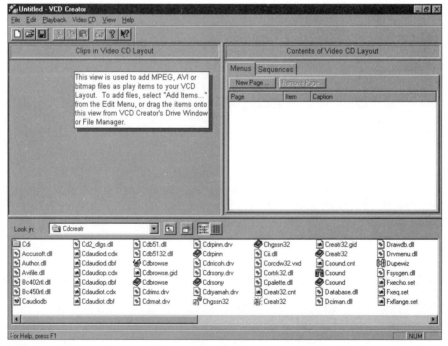

Figure 14-40: A new, empty VCD Creator layout. The layout window is divided into three major sections, each containing a different view.

Loading and Saving VCD Layouts

You can load existing VCD Creator layouts that you've saved to disk from the File menu. Select the Open . . . item on the File menu to display a standard Windows Open File dialog. By default, any layouts saved with VCD Creator have the extension .VCL, and the Open File dialog displays only these files; however, you can view all files regardless of extension by clicking the Files of type drop-down list box and selecting All Files (*.*). Once you've found the VCD Creator layout file you want to load, double-click it, or highlight it and click the Open button.

If your layout design is interrupted or you must record the layout in the future, you need to save it to disk before exiting VCD Creator. If this is the first time you've worked with this layout, select the Save item on the File menu to display a standard Windows Save File dialog. Enter a name in the *File Name* field, and click Save. The .VCL extension is added automatically. If you loaded this layout file from disk, selecting the Save item on the File menu automatically updates the existing file on your disk.

If you want to save an existing layout file under a new name, select the Save As . . . item from the File menu. VCD Creator allows you to rename the file before saving it to disk.

Using the VCD Wizard

By default, VCD Creator displays the Video CD Creator Wizard welcome screen shown in Figure 14-41. As an added bonus, you can prevent the VCD Wizard from running each time you start the program by enabling the *Do not run Wizard at startup* checkbox! The VCD Wizard operates very similarly to the CD Creator Wizard; you also navigate the VCD Wizard with the Next> and <Back buttons. In fact, you can choose to create a video CD as one of the tasks in the CD Creator Wizard list we discussed in Chapter 13; if you select it, CD Creator will launch VCD Creator and run the VCD Wizard for you.

Figure 14-41: The opening screen for the Video CD Creator Wizard.

VIDEO CD STRUCTURES

So what exactly are these two structures I have to choose from, anyway? Well, the Simple Video Sequence structure (often called *sequential* or *linear* display) is designed to show your video clips and still images one after another, from beginning to end, with no viewer control necessary (except to move backwards and forwards through the video that's currently playing). Think of simple sequence as a standard videotape, where you can rewind and fast forward, but you can't jump to another section of the tape or choose an alternate path through the tape. On the other hand, a one-level menu structure is much more complex (as you'll see from the extra steps in our VCD Wizard tutorial) and offers the viewer onscreen menus controllable through the numeric keypad on the Video CD player's remote. When designing a layout using a menu structure, you're actually linking a separate sequence of digital video clips to each menu choice.

Creating a Sequential Video CD

To create a simple sequential Video CD using the Wizard, follow these steps:

1. From the VCD Wizard welcome screen, click Next> to continue. The VCD Wizard displays the screen shown in Figure 14-42. Select the *Simple Video Sequence* option and click Next>.

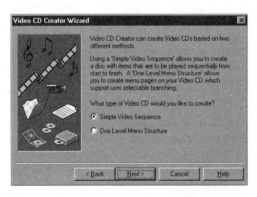

Figure 14-42: You determine the structure of your Video CD from this VCD Wizard screen.

2. Next, the VCD Wizard displays the Adding Play Items screen shown in Figure 14-43. Instead of adding data items as you did in the CD Creator Wizard, the VCD Wizard calls its video clips "*play items.*" You add video play items to your layout using one of two methods:

Figure 14-43: You can add play items to your Video CD layout from this VCD Wizard screen.

✦ First, you can simply click the <u>A</u>dd . . . button to display a standard Windows Open File dialog, where you can navigate through your system and select video clips. Once you've highlighted the file you want added to your layout, click Open.

✦ You can also drag and drop play items to the Adding Play Items screen from Windows Explorer; open an Explorer window, drag the file to the VCD Wizard screen, and release the mouse button.

3. For each video file play item you add, VCD Creator displays the Add New Play Item dialog, as shown in Figure 14-44. Although this dialog has three tabs, I usually don't change much; the defaults are usually correct:

Figure 14-44: The Add New Play Item dialog allows you to set several options for recording a specific play item while you're adding it to your layout.

✦ On the General tab, enter a unique name for the play item; I recommend that you place a number in the name so that you can quickly tell where the video falls in the sequence. You can select an individual frame from the video to appear in your layout by scrolling through the video with the sliding bar. The *Video Data* and *Audio Data* checkboxes allow you to enable and disable the video and audio for the play item; I use this to drop the audio portion of a video file that will be accompanied by a different music source.

✦ On the Video tab, VCD Creator displays a wealth of basic information regarding the video you've selected, including the format, frame rate, frame size, movie size in frames, and the total run time. On the right, you may have multiple choices for the output data format, depending on the source file. If you are offered choices, click the desired format.

✦ On the Audio tab, you can specify the audio track that will accompany your video clip. Typically, the audio is supplied in the same file as the video for MPEG and AVI format video, so select the Video source file option for the *Source of audio information:* field. However, if you want to supply your own audio for the selected video clip, choose the *Other file:* option and click the Browse . . . button. VCD Creator displays a standard Windows File Open dialog, and you can navigate through your system to locate the audio file to use. You may not be able to specify an alternate audio source for some MPEG format video clips. VCD Creator displays the file format, audio format, and play time for the current audio selection.

✦ Once all the information is correct, click OK. These same properties can be displayed from the menu system by highlighting the play item and selecting Properties from the Edit menu. VCD Creator updates the left portion of the layout window with your play item, and you can add additional items. To remove a play item from your layout, click Remove . . . to display the dialog shown in Figure 14-45. Highlight the entry to remove and click the Remove button, or click Cancel to exit the dialog.

Figure 14-45: You can remove play items from your VCD layout from the Remove Play Items dialog.

4. Once you've added all your play items, VCD Creator requires you to arrange them in a play sequence. This order is determined using the next VCD Wizard screen, shown in Figure 14-46. In the left column of the screen are thumbnails representing each selected video clip; to add a clip to the next slot in the sequence in the right column, click the thumbnail to select the play item and click Add> (or simply double-click the item). As you add items

in order to the sequence, they appear in the right side of the layout window. To remove a play item added to the sequence column, click the thumbnail to select the play item and click <u>R</u>emove> (or simply double-click the item). You can also add new play items from this screen: click the Add <u>F</u>ile . . . button, and VCD Wizard takes you through the process described in the last step. When you've added all of your play items in the order you like, click <u>N</u>ext> to continue.

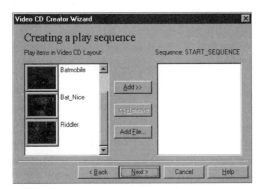

Figure 14-46: VCD Wizard allows you to change the order of your video clips in the sequence from this dialog.

5. As a final step to confirm your layout before recording, VCD Wizard allows you to playback the entire layout sequence. To view your layout, click the Playback . . . button; the VCD Wizard displays a set of standard VCR controls that allow you to pause, stop, or fast forward and rewind through the sequence. When you're ready to record your handiwork, click <u>N</u>ext>.

From this point, the recording process is the same as a data CD-ROM.

Creating a One-Level Menu Video CD

Building the menu structure for a Video CD is much more complex than for a simple sequential disc, and it requires a certain amount of preparation. For example, you should plan the branching structure on paper before you actually run VCD Creator. When designing the menu structure for your disc, keep in mind that a menu with more than 9 or 10 choices is unwieldy! The simpler, the better.

Warning

If you've just picked up your Video CD player or are new to recording, I suggest you read through this tutorial before you try to create a disc with a one-level menu structure! Remember, it's not necessary to build a menu if you're simply storing a number of clips for sequential viewing; the sequential structure is much simpler and requires far less preparation.

To create a Video CD with a one-level menu structure using the Wizard, follow these steps:

1. From the VCD Wizard welcome screen, click <u>N</u>ext> to continue. VCD Wizard displays the screen shown in Figure 14-42. Select the *One Level Menu Structure* option and click <u>N</u>ext>.

2. Next, VCD Wizard displays the Adding Play Items screen, as shown in Figure 14-43. Instead of adding data items as in the CD Creator Wizard, you add video clips, which VCD Wizard calls "*play items.*" As in Step 2 of the previous section, video play items can be added to your layout using one of two methods: either click the Add . . . button to display a standard Windows Open File dialog, or drag and drop play items to the Adding Play Items screen from Windows Explorer. For each play item you add, you can make the changes I described in Step 3 of the previous section from the Add New Play Item dialog. These same properties can be displayed from the menu system by highlighting the play item and selecting Properties from the Edit menu. You remove play items from your layout by clicking the Remove . . . button. After you've added all your play items, click Next> to continue.

3. VCD Creator requires you to arrange your play items in a play sequence called your START_SEQUENCE; this is the first sequence that appears when you load your new disc into your Video CD player. You determine this order in the VCD Wizard screen shown in Figure 14-46. The process is the same as Step 4 of the previous section on creating a sequential disc, so it's not repeated here. Once you've created your sequence and all of your clips are in the desired order, click Next> to continue.

4. To this point, VCD Wizard's steps for a simple sequential structure and a one-level menu structure are almost identical, but now we need to perform additional steps to create our menu. The VCD Wizard displays the screen shown in Figure 14-47. The background for your Video CD menu contains a list of the menu choices for the viewer, who will select from the Video CD player's remote control. However, it's been my experience that you rarely have a video clip that starts with a still image of those choices; therefore, I always click the Add from file . . . button and select an image I prepared with Paint Shop Pro. However, if you do wish to use as your background a frame you specified earlier for one of your video clips, you can select it from the *Play item:* drop-down list box. Click Next> to continue.

Figure 14-47: Selecting the background for a Video CD with a one-level menu structure.

5. Next, the VCD Wizard asks how many menu choices will be on your layout, as shown in Figure 14-48. Generally, you require one menu choice for each separate sequence you add to the disc. Highlight the value in the *Number of menu choices:* field and enter the correct number, or use the up and down arrows for the field to select the number you want; then click <u>N</u>ext> to continue.

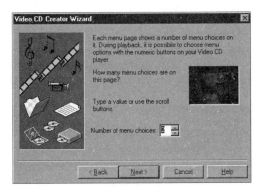

Figure 14-48: Specify the number of menu choices available to the viewer on this VCD Wizard screen.

6. On the next VCD Wizard screen, we link each of your menu choices to a separate sequence. By default, VCD Wizard creates a corresponding sequence name for each menu choice, as in "PLAY_SEQUENCE1" for menu choice 1, and so on. To edit these defaults, highlight the menu number to change and click the Edit button to display the Edit Sequence Name dialog shown in Figure 14-49. You can specify a new name for the play sequence in the *Name:* field, or link the menu choice number to another sequence from the *Available play sequences:* drop-down list box. Once everything is satisfactory, click <u>N</u>ext> to continue.

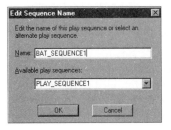

Figure 14-49: This dialog allows you to edit the name and link for any menu item or play sequence.

7. At this point, you've added a single menu page to your layout (at least one is required for the one-level menu structure). However, you can create additional menu pages with their own menu choices from this VCD Wizard screen; the viewer can jump between menu pages with the "<u>N</u>ext >" and "< <u>P</u>revious" buttons on the Video CD player remote control. Sounds familiar, doesn't it? To add a new menu page to your layout, click the Add Page

button; the VCD Wizard returns to Step 4 of this procedure, and will return to this Adding Pages to Menu screen after each page. Once you've added all the menu pages you need, click Next> to continue.

8. Now it's time to build each of the play sequences you created. VCD Creator displays the same dialog you saw in Step 3, when you were building the START_SEQUENCE — however, now you're creating the sequences that are linked to your menu choices. Click Next> after each sequence; VCD Wizard allows you to edit each sequence in turn.

> **Tip**
>
> Here's a few tips to make this process easier! First, keep a sketch of your menu pages, their menu choices, and each linked sequence handy, so that you can refer to it. To avoid getting sequences mixed up, give each sequence a distinct name in Step 6. Finally, always check the *Sequence Name:* field above the right column on the Creating a play sequence screen; it displays the name of the current sequence you're working on. When you're working on a layout with multiple pages, it's easy to lose track of which sequence you **thought** you were editing!

9. You made it! As with the simple sequence procedure, VCD Wizard gives you a chance to playback your layout before you begin the recording process. To watch your layout, click the Playback . . . button; VCD Wizard displays a set of standard VCR controls that allow you to pause, stop, or fast forward and rewind through the sequence. Unlike a sequential layout, you can use the numbered keys under the VCR controls to select a menu choice, just as the viewer will do with the remote control. When you're ready to launch CD Creator, click Next>.

From this point, the recording process is the same as a data CD-ROM.

Adding Play Items Manually to a VCD Layout

There are three ways to add play items to the left side of the VCD Creator window:

✦ Add a play item by selecting Add Item . . . from the Edit menu. VCD Creator displays a standard Windows File Open dialog, allowing you to navigate through your system to find the source file. Double-click the item to add it.

✦ Add a play item by dragging it from the VCD Drive window at the bottom of the layout. The Drive window has a drop-down list box that allows you to change drives on your system. There are standard Explorer-style buttons to move up a directory, create a new directory, or toggle between the list and detail directory views. You can also double-click a directory to open it, just like an Explorer window.

✦ Finally, you can drag and drop a play item directly from Windows Explorer into your VCD layout.

Editing Menus and Sequences Manually

Although the VCD Wizard is the easiest way to create a Video CD, you can edit menus and sequences manually from the right portion of the VCD layout window. The fields are identical to those displayed by the Wizard — in fact, VCD Creator actually runs portions of the Wizard when you add a new page or link a sequence, so I won't repeat the steps here!

You can switch between the Menu and Sequence tabs by clicking the desired tab. When you're displaying the sequences you've created, you can switch between them by clicking the drop-down list box at the top of the tab and selecting the desired sequence to view from the list.

Validating a VCD Layout

Because of the complexity of a Video CD layout, proper validation before recording is even more important than it is within CD Creator. To validate your VCD Creator layout, select Validate Layout . . . from the Video CD menu. VCD Creator displays the dialog shown in Figure 14-50.

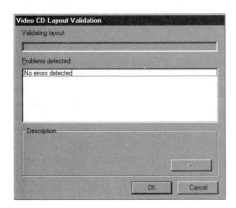

Figure 14-50: Validating a Video CD is recommended before you record it.

If no problems are found, VCD Creator displays the message "No errors detected." If VCD Creator does encounter problems in your layout, you can click the F̲ix . . . button to delete any play items from your layout that can no longer be found.

Selecting VCD Creator Preferences

There are a number of configuration settings you can change in VCD Creator to alter the look and feel of the program. Some of them are similar to their counterparts in CD Creator.

To begin, display the Adaptec VCD Creator Preferences dialog by selecting Preferences . . . from the File menu.

✦ On the General tab, the Startup fields determine what actions VCD Creator takes when you run it. By default, *Show Startup Window* is enabled, so the program displays its welcome banner and copyright information — you can turn the display off by disabling this checkbox. VCD Creator automatically launches the VCD Wizard upon startup, but you can prevent this by disabling the *Open Disc Wizard* checkbox. The New CD Layout option group specifies what happens when you select New CD Layout . . . from the File menu. By default, VCD Creator opens the VCD Wizard, but you can elect to display only the blank layout window by selecting *Create an empty CD layout* instead.

✦ On the Disc Creation tab, you can specify where VCD Creator is to store temporary files during recording. Due to the huge size of most digital video clips, VCD Creator can use multiple directories on several drives to store temporary files (unlike CD Creator, which uses only a single temporary file location). To use the default location assigned for Windows temporary files, enable the *Use Windows TEMP directory* checkbox. If you disable this checkbox, select one or more locations yourself by clicking the Add . . . button, which displays the Add Temporary Files Directory dialog shown in Figure 14-51. Type the full pathname into the *Path:* field, or you select an existing directory by clicking the Browse . . . button to navigate through your system. To limit the amount of temporary space allocated to this directory, enable the <u>L</u>imit disk space usage and enter a maximum size in megabytes.

If you have several hundred megabytes free, I recommend you do **not** limit your temporary space; the more temporary space available, the faster the recording process is. If you must limit your disk space, I recommend a minimum of at least 100 megabytes, with a maximum of three-fourths of your drive's available space. Click OK to accept the new location. You can remove a temporary directory assignment by highlighting the path entry and clicking the Remove . . . button.

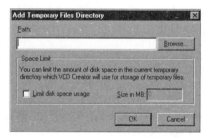

Figure 14-51: This dialog allows you to select a temporary directory for VCD Creator, as well as limit the space that will be used.

Modifying Video CD Properties

A number of changes to the properties for your new Video CD disc can be made from the Video CD Properties dialog, just as you were able to change some of the properties for a data CD-ROM. To begin, display the Properties dialog shown in Figure 14-52 by selecting Properties . . . from the Video CD menu.

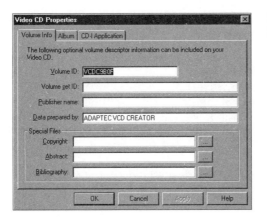

Figure 14-52: The Video CD Properties dialog.

✦ On the Volume Info tab, you can specify the Volume ID, Volume set ID (for multidisc sets), a publisher name, and a preparation ID. All of these fields are optional except for the Volume ID (and possibly the Volume set ID), and VCD Creator supplies a default Volume ID and preparation ID for you. Under Special Files, are the same optional Copyright, Abstract, and Bibliography fields we saw in CD Creator; they identify three text files that exist in the root directory of the disc. The three files contain the disc's copyright information, abstract copy, and bibliography, respectively. If you decide to use these fields, you must create the files manually on your hard drive; you can then select them by clicking the File Browser buttons next to each field, which carry the cryptic ellipsis label (". . .").

✦ On the Album tab, you define the characteristics of a multivolume album set. The same *Album identification:* field value must be used on each volume in the set, and you must specify in advance how many volumes the album set will contain in the *Number of volumes in album:* field. Set the *Ordinal number of the volume:* field to the volume number for the disc you're currently creating. If you feel that the material should be rated for parents, select one of three rating categories in the *Viewing restriction:* drop-down list box. If no rating is required, leave the field set to the default value of None.

✦ On the CD-I Application tab, you can enable or disable Video CD support for CD-I players. If you are certain that your Video CD will not be played on a CD-I player, disable this field. The CD-I application does not interfere with the operation of your Video CD player, so you can leave it enabled. Note that your CD recorder must be able to write mixed Form 1 and Form 2 sectors on a Mode 2 CD-ROM; most drive manufacturers simply state that their recorders support CD-I recording as another format.

Tip If you're not certain whether your drive handles mixed sectors in Mode 2 and there's no mention of CD-I support for Video CDs in the list of formats supported by your recorder, you can still determine whether to use it without ruining a disc! Create a Video CD layout with the *Include CD-I player application on Video CDs* checkbox enabled and try a simulated recording; if it completes successfully without reporting errors due to sector recording problems, then your drive supports this feature.

Once you've made all the changes to the properties for your Video CD, don't forget to click OK to save your changes!

Modifying Display Properties

Need more screen area to work with a really complex VCD layout? VCD Creator allows you to toggle the display of the Drive window, Toolbar, and Status Bar off. Also, if you don't use the Drive window to add play items, there's really no need for it, so you can hide it and expand the other two portions of the VCD layout window.

Pull down the View menu and click the desired item to toggle it; if the display item is on, a check mark appears next to it.

Click the Options . . . item from the View menu to specify the thumbnail image size you prefer; you can select one of three image sizes, or you can choose Custom to enter your own size.

Recording with VCD Creator

Once your VCD layout is ready to go, VCD Creator launches CD Creator for the actual recording. To record, follow these steps:

1. Select Create CD from Layout . . . from the Video CD menu. You can also create a disc image from the same menu if you prefer. You'll see VCD Creator launch CD Creator and build the data layout automatically — it's fun and doesn't cost anything, so sit back and relax while you watch it!

2. CD Creator displays — you guessed it — our old friend, the Disc creation setup dialog! From this point, the recording process is the same as it is for a data CD-ROM.

Recording CD-EXTRA Discs

Now that we've discussed PCD Creator and VCD Creator in detail, let's return to some of the advanced recording formats available within CD Creator itself: for example, the CD-EXTRA disc. As you learned earlier, a CD-EXTRA disc is much like a standard mixed-mode CD-ROM, but the data and audio tracks are recorded in separate sessions. The audio tracks are recorded first, so a standard audio CD player can read them; this prevents your CD player from attempting to play a data track intended for your computer's CD-ROM drive. CD-EXTRA discs can also carry additional text information describing each track, so they're often used to carry both music and digital video clips.

Note

This all sounds great — but, once again, the specter of compatibility raises its ugly head! As mentioned before, not every CD-ROM drive can correctly read a CD-EXTRA multisession disc, so the data session may not be accessible on many computers. If you're more concerned with the audio portion, this isn't a problem; any audio CD player or CD-ROM drive can play the audio tracks on a CD-EXTRA disc. Also, if you already know that the computer that will use the disc supports the CD-EXTRA format, there's no problem. Otherwise, I suggest that you use a CD-EXTRA disc only when you definitely require a separate data session or you absolutely must have the special CD-EXTRA information. If you don't require either of these features, then create a standard audio disc (and a separate standard data CD-ROM if you need it). You may end up with two discs, but you can guarantee that **all** of the information is readable by **any** CD-ROM drive.

To record a CD-EXTRA disc, follow these steps:

1. First, run CD Creator and display a new blank layout.

2. Select the Properties item from the Disc menu to display the Disc Properties dialog, and choose the General tab.

3. Click the *Enable CD EXTRA format* checkbox; the Properties . . . button is no longer grayed out. CD Creator prompts you for confirmation that you wish to create a CD-EXTRA disc, because some CD-ROM drives do not support them. Click Yes to confirm.

4. While we're in this dialog, click Preferences . . . and let's add the general disc data. CD Creator displays the dialog shown in Figure 14-53.

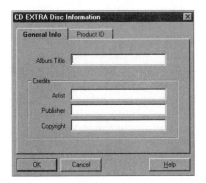

Figure 14-53: The CD EXTRA Disc Information dialog allows you to specify general identifying data for your CD-EXTRA disc.

5. On the General Info screen, enter an album title, artist, publisher name, and copyright date. These fields are optional, but I recommend you enter at least the album title and artist name; these two fields override the *Disc Title:* and *Artist Name:* fields on the Disc Properties dialog.

6. Next, click the Product ID tab. If you need more exotic information like UPC and ISBN product codes, or creation and publishing dates on the disc, enter them here. Both dates must fall between January 1, 1980, and January 18, 2038. Once again, these fields are optional. Click OK to save your changes and return to the Disc Properties dialog, then click OK again to return to the menu system. At this point, CD Creator now knows you're creating a disc in the CD-EXTRA format. CD Creator automatically creates the separate sessions and makes the necessary changes for recording.

HEY, WHERE DID THOSE FILES COME FROM?

If you explore the data layout for a CD-EXTRA disc, you'll see that a directory named CDPLUS was automatically created, and that this directory contains files that are grayed out. You can't modify or delete these files from your layout because they contain the information specific to this CD-EXTRA disc, including the text you added for audio tracks and the general information you added in steps 5 and 6 of the CD-EXTRA tutorial. You can safely ignore this entire directory — now, go about your business, there's nothing more to see here!

7. The next step is to add audio tracks to your layout. Use the procedures learned in Chapter 9 to add tracks until the audio portion of the layout is complete.

8. Now let's add the CD-EXTRA information for each audio track. From the Audio Tracks tab of the layout window, highlight the first track in your layout and select the CD-EXTRA Info item from the Track menu. CD Creator displays the CD-EXTRA Track Information dialog shown in Figure 14-54. It's very similar to the CD-EXTRA Disc Information dialog we saw earlier, but this time all of the fields pertain only to the highlighted track. On the General screen, you can change the track title and enter an artist, composer, publisher name, and copyright date. Click the Miscellaneous tab to specify the ISRC number, creation and publishing dates, the genre, and the musical key for this track. These fields are optional and do not default to the same values entered in the CD-EXTRA Disc Information dialog earlier. If you do change the track name, the CD-EXTRA information is saved with the new name, but the track name in the layout window does not change. Once all the needed information is entered, click OK to save the data and return to the layout window.

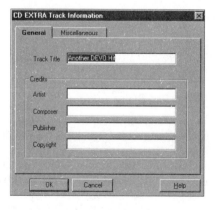

Figure 14-54: You can specify general identifying data for a specific track from the CDEXTRA Track Information dialog.

9. Repeat step 8 with each audio track in your layout.

10. Once you've added all the track-specific information, you're done with the audio portion of your disc. Click the Data Files tab to display the data portion of your layout. Use the procedures learned in Chapter 9 to add data items until the data portion of the layout is complete. To avoid conflicts with the CD-EXTRA files, do not add any data items to the \CDPLUS directory.

11. Done with the data layout? Then you're ready to record! Click the Create CD Toolbar button or select Create CD from Layout . . . from the File menu. From this point, everything is standard operating procedure for recording a mixed-mode disc. CD-EXTRA discs are automatically write-protected, so be certain your layout is correct before you record!

Recording Bootable CDs

Let's turn our attention to recording a truly specialized disc: the "bootable" CD-ROM, that contains the operating system and all the required system files for certain computers! Essentially, a bootable CD-ROM contains the same system information and system files as a bootable floppy, as well as programs and data files. The system BIOS and drive controller in most PCs don't support booting from a CD-ROM, so don't expect your home system to do this, but many "diskless" workstations used on networks have this feature built into their motherboards or drive controllers. The computer boots off the CD-ROM just as if it was booting from a floppy drive; the big difference, of course, is that the boot procedure cannot write any data to the disc. For example, if you're creating an MS-DOS bootable disc, you must make certain that your AUTOEXEC.BAT file doesn't contain any statements or programs that write data to the A: drive during the boot process.

Note

The "El Torito" specification is the official standard for bootable CD-ROMs, and it provides the ability for some computers to boot from any one of several separate floppy or hard drive images stored on a single CD-ROM. Now there's a fun fact to share with others, right?

Before you get started, you need a to create a bootable 1.2, 1.4, or 2.88-megabyte floppy. CD Creator copies the boot information from this disk as a disk image to a special file on the CD-ROM named BOOTIMG.BIN. To create a bootable floppy under MS-DOS 6.22, insert a blank floppy disk into your A: drive and from the DOS prompt type the command:

FORMAT A: /S

If you boot your PC from the A: drive, format the disk in your B: drive instead with the command:

FORMAT B: /S

At the end of the formatting process, DOS adds to the disk the system files required to make it bootable. You should also add whatever special files are needed during the boot process; in other words, you should be able to boot your computer correctly using only this floppy, so make certain that you add mouse drivers, DOS programs, and whatever else is needed.

Now follow these steps to create the CD-ROM:

1. Run CD Creator and open a new CD layout by selecting New CD Layout . . . from the File menu.

2. Insert the bootable floppy in your A: or B: drive; CD Creator can read either drive.

3. Click the Data Files tab of the layout window to display your data layout, then select the Properties item under the Disc menu.

4. Select the ISO 9660 file system from the drop-down list box and click the File system Properties . . . button next to it. You can't create a bootable CD-ROM with the Joliet file system.

5. CD Creator displays the ISO 9660 Properties dialog. At the bottom of the General tab, is the *Make disc bootable* checkbox; enable it and select the source drive that contains the bootable floppy. Click OK to exit the ISO 9660 Properties dialog, and click OK again to return to the menu system.

6. CD Creator immediately begins reading the contents of the loaded boot floppy disk; it's creating a disk image that will be read by the special BIOS I mentioned earlier.

7. Once CD Creator finishes reading the disk, you'll see two special read-only files added to the root of your layout: BOOTCAT.BIN and BOOTIMG.BIN.

From this point, the process is the same as building a standard data CD-ROM.

One final note: If you decide that this disc should not be bootable after all, you need to repeat steps 3 through 5 above, but you must disable the *Make disc bootable* checkbox. CD Creator automatically removes the two special files from your layout, and you can record it as a standard data CD-ROM.

Recording a Master Disc for Duplication

If you need several hundred copies of a single CD-ROM, it's not practical to duplicate them yourself on your PC. Although the prices for blank discs have dropped dramatically, a commercial replication center is still your best bet. You'll save money, headaches, and a heck of a lot of your time!

However, you still have to supply the replication company with a master disc that they can use for duplication, and most companies have a number of requirements for a recordable CD-ROM master disc. Typically, these shops request a write-protected, single-session disc created using the disc-at-once method. Some

companies also require a postgap after each data track on your master disc —
in English, they're requesting that each data track on your disc be followed with
150 blank sectors, which makes the disc easier to duplicate.

A good rule is to check with the replication company before you create your
master disc; find out what their requirements are, and then select those settings
from this list to insure your master disc is acceptable.

✦ First, if a single data track is required (disc-at-once), select Properties from
the CD Creator Disc menu to display the Disc Properties dialog and click the
Disc Optimizer tab. Click the *Preserve normal file ordering* option and then
enable the *Create a master disc (single data track)* checkbox. Click OK to
close the dialog and save your changes.

✦ Need a postgap? Display the same Disc Optimizer tab on the Disc Properties
dialog and enable the *Add 150 sector postgap to data tracks* checkbox. Click
OK to close the dialog and save your changes.

✦ Do not create a multisession master!

✦ Write-protect your master disc by enabling the *Write protect the disc*
checkbox on the Disc Creation Setup dialog.

Recording from Removable or Remote Drives

As mentioned earlier, it's a good practice to avoid recording a CD directly from a
network drive or a removable drive. If at all possible, copy the data to your local
hard drive and use that as the source drive instead. CD Creator attempts to do
this automatically by copying the data to a temporary buffer area it creates on
your hard drive. However, if you don't have enough space to record locally and
the data cannot be staged, remember these tips:

✦ Use the System Tester to determine the transfer rate for the drive you plan
to use as the source. Only tested drives appear in the *Removable/Remote
Drives* drop-down list box on the CD Creator Preferences dialog. You can
display this dialog by selecting the Preferences . . . item from the File menu.

✦ Make recording from a removable drive easier on yourself by minimizing the
number of swaps you have to perform! Select Properties from the CD Creator
Disc menu to display the Disc Properties dialog and click the Disc Optimizer
tab. Enable the *Minimize source media swap* checkbox. Click OK to close the
dialog and save your changes.

✦ Finally, consider writing a disc image to the network or removable drive
instead of attempting to record a disc layout with a large number of small
files. Of course, there must be enough room to hold the image on the
removable or network drive, but if you use a disc image you eliminate the
delays that your system incurs as each small file is opened, read, and closed.
Remember, it's faster to open and transfer a single large file than dozens of
smaller files!

Recording from the Music Cache

If you:

✦ primarily record audio CDs;

✦ have several hundred megabytes of hard drive room to spare; and

✦ record several discs that share some of the same tracks,

then the CD Creator Music Cache is for you! Unlike a temporary file, the Cache stores tracks between sessions; it's more like a disc image, but it automatically stores audio tracks as you use them in layouts. You can selectively delete unneeded tracks whenever you like. The Music Cache can also eliminate disc swapping or the loading of source discs during an audio recording. In this section, we discuss the details and use Music Cache entries to build a layout.

Enabling the Music Cache

By default, CD Creator leaves the Music Cache disabled until you need it. To enable the Music Cache, follow these steps:

1. Run CD Creator and select the Preferences . . . item from the File menu. CD Creator displays the Preferences dialog.

2. Click the Audio tab to display the Audio preference tab. Click the *Enable Music Cache* checkbox.

3. You can enter a path for the Music Cache in the *Path:* field, or click the Browse . . . button to navigate through your system. Make sure you select a hard drive with as much free space as possible! This field can be changed only when the Music Cache is currently empty.

4. Now enter the Cache size in megabytes. Remember, the larger the Music Cache, the more tracks it can hold. As a rough yardstick, every minute of CD-quality digital audio you store takes somewhere around 10 megabytes of hard drive space. The total number of tracks you can store is also dependent upon the length of your average track. If you store small sound bytes, you get many more tracks in 100 megabytes of space than if you store complete songs. Clicking the Contents . . . button displays the contents of the Music Cache if it's already enabled it.

5. Finally, save your changes by clicking the OK button on the CD Preferences dialog. At this point, CD Creator stores all audio tracks you use in your layouts in a "first-in, first-out" manner. Whenever a new audio track is added to a layout and the Music Cache is full, CD Creator automatically deletes the oldest track in the Cache to make room; you can, however, lock a file so that it remains in the Cache indefinitely.

Note   Normally, sound files are much smaller when recorded in 8-bit monaural format. You might think you could save space in the Music Cache by using files such as these. Unfortunately, that's not the case, because CD Creator automatically converts all WAV files to 44KHz, 16-bit stereo format, even though the quality of the sound file is not improved. In other words, all audio tracks are recorded as high quality digital audio, and they take up the same space regardless of original format.

Prerecording Tracks to the Music Cache

Now that the Music Cache is enabled, the audio tracks you record from source discs and WAV files are automatically stored in the Cache. However, you can prerecord tracks you've added to an audio layout to the Cache; this step saves time during the actual recording process, because you won't have to load and read the source disc. To prerecord tracks, follow these steps:

1. Run CD Creator and add an audio track from a source CD in the normal manner.

2. Click the track entry in the layout and select the Pre-record to Music Cache item from the Track menu. Note that the track recording must be small enough to fit within the Cache, or CD Creator will return an error message.

3. If the track will fit, you'll see the Copying CD Track dialog shown in Figure 14-55. CD Creator displays a progress bar and general information about the track as it converts the digital audio into a WAV file for storage in the Music Cache.

Note   You might have noticed that you can also prerecord tracks from source discs and store them as separate WAV files instead of within the Music Cache. If you don't have enough room to maintain a Music Cache, but you still have one or two sound files that you use on almost every recording, you can select Pre-record to WAV file . . . from the Track menu. Once CD Creator converts the source tracks to WAV files, you can add them to your layout from the Add Tracks dialog — click the From WAV File tab. By the way, this is a handy way of creating WAV files from any source disc; for example, if you've got a sound effects audio CD, you can record each track as a separate WAV file for use in Windows!

Figure 14-55: Prerecording an audio track to the Music Cache, where it's stored as a WAV file.

Controlling Your Music Cache

You can unlock, lock, and delete one or more tracks in your Music Cache at any time. To display the Cache, select the Music Cache item from the File menu; CD Creator displays the Music Cache Control dialog you see in Figure 14-56.

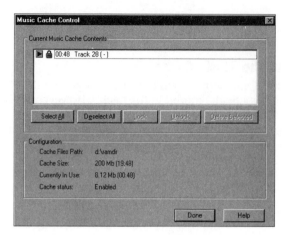

Figure 14-56: You can control the contents of your Music Cache from this dialog.

✦ To play a track, click the play icon next to the track name.

✦ To lock one or more tracks, highlight the desired entries and click the Lock button. You can also press Select All to highlight all the entries in the Cache. The padlock icons change to indicate that the tracks are now locked. CD Creator does not automatically remove a locked track as other tracks are added to the Cache. For safety, tracks that you prerecord from source discs are automatically locked, but you do not have to unlock them to delete them from this dialog. Tracks added automatically during the normal course of recording are not locked.

✦ To unlock one or more tracks, highlight the desired entries and click the Unlock button. You can also press Select All to highlight all the entries in the Cache. The padlock icons change to indicate that the tracks are now unlocked, and in the future they will be deleted to make room for other tracks as you record audio layouts.

✦ To delete one or more tracks, highlight the desired entries and click the Delete button. You can also press Select All to highlight all the entries in the Cache. Note that CD Creator does not prompt for confirmation! Just like when you delete a track from an audio layout, the original WAV file or audio track is not deleted — only its entry in the Music Cache.

The statistics at the bottom of the Music Cache Control dialog are updated each time you delete or add a track, so you can always get an approximate figure on the amount of space remaining in the Music Cache. Once you're done managing your Music Cache, click the Done button to return to the layout window.

Adding Music Cache Files to an Audio Layout

Now let's actually use a file from the Music Cache in an audio layout:

1. From your audio layout, click the Add Tracks Toolbar button to display the Add Tracks dialog.

2. Click the From Music Cache tab to display the tracks currently stored in your Music Cache.

3. Click the desired track and click Add Now to add the track to your layout. Once you're done adding tracks from the Cache, click the Done button to return to the layout window.

That's it! When CD Creator begins the recording process, it won't have to prompt you to load the source disc; instead, it reads the track directly from the Music Cache, and you don't even need to touch the source disc.

What's that you say? You say your Music Cache needs to be moved to another hard drive or partition but you don't want to lose all of the tracks it contains? Follow these steps to move the Cache and its contents:

1. Create the new cache directory and move all files with the prefix "CDMC" into it.

2. Select the Preferences . . . item from the File menu. CD Creator displays the Preferences dialog.

3. Click the Audio tab to display the Audio preference tab.

4. Click the Browse . . . button, navigate to the new directory and select it.

5. Click OK to save your changes and exit the dialog.

"Must-Have" Utilities

In this section, I describe several programs that I find helpful when creating a layout; three are inexpensive shareware, while the other two come with CD Creator version 2. These programs are just what you need to edit and catalog images, WAV files, and audio tracks!

Although we don't exhaustively describe each program, I cover the most common functions to give you a good idea of the features — also, the shareware programs in this section are included on the companion CD-ROM, so you can evaluate them yourself.

If you've read the description of these programs in Chapter 10, you can skip this section; it's repeated here for owners of CD Creator 2.

Using Paint Shop Pro

Of all the shareware programs I've registered and use on a daily basis, Paint Shop Pro from JASC Incorporated is the best. It's a rock-solid image editor, scanning package, paint program, screen capture utility, and image thumbnail browser that supports just about every image format ever encountered. Plus, it converts images between all of them! Paint Shop Pro has been the leading shareware image utility distributed on bulletin board systems and the Internet for years, and because of its success it's also sold in retail stores in its registered form. The program is available in 16-bit and 32-bit versions, and you can always find the latest version on the Web at www.jasc.com (or use FTP at ftp.jasc.com).

Let's look at the interface and the main editing window. Install the program and run it, and you'll see the window shown in Figure 14-57. Paint Shop Pro offers both a standard menu system and a customizable Toolbar, and it supports Adobe plug-ins and Aldus import filters, so you can expand the functionality of the program with external modules. On the right is a complete color palette — changing colors while painting or editing is as simple as clicking the eyedropper cursor on the desired color. Paint Shop Pro can also be configured with "floating" ToolBars.

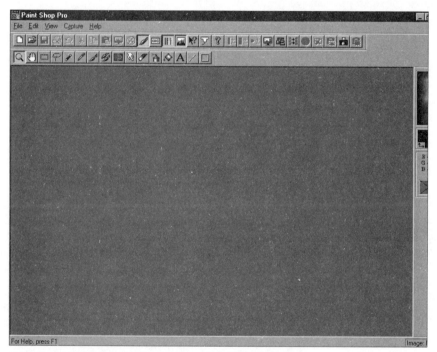

Figure 14-57: The Paint Shop Pro main editing window.

Loading Files

To load files within Paint Shop Pro, select the Open . . . item from the File menu or click the Open Toolbar button. There is a wide range of image types to pick from, so I usually leave the *File type:* field set to All Files. If you highlight an image, Paint Shop Pro provides you with its size and color depth, or you can click the Details . . . button to see the dialog shown in Figure 14-58.

Figure 14-58: Need to see a complete description of an image before you load it? Click the Details . . . button within the Paint Shop Pro Open File dialog.

Once you've selected an image and opened it, Paint Shop Pro displays it within the editing window, and you're ready to work your magic. Like any well-designed Windows program, Paint Shop Pro remembers where you last opened files and what type you were displaying, so it's easy to load more than one file in succession from the same directory.

Converting Between Image Formats

Converting files within Paint Shop Pro from one image format to another is as easy as using the Save As . . . command from the File menu. From the Save As dialog, select the new image format in the *Save as type:* drop-down list box; depending on the new format, you may have to select a format subtype as well (for example, GIF 87a or 89a). You can overwrite the existing filename, or select another to keep the original intact. Paint Shop Pro also offers a batch conversion feature for converting entire directories of images from one format to another automatically; select the Batch Conversion . . . item from the File menu.

Capturing Screen Images

Paint Shop Pro offers a number of different screen capture methods. As shown in Figure 14-59, the Capture Setup dialog, you can capture a window, the entire screen, or a specific area or object. The capture can be triggered from the keyboard, the mouse, or a delay timer. Paint Shop Pro is my favorite screen capture program, and it produced all the screen shots in this book.

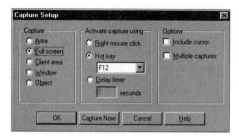

Figure 14-59: The screen capture support within Paint Shop Pro is excellent.

Image Editing

Whether you want to change a single pixel or an entire area of an image, Paint Shop Pro provides a good selection of standard paint tools, such as various brushes, an airbrush, flood fill, line and shape drawing, text objects, and a color replacement tool. You can zoom the image to the pixel level for close editing, or reduce the largest TIF format images so they fit within the window. The program has a number of methods to outline various screen areas for editing, including a neat Magic Wand feature you can use to selectively crop or alter parts of the image according to color. Paint Shop Pro comes with a number of image editing filters, and you can easily add your favorite plug-ins.

Modifying Image Color and Size

Paint Shop Pro performs well the altering of an image's color characteristics: changing the color depth, adjusting brightness, contrast and gamma correction, posterizing, and creating a negative image are all available from the Colors menu. For example, I change the color depth on images when I convert them for use on a Web site, since a 256-color image is still the standard for Internet graphics. Most of these features allow you to preview the change before you make it, so you can avoid the Undo button unless you really need it.

"All this is great, but what if I just want to resize or add a border?" No problem, Paint Shop Pro includes a complete range of sizing features under the Image menu. You can resize (with the same aspect ratio or not), crop, mirror, rotate, flip, and add borders.

Without doubt, Paint Shop Pro is the "Swiss Army Knife" of image editors, and it performs all of its functions as well as better-known commercial packages costing many hundreds of dollars more!

Using Media Center

Our second "must-have" program is also from JASC Incorporated. Media Center is a superb image catalog program — or at least that's its primary function, since I've found it useful in other applications as well! Like Paint Shop Pro, Media Center can convert images, and it can also perform batch manipulation; plus, it's a good slide show engine, and it even prints professional-looking catalogs of all of your multimedia files!

Yes, you read right: Media Center isn't just for images, it also catalogs WAV clips, MIDI music, AVI video, and FLI animation! All of these different formats can be arranged in albums, making it the ideal cataloging system for anyone with an ever-growing library of multimedia files. The program is currently available in a 16-bit version at `www.jasc.com` (or use FTP at `ftp.jasc.com`).

Catalog Those Files!

Media Center's primary job is to organize logically your multimedia files by arranging the files into albums, like the one you see in Figure 14-60. Of course, if that were all it did, I would be less impressed — instead, all the features Media Center provides work within this album environment, so you feel as if you're working with a tangible book. For example, you can:

✦ keep your album current by adding and deleting thumbnails;

✦ arrange the images any way you like using drag and drop;

✦ sort the contents of an album by one of several criteria;

✦ print any image, or the entire album with filenames;

✦ add keywords and descriptions to help locate any file with the Search option;

✦ use a removable drive or a recordable CD to store your images, because Media Center keeps track of disc and CD volume labels.

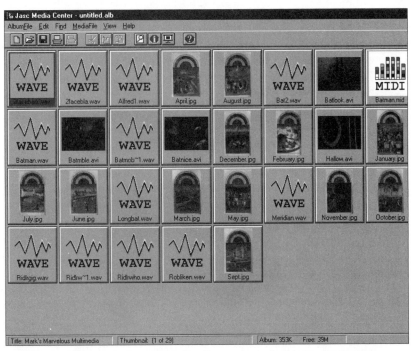

Figure 14-60: A typical multimedia album created with Media Center.

In fact, you can merge albums together, making it a good tool for any office that routinely handles business graphics and clipart.

Slide Show Features

Need a good slide show program for running a demo or displaying your image collection? How about a multimedia slide show? With the Media Center slide show engine, you can link WAV files to your show or pipe in background music directly from an audio CD. The show can repeat a specified number of times or run continuously. You can configure Media Center to move to the next image with the space bar, the mouse, or automatically after a certain delay. Are some of your images larger than the screen resolution? Media Center can automatically scale only those images that need altering for full-screen display.

After using Media Center, you'll wonder how you were ever able to locate a particular sound file, video clip, or image file without it!

Using the Adaptec Sound Editor

We cover two sound editors in this section, either of which can perform basic editing of WAV files before you record them on an audio disc. The first editor is supplied free with CD Creator 2 — it's the Adaptec Sound Editor.

Sound Editor's main window, displayed in Figure 14-61, features a basic Toolbar very similar to its cousin CD Creator; however, notice the addition of standard audio deck controls such as you see on a cassette deck. These include Play, Record, Fast Forward and Rewind, Stop and Pause. There's also a level meter at the bottom of the window that displays the volume of both the left and right channels.

Standard Editing Features

Like any Windows sound editor worth launching, the Adaptec Sound Editor allows you to cut and paste any portion of a WAV file. It even provides a luxury or two, including convenient Toolbar controls for replacing a portion of the file with the Clipboard contents (Paste Over), mixing the Clipboard contents with a highlighted portion of the file (Mix Paste), and playing the contents of the Clipboard. You can also enable an Undo feature if you have sufficient disk space.

Recording and Effects

The Adaptec Sound Editor records directly from your sound card in 8 or 16 bits, mono or stereo, and in 4 standard rates: 8000, 11025, 22050 and 44100Hz. You can select a specific rate other than the standard choices. There's a 10-band graphic equalizer (one feature that Cool Edit 96 doesn't have), and the program can convert a WAV file to another sample rate or sample size. You can also switch a file between stereo and mono.

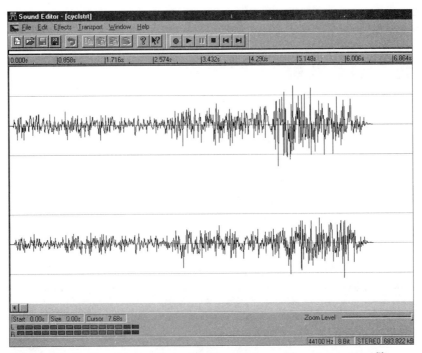

Figure 14-61: The Adaptec Sound Editor window with a stereo WAV file loaded.

The Adaptec Sound Editor offers a healthy selection of effects as well — not as many as Cool Edit 96, but more than I expect in a utility that ships with CD recording software! It includes support for amplify, echo and fade, flange, inversion, pop removal, and pitch shift; plus, each of these effects can be controlled from its own panel, including a number of preset effects. For example, Figure 14-62 shows the Flange settings panel.

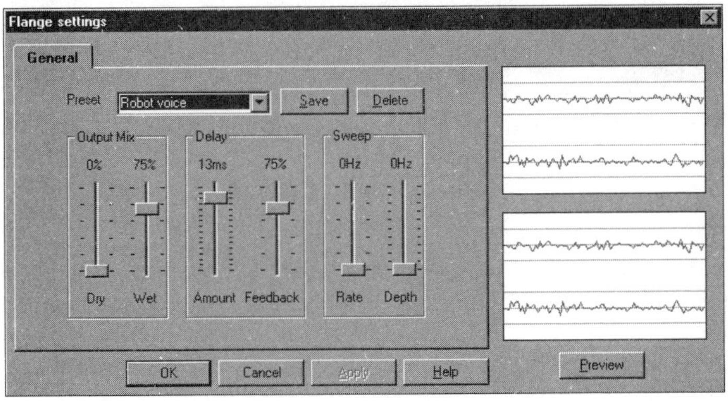

Figure 14-62: Adding a robotic flange effect to a WAV file with the Adaptec Sound Editor.

The Adaptec Sound Editor provides more than enough features for anyone but an audio professional, and it works well as a WAV editing tool.

Using Cool Edit 96

Although the Adaptec Sound Editor is a fine utility, my sound editing program of choice is Syntrillium Software's Cool Edit. Like Paint Shop Pro, it's a shareware success story. Cool Edit has grown up on bulletin boards and through the Internet. Between the two programs, I think of Adaptec Sound Editor as vanilla ice cream and Cool Edit 96 as Fudge Chocolate Chip — either will do the job, but Cool Edit 96 offers a lot more! The program is available in 16-bit and 32-bit versions, and you can download the latest version on the Web at `www.syntrillium.com`. Figure 14-63 illustrates the Cool Edit 96 window.

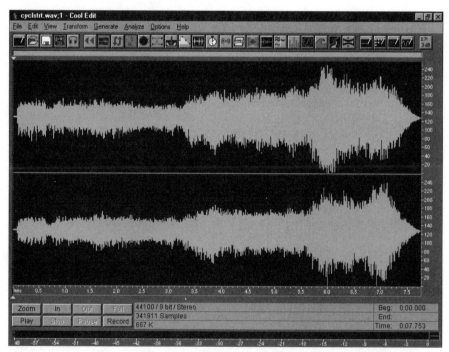

Figure 14-63: The Cool Edit 96 editing window with a stereo WAV file loaded.

Cool Edit 96 Extras

Cool Edit 96 provides almost all of the features of Adaptec Sound Editor, so let's discuss the additional features provided by Cool Edit 96.

First, the interface: You can configure the entire color scheme within Cool Edit 96, as well as customize the Toolbar to your liking. The program includes a very interesting and colorful spectral view, as well as the standard waveform display, or you can choose a frequency analysis. If you're interested in raw data, Cool Edit 96 can display a waveform statistics screen.

Both the Adaptec Sound Editor and Cool Edit 96 provide basic conversion between sampling rates. But unlike Adaptec Sound Editor, which was designed for use only with WAV format files, Cool Edit 96 allows you to load and save files in different formats! For example, you can load a SoundBlaster VOC format sound file, edit it, and then save it as a WAV file for recording with CD Creator. Other file formats supported by Cool Edit include AIF, AU, SND, and VOX, so you can edit files you pick up on the Internet that are meant for other operating systems. There's also a built-in macro scripting language, which allows you to perform multiple functions on one or more files automatically.

Cool Edit 96 Luxuries

Cool Edit 96 offers all the effects that Adaptec Sound Editor offers, and adds noise reduction, custom filters, and an honest-to-goodness brainwave synchronizer for creating your own relaxation sounds! You can put a sound file to music, or harmonize a sound using a particular chord, or generate the same DTMF tones as your telephone and modem. A favorite effect of mine is the distortion feature; try the "Bad FM reception" preset for a nifty effect. Cool Edit 96 can also generate brown, pink, or white noise (I didn't know there was a "brown noise").

Cool Edit 96 also provides a full set of CD-ROM controls, so you can use the program to play audio CDs. The program saves disc and song titles for display, and you can mark and return to a specific point on the audio disc.

In short, Cool Edit 96 is a professional tool for both the novice and advanced user, and it includes a number of unique features that you'll find in no other package. I recommend you give it a try!

Using the Adaptec Music Database Browser

Our final must-have utility is the Adaptec Music Database Browser, CDBrowser for short, and it also comes with CD Creator 2. Remember those artist names, audio CD titles, and track names we entered while adding tracks to our audio layout? CD Creator stores that information within a set of database files, and you can manipulate the contents of those same database files using CDBrowser. CDBrowser references six files; three end in the extension .DBF, and the other three are indexes which end in the extension .CDX. Never delete any of these files, because you'll definitely lose information and you'll have to reenter it again!

Figure 14-64 shows the CDBrowser window, which uses the familiar Toolbar with the addition of buttons for importing a database, adding a new disc to the database, and navigation buttons to move between entries.

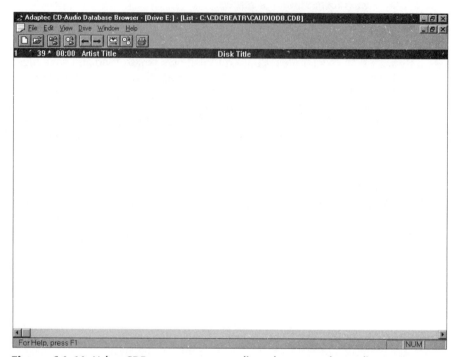

Figure 14-64: Using CDBrowser, you can edit and manage the audio CD information you use within CD Creator.

Adding and Managing CD Information

If you'd like to catalog your entire collection of audio CDs, there's no reason to run CD Creator to add discs. Thank goodness, because I can't imagine anyone going through the recording process and aborting it over and over just to get the CD information into the database! Instead, run CDBrowser and select Add Disc . . . from the Edit menu. You can also delete discs from the same menu. Figure 14-65 illustrates the Add Disc dialog.

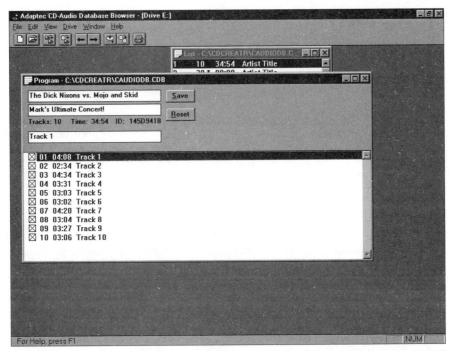

Figure 14-65: Adding a disc to the CD Creator database using the CDBrowser Add disc dialog.

Other Browser Features

CDBrowser offers a number of other features to make it easier to locate a specific disc — you can search for a string of text, insert an audio CD and search for the matching entry, or sort your CD information by title, artist, or tracks. If your friends also use CD Creator, or you use the program at work and at home, the import and merge functions can be helpful. Once the .DBF and .CDX files are copied to a floppy disk, you can trade and import CD information to your database.

Finally, I recommend the database catalog print feature; if you've taken the time to catalog your discs, you can print a complete listing of every track, artist, and disc title in your collection. If you have 25 or so discs of Mozart's work, such a list comes in handy when you visit your local record store!

How often will you use CDBrowser? It depends on how often you record audio tracks and how important it is to catalog your audio CDs. If you're a music lover like I am, and you record at least one or two audio CDs a month, I think you'll find it a "must-have" utility!

Creating Jewel Case Inserts

Our final section discusses another CD Creator advanced feature that you will either love or ignore, depending on whether you need a professional appearance for your finished data and audio discs: the Jewel Case Editor, which creates paper inserts that fit in the front and back of a standard CD-ROM jewel case.

If you have a standard CD-ROM jewel case with inserts handy, you can see how the front insert slides into the front of the case in front of the four tabs, while you must pry off the plastic square that holds the disc to reach the back insert. Normally, this isn't too hard, and you can do it in a few seconds without a tool; if the case is a bit stubborn, I sometimes use a screwdriver with a flat blade to carefully pry the back cover open.

Tip   You may notice that the Jewel Case Editor provides support for a Disc Printer that can print a label directly on the top of a recordable disc. However, for CD Creator version 2 this feature requires a professional CD-ROM disc printer, which you and I aren't likely to have! I recommend the NEATO labeling system we discussed earlier for creating a disc label with a standard inkjet or laser printer.

If you're making archival backups of your hard drive, or simply recording a video clip to take with you on a business trip, there's probably no need to print a jewel case insert. On the other hand, if you're recording an audio CD of harpsichord music or your rare live recording of your kazoo melodies to give as a gift, you probably need an insert. After all, a standard audio CD player can only display the track number, and most of us like to know whether we are listening to Chopin or George Thorogood and the Destroyers! If you're distributing data CDs to beta testers or shareware customers, you should consider the presentation of your work. To make a good first impression, I would both create an insert and use a disc labeler like the NEATO system, or buy a number of blanks that have been screen-printed.

The Jewel Case Editor Window

To use the Jewel Case Editor, run CD Creator and load a layout or create the layout from scratch. When your layout is complete, click the Jewel Case Insert tab at the bottom of the window to display the editor, as shown in Figure 14-66. Any changes that you make to the default insert are saved along with the current layout.

The editor Toolbar includes standard icons for cutting and pasting, as well as icons for switching between the three modes (front cover, back cover, and disc label), column and paragraph formatting, and moving text and graphic objects to the front or back of the design. Along the top and left side of the window are handy rulers that indicate your horizontal and vertical positioning; these rulers move to follow your cursor.

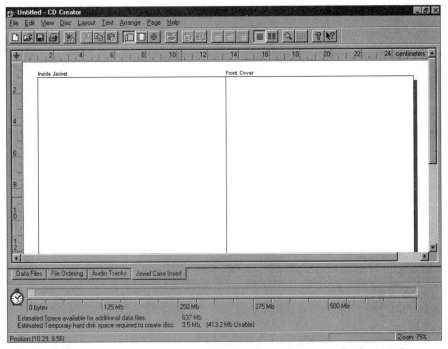

Figure 14-66: The Jewel Case Editor window displaying a simple data CD insert.

What's missing? Well, Jewel Case Editor does not provide drawing tools for creating graphics; instead, it relies on other Windows drawing applications with OLE support to provide graphics, and it can acquire images directly from a scanner. You can, however, alter the font and layout characteristics from inside the editor.

Building a Simple Insert

Let's build a simple insert with a title on the front cover and a version number on the back; we use only text objects in this example. Notice that CD Creator automatically added two text items to the front cover: the file size and total number of files appear at the bottom left corner of the front cover for data layouts. To build a simple insert, follow these steps:

1. Select the Insert text . . . item from the Edit menu, or simply press your Insert key. CD Creator displays the dialog shown in Figure 14-67, where you can configure the font, size, color, and orientation of the text. For this tutorial, let's create a front and back insert for my shareware distribution disc.

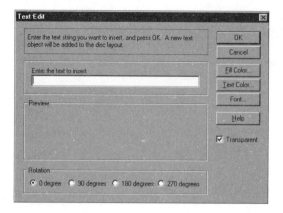

Figure 14-67: The Text Edit dialog contains all the controls you need to add text objects to your inserts.

2. Click the Font . . . button to display the Font selection dialog shown in Figure 14-68. Let's make my title large, bold, and unique, so pick Stencil Sans from the *Font:* drop-down list box, Bold from the *Font Style:* list, and 36 points from the *Size:* list. Once you've made your selections, click OK to return to the Text Edit dialog.

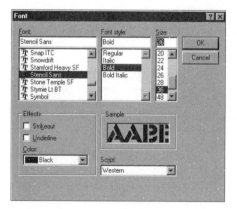

Figure 14-68: It's easy to select font characteristics from this dialog.

3. Next, we specify a fill color for the background behind each character and a text color for the outline of each character by clicking the Fill Color . . . and Text Color . . . buttons, respectively. Each button displays a standard Windows color selection dialog where you can click a color to select it or define a custom color. Let's use black as a text color. However, we want to see the background behind the text; therefore, let's enable the *Transparent* checkbox.

4. Next, we specify the rotation to be applied to this text. Because we want this text to appear with no rotation, we leave it at 0 degrees.

5. Now we're ready to specify the text itself. Enter "Stainless Steel" into the *edit* field; the text appears in the Preview area as well, giving you an idea of what the font and text characteristics you've chosen will look like. When everything is correct, click OK!

6. We've returned to the editor window, and the text now appears on the page — but wait, this was supposed to be a title, and it's not where we want it! Don't panic; remember, these are text objects, and they can be selected, moved, or modified just like objects in a paint program. Click the text and *handles* appear around the object border as shown in Figure 14-69, and you can drag the object to the front cover. Plus, while a text object is selected you can left justify it, right justify it, or center it using the Toolbar buttons, so let's center it as well. Now it looks better! If you need to remove the selected object, just press your Delete key.

Note

If you've never used a drawing package, you might not know that handles are more than just indicators. If you click a specific handle with your mouse and drag it, you can change that dimension of the text object. For example, if I activate a text object and drag the bottom middle handle down, the text object expands to fill the new space; if I click the middle handle on the right side, I can make the text object longer or shorter.

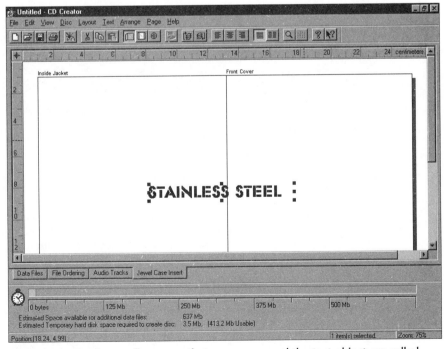

Figure 14-69: The small squares that appear around the text object are called handles, and they indicate that you've selected this text object.

7. For the rest of the title, let's do something a little special. Repeat steps 1 through 5, but select 270-degree rotation instead and enter the string "oftware" in the edit field. Click OK, move the result to the front of the existing title, and voila! You have an interesting title treatment for your front cover, as shown in Figure 14-70.

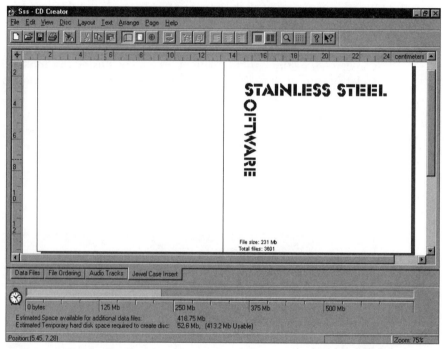

Figure 14-70: The finished front cover with title for my shareware distribution disc.

8. Now we need to switch to the back cover; select Jewel Back from the Page menu, or click the Back Cover Toolbar button. The editor window changes to display the back insert, as shown in Figure 14-71. To add the version number, repeat steps 1 through 5 again, click the text object to select it, and move it wherever you like. Remember to save your layout to disc once your inserts are completed!

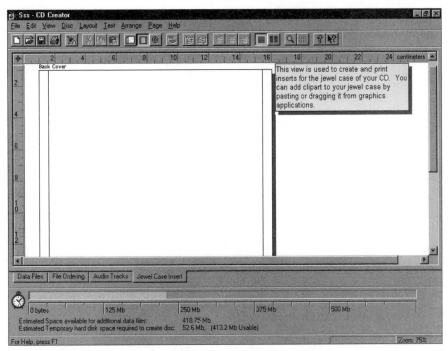

Figure 14-71: The Jewel Case Editor displays this layout screen for the back insert.

Building an Audio Insert

CD Creator adds enough information to an audio CD jewel case insert that you might not need to add any custom text! As shown in Figure 14-72, the front cover lists the Disc Title and Artist Name that you entered in the Disc Properties dialog. If you decide to change these, select Properties from the Disc menu and enter the new text, and CD Creator automatically updates the display. On the inside jacket, CD Creator lists each track and its length; this information is repeated on the back cover.

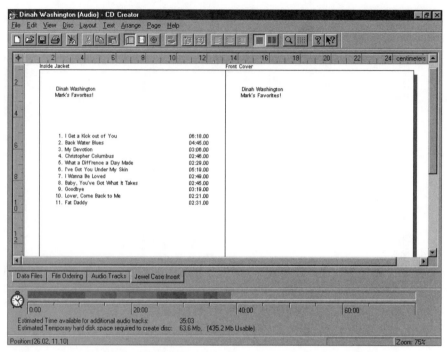

Figure 14-72: An audio CD jewel case insert automatically generated by CD Creator.

If you do decide to make changes, though, you can add, delete, or modify the text on an audio CD insert in the same manner as the simple insert we created in the previous tutorial.

Using Custom Graphics

Since the Jewel Case Editor supports OLE, you can pick just about any existing image to add to your inserts, or even draw your own! There are five methods of adding graphic objects:

✦ Create an OLE object in another application and insert it. Select Insert New Objects from the Edit menu, choose the Create New option, pick your application, and CD Creator launches it automatically.

✦ Insert an existing OLE object. Select Insert New Objects from the Edit menu, choose the Create from File option, and click the Browse . . . button to navigate through your system and open the file.

✦ Add objects using drag and drop from another application.

✦ Cut them from another application and paste them into your layout.

✦ Scan an image directly into your layout. When the scanner is ready, select Acquire Image from the File menu and then click Select Source to pick a scanning device. Select Acquire from the same submenu to display your scanner's control dialog and begin the scanning process.

I tend to use either drag and drop or cut and paste, because they're the easiest methods. As an example, let's use a clipart image and add it to the front cover for a MIDI music disc. To add an image, follow these steps:

1. Open your graphics application and load the image. For me, that means loading Paint Shop Pro.

2. Select the Copy command from the application's Edit menu to copy the graphic into your Windows Clipboard.

3. Click the CD Creator window to activate it and select the Paste item from the Edit menu. The graphic appears within the layout window, but it usually requires you to drag it to the proper location.

4. Resize the graphic if necessary by dragging the handles at the edges of the object.

Printing and Cutting Your Inserts

Finally, you're ready to print the insert pages and cut them out; switch to the Jewel Case Editor, load the layout if it isn't already loaded, and select Print . . . from the File menu. If you don't have a good quality printer, I suggest you visit a friend who does — producing these inserts is not a task for a dot matrix printer!

When cutting my inserts, I get the best results with either an office cutting board, or a modeler's knife and a ruler. Try to cut just inside the lines, or use an existing insert set from a factory-made disc as a cutting guide. A ruler also comes in handy when making the creases for the back cover.

Summary

In this chapter, you gained experience with some of the more complex features of CD Creator!

✦ We first discussed the advanced options and formats offered within CD Creator itself.

✦ Then you learned about the advanced features and recording methods within PCD Creator and VCD Creator.

✦ We also discussed a number of utilities that are indispensable during preparation of your discs.

✦ Finally, we created custom jewel case inserts for those discs that deserve special treatment!

In Chapter 15, we add a professional menu interface to your recorded CDs with help from an unexpected source: the same Hypertext Markup Language (or HTML) that you use on your Web pages!

✦   ✦   ✦

Advanced Recording Topics

In Part III, you learn about some of the professional touches you can add to your finished projects with HTML. Part III also introduces you to a typical multimedia authoring program, Corel's Click & Create, and our final chapter outlines the improvements in disc technology that you can look forward to in the future.

Adding HTML to Your Projects

Now that you're familiar with designing and recording your own CDs in several different formats, you may be wondering, "Is this it?" What other features should be included in a finished disc? Of course, the answer depends on the application and the person using the disc. For example:

✦ If you're creating an audio disc, archival backups, or a simple copy of the source code for a program to take on a trip, your job is essentially done after a successful recording. As we discussed, you could add a disc label and print a jewel case sleeve, but there's really no additional design or enhancements required for these applications.

✦ If you're creating library discs that contain hundreds of files, you can use Media Center or Paint Shop Pro to create a thumbnail catalog, or you can add a simple menu system to make it easier for you to navigate and select files.

✦ If you're creating discs to distribute, you'll want to make your discs as easy to use as possible, and your disc's interface should be more colorful and appealing.

Do appearance and ease-of-use count in your application? If you're a developer, you might consider writing your own custom menu program, or, if you're not a member of the international code-writing guild, you might use a presentation package to create a simple front-end for your disc. However, there are a number of possible problems with custom programming: Can you be sure that the person trying to use your disc will have all of the system requirements necessary to run your program? Will they be comfortable with the controls you've selected? Will you have to build a library of complex functions to let the user select files, display images, run programs, and read text, or will you have to buy an expensive development package?

Because of questions such as these, many developers of disc-based applications have decided on a popular standard for adding features to their finished projects — HTML!

Why HTML?

"Now wait a second, my discs have nothing to do with the Internet or the World Wide Web. Why drag HTML into it?" I understand exactly how you feel. The *Hypertext Markup Language* (or HTML) standard used to create Web pages has taken the computing world by storm. One day I fully expect to open the latest issue of my favorite computer magazine and discover that HTML has been proven to cure the common cold, or that it was actually a gift from ancient astronauts!

Yet, many of the reasons behind the popularity of HTML as a vehicle for transmitting text and graphical content across the Web also make it uniquely suited as a simple programming language for adding functionality to CD-ROMs. The advantages of HTML include:

✦ **Universal standard.** There are now literally thousands of development tools available for HTML programming, including a number of freeware and public domain editors. Plus, you can quickly and easily export text and graphics from your favorite word processing package or desktop publishing package if it supports HTML as an export file type.

✦ **Easy to produce.** If you're familiar with designing your own web pages, you can probably "hack" your HTML code to add or modify features with nothing more exotic than a DOS or Windows text editor. But even if you've never typed a line of HTML code in your life, there's a growing number of "What You See is What You Get" (or WYSIWYG) HTML editors available. My favorite is Microsoft's Front Page, shown in Figure 15-1. Other well-known programs include Adobe PageMill, Claris HomePage, Hot Metal Pro, Fusion, and Netscape's Navigator Gold HTML editor.

✦ **Good variety of functions.** Although many people don't consider HTML a true programming language, it provides most of the functions needed to access programs and content on your CD-ROM. Common HTML functions supported by Web browsers include displaying text, simple branching, file retrieval, image maps for graphic menus, seamless support for playing digital sound and video, and the option to launch your electronic mail application.

✦ **Familiarity.** With the popularity of the World Wide Web, most computer novices can use a Web browser — no long learning curve is required!

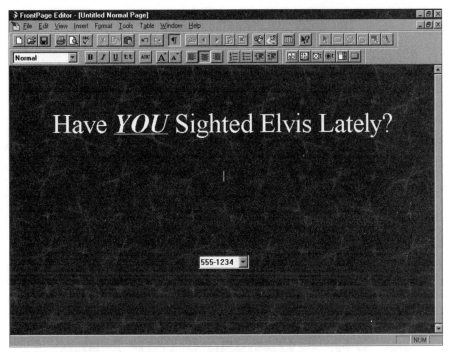

Figure 15-1: Microsoft's Front Page WYSIWYG HTML editor.

HTML IS . . . "BOSS"? "RAD"? COOL!

What do I mean by the "familiarity" of Web technology being an advantage? I recently created a disc for a junior high school that contained a series of long text documents, and I created two distinct copies of the same documents on the disc: One set was pure text, just as I had received it, and the other set was converted into HTML using Microsoft Word's Internet Assistant. As I demonstrated to the class how to use the disc, I showed the students how to load the plain text version into a Windows text editor such as WordPad and search for words and phrases. Their reaction was less than enthusiastic; I think "bored stiff" is a better description. However, when I double-clicked on the colorful main menu I'd created in HTML and they saw Netscape Navigator appear, suddenly everyone wanted a turn at the mouse and the same text became an adventure! Let's face it: Although many of us old-timers who've called or run computer bulletin board systems for the last decade take Web technology for granted, it's just plain *neat* for most PC owners!

✦ **Widespread use.** Finally, if you use HTML as a development tool for your CD-ROM, the web browser suddenly becomes more than just a very popular Internet application: it becomes an inexpensive front-end interface for your CD-ROM! Because just about every operating system supports several browsers these days, you can view an HTML application on an ISO 9660 CD-ROM across a wide variety of different platforms. Also, many browsers are freeware or shareware, so you can distribute a copy of the browser on your CD-ROM in the event that your customer hasn't installed a browser.

For these reasons, many of the discs you find in magazines and accompanying computer books use an HTML interface, and in this chapter we follow their example by designing an attractive HTML menu for a CD-ROM.

Here's an important note: This chapter is not intended to teach you HTML! An entire library's worth of books dedicate themselves to all the nuances of HTML, and I'm not going to try to compete with them in a single chapter. Therefore, I won't be explaining every HTML tag in detail, but we do discuss how you can use specific functions to add features to your CD-ROM projects. For complete information about HTML coding, I'd recommend the excellent *HTML Publishing Bible* by Alan Simpson (IDG Books).

The First Step — Designing Your Menu

Designing the proper HTML menu system for a disc depends on the same criteria you applied to select the type of disc to record in Chapter 7: the nature of the material you're recording and the method of retrieval. However, in the case of on-disc HTML development for CD-ROM, we must add a third factor: the importance of appearance. Before you jump into creating a flashy interface splattered with dozens of animated images, remember that what works online is not necessarily the perfect solution for every disc — not every disc needs to be a multimedia showcase! Even if you're a wizard with an HTML editor and you've designed hundreds of Internet and Intranet pages, you'll still need to make the same design decisions before you start working.

Consider two examples:

✦ First, let's suppose that you're creating an electronic catalog. The material to be recorded is mostly digital video, and there's no need to supply a method of retrieving files; this disc is simply meant to show clips of your work. You expect (at least you *hope*) that the customer will refer to this catalog many times, and it must provide a branching menu to display clips in different categories. Finally, this disc must be colorful and attractive to the user, so it should include all the bells and whistles — in fact, why not include links to your web site and e-mail address so that those with an Internet connection can contact you in cyberspace?

✦ Our second example is an archival library of company information, including press releases, logos, and document templates. Aww, great, now the vice president wants you to add the employee handbook in Adobe Acrobat format! This disc is meant to be used once by new employees, but your boss doesn't want them "wasting time looking at pretty pictures" — the idea is for them to retrieve what they need from the disc as quickly as possible.

OK, now let's determine what type of interface we should design for each of these examples. In example one, we need an attractive interface, and we'd like the customer to spend as much time as necessary reviewing the content — but that content need not be retrieved to hard drive, only presented to the customer. Therefore, the proper design for this application is a complex, multiple-menu interface with the best you can offer: animated graphics, MIDI music, and hotspots galore! Also, we should include HTML functionality for connecting to your Web site and sending you Internet e-mail. In Figure 15-2, I've created the main menu for such a menu system.

Figure 15-2: An on-disc menu system designed for the attractive presentation of material with no time constraint.

In example two, we see the reverse of the coin. First, new employees will only need this information once or twice, and you're not trying to sell a product so there's no need to add multimedia extras to the interface. There's also no need for a multiple menu system — you can display a simple top-level menu that's grouped by file type, as shown in Figure 15-3. In this example, the only HTML function we need is document retrieval (not document display), and our goal is to offer the fastest access.

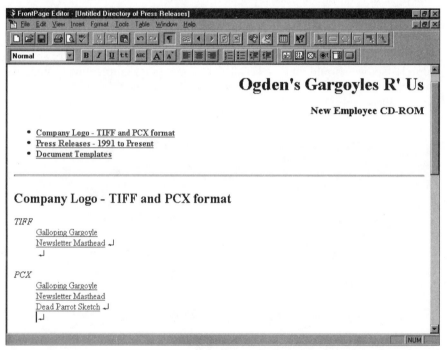

Figure 15-3: A menu system designed for quick retrieval of archival information.

Of course, these are extreme examples! Just like a mixed-mode disc, your application may cross these boundaries, but the basic design decisions you make still rely on these three factors. Remember, you make these decisions at the same time you're selecting the disc type, recording method, and directory structure for your CD-ROM. I generally map out the entire disc at one time, including the layout, disc characteristics, the appearance of the disc sleeve and label, and the structure of the on-disc menu (if needed).

Common HTML Functions

Once you've defined the actions your users will perform, you can select the common HTML functions you need to build your application. In our two examples, the first application required document display, menu branching, mail to, and linking; the second was much simpler, requiring only document retrieval. In this section, we discuss the basic HTML functions you need to build your menu system.

Document Display

Before everyone started labeling the World Wide Web as the answer to all of humanity's problems, its primary purpose was the display of text information, and most of the Web still relies on the basic display of content in HTML format. Note that this function only displays the content — it remains on the source side, whether that source is a Web server or a compact disc. Figure 15-4 shows a typical document display page; nothing fancy, but you'd be surprised how many applications build on this function as a foundation!

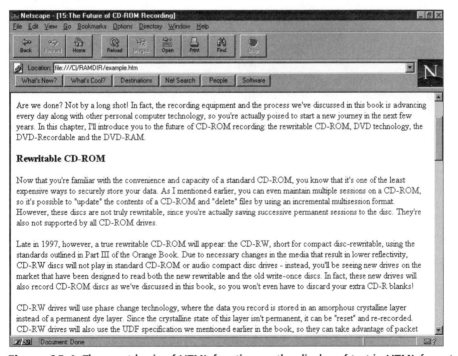

Figure 15-4: The most basic of HTML functions — the display of text in HTML format.

Although you're limited to text and linked graphics, that doesn't mean that you're stuck. HTML allows you to insert headers, separator lines, and italicized and bold text. Whenever possible, I use these formatting devices to highlight important passages and separate paragraphs. The more experience you have in document layout, the better your documents will look. The HTML 3.2 standard also allows you to add color or use an image as a background, which can help hold the reader's interest.

Since the text is in HTML format, your documents can also contain links to other documents on the disc. This takes more time in planning and you'll have to embed the links within the text, but it can transform a simple archival disc containing separate documents into a basic cross-referenced library.

If you're going to display long documents within your menu, keep in mind that most people grow impatient and uncomfortable when they're reading long documents on a computer screen instead of the printed page. This isn't as much of a problem if your documents are designed to be searched instead of read from beginning to end. Figure 15-5 illustrates the Netscape Navigator Find dialog used to search the contents of the current HTML document.

Figure 15-5: Netscape Navigator can search an HTML document to find a specific word or phrase.

HTML displays document text between a beginning and an ending body tag. For example, we could create a text file containing just these lines:

```
<HTML>
<HEAD>
<TITLE>The World's Oldest Computer Joke</TITLE>
<H1>Get Ready to Groan…</H1>
<BODY>
<P>A guy walks into a computer store with a laptop. "Computer
      Salesperson," he says, "ya gotta help me… it hurts like
      the dickens when I type this!"</P>
The Computer Salesperson looks at the guy and says, "Then don't
      type that."
</BODY>
</HTML>
```

Although this an example of an HTML document in its simplest form, that's essentially all there is to document display within your CD-ROM menu system. A branching link from your menu will call the document file in HTML format, and it's displayed within the browser window. Just to make the example a little more elegant, I added a title and heading, but they're not really necessary. Figure 15-6 shows the results.

Figure 15-6: Netscape Navigator displays our simple HTML document.

Another text element I use is a horizontal rule, created with the <HR> tag. It helps to break the text of the document into logical sections, and often works better than the <P> tag I used in our example to create separate paragraphs. Figure 15-7 illustrates the same document using the <HR> tag in a strategic spot.

Later we discuss how to easily export formatted HTML documents using Microsoft Word.

Figure 15-7: The addition of a horizontal rule improves the layout of our HTML document.

Document Retrieval

The next step in HTML functionality is the retrieval of binary files stored elsewhere on the CD-ROM. Remember our example application number two: an employee can load the disc, fire up a Web browser, and download files directly to hard drive? This HTML function is simply a specialized type of link, and it's usually implemented with HTTP (short for *hypertext transfer protocol*) or FTP (short for *file transfer protocol*).

At the simplest level, a CD-ROM retrieval link has these parts:

```
<A HREF="filename.ext">Descriptive text or filename here!</A>
```

The descriptive text portion of this command is called the anchor, and it's the part that's actually displayed by a Web browser. The filename that appears in the first portion of the link typically shows up only in the browser's status line, and only when the mouse cursor is positioned over the anchor.

RELATIVE VS. DIRECT

There are two different methods of specifying the path to a particular file when creating links: *direct* and *relative*. Direct links contain the full pathname to the target file, such as:

```
<A HREF="/files/examples/direct.zip">Direct Link Examples</A>
```

Note that forward slashes ("/") are used instead of the backward slashes ("\") you usually associate with a pathname.

Relative links assume a path relative to the current HTML document you've loaded. In other words, the target file is in the same directory as the HTML file you're viewing that contains the link, or it can be in the parent directory or a subdirectory, as in:

```
<A HREF="relative.zip">Relative Link Examples</A>
```

Which method should you use? It depends on how the target files are arranged on your disc. If all of them are stored in the root or in the same directory as your HTML files, then relative links make sense. However, if your target files are spread throughout a number of directories scattered across your disc, then direct links may make more sense. Personally, I use the relative method when I can, because it allows me to move an entire web page and all of its associated support files stored in one directory tree from one drive to another. This especially comes in handy when you're testing.

Here's our example script with the addition of a relative document retrieval command:

```
<HTML>
<HEAD>
<TITLE>The World's Oldest Computer Joke</TITLE>
<H1>Get Ready to Groan…</H1>
<BODY>
<P>A guy walks into a computer store with a laptop. "Computer
      Salesperson," he says, "ya gotta help me… it hurts like
      the dickens when I type this!"</P>
<A HREF="punchlne.zip">Click here to download the punch
      line!</A>
</BODY>
</HTML>
```

When you click a link, the browser will access the CD-ROM and search for the specific file named in the HTML statement. If the file is located, most browsers allow you to save unknown file types somewhere on your local drive. For example, Netscape Navigator will display the dialog shown in Figure 15-8, where you can choose to save the file to disk or associate the file type with a known application.

Figure 15-8: Netscape Navigator displays this dialog when receiving a file of an unknown type.

On the other hand, if the file type is recognized by its extension, most browsers launch the proper application, such as a sound editor or player for a WAV file or Paint Shop Pro for a JPEG graphic, and you save the file to disk from within this application. One popular application extension is .PDF, which indicates the file is an Adobe Acrobat document (Figure 15-9). Acrobat files display with their original word processing or desktop publishing formatting intact, and you can print them in this format as well. Many online electronic magazines use Acrobat, and if your company has standardized on Acrobat you can store and retrieve that employee handbook just as it was meant to be viewed!

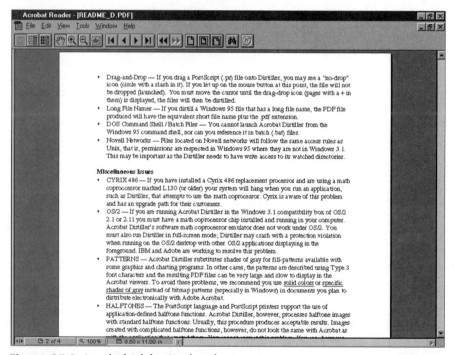

Figure 15-9: A typical Adobe Acrobat document.

Menu Branching Using Links

Building branching menus is an easy task with HTML, since the HTML link function can call other HTML documents and menus. You can use menu link commands inside a document, or jump directly from a menu page to another menu page. A typical link statement looks much like the file transfer HTML code we just used, since you're transferring the contents of a new Web page:

```
<A HREF="pinball.htm">Jump to the Pinball World menu</A>
```

Note the HTM extension on the file, indicating to the Web browser that the link retrieves another HTML page.

Adding Links Within Documents

As I mentioned, adding links within documents makes it easy for your reader to jump to a related topic, either within the same document or another document. If your document is particularly large, you can save the reader a step by creating a simple index or table of contents that allows a jump directly to a specific heading or block of text.

The first type of document link jumps to another point within the current document. To make this possible, you need to create a keyword location with the <A NAME> tag. The keyword should be a single word, and the tag should appear right in front of the target paragraph for the jump. For example, if you want to build a table of contents for a very long HTML document, you might have a statement at the top reading:

```
<A HREF="#pinball">Jump to the Pinball section!</A>
```

Notice the pound sign ("#") prefacing the keyword pinball. Now, at the point where the jump should take the reader, you would add the <A NAME> tag (usually in the form of a header):

```
<H1><A NAME="pinball">Mark's Top Ten Tables</A></H1>
```

Now when the reader wants to jump directly to the pinball section of the document, it's only a click away!

If you'd like to create a jump to a specific spot within another document on your CD-ROM, you'll create the <A NAME> statement within the target document in the same way, but your link within the current document will look something like this:

```
<A HREF="amuse.htm#pinball">Jump to the Pinball section of the
        Amusements list!</A>
```

When the reader clicks on this link, the Web browser loads the amuse.htm document from the current directory and jumps to the point marked with the pinball <A NAME> tag.

Web and Electronic Mail Links

The last basic HTML functions we discuss connect your CD-ROM project to the outside world of cyberspace through the Internet: links to online Web pages and Internet electronic mail. For example, you could offer menu items on your electronic catalog that automatically display certain pages from your company's Web site, or your reader could click a electronic mail icon and send you an order or a product question!

Before you get too enthusiastic about adding these functions to your HTML menu system, however, you must consider whether the person running your CD-ROM has an Internet connection. Without a connection, these features are broken. Of course, the connection need not be active at the time the CD-ROM is loaded, and it doesn't matter whether your user has a direct connection or a dial-up connection to the Internet. With a dial-up connection under Windows 95, for example, clicking an Internet link within a browser when you're not connected to the Internet automatically displays the Connect To dialog shown in Figure 15-10. Although this takes a little more work than a direct connection, eventually your user ends up where you intended!

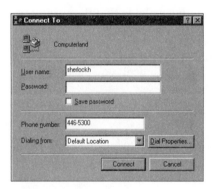

Figure 15-10: If your user has a dial-up Internet connection, clicking an Internet function in your HTML menu displays this dialog in Windows 95.

Adding a Web Link

If you'd like to add a link to an Internet Web page to your CD-ROM menu, you use another variant of the link we've used before. At the simplest level, a CD-ROM Web page link has these parts:

```
<A HREF="http://www.address.com/page.htm">Descriptive text
    here!</A>
```

For example, you can access my home page on the Web with the following link:

```
<A HREF="http://www.geocities.com/Hollywood/5315/index.htm">The
    BatCave!</A>
```

Notice that this link includes the "http://" prefix, which tells your browser to retrieve this HTML page using hypertext transfer protocol. The full Internet address indicates to your browser that this page does not reside in the same directory or on the local CD-ROM.

When you're adding a Web page link, it's important to check your spelling and capitalization: If the URL (short for Universal Resource Locator, and commonly called the Internet address) is wrong by a character or one of the slashes is pointed in the wrong direction, the link will not be recognized. The standard name for the home page on most sites is "index.html," but many sites also use "index.htm" or "welcome.html," so always verify the entire URL.

Tip

Remember, I mentioned at the beginning of the book that one application for creating your own CD-ROMs was to store a complete Internet Web site? If your disc has the space, consider adding your entire site in a separate directory — that way, it doesn't matter whether your users have an Internet connection or not! Your site will load in seconds off the CD-ROM, and there won't be any long wait for animated GIFs or WAV files to load. The only disadvantage to this method is that your users will miss any updates you make to your Internet site after the disc is recorded, so be sure to encourage them to check regularly for updates.

Adding an Electronic Mail Link

The electronic mail link opens a Create Mail dialog within the user's browser, complete with the address specified within the tag, as illustrated in Figure 15-11. Once again, if your user isn't currently connected to the Internet, the outgoing mail will either launch an Internet session immediately to deliver the message, or it will be sent the next time the mail application checks for incoming mail.

A typical mail link looks like this:

```
<A HREF="mailto:sysop@batboard.org">Send me an email
    message!</A>
```

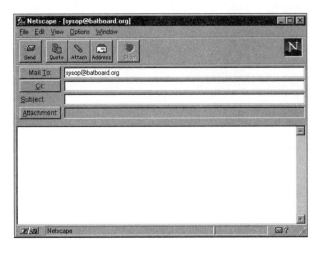

Figure 15-11: A mailto: link within an HTML document has launched the Netscape Navigator Mail dialog.

Adding Graphics, Video, and Music

OK, so you've added the functionality you're looking for within your menu system, and now you'd like to dress it up with a background and animated graphics. But why stop there? How about a toe-tapping background MIDI song that plays while your users are checking out your CD-ROM menu?

Using External and Inline Graphics

Adding an external image download command to your menu can be as simple as inserting the link we used for binary file retrieval and changing the filename, as in this example:

```
<A HREF="apache.jpg">A fearsome Apache helicopter gunship</A>
```

If the user clicks on the description link, the image downloads from the CD-ROM and displays in the graphics viewer or editor associated with the file's extension. Some browsers can also be set to display the image in a separate window.

If you'd like an image to appear as part of the HTML document, however, a link is not required: you need a different type of HTML tag. These graphics are commonly called inline images, and they're the star attractions on many Web pages — especially the animated GIFs that are growing in popularity these days. To add an inline image, you use the <IMG> tag, as in this example:

```
<P><IMG SRC="spotlight.gif" ALIGN=bottom></P>
```

The SRC field specifies the location where the browser will find the image. Just like an HTML document, the location can be relative to the current directory or directly specified through a full pathname. Every graphical browser I know of supports GIF and JPG images, and those are the two standard image formats for Web pages. By the way, the ALIGN attribute specifies the alignment of the image with the text surrounding it. A value of bottom aligns the bottom of the image with the text, but you can also use middle and top, which align the middle and top of the image with the text, respectively. The HTML 3.2 standard also provides left and right alignments that allow you to simulate text wrapping around an image aligned to the left or right side.

Another popular feature added to the HTML 3.2 standard is the ability to use an image or color as the background for your HTML page. To use an image for your background, insert a tag such as this at the top of your page, before the body appears:

```
<BODY BACKGROUND="canebkg.gif">
```

If you do decide to add an image as the background for your menu system, however, make sure the selected image is not too garish or complicated. You should be able to easily read your page's text, and any inline graphics should have the same background color (or a transparent background) to enhance the "seamless" look of your menu.

Perhaps you'd rather have a simple color as your background instead of an image — if so, use the BGCOLOR attribute for the BODY tag. There are two methods of specifying a background color: hexadecimal or one of the recognized keywords. I certainly prefer the keyword format! The HTML 3.2 standard recognizes these keywords for background colors: aqua, black, blue, fuchsia, gray, green, lime, maroon, navy, olive, purple, red, silver, teal, white, and yellow. As an example, here's the statement to use to set a background color of teal:

```
<BODY BGCOLOR="TEAL">
```

Using Digital Video

Another feature that can really add pizzazz to a CD-ROM menu application is the display of digital video. Loading an AVI file from CD-ROM makes the addition of digital video easy for both you and your users! Unlike the interminable delays you find on the Internet, your Web browser can usually display an AVI file from the CD-ROM in just a few seconds.

In its simplest form, you use another variant of the <IMG> tag to display video:

```
<IMG DYNSRC="godzilla.avi" CONTROLS WIDTH=150 HEIGHT=110>
```

Notice the DYNSRC attribute that specifies that the file is a video clip rather than a simple image. I also like to display the controls for the AVI file underneath it, so I add the CONTROLS keyword. Figure 15-12 illustrates an AVI video embedded in an HTML document.

Using Background Sound and Music

Finally, let's not forget the impact of a piece of background MIDI music that matches the mood of your menu system, or a WAV sound that plays when the page is first displayed! Digital sound in WAV format can provide some truly startling effects and CD-quality sound; however, if you remember the size of some of those song-length WAV files we recorded in earlier chapters, you may wish to pick a background tune in MIDI format instead — loading 100 megabytes from a CD-ROM takes some time!

Here's an HTML statement, for example, for background MIDI music that I use on my Web site that would work well on a CD-ROM menu:

```
<BGSOUND SRC="batman.mid" LOOP=INFINITE>
```

Note that we're now using the <BGSOUND> tag, and I'm setting the song to play indefinitely with the LOOP attribute and a value of INFINITE. If you set the LOOP value to a number, the song or sound will loop that number of times and then stop.

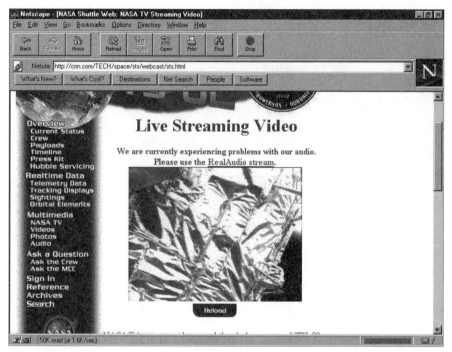

Figure 15-12: The addition of an AVI video clip to your menu attracts the user's attention!

Creating a CD-ROM Menu with FrontPage

As I mentioned, you can create your entire HTML-based CD-ROM menu within a text editor — but *why do so*? After all, there are literally dozens of good-quality HTML editors that cater to every level of HTML experience. Novices can choose a WYSIWYG editor like FrontPage, while HTML old-timers and Webmasters can select a professional editor that allows more control over a project. Whichever package you choose, however, you can use it to build your HTML interface; if you have a favorite program that you're already using on the Web, just open a new page layout and let's get to work!

In this section, I build an example two-page menu system for one of my library discs using Microsoft's FrontPage; by the time we're done, we will have added all of the functions I discussed in the last section.

Ready? Then follow these steps:

1. Select the Microsoft FrontPage folder from the Start menu and click the FrontPage Editor item. FrontPage displays a new, blank page using the Normal template, as shown in Figure 15-13.

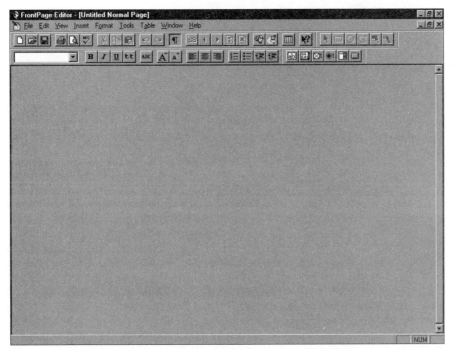

Figure 15-13: When you run the FrontPage Editor, it displays a new blank page, ready for design.

2. First, let's add a background for the main page. Right-click the blank portion of the window and select Page Properties . . . to display the dialog shown in Figure 15-14. If you want to pick a solid color for your background, enable the *Use Custom Background Color:* checkbox, then you click Choose . . . to select the color. However, let's use a tiled image, so enable the *Background Image:* checkbox and click Browse . . ., then click the From File . . . button on the Insert Image dialog. Let's select a favorite pattern of mine, a crumpled paper look. Once you've returned to the Page Properties dialog, click OK to apply the change.

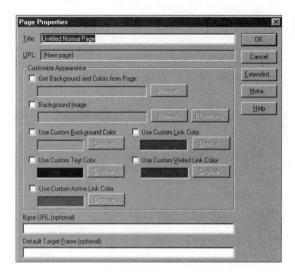

Figure 15-14: The FrontPage Page Properties dialog.

3. Next, we add the menu text. Pull down the Insert menu and select Heading 1 from the Heading submenu. You'll notice that the blinking cursor at the top left of the editing window is now larger, indicating that you're now entering header text. Type "My Library Disc", then click the Center Paragraph button on the Toolbar to align the header in the middle of the page. Press Enter to move down one line, select Heading 3 from the drop-down list box on the far left of the Toolbar, and type "Jump to the AVI Files!" Press Enter again and type "Download the AVI Listing!". Press Enter twice more and type "Connect to My Web Page!". Finally, press Enter one more time and type "Leave Me Internet E-mail!". That's all the menu text we need to demonstrate our functions, and your window should look like Figure 15-15.

4. Now let's build our link to the second page of our CD-ROM menu. Highlight the line "Jump to the AVI Files!" and select the Link . . . item from the Edit menu. FrontPage displays the Create Link dialog shown in Figure 15-16. Click the Current Web tab and enter the name avi.htm in the *Page:* field. Click OK. Notice that the entire line is underlined and colored blue, indicating that you've linked it to something else. If you run your mouse cursor over the line, FrontPage displays the link destination in the status line at the bottom of the window.

5. As an example of a binary file download, let's create a relative link to a file called AVILIST.ZIP. Highlight the line "Download the AVI Listing!" and again select the Link . . . item from the Edit menu. FrontPage displays the Create Link dialog. Click the World Wide Web tab and set the *Protocol:* drop-down list box to (other), which indicates you're creating a relative link. Now we can enter the filename AVILIST.ZIP in the *URL:* field. Click OK.

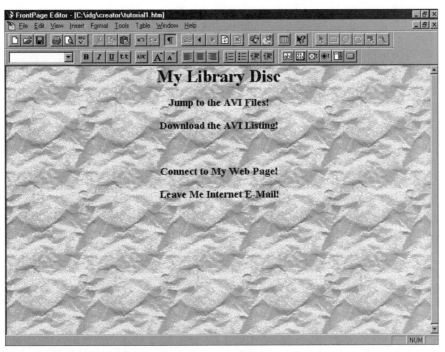

Figure 15-15: FrontPage displays the text we entered for our example menu.

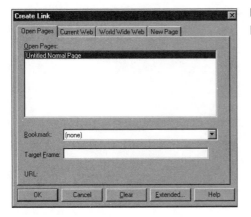

Figure 15-16: Creating a jump to another page within the Edit Link dialog.

6. Next we build a link to my Internet web page. Highlight the line "Connect to My Web Page!" and again select the Link . . . item from the Edit menu. FrontPage displays the Create Link dialog. Click the World Wide Web tab and enter the URL address `http://www.geocities.com/Hollywood/5315/index.htm` in the *URL:* field. The *Protocol:* drop-down list box should be set to http:. Click OK. Now you've added a link to an external page on the World Wide Web.

7. Time to provide a feedback channel! Highlight the line "Leave Me Internet E-Mail!" and again select the Link . . . item from the Edit menu. FrontPage displays the now familiar Create Link dialog. Click the World Wide Web tab and change the *Protocol:* drop-down list box value to mailto:. In the *URL:* field, enter the e-mail address mailto:sysop@batboard.org and click OK. This adds an Internet e-mail link on your menu.

8. Our basic functionality is here, but boy does this menu look plain! An interesting background isn't enough. Click the blank space after the download link to place the cursor at the carriage return, and select Image . . . from the Insert menu. At the Insert Image dialog, click the From File . . . button and select a suitable graphic. Click OK, and suddenly you've got some visual interest, as shown in Figure 15-17!

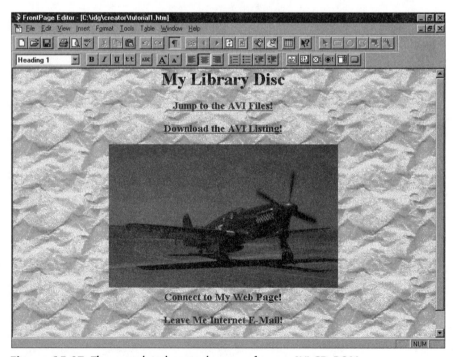

Figure 15-17: The completed example menu for our AVI CD-ROM.

9. Now save your menu page to a separate directory, and make sure you include the contents of that directory in your CD-ROM layout. Depending on the source of your images and music, FrontPage may also ask if you wish to save a copy of each of your support files in the same directory as the menu page. I recommend placing both the menu pages and the support files in the root of the disc, because there usually aren't many files required. This insures that your users will be able to locate the index.htm file using Windows Explorer or their Web browser without too much trouble. Again, this is a good reason to use relative links, since you won't have to modify hard-coded pathnames within your HTML tags.

Tip It's important to remember that the greatest HTML menu will never be touched if your users don't know it's on your CD-ROM! Make sure your installation instructions include the steps necessary to load your main menu page in their browser.

Of course, this short tutorial doesn't begin to cover all of the powerful features of FrontPage — but this book covers CD recording, not HTML page design! The more time and effort you put into your HTML menus, the more professional and appealing your CD-ROMs will be, so learn everything you can about your HTML editor and put it through its paces for your next CD recording project!

One important note before turning to another topic: always test your CD-ROM menu system or HTML application from your hard drive *before* you record your disc! No matter how many times you've successfully designed a menu or used FrontPage, there's always the possibility of a misspelled word or an uppercase/lowercase problem that can result in a broken menu command! You must try every file download, every menu jump, and every specialized HTML function to guarantee that your menu is trouble-free before recording — and even then, if I make multiple copies, I usually record just one at first to load and test.

Converting Text with Internet Assistant

Finally, if you need to convert a document into HTML format and your word processor of choice is Microsoft Word for Windows 95, you're in luck! Thanks to the free Internet Assistant upgrade distributed by Microsoft, Word for Windows 95 can be transformed into a basic HTML editor that works with the existing Word menu system, complete with the ability to add links within documents. To obtain the upgrade, visit the Microsoft site at http://www.microsoft.com/msword/internet/ia/ and download it, and then run the executable to install the upgrade.

Once you've installed Internet Assistant, converting a Word format document into HTML is as easy as exporting text. Follow these steps:

1. Open the desired document in Word and select Save As . . . from the File menu.

2. From the Save As . . . dialog, navigate to the destination for the HTML file and select HTML Document from the *Save as type:* drop-down list box. Select a different filename to make certain that you don't overwrite your original file, and click OK to begin the conversion process.

3. Word displays progress bars as the file converts to HTML. Once it's completed, Word displays the text in the closest format to its original style. Word also displays a new menu system and new Toolbar icons that allow you to modify and preview your HTML code within a browser window. You can select custom link colors, text colors, a background graphic, and background music for your page under the new Format menu. You can also enlarge or reduce the font, specify heading levels, and control bullets and numbering from the Format menu. Under the Insert menu, you can add form fields, special symbols, and graphics to your new page.

4. Don't forget to save any changes you make to the converted text!

Most of the other major Windows word processing programs also allow you to convert documents into basic HTML format. You may have to edit these converted documents before you add them to your CD-ROM, but at least the text and spacing of the converted files — and therefore their appearance — should be roughly equivalent to the layout you used to create the original document.

For complete information on the new commands available with the Internet Assistant upgrade, create an HTML document within Word and then select Internet Assistant for Microsoft Word Help under the Help menu. Note that this menu item only appears when you're editing an HTML document!

Summary

In this chapter, we discussed how you can use HTML to:

✦ provide an easy-to-use interface for your CD-ROMs;

✦ add a professional presentation for your material;

✦ add Internet functions such as electronic mail and Web page links to your CD-ROM menu.

In Chapter 17, we discuss the future of CD recording.

✦   ✦   ✦

Using Corel Click & Create

When the first recorders appeared, CD recording was a luxury; the cost and complexity of recording placed it far beyond the reach of the average PC owner. Besides, CD-ROMs themselves were still relatively new and there weren't many applications that required that huge amount of storage.

However, one particular high-level application did practically require a CD recorder: *multimedia authoring*. If you're not familiar with authoring, here's a quick definition: it's the development of a computer multimedia product, which can include multimedia games, audio or video discs, multimedia presentations, advertising, and pure artwork. The work may involve computer programming, 3D animation, special video and audio effects, or a combination of all these. However, all multimedia authoring is performed on a computer, and the finished work is likely to be seen on a computer as well; the output from a multimedia project might be transferred to video tape for television or film.

Another common characteristic of multimedia authoring is the vast amount of space required to store raw video footage, digital audio, bitmaps, and animation. Because the introduction of multimedia applications occurred about the same time as the CD-ROM, developers of multimedia applications used CD recorders for storage and transportation of all that data!

In this chapter, I introduce you to multimedia authoring for CD-ROM by using one of the better-known development packages — Click & Create from Corel Corporation, a program that allows you to create both 16- and 32-bit multimedia applications. Click & Create is well-known for its ease-of-use and power, and it provides a good overview of the "drag and drop" multimedia development process.

The Click & Create Editors

Click & Create uses a traditional approach to multimedia development. Instead of attempting to integrate all of the program's functions within a single window, it provides you with a number of editors, each specifically designed for a portion of the entire project. You may not need all of these different editors for every project — for example, you may not include animation or morphing — but the Storyboard, Frame, and Event Editors are a requirement for every application. Click & Create's editors are:

✦ **The Storyboard Editor.** Click & Create's Storyboard Editor is very similar to what the film industry means by the term *storyboard*; every project is built from a collection of frames, just like those in a movie. Each frame may display animation, images, or the output from applications that you create. Within the Storyboard Editor, you determine the order your frames appear in and how long they are displayed, actions assigned to mouse buttons, when fade in and out between frames, and play music. Figure 16-1 illustrates a typical project displayed within the Storyboard Editor.

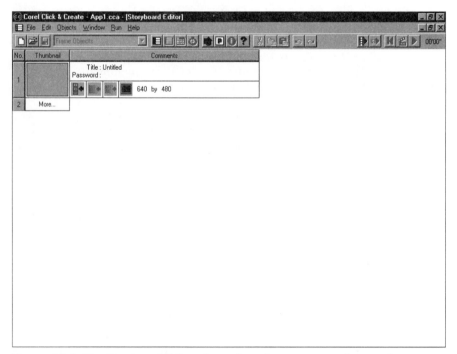

Figure 16-1: The Storyboard Editor determines the sequence of events in your Click & Create project.

✦ **The Frame Editor.** Within the Frame Editor, you can add the contents of each frame — the objects that your user actually sees and the controls that will be used to navigate through your application. Figure 16-2 illustrates the Frame Editor.

Figure 16-2: Using the Frame Editor, you design the contents of each frame.

✦ **The Event Editor.** The Event Editor is used to specify what actions take place as a result of *events* in your project. For example, if you're creating a multimedia presentation, the click of a mouse button is an event, and moving to the next screen might be the action that results. More complicated projects such as video games can assign multiple conditions to an event, so you can check for a number of states — is the player hit by alien fire or did the player just shoot a missile? Figure 16-3 illustrates the Event Editor.

✦ **The Timeline Editor.** If you've ever created a computer presentation, you already know that timing is all-important to a successful conclusion! That's the job of the Timeline Editor, shown in Figure 16-4, which you can use to insert delays, start events at a certain time after your project is launched, and assign automatic actions.

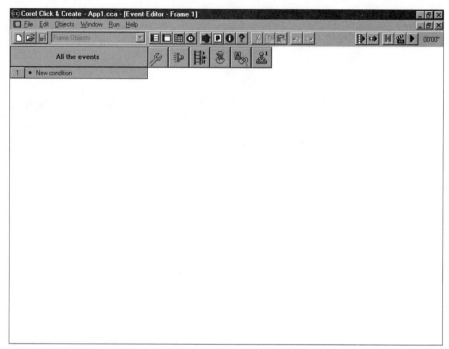

Figure 16-3: The Event Editor specifies the actions that take place within your project.

✦ **The Step Through Editor.** Most computer programmers have been using "step through" editors for years to debug the operation of their programs, and the Click & Create Step Through Editor is very similar. You can use it to run your project event-by-event. This makes it easier to add actions if necessary, change program counters, or modify the events that can trigger actions within your project. Figure 16-5 illustrates the Step Through Editor.

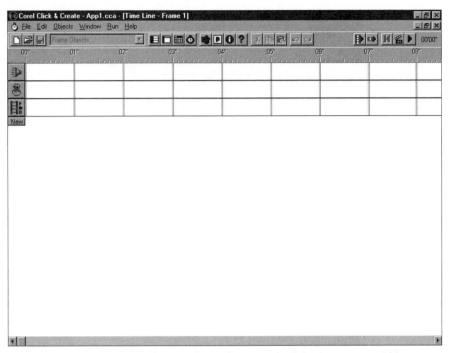

Figure 16-4: You can use the Timeline Editor to schedule the events within your project.

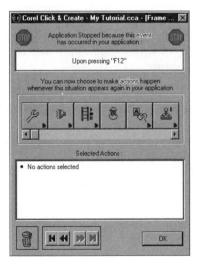

Figure 16-5: The Step Through Editor is your primary debugging environment within Click & Create.

✦ **The Animation Editor.** This is the editor I enjoy using the most! Although Click & Create allows you to import frames from existing animation in FLI format, you can actually create your own animation from your own artwork created with the Picture Editor. Rotate and resize objects easily or "zoom" the camera in on an object. The Animation Editor also makes it easy to manage the individual frames that make up your animation sequences. Figure 16-6 illustrates the Animation Editor.

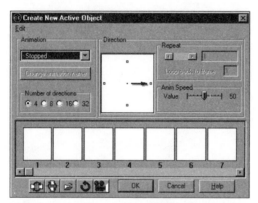

Figure 16-6: If you need animated objects in your project, the Animation Editor is your solution.

✦ **The Picture Editor.** We discussed Paint Shop Pro as an image editor earlier, but the designers of Click & Create didn't know that — therefore, enter the Picture Editor, shown in Figure 16-7, which performs many of the same functions without requiring you to leave Click & Create! You can draw lines or shapes, fill a shape with color, flip or rotate your image, resize it, or cut and paste sections to modify your picture.

✦ **The Icon Editor**. This editor shares many of the same features as the Picture Editor, but the end result is very different. The Icon Editor allows you to create two types of icons: standard Windows icon files to represent your project on the Windows Desktop, and object icons to represent objects within the Frame Editor. If you're creating a multimedia application as a stand-alone program, it's important to spend some time designing an attractive, unique desktop icon for your program. Figure 16-8 illustrates the Icon Editor.

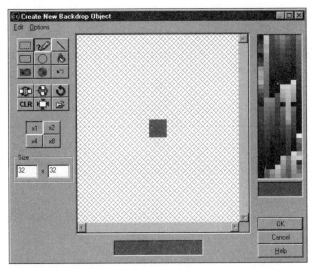

Figure 16-7: Editing an image in the Picture Editor.

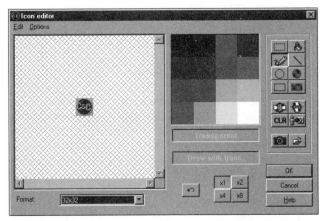

Figure 16-8: Use the Icon Editor to create Windows icons for your program.

✦ **The Morphing Editor.** You've probably seen *morphing* effects on television or in the movies; transformation morphing involves taking a source image and slowly transforming it into another image by blending and reshaping. A good example of this turns up in many science fiction and fantasy films: typically, the hero or villain turns into a tiger or a dragon during a battle (which, I imagine, also helps in some uncomfortable social situations). In Click & Create, the Morphing Editor displays two images and allows you to plot a series of points where the images should blend. Figure 16-9 illustrates the Morphing Editor.

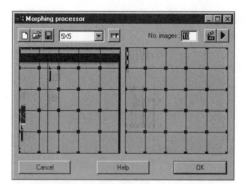

Figure 16-9: Need a magical effect to draw attention to your program? Add a morphing image with the Morphing Editor.

Whew, that's some lineup of editors! Click & Create ties them together, though, so you can easily move from one editor window to another. In fact, you rarely need to load any other application besides a sound editor like Cool Edit 96, since Click & Create has just about everything you'll need. If you missed our discussion of Cool Edit, turn back to Chapter 10 — I'll wait.

Loading and Saving Projects

Because Click & Create can save your projects as stand-alone programs, it's important to understand how to load and save while you're working. Existing projects are loaded from the File menu. Select the Open item on the File menu to display the familiar Windows Open File dialog — you'll also see a thumbnail image of the first frame in your project. Alternately, click the Open button on the Toolbar, which looks like a folder being opened.

By default, any application projects you save will have the extension .CCA, while games have the extension .GAM. The Open File dialog displays only these files; however, you can view all files regardless of extension by clicking the *Files of type* drop-down list box and selecting the All Files wildcard (*.*). Once you've found the layout file you want to load, click to highlight it, and click the Open button.

If you need to continue working on a project later, you need to save it to disk before you exit Click & Create. If this is the first time you've worked with this project, select the Save item on the File menu to display a standard Windows Save File dialog, or click the Save button on the Toolbar, which looks like a floppy disk. Enter a name in the File Name field, and click Save. The extension .CCA is automatically added to the filename you entered.

If you loaded this project from disk, selecting the Save item on the File menu automatically updates the existing file on your disk.

If you want to save an existing project file under a new name, select the Save As . . . item from the File menu. Click & Create allows you to rename the project file before saving it to disk — this is a good way of creating a copy of an existing project.

Creating a Multimedia Project

So far, you've learned that Click & Create ties together a number of separate powerful editors, each of which takes care of a particular part of the entire project. But how does one actually *create* a project? Is there a large amount of computer programming? And where will you find the graphics and clip art you need to build your project?

In this section, we build a basic multimedia presentation with three screens — this presentation is a perfect candidate for CD recording, because it involves digital video and digital sound read from a CD, and probably the only practical way to transport it to a meeting is on a hard drive or a CD-ROM!

First, launch Click & Create to display the Storyboard Editor, empty and ready for a new project. Then follow these steps:

1. Click the frame number to edit it — of course, we start with the first frame, so click the box marked 1 at the far left of the screen.

2. Click & Create displays the Frame Editor window, where you place the objects you use.

3. Now we get to have some real fun! Click & Create comes with a huge library of clip art and backgrounds that range from business to screensavers to games, so you can build an entire project without loading a single external image. Click the *Frame Objects* drop-down list box and select Media:Presentation Backdrops. This loads the Backdrops clip art library and displays a thumbnail representing each piece of artwork at the left side of the Frame Editor, as shown in Figure 16-10. To display the name of a piece of artwork, place your mouse cursor over the thumbnail and leave it there for a second or two.

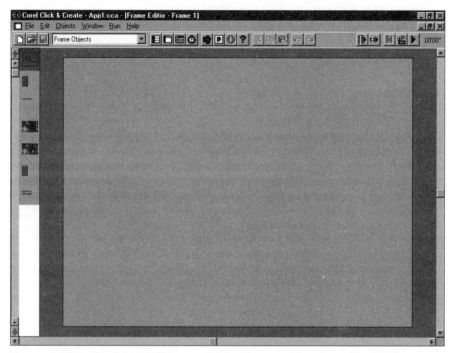

Figure 16-10: The Frame Editor can display the contents of any clip art library supplied with Click & Create.

4. Next, click the piece of artwork called Titled Boxout, and drag it into the Editor. Because it's a backdrop, it completely fills the Editor screen; align it and release the mouse button to drop it. You've added the background for your first frame, as shown in Figure 16-11.

5. Now let's add a button to advance to the next frame of the presentation. Click the *Frame Objects* list box and select Media:Circular Buttons. Select Button 14 and add it to the Frame Editor at the lower edge of the screen.

6. Ready for something neat? Select Media:3D Font 2 from the *Frame Objects* list box, and add a spinning, three-dimensional letter C and D to your first frame. Your finished first frame should look something like Figure 16-12.

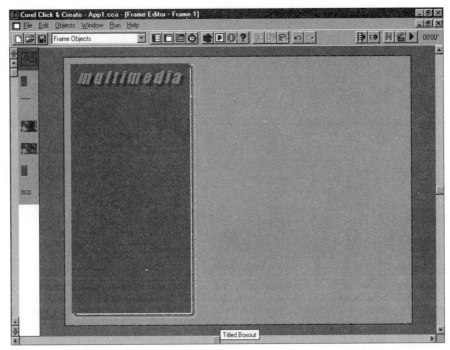

Figure 16-11: Adding a background for your frames is as easy as drag and drop!

7. Time to add our second frame. Return to the Storyboard Editor by selecting Storyboard Editor from the Window menu. From the Toolbar, click the Create New Frame button, and then select Add A New Frame. Finally, click in the More . . . box next to the number 2. You'll see that a thumbnail image of the first frame's contents appears next to the number 1, and you're ready to edit frame 2.

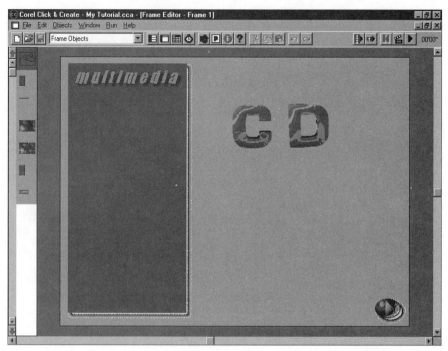

Figure 16-12: The first frame of our quick tutorial, displayed in the Frame Editor.

8. Follow steps 1 through 5 above, but select a different backdrop for variety. On this frame, instead of spinning letters, let's add a digital video clip. From the Toolbar, click the Create New Object button to display the Create New Object dialog shown in Figure 16-13. From this dialog, you can select from a wide variety of objects to add to your frame.

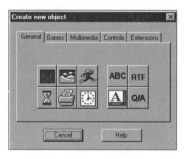

Figure 16-13: You can select from many different objects to add to a Click & Create frame.

9. One of the powerful features of Click & Create is its comprehensive support for many different types of digital video, including Windows AVI, MPEG, QuickTime, and QuickTime VR (for 360-degree virtual reality)! Click the Multimedia tab and select AVI to display the Setup AVI dialog shown in Figure 16-14. Here you can specify the characteristics of your video clip. Click Browse . . . and select a file from the AVI directory on the Click & Create CD-ROM, then click OK to add the clip. Move the clip around the frame like any other object. Note, however, that the video clip is not saved within your stand-alone program when you compile this project, so it's important to make sure that it exists in the same directory on the same drive when the program runs.

Tip   "Where can I find digital video?" Actually, it's much easier to locate video clips these days because of the Web, where the medium is flourishing, but you can also find video clip art discs especially made for presentations and multimedia programs. Also, you can record your own video from television or a VCR with an internal digitizer card, but they're still pretty expensive and you run into the same copyright problems we discussed earlier. Your best bet is to record live digital video on a digital camera connected to your computer. With the popularity of Internet videoconferencing, these digital cameras are dropping in price — and they're a great way to create your own royalty-free video.

Figure 16-14: From the Setup AVI dialog, you can specify how digital video plays in your project.

10. Once you've added the video clip, add a third frame and then add a different backdrop as you did before. However, for our third frame let's add text, digital audio from a CD, and a button back to our first frame.

11. Click the Create New Object button and display the dialog, but this time select the General tab and click the button marked ABC to add text. The Frame Editor displays a text insertion cursor, and a separate control bar where you can change the font, color, and alignment of your text. Type "Thanks for watching!" and click OK on the text control bar to accept your new text object.

12. Next, let's play a music track from the CD. Click the Create New Object button and display the dialog, select the Multimedia tab and click the button marked with a CD-ROM symbol. Once you've added the CD-ROM icon, right-click it and select Setup . . . to display the CD Setup dialog shown in Figure 16-15. By default, Click & Create plays track 1 from the CD as long as you display this frame.

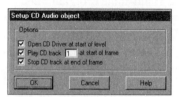

Figure 16-15: Use the CD Setup dialog to select a CD audio track to play while your presentation runs.

Now all that remains before we test this project is to build the links between buttons so that users can travel between frames in the finished application.

13. Return to the Storyboard Editor by selecting Storyboard Editor from the Window menu. Click the number 1 to select the first frame and display the Frame Editor.

14. It's time to run another editor — from the Window menu, select the Event Editor.

15. Click the number 1 next to the New Condition box to set up an event for the button.

16. The Editor displays the New Condition dialog shown in Figure 16-16. Each of these icons represents a specific condition within the program that can trigger an event.

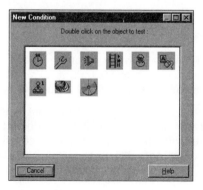

Figure 16-16: The New Condition dialog makes it easy to set up an event.

17. We're going to add a mouse condition, so right-click the icon with the mouse and key icon. From the first submenu, select The Mouse, and from the next submenu, select User Clicks on an Object.

18. Our next dialog, shown in Figure 16-17, allows you to specify which mouse button and which type of click triggers the event. Let's use a standard single click of the left button, so click OK to select the default values.

Figure 16-17: Specifying a mouse button and click type for a mouse condition.

19. Next, the Event Editor displays a window that shows the items added to this frame. In this case, there are the spinning letters C and D and the next button, so select the button we added and click OK. The event is added to the column marked All the events.

20. Now that we have an event, you must tell the Editor what to do when the event occurs. Next to the box for Event 1 are several empty boxes under a series of icons, as in Figure 16-18; right-click in the third box, which carries an icon of a film strip. From the submenu that pops up, select Jump to Frame.

21. Now a thumbnail list of all the frames in your project appears — simply select frame 2 and click OK. A blue dot appears in the box indicating that condition 1 results in a storyboard control action.

22. To link the other buttons, repeat steps 13 through 21, and select each of the other two frames. Remember, your third frame should loop back to the first frame, so select the thumbnail for frame 1 when you select a target.

You're done! Of course, that was an extremely simple example that didn't really demonstrate the full capabilities of Click & Create, but now you have an idea of just how easy it is, and how little actual programming is involved — none at all!

Tip If your application will be distributed as shareware or as a commercial product, you should certainly use the Click & Create Icon Editor to create an attractive program icon before you compile your project. This is the icon that users see within the Start menu and Windows Explorer after your program is installed.

Now let's save the project to disk before we test it, just in case. Click the Save button on the Toolbar, enter a name in the File Name field, and click Save.

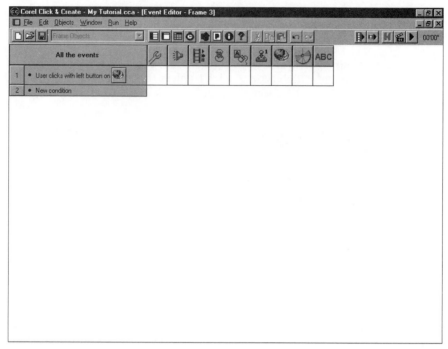

Figure 16-18: The Event Editor action icons indicate which action each condition triggers.

Testing a Project

Like any new program, extensively test your Click & Create project before distributing it. Click & Create makes testing easy! Follow these steps:

1. Load your project and display the Storyboard Editor.

2. Select Run Application from the Run menu. Click & Create launches your project in its own window, as shown in Figure 16-19.

3. Check each action that you've programmed by clicking every button and selecting each item that should respond to user control. Also, check to make sure that all digital audio and video clips play correctly.

If necessary, you can pause or quit your application from the File menu.

You can also test an individual frame of your project; instead of choosing Run Application, select Run Frame from the Run menu. Because Click & Create jumps to and runs only the currently selected frame, this is a great way to test a change you've made halfway through a long project!

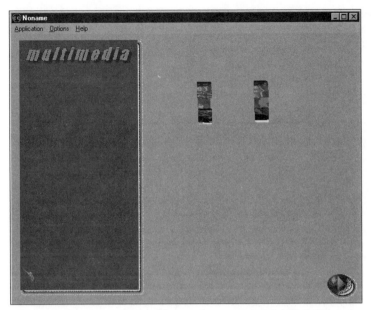

Figure 16-19: Test your application by running it within Click & Create.

Compiling Your Application

Once your project is thoroughly tested, you're ready to compile it into a stand-alone program. This is the distribution format for Click & Create projects; even if you don't plan on circulating your program among the teeming masses, I still recommend compiling your project for speed, convenience, and ease-of-use!

There are two methods of compiling your application:

✦ **Install compile.** Click & Create programs saved with this method include a SETUP.EXE executable file, a SETUP.DAT data file, and your program stored as a data file. This configuration allows you to copy these files later to a CD-ROM for distribution, complete with a professional installation routine.

✦ **Standard compile.** The standard compile method is better if you'll be the only person using your application. No installation files are created, but you can run your application directly from Windows Explorer instead of first loading Click & Create.

To compile your project into a finished application, follow these steps:

1. Load your finished project within Click & Create.

2. Select Save as stand-alone application from the File menu. Click & Create displays the Save Stand-Alone Application dialog, as shown in Figure 16-20.

Figure 16-20: You compile your Click &
Create projects into stand-alone applications
from this dialog.

3. If you'd like to create the installation files, enable the *Save with installer*
   checkbox at the bottom of the dialog.

4. Enter a new, unique filename for your application in the *File name:* field. Do
   not add an extension, as the .EXE extension is automatically added.

5. Click Save to create your application. As your application is built, a progress
   bar is displayed, and the program prompts you for any external files it
   requires during the compilation process.

Tip   I recommend that you create a new directory as the destination for your
application. Also, I name the completed executable differently than the source
.CCA file! Separation of program source files and compiled code is a traditional
rule in computer programming, and it makes just as much sense within Click &
Create. This is especially important if you're compiling an application with all of
the required installation files, because you should only distribute the files
generated by Click & Create.

Summary

In this chapter, I introduced you to multimedia authoring, using Corel's Click & Create as an example. You learned:

✦ how a traditional multimedia authoring program uses multiple editors to build portions of your application;

✦ how to use the Storyboard Editor and the Event Editor to build a simple presentation, complete with digital video, CD audio, and basic animation;

✦ how to test your new application within Click & Create;

✦ how to compile your project into an application for personal use or distribution on CD-ROM.

✦   ✦   ✦

CHAPTER

17

Rewritable CD-ROM

DVD Drives

The Future of CD-ROM Recording

Congratulations! You've reached the end of a long road, and you're the master of a rather cantankerous computer peripheral and its accompanying software. We discussed the installation and configuration of your recorder and its SCSI support, explained the inner workings of three of the most popular recording programs, and discussed the proper design of a CD-ROM layout, jewel case insert, and an HTML menu interface.

Are we done? Not by a long shot! In fact, the recording equipment and the process we discussed is advancing every day along with other personal computer technology, so you're actually poised to start a new journey in the next few years. In this chapter, I introduce you to the future of CD recording: the rewritable CD-ROM, DVD technology, the DVD-Recordable, and the DVD-RAM.

Rewritable CD-ROM

Now that you're familiar with the convenience and capacity of a standard CD-ROM, you know that it's one of the least expensive ways to store your data securely. As mentioned earlier, you can maintain multiple sessions on a CD-ROM, so it's possible to "update" the contents of a CD-ROM and "delete" files by using an incremental multisession format. However, these discs are not truly rewritable, since you're actually saving successive permanent sessions to the disc and not all CD-ROM drives are capable of reading these multisession discs.

Because packet writing will soon be generally accepted and supported by all hardware and software manufacturers, it will add to the functionality and convenience of CD recording — once again, though, these discs are not rewritable.

In 1997, however, a true rewritable CD-ROM appeared: the CD-RW, short for compact disc-rewritable, using the standards outlined in Part III of the Orange Book. Because of necessary changes in the media that result in lower reflectivity, CD-RW discs will not play in standard CD-ROM or audio compact disc drives. Instead, you'll see new "multiread" drives designed to read **both** the new rewritable and the old write-once discs. In fact, these new drives will also record CDs as we've discussed in this book, so you won't even have to discard your extra CD-R blanks!

CD-RW drives will use phase change technology, where the data you record is stored in an amorphous/crystalline layer instead of a permanent dye layer. Because the crystalline state of this layer isn't permanent, it can be "reset" and re-recorded. CD-RW drives also use the UDF specification we mentioned earlier, so they can take advantage of packet writing; in fact, you may not even require a separate recording program to use these drives, because programs like Adaptec's DirectCD allow your CD-RW drive to appear just like a standard hard drive! You'll be able to drag and drop to your CD-RW drive, as well as copy and delete files transparently within your Windows applications.

Initially, these drives will be more expensive than their write-once cousins, but prices will probably fall to a level comparable to current CD-R drive prices. CD-RW media will also be more expensive as well. Look for initial offerings from Hewlett Packard, Philips, Ricoh, Sony, and Mitsubishi.

DVD Drives

Are you beginning to feel claustrophobic when you record a mere 600 megabytes on a CD-ROM? Personally, I'm happy with the current capacity of my recorded discs, but the computer and audio industry are busy working on the successor to the venerable compact disc. Soon you'll be able to access a whopping 4.7 GIGABYTES, or more than 4,700 megabytes, on a single-sided disc. That's the equivalent of seven standard CD-ROMs, or an incredible 3,267 high-density 1.44 megabyte floppies! Welcome to DVD, the next generation of compact disc.

DVD-Video and DVD-ROM

The 4.7-gigabyte DVD disc is actually the same size and generally looks much like our current compact discs, but its structure includes some significant improvements:

✦ DVD discs pack more information on the disc by decreasing the size of the pits that hold the encoded data, and the tracks are compressed together so there's less space between them. As shown in Figure 17-1, this results in a much higher density and more data storage, even though the size of the disc itself hasn't changed.

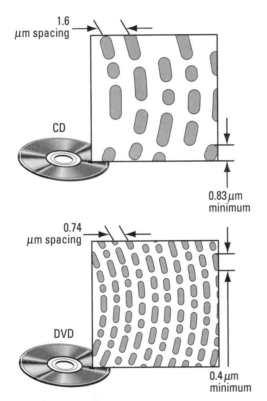

Figure 17-1: DVD provides a much denser data structure, as as shown by this comparison to a standard CD-ROM.

✦ Instead of the single reflective layer used in a CD-ROM, DVD discs can take advantage of multiple layers of data on the same disc. Figure 17-2 illustrates how the laser in a DVD drive can actually penetrate the first layer of the disc to read the second layer. Single-layer DVD discs hold 4.7 gigabytes, while dual-layer single-sided discs hold 8.5 gigabytes. Also planned are double-sided discs; although you'll have to turn these discs over manually to access the second half of the disc, one disc can hold an incredible 17 gigabytes of data!

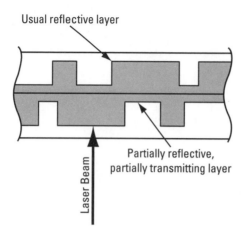

Usual reflective layer

Laser Beam

Partially reflective,
partially transmitting layer

Figure 17-2: A DVD drive can access two data
layers from one side of the disc.

✦ DVD drives are several times faster than even the 12x and 16x CD-ROM
drives we see, which should help eliminate problems with full motion video
display.

✦ Finally, DVD drives make use of a higher frequency, highly-focused laser that
can distinguish the denser pattern on the new discs.

So why do we need all this space? For several reasons:

✦ DVD makes use of MPEG 2 video compression, so desktop video benefits
from the same technology used in today's consumer digital satellite services.
In fact, MPEG 2 is far superior in quality to standard VHS.

✦ DVD discs provide support for Dolby Digital surround sound audio, with five
channels and a separate subwoofer channel.

✦ The DVD specification includes support for multiple languages and parental
lockout.

✦ Finally, the ongoing fascination that computer owners have with high-
resolution 3D video — especially game players — has stretched the current
capacity of a standard CD-ROM to the limit. Game, reference, and educational
titles that require multiple discs fit comfortably on a single DVD disc.

DVD-ROM is the computer version of DVD, and it's likely to be compatible with
older audio compact discs and CD-ROMs. However, to play the video CDs slated to
appear first on the market, these drives will have to be accompanied by a separate
MPEG 2 and Dolby Digital decoder card.

DVD-Recordable

The write-once recordable variety of DVD is due before the end of 1997. Pioneer has already announced a DVD-R drive for release in the summer of 1997, but the initial machines are limited to 3.9 gigabytes. DVD-R continues to be a source of concern for movie studios and record companies, who argue that the DVD-R industry could result in copyright protection problems.

DVD-RAM

Potentially the most exciting of all of the DVD-based drives, DVD-RAM is the ultimate: rewritable DVD format. (Why is it called "DVD-RAM" instead of "DVD-RW"? Because life just isn't that simple, I guess!) Initial DVD-RAM drives are limited to 2.6 gigabytes, but expect that figure to increase once DVD makes an inroad into the CD-ROM world. As with DVD-R, these drives are also the target of copyright protection discussions. Prices for these drives start in the thousands of dollars, so it might be prudent to hang on to your old-fashioned, archaic CD-ROM recorder for a few more years!

Summary

Although it took several years to reach the mainstream computer public, PC owners like you and I can finally record our own CDs — a technology that many industry critics once claimed would never be affordable enough for widespread use! This book helps familiarize you with the recording process, and it helps clear some of the mystery that surrounds CD recording. I hope it helps you avoid mistakes and improve the content of your discs. "Death to coasters!"

As we look to the future, I expect that the advancements outlined in this chapter will someday be within our grasp. After all, "no one could possibly need more than 17 gigabytes worth of storage space!" I wonder how long it will take before that phrase sounds quaint?

Good luck and good recording — and remember, always make your next CD recording project better than your last!

✦   ✦   ✦

Appendixes

Part IV has a number of helpful resources, including a glossary, contact information for hardware and software vendors, and a technical appendix.

CD-ROM Recording Software

Just a few years ago, only a professional developer or multimedia author could afford the equipment necessary to create a CD-ROM on a personal computer. Even if you could afford a first-generation recorder, there were only a handful of recording programs available, and most were prohibitively expensive. The explosive growth in popularity of CD recordable technology has changed all that forever, attracting software developers and fostering competition.

Although this book focuses primarily on the Adaptec product line of CD-ROM recording software, you can choose from a wide range of mastering software, with titles to match just about every budget. Some of these programs recently arrived on the scene, while others date back to the beginnings of the CD-ROM recording revolution.

In this appendix, I discuss many of the more popular CD-ROM recording packages for Windows, Macintosh, OS/2, and UNIX. Some recorder manufacturers distribute bundled kits with their own software, but all of the packages discussed here are available separately. If you're looking for a recording package with a specific set of features, these reviews should help narrow your choices. I also provide contact information so that you can request literature or download a demonstration of the latest version.

Gear for Windows

✦ Manufacturer: Elektroson, Inc
   2105 South Bascom Avenue
   Suite 160
   Campbell, California 95008

✦ Current version: 4.01.

✦ Supported platforms: Windows 3.1/95/NT, Macintosh (including Power Mac),
   UNIX, and OS/2.

✦ Website: www.elektroson.com.

✦ Telephone: 408-371-4800.

Gear is one of the "old-timers" in CD-ROM recording; Elektroson introduced Gear
in 1993, and it ranks along with CD Creator and Easy-CD Pro as one of the top
recording programs available. It's also popular with recorder manufacturers, and
is often bundled with recording kits — and no wonder, since Gear is available for
practically every computer platform that can use a CD-ROM recorder! The main
menu from the Windows 95 version is shown in Figure A-1; it may look simple, but
there's quite a bit of power lurking on that toolbar!

Figure A-1: The Gear main menu.

Gear is well-known for supporting a huge array of recorders, including some older
drives that are not recognized by other packages. The program also offers a
number of advanced features that appeal to professional recording shops, like
DDP Premaster support for generating glass master discs, multisession cross-
platform mastering, and multidisc support for Pioneer and Kodak "jukebox"
drives. Gear can also save premaster output on a SCSI tape drive.

The Gear interface allows you to drag and drop files within separate data and
audio editors to build ISO tracks; Figure A-2 illustrates the data editor. This
method of defining the contents of a disc is a little less elegant and a little harder
to use than the layout method offered in CD Creator, but it can be significantly
faster, and some people naturally prefer it.

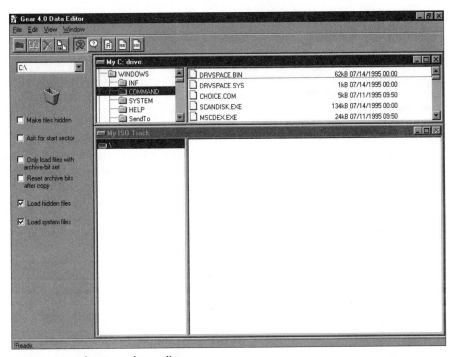

Figure A-2: The Gear data editor.

Gear can create all of the popular formats I've mentioned, offers both disc-at-once and track-at-once recording, and allows for long filenames. Besides WAV sound files, Gear can convert sounds in AIFF format. It supports recording speeds up to 6x.

My hands-down favorite feature offered by Gear is its advanced cyclic buffering, where the program creates a large number of smaller buffers and "cycles" data in a pattern to store it for recording. Unlike the standard two-buffer system used by most recording programs that uses a single read and a single write buffer, the Gear cyclic buffering system helps minimize buffer underrun errors.

If you're looking for CD-ROM recording software with professional features, give Gear a close look!

CDR Publisher HyCD

✦ Manufacturer: Creative Digital Research
   7291 Coronado Drive
   San Jose, CA 95129

✦ Current version: 4.72.

✦ Supported platforms: Windows 3.1/95/NT, Sun, and Silicon Graphics.

✦ Website: www.cdrl.com.

✦ Telephone: 408-225-0999.

CDR Publisher's claim to fame is its ability to create "hybrid" discs that can be read on both Macintosh and PC systems, as well as the UNIX RRIP format. It features a very simple user interface that novices find easier to understand than some of the better-known commercial competition. As shown in Figure A-3, the main program window is dominated by two visual drop-down list boxes: one specifying the source drive, image file, or tape, and the other specifying the destination for the data. There also is an arrow pointing to the next step in the recording process; although not as convenient or as informative as a true Windows 95 wizard, it does help guide you through the recording process.

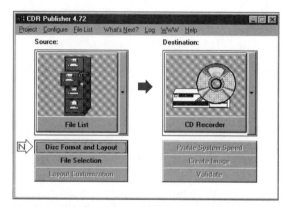

Figure A-3: The CDR Publisher main window.

You add files within CDR Publisher using either drag and drop from Explorer or a custom file selection dialog. Like CD Creator, CDR Publisher allows you to order the files as you wish on your final disc, or you can choose to sort by file size. Other powerful features include a full selection of ID information and volume dates, the ability to write premaster tapes, barcode support, the ability to create bootable discs, and support for UNIX symbolic links.

On the downside, CDR Publisher doesn't offer support for many drives (particularly older recorders), and its transfer testing is rather rudimentary. CDR Publisher doesn't have a true Windows online help system; it launches Adobe Acrobat and loads the program's entire manual, which takes extra time and doesn't provide much of the search functionality of a true online help system.

If you need the ability to create PC/Mac hybrid discs and you have a Macintosh handy to provide the HFS partition, CDR Publisher HyCD might be the answer to your mastering needs — it has a few rough edges, but it's a solid product that's constantly updated and improved.

QuickTOPiX

- ✦ Manufacturer: Microtest

  4747 North 22nd Street

  Phoenix, AZ 85016-4708

- ✦ Current version: 2.2.

- ✦ Supported platforms: Windows 3.1/95/NT and Macintosh.

- ✦ Website: www.microtest.com.

- ✦ Telephone: 800-526-9675.

As illustrated in Figure A-4, QuickTOPiX presents yet another angle on the user interface problem that distinctly reminds you of its Macintosh sibling. Its simple main window allows you to specify a template (the type of disc to record), the data source, and the target. Next to these three drop-down list boxes are six buttons that toggle important functions like testing before writing, closing the session, finalizing the disc, and ejecting it. Once you're ready, you can start the recording process by clicking on the large Make button. It's not particularly intuitive, but it's definitely the fastest program in terms of setting up a recording!

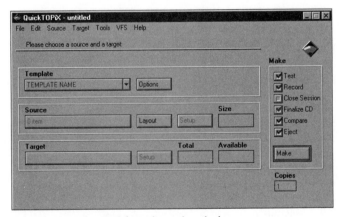

Figure A-4: The QuickTOPiX main window.

Like CDR Publisher, QuickTOPiX can create Mac HFS discs on your PC. The PC version supports a wide range of digital sound formats (including AIF, QT, and WAV formats), and you can preview sound files before you add them to your layout. The Macintosh version also supports WAV format sound files!

Unfortunately, QuickTOPiX doesn't include support for drag-and-drop, so you have to use the program's cryptic custom file selection dialog. Also, the program has no option for disc-at-once recording or custom file placement.

QuickTOPiX fills a niche for those who prefer its fast interface and need to write HFS discs on a PC, but other programs offer more functionality.

Toast CD-ROM Pro

✦ Manufacturer: Adaptec

✦ Current version: 3.0.

✦ Supported platforms: Macintosh.

✦ Website: www.astarte.de.

✦ Telephone: 800-255-4020.

Toast is considered to be the premiere Mac-only mastering program. It has a long list of features, including an impressive variety of supported recorders, CD-EXTRA, CD-I, and Video CD support, bootable CD-ROM support, customized file placement, and drag and drop file selection. Toast can also create Mac/PC hybrid discs. Although Toast has a conventional Macintosh look and feel, the interface is colorful and easy to use, and options can be found and set without digging through multiple menu levels. Figure A-5 shows Toast's main screen.

Figure A-5: The main screen from the Toast mastering program for the Macintosh.

One unique feature of Toast that I've yet to see offered in any other program is its "on-the-fly optimization": you can literally forget about defragmenting your source drive, because Toast does it for you! This automatic optimization extends to the finished disc, too. Like CD Creator, Toast can determine the optimum block size and file position so that files can be located and loaded faster from your finished disc.

You can also improve the performance of your CD-ROM recorder by using Toast's RAM cache feature, which sets aside a portion of your Mac's system memory as additional data buffer space. Naturally, you can specify the amount of memory to be reserved for recording. You can display the performance of both the RAM cache and your recorder's cache to check the speed of your system, or you can perform a full simulation before recording. Toast can also automatically verify your new CD-ROM after recording is complete.

Without a doubt, Toast will take you just about anywhere you'd like to go in Macintosh CD-ROM recording! About the only feature I found wanting was the lack of WAV support — because the WAV format is becoming more popular on the Internet, it would be nice to have internal support for WAV format sound files within Toast. Oh, and it would also be nice if Adaptec would consider a Windows 95 version — are you listening, people?

CD-Maker Pro

✦ Manufacturer: NewTech Infosystems
2081 Business Center Drive, Suite #250
Irvine, CA 92715

✦ Current version: 2.5.

✦ Supported platforms: Windows 3.1/95/NT.

✦ Website: www.ntius.com.

✦ Telephone: 714-622-6970.

Although CD-Maker Pro is the least expensive recording program in this appendix, it has one thing that most of the other programs don't: an honest-to-goodness Windows interface! If you're a fan of the conventional Windows Toolbar, both CD Creator and CD-Maker Pro will put you at ease. CD-Maker Pro also features a one-line Tip under its Toolbar that helps novices learn how to use the program by indicating logical choices. For example, when you first run the program the Tip tells you the menu items to pick to create a new disc or load an existing image.

CD-Maker Pro doesn't create HFS or hybrid discs, so if you're creating discs with Macintosh support, you need to look elsewhere. The program does have all the standard features, however, that make it a good choice for low-end recording: drag-and-drop file selection (including direct launching of Windows Explorer from the menu), file ordering, a good collection of supported drives, and the ability to write to an open session. The program also includes a SCSI device scanning utility and a session selector for multisession discs. CD-Maker Pro supports track-at-once, disc-at-once, and packet recording.

On the downside, the only supported sound format is WAV, and the online help is less than helpful in documenting several of the program's features.

As an inexpensive recording package, there is much to like about CD-Maker Pro, and I give it a definite "thumbs-up"! Other programs discussed here can do more, but the CD-Maker Pro feature set is very well-suited to casual recording, and you won't have to learn how to use a new proprietary interface.

SimpliCD

✦ Manufacturer: YMI
1906 Orange Tree Lane, Suite 240
Redlands, CA 92374

✦ Current version: 3.1.

✦ Supported platforms: Windows 3.1.

✦ Website: www.ymi.com.

✦ Telephone: 909-335-1350.

SimpliCD is the only Windows program in this appendix without a true 32-bit version, but the program does run under Windows 95. As shown in Figure A-6, SimpliCD provides an enlarged, rather outdated Toolbar interface designed to simplify CD-ROM recording — either you like the controls or they irritate you. I use the menu commands within SimpliCD, because I prefer a standard-sized Toolbar with more buttons.

SimpliCD offers a number of exceptionally powerful features that might make the interface easier to tolerate. It provides support for disc-at-once recording, barcodes, 6x speed recording, drag and drop from File Manager (as well as popular alternate desktops for Windows 3.1 like Norton Desktop), tape output, WAV and AIFF sound formats, and a good variety of supported recorders. I especially like the comprehensive online help system.

Another unique feature of SimpliCD is its support for a separate optional compression module called capaCD Pro that provides up to 4 gigabytes of storage on a single disc; such storage rivals even the upcoming DVD drives! The program also includes SimpliStor, a backup/restore utility.

This is a 16-bit program, so SimpliCD doesn't support long file names or the Joliet structure, and it doesn't take advantage of the Windows 95 32-bit architecture. A lack of support for file ordering handicaps the program. Also, recording sessions do not launch automatically after a successful simulated recording.

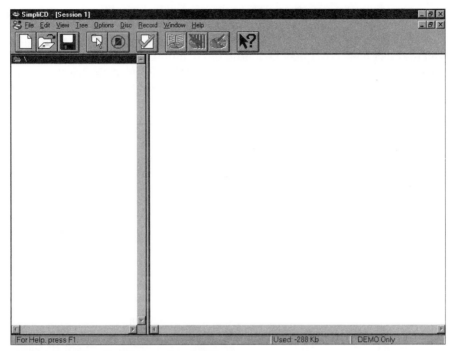

Figure A-6: The SimpliCD main window.

Although SimpliCD is showing its age, it's a solid performer with much to offer — in fact, if you're still running Windows 3.1, this program is one of the few remaining competitors to CD Creator! Within Windows 95, I experienced no problems running SimpliCD, but it wasn't the fastest performer, and the lack of support for long filenames will be a major shortcoming in the years to come.

WinOnCD

✦ Manufacturer: CeQuadrat
1804 Embarcadero Road, #101
Palo Alto, CA 94303

✦ Current version: 3.0.

✦ Supported platforms: Windows 95/NT.

✦ Website: www.cequadrat.com.

✦ Telephone: 800-330-MPEG.

Our final program is WinOnCD, one of the better-known recording programs that's generally highly regarded as a professional mastering program for Windows 95. The windowed interface provides you with all the information you need and allows you to select files, but it may be a little too daunting for novice users. It can handle HFS and hybrid discs, Video CD and CD-EXTRA formats, and bootable CDs. The program can perform advanced disc-at-once and open session writing. File ordering is supported, and WinOnCD automatically converts AVI digital video to MPEG format for Video CDs, just like VCD Creator.

WinOnCD also shines in the audio department; it even includes an audio editor somewhat similar to the Adaptec Sound Editor, allowing you to play and modify your WAV files, add silent delay, and insert sounds from other files. The program supports WAV and AIFF formats, and like Gear for Windows you can specify the gap delay in between audio tracks.

Is there anything that WinOnCD doesn't do? Actually, yes — for example, it doesn't support PhotoCD or CD-I, and you can't use Explorer to select files (instead, you drag and drop files from a similar tree display within the program's window). WinOnCD also doesn't have a Wizard to lead you through its functions.

Feature-for-feature, WinOnCD equals Gear for Windows, and it's actually a step or two in front of CD Creator in terms of Mac HFS and advanced hybrid formatting. If you're looking for a professional-quality mastering program and you're experienced with recording discs, make sure you give WinOnCD a test drive!

CD-R Hardware and Media Vendors

This appendix provides the contact information for companies manufacturing CD-R hardware and media.

Dynatek
800-461-0052
www.dynatek.ca

Eastman Kodak Company
800-235-6325
www.kodak.com

Hewlett-Packard
800-810-0134
www.hp.com

JVC Information Products
714-816-6500
www.jvcinfo.com

Meridian Data
800-342-1129
www.meridian-data.com

MicroTech Conversion Systems
415-596-1900
www.microtech.com

Mitsui Toatsu
800-MTC-CDRS
www.mtchem.co.jp/english/index.htm

Mitsumi
516-752-7730
www.mitsumi.com

Olympus
800-347-4027
www.olympus.com

Panasonic
201-348-7000
www.panasonic.com

Phillips Professional Solutions
800-235-7373
www.pps.philips.com

Pinnacle Micro
800-553-7070
www.pinnaclemicro.com

Pioneer
800-444-6784
www.pioneerusa.com

Plasmon
800-451-6845
www.plasmon.com

Plextor
800-886-3935
www.plextor.com

Ricoh
800-955-3453
www.ricoh.com

Sony Electronics
800-352-7669
www.sony.com

Taiyo Yuden
800-348-2496
www.yuden.co.jp

TDK Electronics
800-835-8273
www.tdk.com

Teac
213-726-0303
www.teac.com

Todd Enterprises
800-445-8633
www.toddent.com

Verbatim
704-547-6628
www.verbatimcorp.com

Yamaha
800-543-7457
www.yamahayst.com

Glossary

This appendix provides an alphabetical listing of the terms used throughout the book.

AIFF One of the most common Internet standards for digital audio. Most Windows CD recording programs can read digital audio from an AIFF file and record that audio onto a blank disc.

ASPI Acronym for *Advanced SCSI Programmer's Interface*. A standard low-level programming interface that allows software to access SCSI devices using any SCSI adapter card.

Buffer A portion of memory reserved to hold data temporarily before it's transferred to your CD recorder. Buffers come in many forms: your CD recorder has a dedicated hardware buffer. Many recording programs also allow you to reserve a portion of your system memory for use as a buffer. Generally, the larger the buffer, the less problems you have with recording, especially on a slower system.

Caddy A thin, square box slightly larger than a CD-ROM that holds and protects discs. Many CD recorders and read-only drives require caddies, while others use trays that hold the disc without a caddy.

CD-DA Acronym for *compact disc-digital audio*. Commonly referred to as a compact disc. These discs store audio and are playable on any audio CD player or computer CD-ROM drive. CD-DA discs conform to the Red Book standard.

CD-R Acronym for *compact disc-recordable*. CD-R discs are writable on a PC or Macintosh with a CD recorder and readable by any standard CD-ROM drive (or, in the case of an audio disc, any standard audio compact disc player).

CD-ROM Acronym for *compact disc-read only memory*. Typically refers to a compact disc that stores data for use on a computer and conforms to the Yellow Book standard. This data can be in the form of audio, video, or computer files.

Close disc Sometimes called "write protection." Closing a recordable CD prevents recording any additional data to it. Closing a disc also automatically closes the current session.

Close session Closing an open session stores directory and file information about the session within the disc's Table of Contents, preventing recording further information to that session. However, you can write another session to that same disc in the future.

Digital audio extraction A method of copying audio tracks from a standard audio compact disc to your hard drive or CD recorder. Most CD recorders and computer CD-ROM drives can extract digital audio.

Disc-at-once A method of recording CD-ROMs where all of the data is written to the disc at once in a single session and the disc is write-protected to prevent further recording. The disc's Table of Contents is recorded before the data. If you're creating a master disc for use in manufacturing copies, you should use disc-at-once recording. Not all recording software and CD recorders support disc-at-once!

Dye layer The dye layer on a recordable CD-ROM stores digital data, much like the reflective layer on a mass-produced disc. Instead of physical pits and flats, however, your CD recorder changes the transparency level of the disc by distorting the dye layer, creating the same pattern that your CD-ROM drive translates into digital data.

El Torito The standard specification for bootable CD-ROM discs. These discs contain all of the system files necessary to load one or more operating systems on a computer without the need for a hard drive or floppy disk.

External recorder A CD recorder with a separate case and power supply that is attached to the external SCSI connector on your SCSI adapter card.

Glass master A glass original disc created as a first step in the mass production of commercial compact discs and blank recordable discs. The glass master is used to build the metal molds used in the injection molding process.

HFS Acronym for *Hierarchical File System*. The Macintosh file system for storing data on either magnetic disks (such as hard drives and floppy disks) or CD-ROM.

Hybrid A CD-ROM that can be read by both a Macintosh and an IBM PC. Hybrid discs contain both a Mac HFS partition and an ISO 9660 partition.

Internal recorder A CD recorder that fits inside one of the device bays in your computer's case, much like a floppy disk drive; it does not require a separate power supply.

ISO 9660 The widely-recognized international logical file format standard for CD-ROMs developed by the High Sierra Group. ISO 9660 discs are readable by nearly all computers and under a wide variety of operating systems.

Jewel case A clear plastic storage box that holds and protects a disc when you're not using it.

Joliet A Microsoft-specific extension of the ISO 9660 standard developed for Windows 95 and Windows NT. It supports long filenames of up to 64 characters (including spaces). Joliet also supports the Unicode international character set.

Kodak PhotoCD A disc containing high-resolution images developed from a film camera, viewable on any Kodak PhotoCD player. PhotoCDs conform to a proprietary Kodak standard and cannot be created with a CD recorder.

Land A flat area in between pits in the reflective surface of a compact disc. Lands reflect laser light better than the pits on a CD-ROM, allowing the laser read head of your CD-ROM drive to distinguish between them. Your drive assigns the pits and lands on a CD-ROM the binary value of zero and the transitions between them the value of one; the resulting stream of ones and zeros is then interpreted as digital data or audio.

Laser A device that produces a tightly focused beam of coherent light used by a CD-ROM read-only drive to read the data stored on a disc. Your CD recorder contains a higher powered laser than a standard CD-ROM drive or CD player; the recorder's laser creates the imperfections in the surface of a blank disc to store data.

Mixed-mode A CD that merges digital audio tracks and computer data, typically used for entertainment and educational programs. The first track contains data, while the remaining tracks store digital audio.

Modes 1 and 2 Two data structures defined within the Yellow Book specification for CD-ROMs. Mode 1 discs hold text and computer data and include error correction, while Mode 2 discs do not contain the extra error correction data. Nearly all available CD-ROMs are written in Mode 1.

MPEG Acronym for *Motion Picture Experts Group*. The common name for a standard format of compressed full-motion digital video used in Video CDs.

MSCDEX A DOS driver supplied by Microsoft that allows DOS programs and the operating system to access a CD-ROM drive.

Multisession A method of recording CD-ROMs that allows multiple recording sessions, up to the total storage space on the disc. Multisession discs are readable on most CD-ROM drives.

Orange Book The standard specification for CD-R (or recordable CD-ROM) discs.

Packet recording A method of recording CD-ROMs that allows one or more files to be saved to the disc incrementally in packets, without the wasted space that occurs in between sessions on a multisession disc. Unlike track-at-once recording, packet recording is not limited to a maximum of 99 tracks per disc.

Pit A minute depression in the reflective surface of a compact disc. Pits do not reflect laser light as well as the lands on a CD-ROM, allowing the laser read head of your CD-ROM drive to distinguish between them. Your drive assigns the pits and lands on a CD-ROM the binary value of zero and the transitions between them the value of one; the resulting stream of ones and zeros is then interpreted as digital data or audio.

Red Book Developed in 1980 by Philips and Sony, it is the standard specification for audio compact discs.

SCSI Acronym for *Small Computer System Interface*. A hardware interface that allows you to connect devices like hard drives, scanners, and CD-ROM recorders to your computer. SCSI is standard on the Macintosh, and an optional hardware upgrade on most PCs.

SCSI ID A numeric ID that identifies a specific SCSI device in a SCSI chain. Each device in a SCSI chain must have a unique ID number.

Sector Much like a hard drive, data is stored on compact discs in sectors — each sector represents a single unit (or block) of data. Most standard CD-ROMs available today hold 2,048 bytes of data per sector.

Session A separate, distinct recording session that stores one or more tracks of data or audio on a CD-DA or CD-ROM disc. CD-DA discs that store digital audio for playback on a standard audio disc player are always single-session (where all the data is recorded in one session and the disc is write-protected afterwards). CD-ROM discs can be either single-session or multisession (where multiple sessions are recordable on a single disc as needed).

Silk-screening A process whereby successive layers of paint are applied to the top of a compact disc to form a label. For those copying a large number of discs, a silk-screened label provides a professional finished appearance to a disc.

Simulated recording Most CD-ROM recording programs allow you to simulate the recording of a disc without actually writing data. The program toggles the recorder's laser write head to a lower power setting, allowing the program to test for possible throughput or file structure problems.

Sleeve The paper inserts commonly used on the front and back of a jewel case; they usually identify the disc and its contents.

Terminator No, not the intelligent cyborg that made Arnold famous — we're talking about a SCSI terminator! It's a setting, jumper, or switch that you add or enable on a SCSI device to indicate that it's the end device in a SCSI chain.

TOC Acronym for *Table of Contents*. A CD-ROM TOC holds information used by a CD-ROM drive to determine how many tracks have been recorded on the disc and where they are located.

Track A discrete amount of data recorded on a CD. Tracks can hold either computer data or digital audio, and a track can vary in size from a single song to the entire contents of a CD-ROM. A CD-ROM must contain at least one session, and that session must include at least one track.

Track-at-once A method of recording CD-ROMs where the laser is turned off between data and audio tracks, and the data is written before the Table of Contents. Track-at-once is the standard recording method for most recording software.

UDF Acronym for *Universal Disc Format*. A new file system standard approved by the Optical Storage Technology Association, it's designed to overcome some of the shortcomings of the ISO 9660 standard, including support for the packet writing recording method.

Validation The process of verifying the contents of a CD-ROM layout before recording. During validation, the mastering program checks to make sure all of the files to be recorded still exist in their proper path and that they can be read without access problems.

Video CD A disc containing digital video in MPEG format that can be viewed on Video CD players and most computer CD-ROM drives. Video CDs conform to the White Book standard.

WAV The Windows standard for digital audio. WAV files range in fidelity from 8-bit mono to CD-quality stereo. Most Windows CD recording programs can extract digital audio from an audio disc, save it as a WAV file, and record that WAV file onto a blank disc.

White Book The standard specification for Video CD discs.

Yellow Book Developed in 1983 by Philips and Sony, it is the standard specification for computer CD-ROM discs.

CD-ROM Recorders

This appendix provides details on available popular CD-ROM recorders. Many of these recorders sell under different names and brands, so if a particular recorder doesn't appear, it may be because that recorder is represented by another brand. I also provide contact information so that you can request literature or specifications from the manufacturer.

All the recorders listed here are capable of multisession and packet recording.

HP Surestore

✦ Manufacturer: Hewlett-Packard

   3000 Hanover Street

   Palo Alto, CA 94304

✦ Current model: 6020 series.

✦ Website: www.hp.com.

✦ Telephone: 800-810-0134.

✦ Interface: SCSI-2 and parallel.

✦ Speed: 2x write, 6x read.

✦ Loading mechanism: Tray.

✦ Cache RAM: 1 megabyte.

✦ Audio: Headphone jack.

✦ Panel lights: Busy, Recording.

✦ Warranty: 2 years.

JVC Personal RomMaker

- ◆ Manufacturer: JVC Information Products

  5665 Corporate Ave.

  Cypress, CA 90630
- ◆ Current model: n/a.
- ◆ Website: www.jvcinfo.com.
- ◆ Telephone: 714-816-6500.
- ◆ Interface: SCSI-2.
- ◆ Speed: 2x write, 4x read
- ◆ Loading mechanism: Tray.
- ◆ Cache RAM: 1 megabyte.
- ◆ Audio: Headphone jack, external outputs.
- ◆ Panel lights: Busy, Recording, Speed.
- ◆ Warranty: 1 year.

Panasonic CD-Rtist

- ◆ Manufacturer: Matsushita Electric Corporation of America

  One Panasonic Way

  Secaucus, NJ 07094
- ◆ Current model: LK-MW602BPK.
- ◆ Website: www.panasonic.com.
- ◆ Telephone: 201-348-7000.
- ◆ Interface: SCSI-2.
- ◆ Speed: 2x write, 4x read.
- ◆ Loading mechanism: Tray.
- ◆ Cache RAM: 1 megabyte.
- ◆ Audio: Headphone jack, external outputs.
- ◆ Panel lights: Busy, Recording.
- ◆ Warranty: 2 years.

Phillips Professional Solutions

✦ Manufacturer: Phillips Professional Solutions

  100 East 42nd Street

  New York, NY 10017-5699

✦ Current model: CDD2000.

✦ Website: www.pps.philips.com.

✦ Telephone: 800-235-7373.

✦ Interface: SCSI-2.

✦ Speed: 2x write, 4x read.

✦ Loading mechanism: Tray.

✦ Cache RAM: 1 megabyte.

✦ Audio: headphone jack, external outputs.

✦ Panel lights: Busy, Recording.

✦ Warranty: 2 years.

Pinnacle Micro

✦ Manufacturer: Pinnacle Micro

  19 Technology

  Irvine, CA 92618

✦ Current model: RCD 4x4.

✦ Website: www.pinnaclemicro.com.

✦ Telephone: 800-553-7070.

✦ Interface: SCSI-2.

✦ Speed: 4x write, 4x read.

✦ Loading mechanism: Tray.

✦ Cache RAM: 1 megabyte.

✦ Audio: headphone jack, external outputs.

✦ Panel lights: Busy.

✦ Warranty: 1 year.

Plasmon AFTERBURNER

✦ Manufacturer: Plasmon Data

9625 West 76th Street

Eden Prairie, MN 55344

✦ Current model: CDR4240.

✦ Website: www.plasmon.com.

✦ Telephone: 800-451-6845.

✦ Interface: SCSI-2.

✦ Speed: 2x write, 4x read.

✦ Loading mechanism: Tray.

✦ Cache RAM: 1 megabyte.

✦ Audio: headphone jack, external outputs.

✦ Panel lights: Busy, Recording.

✦ Warranty: 1 year.

Plextor PlexWriter

✦ Manufacturer: Plextor

4255 Burton Drive

Santa Clara, CA 95054

✦ Current model: PX-R24CS.

✦ Website: www.plextor.com.

✦ Telephone: 800-886-3935.

✦ Interface: SCSI-2.

✦ Speed: 2x write, 4x read.

✦ Loading mechanism: Caddy.

✦ Cache RAM: 512K.

✦ Audio: headphone jack, external outputs.

✦ Panel lights: Busy.

✦ Warranty: 1 year.

Ricoh

✦ Manufacturer: Ricoh

   5 Dedrick Place

   West Caldwell, NJ 07006

✦ Current model: RO-142OC.

✦ Website: www.ricoh.com.

✦ Telephone: 800-955-3453.

✦ Interface: SCSI-2.

✦ Speed: 2x write, 4x read.

✦ Loading mechanism: Caddy.

✦ Cache RAM: 2 megabytes.

✦ Audio: headphone jack, external outputs.

✦ Panel lights: Busy.

✦ Warranty: 1 year.

Smart and Friendly

✦ Manufacturer: Smart and Friendly

   20520 Nordhoff Avenue

   Chatsworth, CA 91311

✦ Current model: CD-R 2006.

✦ Website: www.smartandfriendly.com.

✦ Telephone: 800-366-6001.

✦ Interface: SCSI-2.

✦ Speed: 2x write, 6x read.

✦ Loading mechanism: Caddy.

✦ Cache RAM: 512K.

✦ Audio: headphone jack, external outputs.

✦ Panel lights: Busy.

✦ Warranty: 1 year.

TEAC

✦ Manufacturer: Teac

7733 Telegraph Road

Montebello, CA 90640

✦ Current model: CD-R50S.

✦ Website: www.teac.com.

✦ Telephone: 213-726-0303.

✦ Interface: SCSI-2.

✦ Speed: 4x write, 4x read.

✦ Loading mechanism: Tray.

✦ Cache RAM: 1 megabyte.

✦ Audio: headphone jack, external outputs.

✦ Panel lights: Busy.

✦ Warranty: 1 year.

Turtle Beach

✦ Manufacturer: Turtle Beach Systems

5 Odell Plaza

Yonkers, NY 10701-1406

✦ Current model: TBS-2040R.

✦ Website: www.tbeach.com.

✦ Telephone: 914-966-0600.

✦ Interface: SCSI-2.

✦ Speed: 2x write, 4x read.

✦ Loading mechanism: Caddy.

✦ Cache RAM: 1 megabyte.

✦ Audio: headphone jack, external outputs.

✦ Panel lights: Busy.

✦ Warranty: 1 year.

Yamaha

✦ Manufacturer: Yamaha

    100 Century Center Court

    San Jose, CA 95112

✦ Current model: CDR400.

✦ Website: www.yamahayst.com.

✦ Telephone: 800-543-7457.

✦ Interface: SCSI-2.

✦ Speed: 4x write, 6x read.

✦ Loading mechanism: Tray.

✦ Cache RAM: 2 megabytes.

✦ Audio: headphone jack, external outputs.

✦ Panel lights: Busy, Recording, Speed.

✦ Warranty: 1 year.

Technical Information

The High Sierra/ISO 9660 Standard

The High Sierra (also known as the ISO 9660) file standard allows logical organization of the data on a CD-ROM. ISO 9660 was designed as a read-only, high-capacity file standard, where:

+ each individual CD is a volume that can contain standard file structures, coded character set file structures for character encoding other than ASCII, or boot records. Each volume has a root directory which serves as an ancestor to all other directories or files in the volume;

+ several CDs may be grouped together in a volume set;

+ the smallest addressable space on a disc is the logical block. Each logical block is identified by a unique Logical Block Number (LBN), assigned in order starting from 0 at the beginning of the disc. Under the ISO 9660 standard, all data on a CD is addressed in terms of Logical Block Numbers.

ISO 9660 specifies that each volume must contain a path table in addition to its directories and files. The path table describes the directory hierarchy in a compact form that is easily cached to improve performance. The path table contains entries for the volume's directories in a breadth-first order; directories with a common parent are listed in lexicographic order. Each entry contains only the location of the directory it describes, its name, and the location in the path table of its parent. This mechanism allows any directory to be accessed with only a single CD seek.

ISO 9660 directories contain more detailed information than the path table. Each directory entry contains:

✦ directory or file location;

✦ file length;

✦ date and time of creation;

✦ name of the file;

✦ flags including whether the entry is for a file or a directory, whether it is an associated file, whether it has records, whether it has read protection, and whether it has subsequent extents;

✦ interleave structure of the file. Interleaving is required to present the contents of multiple files simultaneously; for example, the presentation of video with synchronized sound.

Files themselves are recorded in contiguous (or interleaved) blocks on the disc. A file is also recordable in a series of noncontiguous extents with a directory entry for each extent.

Choice of Filename Characters

Valid ISO 9660 filename characters are the letters "A" through "Z," the digits "0" through "9," and the underscore character ("_"). Note that the letters "a" through "z" are not included so that file names are not case sensitive.

Depth of Path

The ISO 9660 format permits pathnames up to eight levels deep.

Length of Path

The ISO 9660 format permits the entire pathname to be a maximum of 255 characters.

UNIX Rock Ridge Extensions

Rock Ridge extensions to the ISO 9660 standard allow all the features of the UNIX file system to be used. The additional data is stored in the System Use fields defined in the ISO 9660 standard. The information that is stored there for UNIX/POSIX include:

✦ uid;

✦ gid;

- ✦ permissions;

- ✦ file mode bits;

- ✦ file types;

- ✦ setuid;

- ✦ setgid;

- ✦ sticky bit;

- ✦ file links;

- ✦ device nodes;

- ✦ symbolic links;

- ✦ POSIX filenames;

- ✦ reconstruction of deep directories;

- ✦ time stamps.

ISO 9660 Directory Record Format

The format of the directory record for an ISO 9660 disc is:

```
/* ISO-9660 directory entry structure */
typedef struct iso_dir_entry {
uchar len_dr; /* length of this directory entry */
uchar XAR_len; /* length of XAR in LBN's */
ulong loc_extentI; /* LBN of data Intel format */
ulong loc_extentM; /* LBN of data Molorola format */
ulong data_lenI; /* length of file Intel format */
ulong data_lenM; /* length of file Motorola format */
uchar record_time[7];/* date and time */
uchar file_flags_iso;/* 8 flags */
uchar il_size; /* interleave size */
uchar il_skip; /* interleave skip factor */
ushort VSSNI; /* volume set sequence num Intel */
ushort VSSNM; /* volume set sequence num Motorola*/
uchar len_fi; /* length of name */
uchar file_id[...]; /* variable length name upto 32 chars */
uchar padding; /* optional padding if file_id is odd length*/
uchar sys_data[...] /* variable length system data */
} iso_dir_entry;
```

CD-ROM Structure

Figure E-1 illustrates the relationship of the different Book standards and their approximate development timeline:

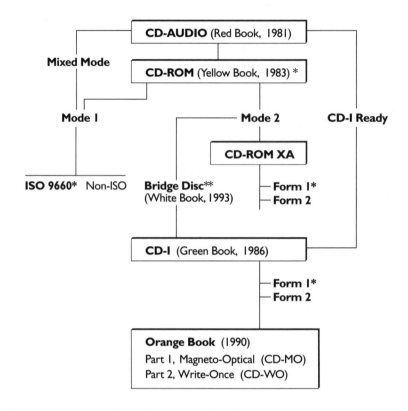

* Implements Third Layer of Error Detection and Error Correction
** Kodak PhotoCD and Video CD are Bridge Discs

Figure E-1: Family tree of CD format standards

Data Track Structure

Each data track on a CD-ROM is divided into individually addressable blocks of 2352 data bytes (one subcoding block or 98 frames). A header in each block contains the block address and the mode of the block. The block address is identical to the encoding of minute, second, and frame number in subcode channel Q.

The modes defined in the CD-ROM specification are:

Mode 0 — all data bytes are zero.

Mode 1 — (CD-ROM Data):

Sync Field — 12 bytes

Header Field — 4

User Data Field — 2048

Error Detection Code — 4

Reserved — 8

Error Correction — 276

Mode 2 — (CD Audio or Other Data):

Sync Field — 12 bytes

Header Field — 4

User Data Field — 2048

Auxiliary Data Field — 288

Figure E-2 illustrates the block structure of the various Book standards:

✦ A CD recorder writes **link blocks** each time the laser write head is turned on or off during the recording of a track or packet. These link blocks contain no usable data.

✦ Tracks are divided by **pregap** and **postgap** spaces. Pregap is written before the track actually begins, while postgap is recorded within the end of the track data area. Postgap spaces are 150 sectors long (or 2 seconds in duration); they are used only if successive tracks are of different types. Where successive tracks are both of data, one track is separated from another by a track pregap of 150 sectors. Where successive tracks are of different types, the pregap is usually of 225 sectors (or three seconds in duration). If two successive tracks are audio, there may be no pregap at all.

Session Structure

Each session on a CD-R disc is preceded by a Lead In area, which is left blank for the session's Table of Contents (track numbers and start-and-stop points). The lead-in is written when a session is closed, and occupies 4500 sectors on disc (1 minute, or roughly 9 megabytes). The lead-in also indicates whether the disc is multisession by giving, and if the disc is not closed, the next recordable address on the disc.

Red Book Specifications (Philips and Sony, 1981)

CD-Audio Sector = 2352 bytes.

User Data
2352 Bytes

Yellow Book Specifications (Philips and Sony, 1983)

CD-ROM, Mode 1 Sector = 2352 bytes.

Sync	Header	User Data	EDC	Blank	ECC
12	4	2048	4	8	276

CD-Mode 2 Sector = 2352 bytes.

Sync	Header	User Data
12	4	2336

CD-ROM XA (Extended Architecture)

(All tracks are CD-ROM, Mode 2)

CD-XA Sector, Form 1 = 2352 bytes.

Sync	Header	Sub-Header	User Data	EDC	ECC
12	4	8	2048	4	276

CD-XA Sector, Form 2 = 2352 bytes.

Sync	Header	Sub-Header	User Data	EDC
12	4	8	2324	4

Green Book Specifications (Philips and Sony, 1986)

(All tracks are CD-ROM, Mode 2)

CD-I Sector, Form 2 = 2352 bytes.

Sync	Header	Sub-Header	User Data	EDC	ECC
12	4	8	2048	4	276

CD-I Sector, Form 2 = 2352 bytes.

Sync	Header	Sub-Header	User Data	EDC
12	4	8	2324	4

Figure E-2: Comparing the block structure of the various CD standards

In a similar fashion, the Lead Out is written at the end of a session to signal the end of the data. The first lead-out on a disc is 6,750 sectors (1.5 minutes, about 13 megabytes) long; any subsequent lead-outs are 2,250 sectors (.5 minute, about 4 megabytes).

Error Correction

The various standard formats of CD and CD-ROM employ one or both of two levels of error correction.

Level 1 Error Correction

Motion during reading, stains, damage, and production defects can all result in data errors, which typically occur in a series. Error correction on compact discs is based on a two-level system called Cross Interleave Reed-Solomon Coding (CIRC). The cross interleave component breaks up the long error bursts into several short errors; the Reed-Solomon component provides the error correction. The process includes these steps:

1. As each frame is read from the disc, it's converted into 8-bit data bytes.

2. The bytes from each frame (24 data bytes and 8 error correction bytes) are passed to the first Reed-Solomon decoder.

3. Checks are made against 4 of the error correction bytes. If there are errors, the data is marked as being in error at this stage of decoding.

4. The 24 data bytes and 4 remaining error correction bytes are then passed through unequal delays before going through another Reed-Solomon decoder, which result in an interleaving of the data that makes it easier to identify errors in series.

5. The second Reed-Solomon decoder uses the last 4 error correction bytes to correct any remaining errors in the 24 data bytes. At this point, the data goes through a de-interleaving process to restore the correct byte order.

Level 2 Error Correction

The Mode 1 standard adds a second level of error detection and error correction (EDC/ECC) for data. This error detection data is stored in the auxiliary data field, and it consists of a cyclic redundancy check (CRC) on the sync, header, and user data. It occupies the first 4 bytes of the auxiliary data field and provides a very high probability that uncorrected errors will be detected.

The error correction code uses the same interleaving and Reed-Solomon coding technique used in Level 1 Error Correction. It occupies the final 276 bytes of the auxiliary data field.

Kodak PhotoCD Format

Kodak's PhotoCD format is a proprietary system developed jointly by Eastman Kodak Company and Philips. The CD-Bridge standard expands on the CD-ROM/XA specification, adding specific proprietary information at the track level.

There are 5 image resolutions stored on a Photo CD, ranging from 128 x 192 to 2,048 x 3,072. All 5 resolutions are in 24-bit color, with the largest image at the highest resolution reaching about 20 megabytes in size.

The five picture formats are:

Image	Resolution
Base/16	128 x 192 pixels
Base/4	256 x 384 pixels
Base	512 x 768 pixels
4Base	1,024 x 1,536 pixels
16Base	2,048 x 3,072 pixels

On the CD-ROM

When the good folks at IDG Books Worldwide told me that I had considerable freedom to select just what you would find on the companion CD-ROM, they weren't kidding. I'm proud to say that there's a wide range of software included on the CD-ROM; in fact, I'd like to think that it provides a good cross section of the applications available today for CD recording, including specialized areas such as Web content storage and digital video editing. I've been using some of these programs for years, while others were recommended by friends and professionals. All in all, I hope I've reached my goal, which was to create a companion CD-ROM so good that your friends will beg to borrow it.

Make 'em wait in line!

A Word About Shareware

Most of these programs are shareware, but don't fall prey to the common misconception that shareware is inferior. I selected each of these titles because they were the best-known and most powerful programs in their class. As a shareware game developer myself, I'm a firm believer that well-written shareware can equal (and sometimes surpass) the quality of its commercial competitors — in fact, many successful commercial programs got their start as shareware.

There's another common misconception that dates back to the days when bulletin board systems ruled Cyberspace and acted as shareware distribution centers. That is, the old belief that shareware is free. *Wrong.* Shareware is *not* free — someone worked long and hard to write a professional, solid program that works, and that person deserves to be paid for their time. Instead of paying for a fancy box and big advertisements in all the national magazines, you typically pay the author directly, and your registration fee is usually a minor fraction of what you would pay for a similar commercial product.

"How do I register?" The shareware programs on the CD-ROM all include complete instructions on how to register, and most of them also offer registration information from within the program. Make sure you read the README file, and pull up the online help if you need it. My sincere thanks for buying this book, but that didn't register any of these shareware programs — that's your obligation if you decide to use them.

I strongly encourage you to help maintain these shareware programs with your registration fee; you'll gain technical support for the program, and you'll help ensure the continued development of these fine applications!

What's on the CD-ROM?

Here's a quick list of the different types of programs you'll find on the companion disc:

✦ **Recording and duplicating software.** Programs that enable you to create your own discs or replicate existing discs on a variety of platforms and operating systems.

✦ **Image, sound, and video editing software.** These applications make it easy to load, edit, and modify many of the multimedia files you'll be recording on CD, including the digital WAV files used to record audio CDs.

✦ **Multimedia cataloging software.** Software that stores and displays your images, sounds, and video clips, enabling you to search and retrieve files from CD.

✦ **Web content software.** Software that records information and data from Web pages directly to CD.

✦ **CD audio software.** Software that enables you to play audio CDs on your computer's CD-ROM drive.

✦ **Tutorials and Tours.** Video tutorials and product demonstrations that present features and benefits.

Running the CD-ROM

To browse the disc in Windows 95:

1. Launch Windows Explorer.

2. Select the letter for your CD-ROM drive in the directory tree. Explorer will display the contents of the disc. Note that the files on the CD are arranged in directories by program name.

3. Check the launch information for the specific program. Most programs can be installed by running the program SETUP.EXE in the desired directory.

The CD-ROM Programs

I've already mentioned several of these programs within the body of the book, but I'll give you a short description of each in this section, as well as information on how to begin the installation process. Most of these programs require Windows 95 or Windows NT to run; for complete details on system requirements, refer to the documentation supplied with the program.

I've also included the developer's Web site address whenever possible. You can typically register from the home page, or you might check to see if a new version has been released since this book went to press.

Adobe Acrobat Reader

This free utility from Adobe enables you to read and print electronic documents saved as .PDF (Portable Document Format) files. Many of the applications that appear on this disc include manuals in .PDF format, and you'll also find that Acrobat files are a popular method of presenting documents on the Internet.

The CD contains versions of the program for both Macintosh and Windows 95. You'll find the installation files in the **Acrobat** directory; there are separate subdirectories, labeled **Macintosh** and **Windows**.

You can visit the Adobe site at **www.adobe.com/prodindex/acrobat/** for more information about Adobe Acrobat.

Cool Edit 96

This shareware digital audio editor has been a favorite of mine for a long time now. For more details on the many features offered by Cool Edit, see Chapter 10.

The CD contains versions of the program for both 16- and 32-bit platforms for Windows 3.1 and Windows 95/NT. You'll find the installation files in the **Cooledit** directory; there are separate subdirectories, labeled **16bit** and **32bit**.

To install the Windows 95 version of Cool Edit, change to the **Cooledit\\32bit** directory and run the program C96SETUP.EXE.

To install the Windows 3.1 version of Cool Edit, change to the **Cooledit\\16bit** directory and run the program COOL153Z.EXE.

Visit the Syntrillium Web site at **www.syntrillium.com/index.htm** for the latest information on Cool Edit and Cool Edit 96.

GEAR Replicator

This is the demonstration version of Elektroson's GEAR Replicator, a program that enables you to replicate existing CDs. The demonstration version will record a maximum of three CDs of almost any type.

GEAR Replicator requires Windows 95. Documentation for this program is supplied in Adobe Acrobat .PDF format.

You'll find the installation files in the **\Elektrsn\Win95NT\Replic** directory. To install GEAR Replicator, run the program SETUP.EXE.

Visit the Elektroson Web site at **www.elektroson.com** for complete information on the current version of CD-Replicator.

CD/Spectrum Pro

CD/Spectrum Pro is one of the best-known shareware audio CD player programs for your computer CD-ROM drive, and it includes a number of features you won't find in the Windows 95 CD player — for instance, how about a full graphical spectrum analyzer?

CD/Spectrum Pro requires Windows 95 or Windows NT 4.0.

You'll find the installation files in the **\Spectrum** directory. To install CD/Spectrum Pro, run the program CDSPRO31.EXE.

Visit the CD/Spectrum home page at **www.halcyon.com/gator/cdspro.htm** for the latest information and upgrades.

CD Worx

This program from Cyberdyne Software specializes in reading digital audio tracks from audio CDs and saving them as WAV format sound files on your hard drive. Plus, you can examine data from a single sector of any CD-ROM.

CD Worx requires Windows 95.

You'll find the installation files in the **\CDWorx** directory. To install CD Worx from the Windows 95 Explorer, right-click the file INSTALL.INF and then choose Install in the pop-up menu that appears.

For full information on CD Worx, visit the CD Worx Homepage at **www.b.shuttle.de/cyberdyne/cdworx.html** and download the latest version, the hardware compatibility list, and the program FAQ.

Easy CD Creator Tour

This animated Macromedia tour of the new Easy CD Creator recording software from Adaptec will introduce you to the main features of the program, including the additional features available within the Deluxe edition.

The tour requires Windows 95, and you will need at least 63MB of free hard drive space to run it.

You'll find the installation files in the **Tour** directory. To install the program, create a temporary directory on your hard drive named **easycd** and copy all of the files from the **Tour** directory into it. To begin the tour, run TOUR.EXE from this temporary directory. When you're done with the program, you can delete the **easycd** directory and everything in it from your hard drive.

For more information on Easy CD Creator, visit the Adaptec site at **www.adaptec.com**.

firstGEAR

This is the working version of firstGEAR from Elektroson, the makers of the popular GEAR for Windows recording program. Although some menu items are disabled, you'll find this excellent program more than powerful enough to record mode 1 Data and audio CDs!

firstGEAR requires Windows 95 or Windows NT 4.0. Documentation for this program is supplied in Adobe Acrobat .PDF format.

You'll find the installation files in the **Elektrsn\Win95NT\1stGear** directory. To install firstGEAR, run the program SETUP.EXE.

The Elektroson Web site at **www.elektroson.com** offers upgrade information and technical support for all of the company's products.

GEAR for MacOS

Here's the demonstration version of Elektroson's GEAR recording program for Macintosh and PowerMac users. Although the program can create almost any type of CD, each disc is limited in the demonstration version to a total of 6MB of data.

Documentation for this program is supplied in Adobe Acrobat .PDF format.

You'll find the installation files in the **Elektrsn\Mac** directory. The Mac version is in HQX format; to install GEAR, run the file GEAR Demo Installer (MM).

You'll find complete information for all versions of the GEAR line of recording software on the Elektroson Web site at **www.elektroson.com** — this includes GEAR for OS/2 and UNIX.

GEAR for OS/2

This is the demonstration version of Elektroson's GEAR recording program for OS/2. Like GEAR for MacOS, this version is fully functional, but it's limited to writing a total of 6MB of data on a CD.

Documentation for this program is supplied in Adobe Acrobat .PDF format.

You'll find the installation files in the **\Elektrsn\Os2** directory. To install GEAR, run the program SETUP.EXE.

GEAR for UNIX

GEAR for UNIX is the UNIX version of the award-winning GEAR recording program from Elektroson. This demonstration version is fully functional, but it carries only a 15-day license; once this evaluation period has passed, the software expires automatically.

This demonstration version of GEAR for UNIX supports SunOS 4.1.4, Solaris 2.5, Silicon Graphics v5.3 & v6.2, IBM AIX v4.2, and DEC Digital UNIX v4.0. Documentation for this program is supplied in Adobe Acrobat .PDF format.

You'll find the installation files in the **\Elektrsn\Unix** directory. The Unix version is in tar format; to install GEAR, untar the file gearunix.tar and then run the installer.

Media Center

I use this shareware multimedia catalog program to organize and manage my growing collection of audio, video, and images. For more details on using Media Center, see Chapter 10.

You'll find the installation files in the **\Media** directory. To install Media Center, run the program SETUP.EXE.

The JASC Web site at **www.jasc.com** provides online ordering, technical support, and upgrade downloads for Media Center.

Paint Shop Pro

Paint Shop Pro, from JASC Inc., is the reigning king of shareware image editing software, and I find myself using it daily for one task or another involving images. It supports and converts over 30 file formats, and even uses Adobe and Aldus plug-ins. Chapter 10 includes more detail on this great program.

Paint Shop Pro requires Windows 95 or Windows NT 4.0.

You'll find the installation files in the **\Paint** directory. To install Paint Shop Pro, run the program SETUP.EXE.

Contact the JASC Web site at **www.jasc.com** for more information — you'll find online ordering, technical support, and upgrade downloads for Paint Shop Pro.

Personal AVI Editor

Here's a shareware program from FlickerFree Multimedia Products A/S that enables you to edit Windows AVI format digital video. You can add sophisticated special effects, including Fade in, Fade out, Cross fade, and wipe, and you can even mix audio effects from WAV files. Personal AVI Editor includes support for recording video and audio, and you can synchronize tracks.

Version 1.5 of Personal AVI Editor requires Windows 95 or Windows NT 4.0.

You'll find the installation files in the **\AVIedit** directory. To install Personal AVI Editor, run the program INSTALL.EXE.

Visit the excellent company Web site at **www.flickerfree.com** for updates, product information, and online ordering.

ThreadMark

This is a working version of Adaptec's new multithreaded benchmarking utility software, with which you can measure the performance of your SCSI or IDE hard drives to determine if their performance will support your CD-write speeds.

ThreadMark 2.0 runs on Windows 95 and NT.

You'll find the installation files in the **\ThreadMark** directory. To install ThreadMark, run the program THRDMK20.EXE. Information on the program is in the files README.TXT and THREADMARK DESCRIPTION.TXT.

Visit the ThreadMark Web site at **www.adaptec.com/threadmark** for more info on the software.

WebGrabber

This is the full working version 1.0 of WebGrabber from Elektroson — it attaches a menu to Netscape Navigator that allows you to record Web content directly to CD.

WebGrabber requires Windows 95. Documentation for this program is supplied in Adobe Acrobat .PDF format.

You'll find the installation files in the **\Elektrsn\Win95NT\Webgrab** directory. To install WebGrabber, run the program SETUP.EXE.

Visit the Elektroson Web site at **www.elektroson.com** for additional information on the newest version of WebGrabber,.

INDEX

The Fun & Easy Way™ to learn about computers and more!

Here's a complete listing of IDG Books' ...For Dummies® titles

Title	Author	ISBN	Price
DATABASE			
Access 2 For Dummies®	by Scott Palmer	ISBN: 1-56884-090-X	$19.95 USA/$26.95 Canada
Access Programming For Dummies®	by Rob Krumm	ISBN: 1-56884-091-8	$19.95 USA/$26.95 Canada
Approach 3 For Windows® For Dummies®	by Doug Lowe	ISBN: 1-56884-233-3	$19.99 USA/$26.95 Canada
dBASE For DOS For Dummies®	by Scott Palmer & Michael Stabler	ISBN: 1-56884-188-4	$19.95 USA/$26.95 Canada
dBASE For Windows® For Dummies®	by Scott Palmer	ISBN: 1-56884-179-5	$19.95 USA/$26.95 Canada
dBASE 5 For Windows® Programming For Dummies®	by Ted Coombs & Jason Coombs	ISBN: 1-56884-215-5	$19.99 USA/$26.95 Canada
FoxPro 2.6 For Windows® For Dummies®	by John Kaufeld	ISBN: 1-56884-187-6	$19.95 USA/$26.95 Canada
Paradox 5 For Windows® For Dummies®	by John Kaufeld	ISBN: 1-56884-185-X	$19.95 USA/$26.95 Canada
DESKTOP PUBLISHING/ILLUSTRATION/GRAPHICS			
CorelDRAW! 5 For Dummies®	by Deke McClelland	ISBN: 1-56884-157-4	$19.95 USA/$26.95 Canada
CorelDRAW! For Dummies®	by Deke McClelland	ISBN: 1-56884-042-X	$19.95 USA/$26.95 Canada
Desktop Publishing & Design For Dummies®	by Roger C. Parker	ISBN: 1-56884-234-1	$19.99 USA/$26.99 Canada
Harvard Graphics 2 For Windows® For Dummies®	by Roger C. Parker	ISBN: 1-56884-092-6	$19.95 USA/$26.95 Canada
PageMaker 5 For Macs® For Dummies®	by Galen Gruman & Deke McClelland	ISBN: 1-56884-178-7	$19.95 USA/$26.95 Canada
PageMaker 5 For Windows® For Dummies®	by Deke McClelland & Galen Gruman	ISBN: 1-56884-160-4	$19.95 USA/$26.95 Canada
Photoshop 3 For Macs® For Dummies®	by Deke McClelland	ISBN: 1-56884-208-2	$19.99 USA/$26.99 Canada
QuarkXPress 3.3 For Dummies®	by Galen Gruman & Barbara Assadi	ISBN: 1-56884-217-1	$19.99 USA/$26.99 Canada
FINANCE/PERSONAL FINANCE/TEST TAKING REFERENCE			
Everyday Math For Dummies™	by Charles Seiter	ISBN: 1-56884-248-1	$14.99 USA/$22.99 Canada
Personal Finance For Dummies™ For Canadians	by Eric Tyson & Tony Martin	ISBN: 1-56884-378-X	$18.99 USA/$24.99 Canada
QuickBooks 3 For Dummies®	by Stephen L. Nelson	ISBN: 1-56884-227-9	$19.99 USA/$26.99 Canada
Quicken 8 For DOS For Dummies,® 2nd Edition	by Stephen L. Nelson	ISBN: 1-56884-210-4	$19.95 USA/$26.95 Canada
Quicken 5 For Macs® For Dummies®	by Stephen L. Nelson	ISBN: 1-56884-211-2	$19.95 USA/$26.95 Canada
Quicken 4 For Windows® For Dummies,® 2nd Edition	by Stephen L. Nelson	ISBN: 1-56884-209-0	$19.95 USA/$26.95 Canada
Taxes For Dummies,™ 1995 Edition	by Eric Tyson & David J. Silverman	ISBN: 1-56884-220-1	$14.99 USA/$20.99 Canada
The GMAT® For Dummies™	by Suzee Vlk, Series Editor	ISBN: 1-56884-376-3	$14.99 USA/$20.99 Canada
The GRE® For Dummies™	by Suzee Vlk, Series Editor	ISBN: 1-56884-375-5	$14.99 USA/$20.99 Canada
Time Management For Dummies™	by Jeffrey J. Mayer	ISBN: 1-56884-360-7	$16.99 USA/$22.99 Canada
TurboTax For Windows® For Dummies®	by Gail A. Helsel, CPA	ISBN: 1-56884-228-7	$19.99 USA/$26.99 Canada
GROUPWARE/INTEGRATED			
ClarisWorks For Macs® For Dummies®	by Frank Higgins	ISBN: 1-56884-363-1	$19.99 USA/$26.99 Canada
Lotus Notes For Dummies®	by Pat Freeland & Stephen Londergan	ISBN: 1-56884-212-0	$19.95 USA/$26.95 Canada
Microsoft® Office 4 For Windows® For Dummies®	by Roger C. Parker	ISBN: 1-56884-183-3	$19.95 USA/$26.95 Canada
Microsoft® Works 3 For Windows® For Dummies®	by David C. Kay	ISBN: 1-56884-214-7	$19.99 USA/$26.99 Canada
SmartSuite 3 For Dummies®	by Jan Weingarten & John Weingarten	ISBN: 1-56884-367-4	$19.99 USA/$26.99 Canada
INTERNET/COMMUNICATIONS/NETWORKING			
America Online® For Dummies,® 2nd Edition	by John Kaufeld	ISBN: 1-56884-933-8	$19.99 USA/$26.99 Canada
CompuServe For Dummies,® 2nd Edition	by Wallace Wang	ISBN: 1-56884-937-0	$19.99 USA/$26.99 Canada
Modems For Dummies,® 2nd Edition	by Tina Rathbone	ISBN: 1-56884-223-6	$19.99 USA/$26.99 Canada
MORE Internet For Dummies®	by John R. Levine & Margaret Levine Young	ISBN: 1-56884-164-7	$19.95 USA/$26.95 Canada
MORE Modems & On-line Services For Dummies®	by Tina Rathbone	ISBN: 1-56884-365-8	$19.99 USA/$26.99 Canada
Mosaic For Dummies,® Windows Edition	by David Angell & Brent Heslop	ISBN: 1-56884-242-2	$19.99 USA/$26.99 Canada
NetWare For Dummies,® 2nd Edition	by Ed Tittel, Deni Connor & Earl Follis	ISBN: 1-56884-369-0	$19.99 USA/$26.99 Canada
Networking For Dummies®	by Doug Lowe	ISBN: 1-56884-079-9	$19.95 USA/$26.95 Canada
PROCOMM PLUS 2 For Windows® For Dummies®	by Wallace Wang	ISBN: 1-56884-219-8	$19.99 USA/$26.99 Canada
TCP/IP For Dummies®	by Marshall Wilensky & Candace Leiden	ISBN: 1-56884-241-4	$19.99 USA/$26.99 Canada

10/31/95

The Internet For Macs® For Dummies® 2nd Edition	by Charles Seiter	ISBN: 1-56884-371-2	$19.99 USA/$26.99 Canada
The Internet For Macs® For Dummies® Starter Kit	by Charles Seiter	ISBN: 1-56884-244-9	$29.99 USA/$39.99 Canada
The Internet For Macs® For Dummies® Starter Kit Bestseller Edition	by Charles Seiter	ISBN: 1-56884-245-7	$39.99 USA/$54.99 Canada
The Internet For Windows® For Dummies® Starter Kit	by John R. Levine & Margaret Levine Young	ISBN: 1-56884-237-6	$34.99 USA/$44.99 Canada
The Internet For Windows® For Dummies® Starter Kit, Bestseller Edition	by John R. Levine & Margaret Levine Young	ISBN: 1-56884-246-5	$39.99 USA/$54.99 Canada

MACINTOSH

Mac® Programming For Dummies®	by Dan Parks Sydow	ISBN: 1-56884-173-6	$19.95 USA/$26.95 Canada
Macintosh® System 7.5 For Dummies®	by Bob LeVitus	ISBN: 1-56884-197-3	$19.95 USA/$26.95 Canada
MORE Macs® For Dummies®	by David Pogue	ISBN: 1-56884-087-X	$19.95 USA/$26.95 Canada
PageMaker 5 For Macs® For Dummies®	by Galen Gruman & Deke McClelland	ISBN: 1-56884-178-7	$19.95 USA/$26.95 Canada
QuarkXPress 3.3 For Dummies®	by Galen Gruman & Barbara Assadi	ISBN: 1-56884-217-1	$19.95 USA/$26.99 Canada
Upgrading and Fixing Macs® For Dummies®	by Kearney Rietmann & Frank Higgins	ISBN: 1-56884-189-2	$19.95 USA/$26.95 Canada

MULTIMEDIA

Multimedia & CD-ROMs For Dummies® 2nd Edition	by Andy Rathbone	ISBN: 1-56884-907-9	$19.99 USA/$26.99 Canada
Multimedia & CD-ROMs For Dummies® Interactive Multimedia Value Pack, 2nd Edition	by Andy Rathbone	ISBN: 1-56884-909-5	$29.99 USA/$39.99 Canada

OPERATING SYSTEMS:

DOS

MORE DOS For Dummies®	by Dan Gookin	ISBN: 1-56884-046-2	$19.95 USA/$26.95 Canada
OS/2® Warp For Dummies® 2nd Edition	by Andy Rathbone	ISBN: 1-56884-205-8	$19.95 USA/$26.95 Canada

UNIX

MORE UNIX® For Dummies®	by John R. Levine & Margaret Levine Young	ISBN: 1-56884-361-5	$19.99 USA/$26.99 Canada
UNIX® For Dummies®	by John R. Levine & Margaret Levine Young	ISBN: 1-878058-58-4	$19.95 USA/$26.95 Canada

WINDOWS

MORE Windows® For Dummies® 2nd Edition	by Andy Rathbone	ISBN: 1-56884-048-9	$19.95 USA/$26.95 Canada
Windows® 95 For Dummies®	by Andy Rathbone	ISBN: 1-56884-240-6	$19.95 USA/$26.99 Canada

PCS/HARDWARE

Illustrated Computer Dictionary For Dummies® 2nd Edition	by Dan Gookin & Wallace Wang	ISBN: 1-56884-218-X	$12.95 USA/$16.95 Canada
Upgrading and Fixing PCs For Dummies® 2nd Edition	by Andy Rathbone	ISBN: 1-56884-903-6	$19.99 USA/$26.99 Canada

PRESENTATION/AUTOCAD

AutoCAD For Dummies®	by Bud Smith	ISBN: 1-56884-191-4	$19.95 USA/$26.95 Canada
PowerPoint 4 For Windows® For Dummies®	by Doug Lowe	ISBN: 1-56884-161-2	$16.99 USA/$22.99 Canada

PROGRAMMING

Borland C++ For Dummies®	by Michael Hyman	ISBN: 1-56884-162-0	$19.95 USA/$26.95 Canada
C For Dummies® Volume 1	by Dan Gookin	ISBN: 1-878058-78-9	$19.95 USA/$26.95 Canada
C++ For Dummies®	by Stephen R. Davis	ISBN: 1-56884-163-9	$19.95 USA/$26.95 Canada
Delphi Programming For Dummies®	by Neil Rubenking	ISBN: 1-56884-200-7	$19.99 USA/$26.99 Canada
Mac® Programming For Dummies®	by Dan Parks Sydow	ISBN: 1-56884-173-6	$19.95 USA/$26.95 Canada
PowerBuilder 4 Programming For Dummies®	by Ted Coombs & Jason Coombs	ISBN: 1-56884-325-9	$19.99 USA/$26.99 Canada
QBasic Programming For Dummies®	by Douglas Hergert	ISBN: 1-56884-093-4	$19.95 USA/$26.95 Canada
Visual Basic 3 For Dummies®	by Wallace Wang	ISBN: 1-56884-076-4	$19.95 USA/$26.95 Canada
Visual Basic "X" For Dummies®	by Wallace Wang	ISBN: 1-56884-230-9	$19.99 USA/$26.99 Canada
Visual C++ 2 For Dummies®	by Michael Hyman & Bob Arnson	ISBN: 1-56884-328-3	$19.99 USA/$26.99 Canada
Windows® 95 Programming For Dummies®	by S. Randy Davis	ISBN: 1-56884-327-5	$19.99 USA/$26.99 Canada

SPREADSHEET

1-2-3 For Dummies®	by Greg Harvey	ISBN: 1-878058-60-6	$16.95 USA/$22.95 Canada
1-2-3 For Windows® 5 For Dummies® 2nd Edition	by John Walkenbach	ISBN: 1-56884-216-3	$16.95 USA/$22.95 Canada
Excel 5 For Macs® For Dummies®	by Greg Harvey	ISBN: 1-56884-186-8	$19.95 USA/$26.95 Canada
Excel For Dummies® 2nd Edition	by Greg Harvey	ISBN: 1-56884-050-0	$16.95 USA/$22.95 Canada
MORE 1-2-3 For DOS For Dummies®	by John Weingarten	ISBN: 1-56884-224-4	$19.99 USA/$26.99 Canada
MORE Excel 5 For Windows® For Dummies®	by Greg Harvey	ISBN: 1-56884-207-4	$19.95 USA/$26.95 Canada
Quattro Pro 6 For Windows® For Dummies®	by John Walkenbach	ISBN: 1-56884-174-4	$19.95 USA/$26.95 Canada
Quattro Pro For DOS For Dummies®	by John Walkenbach	ISBN: 1-56884-023-3	$16.95 USA/$22.95 Canada

UTILITIES

Norton Utilities 8 For Dummies®	by Beth Slick	ISBN: 1-56884-166-3	$19.95 USA/$26.95 Canada

VCRS/CAMCORDERS

VCRs & Camcorders For Dummies™	by Gordon McComb & Andy Rathbone	ISBN: 1-56884-229-5	$14.99 USA/$20.99 Canada

WORD PROCESSING

Ami Pro For Dummies®	by Jim Meade	ISBN: 1-56884-049-7	$19.95 USA/$26.95 Canada
MORE Word For Windows® 6 For Dummies®	by Doug Lowe	ISBN: 1-56884-165-5	$19.95 USA/$26.95 Canada
MORE WordPerfect® 6 For Windows® For Dummies®	by Margaret Levine Young & David C. Kay	ISBN: 1-56884-206-6	$19.95 USA/$26.95 Canada
MORE WordPerfect® 6 For DOS For Dummies®	by Wallace Wang, edited by Dan Gookin	ISBN: 1-56884-047-0	$19.95 USA/$26.95 Canada
Word 6 For Macs® For Dummies®	by Dan Gookin	ISBN: 1-56884-190-6	$19.95 USA/$26.95 Canada
Word For Windows® 6 For Dummies®	by Dan Gookin	ISBN: 1-56884-075-6	$16.95 USA/$22.95 Canada
Word For Windows® For Dummies®	by Dan Gookin & Ray Werner	ISBN: 1-878058-86-X	$16.95 USA/$22.95 Canada
WordPerfect® 6 For DOS For Dummies®	by Dan Gookin	ISBN: 1-878058-77-0	$16.95 USA/$22.95 Canada
WordPerfect® 6.1 For Windows® For Dummies® 2nd Edition	by Margaret Levine Young & David Kay	ISBN: 1-56884-243-0	$16.95 USA/$22.95 Canada
WordPerfect® For Dummies®		ISBN: 1-878058-52-5	$16.95 USA/$22.95 Canada

Fun, Fast, & Cheap!™

The Internet For Macs® For Dummies® Quick Reference

by Charles Seiter

ISBN:1-56884-967-2
$9.99 USA/$12.99 Canada

Windows® 95 For Dummies® Quick Reference

by Greg Harvey

ISBN: 1-56884-964-8
$9.99 USA/$12.99 Canada

Photoshop 3 For Macs® For Dummies® Quick Reference

by Deke McClelland

ISBN: 1-56884-968-0
$9.99 USA/$12.99 Canada

WordPerfect® For DOS For Dummies® Quick Reference

by Greg Harvey

ISBN: 1-56884-009-8
$8.95 USA/$12.95 Canada

Title	Author	ISBN	Price
DATABASE			
Access 2 For Dummies® Quick Reference	by Stuart J. Stuple	ISBN: 1-56884-167-1	$8.95 USA/$11.95 Canada
dBASE 5 For DOS For Dummies® Quick Reference	by Barrie Sosinsky	ISBN: 1-56884-954-0	$9.99 USA/$12.99 Canada
dBASE 5 For Windows® For Dummies® Quick Reference	by Stuart J. Stuple	ISBN: 1-56884-953-2	$9.99 USA/$12.99 Canada
Paradox 5 For Windows® For Dummies® Quick Reference	by Scott Palmer	ISBN: 1-56884-960-5	$9.99 USA/$12.99 Canada
DESKTOP PUBLISHING/ILLUSTRATION/GRAPHICS			
CorelDRAW! 5 For Dummies® Quick Reference	by Raymond E. Werner	ISBN: 1-56884-952-4	$9.99 USA/$12.99 Canada
Harvard Graphics For Windows® For Dummies® Quick Reference	by Raymond E. Werner	ISBN: 1-56884-962-1	$9.99 USA/$12.99 Canada
Photoshop 3 For Macs® For Dummies® Quick Reference	by Deke McClelland	ISBN: 1-56884-968-0	$9.99 USA/$12.99 Canada
FINANCE/PERSONAL FINANCE			
Quicken 4 For Windows® For Dummies® Quick Reference	by Stephen L. Nelson	ISBN: 1-56884-950-8	$9.95 USA/$12.95 Canada
GROUPWARE/INTEGRATED			
Microsoft® Office 4 For Windows® For Dummies® Quick Reference	by Doug Lowe	ISBN: 1-56884-958-3	$9.99 USA/$12.99 Canada
Microsoft® Works 3 For Windows® For Dummies® Quick Reference	by Michael Partington	ISBN: 1-56884-959-1	$9.99 USA/$12.99 Canada
INTERNET/COMMUNICATIONS/NETWORKING			
The Internet For Dummies® Quick Reference	by John R. Levine & Margaret Levine Young	ISBN: 1-56884-168-X	$8.95 USA/$11.95 Canada
MACINTOSH			
Macintosh® System 7.5 For Dummies® Quick Reference	by Stuart J. Stuple	ISBN: 1-56884-956-7	$9.99 USA/$12.99 Canada
OPERATING SYSTEMS:			
DOS			
DOS For Dummies® Quick Reference	by Greg Harvey	ISBN: 1-56884-007-1	$8.95 USA/$11.95 Canada
UNIX			
UNIX® For Dummies® Quick Reference	by John R. Levine & Margaret Levine Young	ISBN: 1-56884-094-2	$8.95 USA/$11.95 Canada
WINDOWS			
Windows® 3.1 For Dummies® Quick Reference, 2nd Edition	by Greg Harvey	ISBN: 1-56884-951-6	$8.95 USA/$11.95 Canada
PCs/HARDWARE			
Memory Management For Dummies® Quick Reference	by Doug Lowe	ISBN: 1-56884-362-3	$9.99 USA/$12.99 Canada
PRESENTATION/AUTOCAD			
AutoCAD For Dummies® Quick Reference	by Ellen Finkelstein	ISBN: 1-56884-198-1	$9.95 USA/$12.95 Canada
SPREADSHEET			
1-2-3 For Dummies® Quick Reference	by John Walkenbach	ISBN: 1-56884-027-6	$8.95 USA/$11.95 Canada
1-2-3 For Windows® 5 For Dummies® Quick Reference	by John Walkenbach	ISBN: 1-56884-957-5	$9.95 USA/$12.95 Canada
Excel For Windows® For Dummies® Quick Reference, 2nd Edition	by John Walkenbach	ISBN: 1-56884-096-9	$8.95 USA/$11.95 Canada
Quattro Pro 6 For Windows® For Dummies® Quick Reference	by Stuart J. Stuple	ISBN: 1-56884-172-8	$9.95 USA/$12.95 Canada
WORD PROCESSING			
Word For Windows® 6 For Dummies® Quick Reference	by George Lynch	ISBN: 1-56884-095-0	$8.95 USA/$11.95 Canada
Word For Dummies® Quick Reference	by George Lynch	ISBN: 1-56884-029-2	$8.95 USA/$11.95 Canada
WordPerfect® 6.1 For Windows® For Dummies® Quick Reference, 2nd Edition	by Greg Harvey	ISBN: 1-56884-966-4	$9.99 USA/$12.99/Canada

For scholastic requests & educational orders please call Educational Sales at 1. 800. 434. 2086

FOR MORE INFO OR TO ORDER, PLEASE CALL ▶ 800. 762. 2974

For volume discounts & special orders please call Tony Real, Special Sales, at 415. 655. 3048

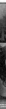

IDG BOOKS WORLDWIDE

Order Center: **(800) 762-2974** *(8 a.m.–6 p.m., EST, weekdays)*

Quantity	ISBN	Title	Price	Total

Shipping & Handling Charges

	Description	First book	Each additional book	Total
Domestic	Normal	$4.50	$1.50	$
	Two Day Air	$8.50	$2.50	$
	Overnight	$18.00	$3.00	$
International	Surface	$8.00	$8.00	$
	Airmail	$16.00	$16.00	$
	DHL Air	$17.00	$17.00	$

*For large quantities call for shipping & handling charges.
**Prices are subject to change without notice.

Ship to:

Name _____

Company _____

Address _____

City/State/Zip _____

Daytime Phone _____

Payment: ☐ Check to IDG Books Worldwide (US Funds Only)

☐ VISA   ☐ MasterCard   ☐ American Express

Card # _____ Expires _____

Signature _____

Subtotal _____

CA residents add
applicable sales tax _____

IN, MA, and MD
residents add
5% sales tax _____

IL residents add
6.25% sales tax _____

RI residents add
7% sales tax _____

TX residents add
8.25% sales tax _____

Shipping _____

Total _____

Please send this order form to:

IDG Books Worldwide, Inc.
7260 Shadeland Station, Suite 100
Indianapolis, IN 46256

Allow up to 3 weeks for delivery.
Thank you!

IDG BOOKS WORLDWIDE, INC.
END-USER LICENSE AGREEMENT

READ THIS. You should carefully read these terms and conditions before opening the software packet(s) included with this book ("Book"). This is a license agreement ("Agreement") between you and IDG Books Worldwide, Inc. ("IDGB"). By opening the accompanying software packet(s), you acknowledge that you have read and accept the following terms and conditions. If you do not agree and do not want to be bound by such terms and conditions, promptly return the Book and the unopened software packet(s) to the place you obtained them for a full refund.

1. **License Grant.** IDGB grants to you (either an individual or entity) a nonexclusive license to use one copy of the enclosed software program(s) (collectively, the "Software") solely for your own personal or business purposes on a single computer (whether a standard computer or a workstation component of a multiuser network). The Software is in use on a computer when it is loaded into temporary memory (RAM) or installed into permanent memory (hard disk, CD-ROM, or other storage device). IDGB reserves all rights not expressly granted herein.

2. **Ownership.** IDGB is the owner of all right, title, and interest, including copyright, in and to the compilation of the Software recorded on the disk(s) or CD-ROM ("Software Media"). Copyright to the individual programs recorded on the Software Media is owned by the author or other authorized copyright owner of each program. Ownership of the Software and all proprietary rights relating thereto remain with IDGB and its licensers.

3. **Restrictions On Use and Transfer.**

   (a) You may only (i) make one copy of the Software for backup or archival purposes, or (ii) transfer the Software to a single hard disk, provided that you keep the original for backup or archival purposes. You may not (i) rent or lease the Software, (ii) copy or reproduce the Software through a LAN or other network system or through any computer subscriber system or bulletin-board system, or (iii) modify, adapt, or create derivative works based on the Software.

   (b) You may not reverse engineer, decompile, or disassemble the Software. You may transfer the Software and user documentation on a permanent basis, provided that the transferee agrees to accept the terms and conditions of this Agreement and you retain no copies. If the Software is an update or has been updated, any transfer must include the most recent update and all prior versions.

4. **Restrictions On Use of Individual Programs.** You must follow the individual requirements and restrictions detailed for each individual program in Apendix F of this Book. These limitations are also contained in the individual license agreements recorded on the Software Media. These limitations may include a requirement that after using the program for a specified period of time, the user must pay a registration fee or discontinue use. By opening the Software packet(s), you will be agreeing to abide by the licenses and restrictions for these individual programs that are detailed in Appendix F and on the Software Media. None of the material on this Software Media or listed in this Book may ever be redistributed, in original or modified form, for commercial purposes.

5. Limited Warranty.

(a) IDGB warrants that the Software and Software Media are free from defects in materials and workmanship under normal use for a period of sixty (60) days from the date of purchase of this Book. If IDGB receives notification within the warranty period of defects in materials or workmanship, IDGB will replace the defective Software Media.

(b) **IDGB AND THE AUTHOR OF THE BOOK DISCLAIM ALL OTHER WARRANTIES, EXPRESS OR IMPLIED, INCLUDING WITHOUT LIMITATION IMPLIED WARRANTIES OF MERCHANTABILITY AND FITNESS FOR A PARTICULAR PURPOSE, WITH RESPECT TO THE SOFTWARE, THE PROGRAMS, THE SOURCE CODE CONTAINED THEREIN, AND/OR THE TECHNIQUES DESCRIBED IN THIS BOOK. IDGB DOES NOT WARRANT THAT THE FUNCTIONS CONTAINED IN THE SOFTWARE WILL MEET YOUR REQUIREMENTS OR THAT THE OPERATION OF THE SOFTWARE WILL BE ERROR FREE.**

(c) This limited warranty gives you specific legal rights, and you may have other rights that vary from jurisdiction to jurisdiction.

6. Remedies.

(a) IDGB's entire liability and your exclusive remedy for defects in materials and workmanship shall be limited to replacement of the Software Media, which may be returned to IDGB with a copy of your receipt at the following address: Software Media Fulfillment Department, Attn.: *Recordable CD Bible*, IDG Books Worldwide, Inc., 7260 Shadeland Station, Ste. 100, Indianapolis, IN 46256, or call 1-800-762-2974. Please allow three to four weeks for delivery. This Limited Warranty is void if failure of the Software Media has resulted from accident, abuse, or misapplication. Any replacement Software Media will be warranted for the remainder of the original warranty period or thirty (30) days, whichever is longer.

(b) In no event shall IDGB or the author be liable for any damages whatsoever (including without limitation damages for loss of business profits, business interruption, loss of business information, or any other pecuniary loss) arising from the use of or inability to use the Book or the Software, even if IDGB has been advised of the possibility of such damages.

(c) Because some jurisdictions do not allow the exclusion or limitation of liability for consequential or incidental damages, the above limitation or exclusion may not apply to you.

7. U.S. Government Restricted Rights. Use, duplication, or disclosure of the Software by the U.S. Government is subject to restrictions stated in paragraph (c)(1)(ii) of the Rights in Technical Data and Computer Software clause of DFARS 252.227-7013, and in subparagraphs (a) through (d) of the Commercial Computer—Restricted Rights clause at FAR 52.227-19, and in similar clauses in the NASA FAR supplement, when applicable.

8. General. This Agreement constitutes the entire understanding of the parties and revokes and supersedes all prior agreements, oral or written, between them and may not be modified or amended except in a writing signed by both parties hereto that specifically refers to this Agreement. This Agreement shall take precedence over any other documents that may be in conflict herewith. If any one or more provisions contained in this Agreement are held by any court or tribunal to be invalid, illegal, or otherwise unenforceable, each and every other provision shall remain in full force and effect.

CD-ROM Installation Instructions

To browse the disc in Windows 95:

1. Launch Windows Explorer.

2. Select the letter for your CD-ROM drive in the directory tree. Explorer will display the contents of the disc. Note that the files on the CD-ROM are arranged in directories by program name.

3. Check the launch information for the specific program in Appendix F. Most programs can be installed by running the program SETUP.EXE in the desired directory.

Files ending in .PDF are Adobe Acrobat electronic documents, and you must install Adobe Acrobat before you can read or print them.

Always check the README files provided with each program on the disc before you run the application for the first time.

IDG BOOKS WORLDWIDE REGISTRATION CARD

RETURN THIS REGISTRATION CARD FOR FREE CATALOG

Title of this book: **Recordable CD Bible**

My overall rating of this book: ❑ Very good [1] ❑ Good [2] ❑ Satisfactory [3] ❑ Fair [4] ❑ Poor [5]

How I first heard about this book:

❑ Found in bookstore; name: [6]   ❑ Book review: [7]

❑ Advertisement: [8]   ❑ Catalog: [9]

❑ Word of mouth; heard about book from friend, co-worker, etc.: [10]   ❑ Other: [11]

What I liked most about this book: _____
_____
_____

What I would change, add, delete, etc., in future editions of this book: _____
_____
_____

Other comments: _____
_____

Number of computer books I purchase in a year: ❑ 1 [12] ❑ 2-5 [13] ❑ 6-10 [14] ❑ More than 10 [15]

I would characterize my computer skills as: ❑ Beginner [16] ❑ Intermediate [17] ❑ Advanced [18] ❑ Professional [19]

I use ❑ DOS [20] ❑ Windows [21] ❑ OS/2 [22] ❑ Unix [23] ❑ Macintosh [24] ❑ Other: [25]_____
(please specify)

I would be interested in new books on the following subjects:
(please check all that apply, and use the spaces provided to identify specific software)

❑ Word processing: [26]   ❑ Spreadsheets: [27]

❑ Data bases: [28]   ❑ Desktop publishing: [29]

❑ File Utilities: [30]   ❑ Money management: [31]

❑ Networking: [32]   ❑ Programming languages: [33]

❑ Other: [34]

I use a PC at (please check all that apply): ❑ home [35] ❑ work [36] ❑ school [37] ❑ other: [38] _____

The disks I prefer to use are ❑ 5.25 [39] ❑ 3.5 [40] ❑ other: [41]_____

I have a CD ROM: ❑ yes [42] ❑ no [43]

I plan to buy or upgrade computer hardware this year: ❑ yes [44] ❑ no [45]

I plan to buy or upgrade computer software this year: ❑ yes [46] ❑ no [47]

Name: _____ Business title: [48] _____ Type of Business: [49] _____

Address (❑ home [50] ❑ work [51]/Company name: _____)

Street/Suite# _____

City [52]/State [53]/Zipcode [54]: _____ Country [55] _____

❑ **I liked this book!** You may quote me by name in future
IDG Books Worldwide promotional materials.

My daytime phone number is _____

IDG BOOKS

THE WORLD OF
COMPUTER
KNOWLEDGE

 **YES!**

Please keep me informed about IDG's World of Computer Knowledge.
Send me the latest IDG Books catalog.

BUSINESS REPLY MAIL
FIRST CLASS MAIL   PERMIT NO. 2605   FOSTER CITY, CALIFORNIA

IDG Books Worldwide
919 E Hillsdale Blvd, STE 400
Foster City, CA 94404-9691

NO POSTAGE
NECESSARY
IF MAILED
IN THE
UNITED STATES